# ASPECTS OF EDUCATIONAL TECHNOLOGY

Volume VIII
Communication and Learning

# ASPECTS OF
# EDUCATIONAL TECHNOLOGY

## Volume VIII
## Communication and Learning

Edited for the Association for
Programmed Learning and
Educational Technology by:

JON BAGGALEY

G. HARRY JAMIESON

HARRY MARCHANT

General Editor:
JOIIN LEEDHAM

Pitman Publishing

First published 1975


SIR ISAAC PITMAN AND SONS LTD.
Pitman House, Parker Street, Kingsway, London WC2B 5PB
P.O. Box 46038, Banda Street, Nairobi, Kenya

PITMAN PUBLISHING PTY. LTD.
Pitman House, 158 Bouverie Street, Carlton, Victoria 3053, Australia

PITMAN PUBLISHING CORPORATION
6 East 43rd Street, New York, N.Y. 10017, U.S.A.

SIR ISAAC PITMAN (CANADA) LTD.
495 Wellington Street West, Toronto 1ᵒ5, Canada

THE COPP CLARK PUBLISHING COMPANY
517 Wellington Street West, Toronto 135, Canada

ISBN: 0 273 00422 0

Reproduced and printed by photolithography and bound in
Great Britain at The Pitman Press, Bath
(G.4699:15)

# Foreword

As it was held at the University of Liverpool, it was natural that the 1974 Conference of the Association for Programmed Learning and Educational Technology should reflect the growing discipline devoted to the study of communication processes generally. Liverpool's particular activities in the field were highlighted in the opening address to the Conference (8 April, 1974) by Professor F.B.R. Smallman, University Pro-Vice-Chancellor.

"It gives me great pleasure to welcome you here today on behalf of the University of Liverpool as delegates to this International Conference on 'Communication and Learning'. I understand that we have present representatives from many parts of the world: from several European countries, from the United States and Canada, and from India, Malaysia and Australasia. I hope that you will find your visit to Liverpool an enjoyable and profitable one and that, when you eventually return home, you will carry away with you happy memories of your stay here.

It was in 1967 that a unit for Audio Visual Aids and Programmed Learning was originally established in this University. It was, in fact, one of the first of its kind in the country and from the outset it gained a reputation as a high-activity centre and — so we modestly like to believe — as something of a model for other similar units which were founded later. In this University it is our belief that detailed research into the problems of communication is of crucial importance to the development of educational technology — particularly, but by no means solely, in the Sciences and the Medical Sciences. With this in mind we have encouraged within the unit here an academic bias towards the understanding of Communication as a Science in itself, placing special emphasis on the development of teaching methods. Already, valuable postgraduate work is being undertaken, and recently, with the agreement of Senate, undergraduate courses have been planned and it is hoped that these will be started very soon. In parallel to, and springing from, their academic research function, the staff of our unit also provide full-scale technical services for many academic departments in the university, by producing teaching materials involving television and other media such as film and tape-slide. Not least amongst these services is the use of closed-circuit television for instructing medical students in the techniques of surgery and the diagnosis of disease.

We are delighted and honoured that APLET has chosen to hold this International Conference in Liverpool and, in particular, it gives us the greatest pleasure that the President of your Association, Sir James Pitman, is able to be present here today. I should like to extend to him our warmest greetings and to wish the Conference every success in the interesting and intensive programme of lectures and discussions which are to follow."

The Conference theme 'Communication and Learning' was adopted with the following intentions :

(a)  to present developments in educational technology in juxtaposition with principles relating to the communication process; and thereby

(b)  to enable educational technology to derive benefit from the theoretical and practical approaches to communication problems in other disciplines.

Attention has been paid to communication problems by psychologists, sociologists, engineers, and graphic designers since the war; and the significance of their work is equally recognized in commercial and occupational contexts, in the press, the media and advertising. In education the need for methods improving and guaranteeing the effectiveness of teacher-student communication was commendably indicated by the programmed learning specialists. They recognized that communication, being essentially a two-way process, is incomplete if the student is not actively involved in the process of learning, if he does not receive continual knowledge of his progress and remedial treatment in the event of error. While methods and media for the improvement of communication have been provided by the technologists working within education, the value that any development claims to represent is difficult to guarantee. And as logistic and economic problems in education multiply, guarantees become crucial. An attention to Communication and Learning must thus aim particularly for a better understanding of the factors contributing to educational effectiveness, and on which improvement depends.

Edited together as 'Aspects of Educational Technology VIII', the proceedings of the 1974 Conference have been divided into three sections. The first deals with particular problems arising within educational technology in the development of effective media; the second presents a number of the approaches to instructional design currently employed; and in the third, theory and practice in educational technology are related in terms of wider concepts of communication than are generally associated with the field. Several papers are included additional to those actually scheduled at the Conference.

In an important sense, educational technology is in itself an aspect of the science of communication that is developing. As the awareness of problems relating to the communication and learning processes deepens, the inability of conventional educational technology to offer definite solutions becomes increasingly apparent. The halo effect which originally surrounded the new technology is wearing off; and the plain realization that the major educational problems remain is a notable feature of the present volume. The close relationships between sections of the book, and in particular the implications for educational development of Section C indicate the need for a deliberate integration of ideas within a broad communication framework. A number of the papers thus have a wider significance than for educational technology alone; and in a historical perspective, the catalytic role played by educational technology in the evolution of a more integrated approach to communication problems, may prove as significant as its promised role at the applied level.

JPB
GHJ
HM

Audio-Visual Aids & Programmed Learning Unit,
The University of Liverpool.

April 1974.

# Contents

# List of Contributors

(All addresses in United Kingdom unless otherwise stated)

Allan, Prof. T.S.  Department of Education, Sir George Williams University, Montreal 107, Canada.

Baggaley, Dr. J.P.  Audio-Visual Aids and Programmed Learning Unit, The University, Liverpool.

Bates, Dr. A.W.  Institute of Educational Technology, The Open University, Milton Keynes, Bucks.

Bingham, Elspeth  Civil Engineering Learning Unit, Heriot-Watt University, Edinburgh.

Burnhill, P.  Staffordshire College of Further Education, Tenterbanks, Stafford.

Byrne, Dr. C.J.  Institute of Educational Technology, Open University, Milton Keynes, Bucks.

Catlow, Sq.Ldr. G.R.  RAF School of Education, Upwood, Huntingdon.

Cherry, Prof. C.  Department of Electrical Engineering, Imperial College of Science and Technology, Exhibition Road, London SW7 2BT.

Clarke, J.  Dundee College of Education, Park Place, Dundee, Angus, Scotland.

Coldevin, Dr. G.O.  Department of Education, Sir George Williams University, Montreal 107, Canada.

Cook, Dr. R.M.  Université des Sciences et Techniques du Languedoc, Montepelier, France.

Cowan, J.  Department of Civil Engineering, Heriot-Watt University, Edinburgh.

Davies, Prof. I.K.  2447 Rock Creek Drive, Bloomington, Indiana, U.S.A.

Denis, J.P.  Imago Centre, Catholic University of Louvain, B-3030 Heverle-Louvain, Belgium.

Dodd, B.  Applied Psychology Unit, Admiralty Research Laboratory, Teddington, Middlesex.

Duck, Dr. S.W.  Department of Psychology, University of Lancaster, Bailrigg, Lancaster.

Ellis, P.  Middlesex Polytechnic, Queensway, Enfield, Middlesex.

Elton, Prof. L.R.B.  Institute of Educational Technology, University of Surrey, Guildford, Surrey.

Hancock, A.  Division of Development and Application of Communication, UNESCO, Place de Fontenoy, Paris, France.

Hartley, Dr. J.  Department of Psychology, The University, Keele, Staffordshire.

| | |
|---|---|
| Hooper, R. | National Development Programme in Computer Assisted Learning, 37-41 Mortimer Street, London W1A 2JL. |
| Houlton, Dr. R. | Institute of Extension Studies, The University, Liverpool. |
| Howe, Miss A. | Middlesex Polytechnic, Queensway, Enfield, Middlesex. |
| Howland, Dr. R.J. | Department of Biological Sciences, University of Surrey, Guildford, Surrey. |
| Jamieson, Dr. G.H. | Audio-Visual Aids and Programmed Learning Unit, The University, Liverpool. |
| Jones, R.W. | Radio Merseyside, Commerce House, 13-17 Sir Thomas Street, Liverpool. |
| Lawton, P.J. | School of Electronic & Electrical Engineering, City of Leicester Polytechnic, Leicester. |
| Leedham, Dr. J. | Centre for Educational Technology, Martin Hall, Loughborough. |
| LeHunte, R.J.G. | Inbucon Learning Systems, Ancaster Lodge, Queens Road, Richmond, Surrey. |
| Lombaerde, J. | IMAGO Centre, Catholic University of Louvain, B-3030 Heverle-Louvain, Belgium. |
| Marchant, H. | Audio-Visual Aids and Programmed Learning Unit, The University, Liverpool. |
| Maskill, Dr. R. | Institute of Educational Technology, The Open University, Milton Keynes, Bucks. |
| Meredith, Prof. G.P. | Epistemic Communication Research Unit, Department of Psychology, The University, Leeds. |
| Midson, A.J. | Audio-Visual Aids Unit, University of Surrey, Guildford, Surrey. |
| Mitchell, Prof. P.D. | Department of Education, Sir George Williams University, Montreal 107, Canada. |
| Morgan, Dr. A. | Institute of Educational Technology, The Open University, Milton Keynes, Bucks. |
| Morton, Dr. J. | Department of Civil Engineering, Heriot-Watt University, Edinburgh. |
| Moss, Dr. G.D. | Centre for Educational Technology, University College, Cardiff, South Wales. |
| O'Hare, Sq.Ldr. B. | RAF School of Education, Upwood, Huntingdon. |
| Pitman, Sir James | ita Foundation, 154 Southampton Row, London WC1B 5AX. |
| Richardson, Major J.C. | HQ, REME, Havannah Barracks, Bordon, Hants. |
| Romiszowski, A. | Middlesex Polytechnic, Queensway, Enfield, Middlesex. |
| Rowntree, D. | Institute of Educational Technology, The Open University, Milton Keynes, Bucks. |
| Sheppard, C. | Applied Psychology Unit, Admiralty Research Laboratory, Teddington, Middlesex. |
| Williams, Dr. E. | JUPR, University College, Tottenham Court Road, London W1P OBS. |
| Williams, Miss R. | Department of Biological Sciences, University of Surrey, Guildford, Surrey. |

# SECTION A

# Problems in media development

## INTRODUCTION

The first section of the book contains papers in which a number of the problems within current educational technology are discussed. Davies, whose paper opens the section, emphasizes that technology is a process characterized by the ways in which machines and software are used. Past over-emphasis on 'efficiency' to the neglect of 'effectiveness' has led to a rigidity of viewpoints and inflexibility of minds in the field; and a revised approach is required, involving the integration of values and processes as well as techniques. The papers by Bates, Jones, and Moss et al. develop this contribution. Bates points out that the media require new methods of teaching, which in turn demand new organizational structures to ensure their success. Jones, in his discussion of the use of radio in schools, lays stress on the need to select appropriate media for given learning situations; while in the Open University paper by Moss, Maskill and Morgan, particular problems concerned with the teaching of practical skills are highlighted.

Identifying media learning difficulties is a major problem to be overcome. Advancement in educational technology will only occur if research and evaluation projects are given priority and their results made generally known, as in the papers of Marchant, Coldevin, and Burnhill & Hartley. The need to develop to a wider behavioural standpoint is underlined in Marchant's work concerning a presentation strategy with instructional films. Coldevin has rightly moved away from the traditional comparative approach to media study, to investigate the question of how in a given learning situation television can be used more effectively. And Burnhill & Hartley discuss the issue of layout assessment in printed materials.

The role that Instructional Systems Design might play in educational television production is outlined by Allan. He emphasizes the need for evaluation but argues that precise specification of terminal objectives is not always possible, or indeed desirable. This latter topic is dealt with by Hooper whose paper, although closing this section of the book, opens a number of wider problems concerning the application of technological principles to education in general.

# Educational technology at the crossroads:
# Efficient message design or effective communication

I. K. DAVIES, Indiana University

**Abstract:** 'Educational technology at the crossroads' examines the development of the concept within a communications framework. Two central issues are explored, the one of efficiency which entails 'doing things right', and the other of effectiveness which involves 'doing the right things'. It is argued that an educational technology built on the former reduces it to a peripheral and subservient role in education and training.

The skills and indicators of effectiveness are then postulated (at the personal, group, organizational and societal levels), on the basis of which an educational technology built on effectiveness is outlined. This model places educational technology in a more central and critical role. It is suggested that message design now becomes subsidiary to educational or **instructional development**, which relates to long-range efforts to improve the overall quality of education and training, both in terms of content and process. Such a view of educational technology (involving the integration of values and processes as well as techniques) enhances the promise of what can be achieved, whilst providing opportunities for teachers and students to function as people rather than as resources in a task-orientated, mechanistic process.

> 'In spite of all similarities, every living situation has, like a newborn child, a new face that has never been before and will never come again. It demands of you a reaction which cannot be prepared beforehand. It demands nothing of what is past. It demands presence, responsibility; it demands you.'
>
> Martin Buber

Communication is orientated to the future, or — at the very least — to the imminently impending future that we call 'the present'. It is anticipatory, its goal is prediction. But prediction is only part of the process. Communication is prediction orientated so that the primary objective can be realized. This objective is influence. Communication involves exchange. It implies participation and adaptation. It includes sharing. For this reason, if for no other teaching involves the very essence of the communication process, and the communication process involves teaching. Sharing and influence, teaching and learning, are what communication is really about. As Mark Harris once remarked 'teaching is a form of loving'.

## Development of an Educational Technology

Many of the developments that have taken place in education and training in the last 70 years have largely been concerned with attempts to enhance this communication aspect. Developments in the audio-visual field, more lately referred to as media, are an obvious example of this interest, stemming from the contributions of the physical sciences and technologies to the problems of teaching and instruction. Developments in mathematics have also contributed to greater efficiency, influencing experimental design and evaluation but also selection and testing as well as a more precise analysis of data and the communication of results. Finally, developments in the behavioural sciences have contributed to a knowledge of individual differences, group processes, learning theory and motivation problems as well as specific technologies like programmed instruction, mathetics, and behavioural control and management. These three converging streams of influence (from the physical sciences, mathematics and the behavioural sciences) have affected awareness of, as well as knowledge and practices in education and training. They have deepened our understanding of what we are about, and have contributed to the development of a concept of an educational technology.

To a very large extent the major message of educational technologists has been concerned with efficiency. They have attempted to demonstrate that their procedures, and that their teaching aids, will help increase the efficiency of the teaching process. Identifying objectives and analysing tasks (where am I going?), sequencing information, selecting resources and organizing learning environments (how shall I get there?), and evaluating results as well as improving what has been accomplished (how will I know I've arrived?), obviously can improve the efficiency of education and training. If this process can then be partly or wholly mechanized or even automated by means of teaching machines, projectors, language laboratories, computers, telephone, radio, or television, further efficiencies, if not real economies, can probably be realized. This is certainly the potential of educational technology, and a great deal of this potential is already being realized. What we have to ask ourselves is 'Is this enough?', or to put it more bluntly 'Is this what educational technology is really about?'.

## TWO ROLES FOR EDUCATIONAL TECHNOLOGY

Contributing to the **efficiency** of teaching and instruction is a commendable and necessary goal, but to contribute to the **effectiveness** of education and training may well be a more critical concern. This is the crossroads that educational technology faces. Educational technologists can decide to concentrate primarily on making further contributions to efficient message design (i. e. , designing and creating better instructional materials, which help teachers to be more efficient) or educational

4

technologies can decide to concentrate on efficiency and effectiveness
(i. e. , developing teaching and instruction). The one decision, as we
shall see, is quite different to the other, and two quite different futures
are involved. Efficiency casts educational technologists in a peripheral
role in education and training. Effectiveness casts educational technologists in a central role, for which their present inclinations and training
may not necessarily prepare them.

## Efficiency and Effectiveness

The decision, therefore, facing educational technologists, is whether
the central concern is to be efficiency or efficiency and effectiveness.
Efficiency involves doing things right; effectiveness involves doing the
right things (see Davies, 1972). Well designed classrooms, a plenteous
supply of audio-visual aids, well qualified and prepared teachers and
instructors, good question technique, excellent chalkboard work, well
defined objectives, proper evaluation, a sympathetic manner, up-to-
date record keeping, etc. , are all commendable in themselves, but
they do not necessarily ensure that an education or training programme
will be effective. It will probably be an efficient programme, but its
effectiveness remains to be demonstrated.

| EFFECTIVENESS is doing the right things | | EFFICIENCY is doing things right |
|---|---|---|
| this involves: | | this involves: |
| creating alternatives | rather than | solving problems |
| optimizing resource utilization | rather than | safeguarding resources |
| realizing responsibilities | rather than | following procedures |
| meeting criterion | rather than | increasing pass rates |
| satisfying needs | rather than | reducing costs |
| using a systems approach | rather than | treating things separately |

Figure 1:   Effectiveness and efficiency in education and training.

Effectiveness, see figure 1, does not necessarily involve a teacher's personality, the quality of a teacher's administration, or the efficiency of a teacher's instruction. It is a direct function of what a teacher **does**, the extent to which a teacher realizes the responsibilities of the position or role which the teacher occupies. If teachers fail to realize the potential that stems from their role, they are ineffective — no matter how efficient they may be. Since teachers are meant to be effective, they can only really be judged by what they accomplish. In the same way, students and trainees, too, are expected to be effective, and they must also be judged by the same criterion as the teacher.

## Skills of Effectiveness

Fortunately, effectiveness can be learned. It is rarely a quality that is brought to a situation. It is something that is consciously done or achieved by learning how to manage learning **appropriately** according to the demands of the situation. This involves competency, which depends as Peter Drucker (1967) remarks, upon four habits of mind. Transferring his remarks to education and training, teachers and instructors, students and trainees, acquire effectiveness by:

(1) Knowing where their time goes. This enables them to manage the one resource that cannot be expanded.

(2) Gearing effort to results. This is achieved by concentrating on what is expected of them, rather than on the work to be done.

(3) Knowing when, and where to apply their effort. This involves building on strengths rather than weaknesses.

(4) Setting up the right priorities. This means concentrating on those few key tasks that are most likely to produce outstanding results.

All of this involves making effective decisions about time, effort and priorities, and this in turn demands a very clear view of the nature of the objectives to be realized.

## Indicators of an Effective Educational Technology

The skills underlying effectiveness, of course, are not new. Implementing these rather obvious and commonplace concepts, however, is often so difficult that effectiveness remains a dream. In such circumstances, human weakness encourages us to replace effectiveness with efficiency. This problem is well described by the Queen in 'Alice's Adventures in Wonderland' for:

> ' ".... how can you possibly award prizes when everybody missed the target?" said Alice. "Well" said the Queen, "Some missed

6

by more than others, and we have a fine normal distribution of misses, which means we can forget the target." '

(Lewis Carroll, 1907)

So the problem of effectiveness involves concentrating on the target. But what is this target? How will we know when we are effective?

Educators and trainers can use a number of indicators to determine whether or not an effective learning situation has been created. These indicators involve three different, but related levels : individual effectiveness, group or team effectiveness, and effectiveness in terms of society (for education) and an organization (in the case of training). In other words, effectiveness involves dealing with all three levels simultaneously, for most students and teachers work in groups or teams and most groups or teams exist in the context of a larger social organization. Concentrating on individual or group effectiveness alone makes little sense, for all of us are part of a larger social system. Effectiveness demands, therefore, that each level is recognized, and the necessary inter-relationships between levels strenthened and nurtured. (See figure 2, page 8)

Once the existence and importance of this hierarchy of levels is recognized, the indicators of effectiveness can be examined from the perspective of each level. Personal effectiveness does not necessarily imply group effectiveness, neither does group effectiveness imply organizational effectiveness. A decision has to be made, therefore, as to which of the three levels are the most important, sometimes it will be one level and sometimes it will be a combination — if not all three. Regardless of the level involved, the indicators of effectiveness are similar, if not the same. They are five-fold, and consist of :

(1) Achievement of the agreed objectives. (These may or may not be stated in a behavioural form). Individuals, groups and larger social organizations should have a fairly clear view of what has to be achieved in terms of any learning task. Effectiveness in terms of achievement involves the realization of all or most of these goals.

(2) Satisfaction with what has been experienced. Whether or not the learning objectives of an individual, group or larger organization have been achieved, a learning situation should be an enriching one. Individual, group and society or organizational needs should be satisfied, in the sense that people or groups experience a sense of achievement, recognition, responsibility and reward. Learning devoid of these feelings of inner satisfaction is a sterile experience.

(3) Growth and development. The overall aim of education and training is to bring about some larger change in people, groups and organizations or society. This involves a larger scale of growth and development than would be reflected by most long lists of learning objectives.

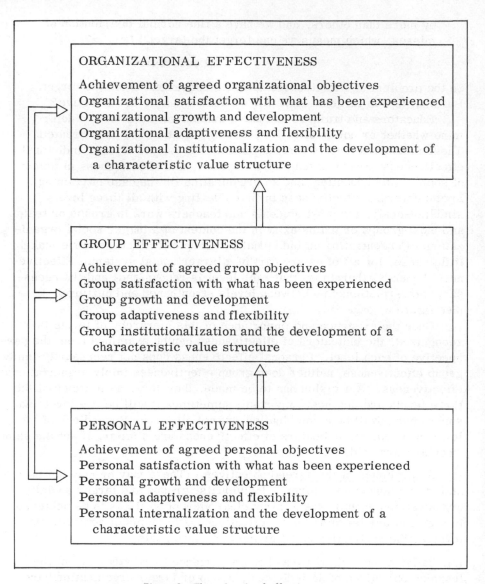

ORGANIZATIONAL EFFECTIVENESS

Achievement of agreed organizational objectives
Organizational satisfaction with what has been experienced
Organizational growth and development
Organizational adaptiveness and flexibility
Organizational institutionalization and the development of
   a characteristic value structure

GROUP EFFECTIVENESS

Achievement of agreed group objectives
Group satisfaction with what has been experienced
Group growth and development
Group adaptiveness and flexibility
Group institutionalization and the development of a
   characteristic value structure

PERSONAL EFFECTIVENESS

Achievement of agreed personal objectives
Personal satisfaction with what has been experienced
Personal growth and development
Personal adaptiveness and flexibility
Personal internalization and the development of a
   characteristic value structure

Figure 2: Three levels of effectiveness

Indeed, this indicator may well be the most important of all, since it
involves the very essence of education itself.

(4) <u>Adaptiveness and flexibility.</u> Flexibility and adaptiveness, the
ability to respond quickly and appropriately to changing situations, are
essential ingredients of both an effective educational and training programme. Rigidity of viewpoint, and inflexibility of mind, are some of the
dangers that an over-emphasis on efficiency can nurture.

(5)  <u>Internalization or institutionalization.</u>  This is the last of the five
measures relating to effectiveness, and involves the survival or permanency of what has been achieved.  At the personal level, educational
achievement hopefully involves some sort of internalization, in the sense
that learning is organized into some sort of coherent and consistent value
system.  In terms of a group or larger organization, real achievement
involves some sort of institutionalization, in the sense that what has been
learned is so valued by the group or oganization that it accepted and supported.  Evidence of internalization and institutionalization would be indicated by positive attitudes, interest and commitment.

These five indicators, examined from the perspective of the individual, group and organizational or society levels, can be used to determine
whether or not an effective and efficient learning situation has been
created.  Their realization demands a level of commitment, knowledge
and skill that takes education and training far beyond the craft level.
They pose a series of challenges for educational technology and educational technologists that is quite different in kind and character to the old
audio-visual and programmed learning background from which we sprang.

## EDUCATIONAL TECHNOLOGY FOR EFFECTIVENESS

Drawing the vital distinction between efficiency and effectiveness in
terms of 'doing things right' and 'doing the right things' highlights the
two roles or responsibilities that can be accepted by educational technologists.  The path of efficiency leads us to an important, but peripheral
role, concerned with helping to increase and enhance the power of message design.  Efficiency is concerned with ensuring that the probability
of what is predicted is increased, that a teacher's or instructor's
anticipations and expectations are actually realized.  Such a view puts
us squarely in the media field, which incidently includes printed books
and duplicated papers as well as the more esoteric problems of band
width and cable TV.

Effectiveness, as we have seen, leads us along another path, where
the role of educational technology is not only critical, but central to the
whole communication process.  Message design is now subservient to
what can only be called 'educational development' or what is now being
increasingly referred to as 'instructional development'.  This involves
every aspect of communication, and is centered on the concepts of
sharing and influence.  Such a view lacks the mechanistic flavour which
some see in the media approach, and introduces a more organic,
humanistic view of both education and training based upon the total rich-
ness and diversity of the behavioural sciences.

## Instructional Development

The basic value underlying all instructional development, theory and practice, is that of choice. Educational or instructional development is nothing more than a harnessing of all of our basic skills involved in answering our three traditional, task-centered questions of:

    a.  'Where are we going?'
    b.  'How shall we get there?'
    c.  'How will we know when we've arrived?'

to the more fundamental people-orientated question of planned growth and development founded on choice and appropriateness. Such a view enables us to deal with such questions as 'Why are we going there?' (i. e. , where have the objectives come from?), 'How many ways can we choose to get there?' (i. e. , let's make decisions rather than judgements), and 'Can we ever be sure we have arrived?' (i. e. , it may be better to have travelled, than to have arrived. ) The products may be **concrete** (e. g. , a discussion or lecture; a book or programmed text; film or video tape; simulation or game) or **abstract** (e. g. , team building; improved interpersonal competence and influence; better planning, problem solving and goal setting; more appropriate conflict management, etc. ) Indeed, since the main problems facing schools today appear to involve problems of identity, mission discipline, and competence, it may well be that the abstract products of educational development may be more relevant than the more typical concrete ones.

Instructional development, within the context of an effective educational technology, refers to a long-range effort to improve the overall quality of education and training, both in terms of **what** is experienced (i. e. , the content) as well as in terms of **how** it is experienced (i. e., the process). See figure 3. It is concerned with planned growth, with increased effectiveness as well as efficiency, and with deliberate rather than with chance interventions, using the concepts of behavioural science, into the total people and task system that is the context of education and training. Such a change towards more effective educational or training programmes, however, will be short lived, unless continuous renewal or permanency are included in the objectives. For this reason, as Lewin (1947) suggests, preparing people for change (i. e. , unfreezing the situation) and then bringing about the desired change, must be followed by some type of refreezing — otherwise all that has been gained may be lost. How often have we forgotten this simple truism?

The aims of instructional development are basically quite simple. Overall the objective is to develop a self-renewing, viable educational or training programme that can be presented in a rich and diverse number of ways, depending upon what is to be achieved and the people who are involved. In this way, 'form follows function', so that collaboration

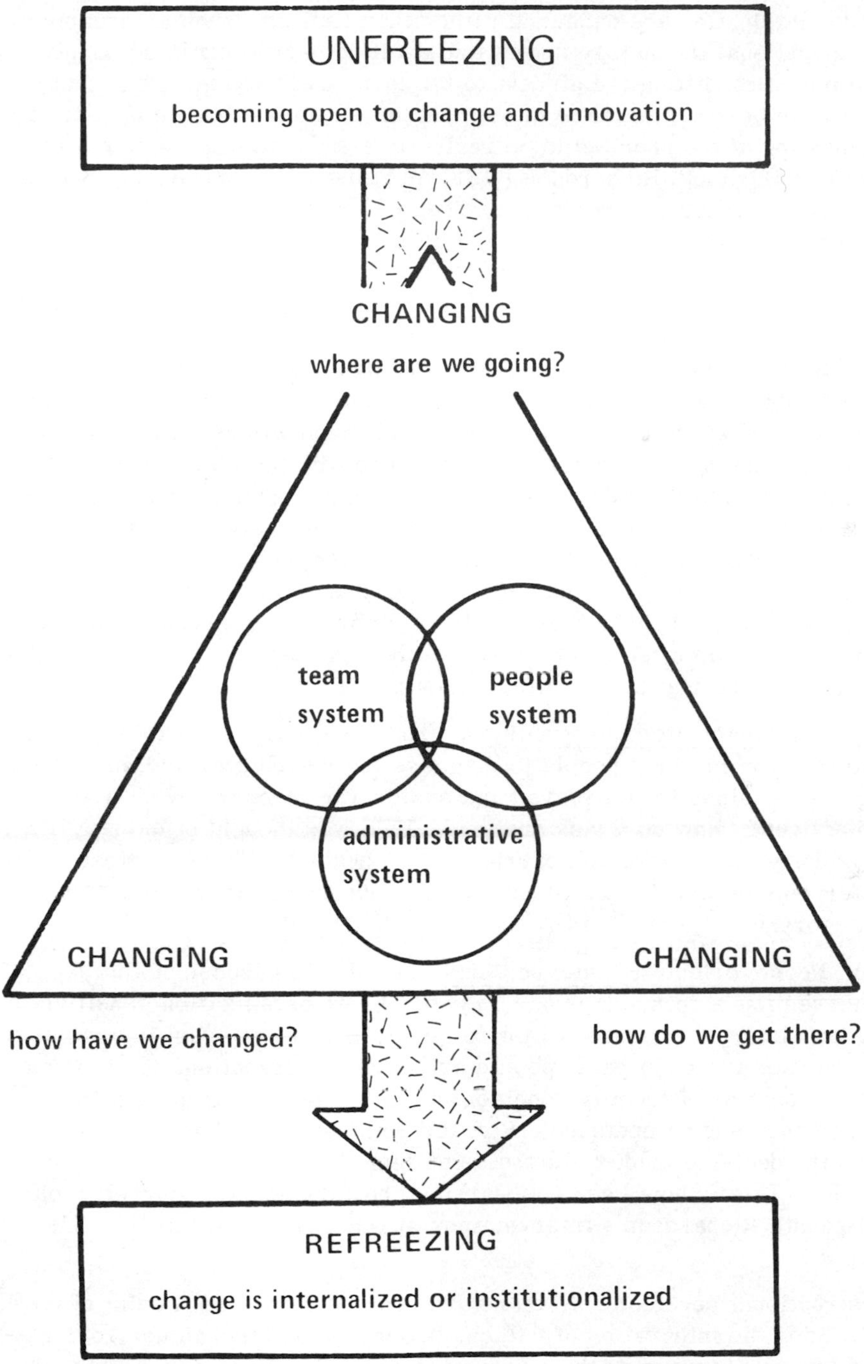

# UNFREEZING

## becoming open to change and innovation

## CHANGING

### where are we going?

team
system

people
system

administrative
system

CHANGING

CHANGING

how have we changed?

how do we get there?

# REFREEZING

## change is internalized or institutionalized

Figure 3 : Some of the concerns of instructional development.

and participation are enhanced rather than limited. Such an organic view in educational technology is new and exciting, and contrasts sharply with the model of 'fitting the student to the task' (see Davies, 1971) that seems to be characteristic of so many of the things that we appear to do. Something of the promise to be realized is suggested in the perceptive work of Elizabeth Richardson (1973) at Nailsea Comprehensive School in Somerset. There, under the auspices of Bristol University and the Schools Council, she has worked for three years as a consultant to the human system, helping teachers clarify their problems, so that they could arrive at personal solutions which enabled them to provide better for the children in their charge.

Such a view highlights another objective of instructional development. There is a fundamental need to integrate the task system (with which educational technologists have traditionally concerned themselves) with both the administrative system (concerned with policies, rules and regulations; roles and responsibilities) and the human system (concerned with individual, group and organizational needs, values and satisfactions). The integration of these three systems affects the effectiveness of the system as a whole. Any planned change must consider the potential impact on each of these three systems before any intervention is made. Interventions into the three systems, too, can take many forms. Although they cannot be rigidly classified, they might include:

(a) Task orientated interventions. The basic purpose of this type of intervention is to get people to diagnose their problems and make appropriate decisions in an ordered and systematic manner. What are your objectives? Now do a task analysis. Have you thought of using a film? Try doing this. Have you carried out an evaluation? etc. Most of the interventions in educational technology have tended to fall into this category.

(b) People orientated interventions. The basic purpose of this type of intervention is to make people, a group or an organization sensitive to its own internal processes, and to generate some interest in analysing them. For the most part, people orientated interventions tend to deal with problems of identity, control and influence, needs and goals, acceptance and competence. How did you feel about that decision? How was the decision made? How did you feel about how the decision was made? This is how I see you working, how do you see yourself? etc. Elizabeth Richardson's interventions at Nailsea School fall into this class.

Instructional development, therefore, can be viewed as a point of view, involving the integration of values, processes and techniques, orientated towards increasing the effectiveness of education and training. In order to accomplish this objective, it uses the concepts and procedures of educational technology and the social sciences.

**Technology**

Some people will probably feel that such a view has little or anything to do with the term 'technology', since the very word involves a more restricted and specialized meaning. Such a view, however, ignores an older meaning of the word. Machines and equipment (e. g. , computers and projectors) are merely tools, they are not the technology itself. Similarly, software (e. g. , programmes and film) are not the technology. Technology is concerned with 'know-how'. It is characterized by **how** the machines and software are used. Technology is a process, rather than an object. As such, it is more closely related to effectiveness than to efficiency, with people rather than with things.

## CONCLUSION

Underlying all human endeavour are sets of values and assumptions, which exert a powerful influence on beliefs and behaviour. Nowhere are these values and assumptions more evident and pervasive than in the communication process. Education and training, which are but specific applications of communication, suffer from all the problems and difficulties characteristic of human communication. Problems and difficulties which educational technology seeks to mitigate, if not to solve. Unfortunately, educational technologists often fail to recognize that educational technology itself is founded on underlying values and assumptions (see Davies, 1973) of which they are sometimes unaware.

One set of values and assumptions related to efficiency limits educational technology to a subordinate role. An alternative set of values and assumptions related to effectiveness enhances the promise of educational technology by placing it in a central position in education and training. There its concepts and procedures are employed from the point of view of instructional development, which integrates values, processes and techniques so as to increase the effectiveness of what is achieved.

In this way, through the perspective of instructional development, educational technologists provide opportunities for people to function as human-beings rather as resources in a task-orientated process. Such a view enables the educational technologist to create learning environments and opportunities in which learning becomes an exciting, challenging, creative activity. People can be given an opportunity for influencing both the content and process of education and training, as well as being treated as a human-being with complex sets of needs – all of which are important. Such a concept 'demands nothing of what is past. It demands presence, responsibility; it demands you'.

REFERENCES

Buber, M. (1955) <u>Between Man and Man</u>. New York: Beacon Press.

Carroll, L. (1907) <u>Alice's Adventures in Wonderland</u>. London: Rackham.

Davies, I.K. (1971) <u>The Management of Learning.</u> London: McGraw-Hill.

Davies, I.K. (1972) Style and effectiveness in education and training: a model for organizing teaching and learning. <u>Instructional Science</u> **1**, 1, 45-88.

Davies, I.K. (Ed.) (1973) <u>The Organization of Training</u>. London: McGraw-Hill.

Drucker, P.F. (1967) <u>The Effective Executive</u>. London: Heinemann.

Harris, M. (1973) Teaching as a form of loving. <u>Psychology Today</u> **7**, 4, 59.

Lewin, K. (1947) Frontiers in group dynamics. <u>Human Relations</u> **1**, 1, 5-41.

Richardson, E. (1973) <u>The Teacher, the School, and the Task of Management</u>. London: Heinemann.

# Obstacles to the effective use of communication media in a learning system

A. W. BATES, The Open University

**Abstract:** There is strong evidence that in many cases, new teaching media are under-used, and where used, frequently fail to achieve their potential. Some reasons for this are: lack of clear teaching objectives in setting up a media system; inappropriate organizational structures for the integration of media and curriculum; an ignorance of the problems and possible solutions in the use of media for teaching; and insufficient expenditure, usually recurrent, but in some cases capital as well. The two most serious of these are the lack of an appropriate organizational structure, and ignorance of the problems of using media.

Communication media will not achieve their potential if they are merely added as separate and extra components to an existing structure which already has its own internal dynamic. The graft will not take. New media require new methods of teaching, which in turn demand new organizational structures to support them. Also, there are a great many unknown or unsolved problems in using media for teaching, among which are: identifying the most appropriate teaching uses of various media, when they are used in conjunction, and identifying and solving the problems encountered by students in learning from media.

The lack of appropriate organizational structures and the difficulties in identifying media learning difficulties could be overcome by determined action by funding bodies. Organizational changes could be demanded as a precondition of capital or renewed current expenditure; and a much greater proportion of recurrent expenditure should be devoted to systematic monitoring, research and evaluation.

First of all, I would like to begin by defining — very crudely — what I mean by 'media'. I consider the term 'medium' describes various methods of distributing information. It would include books and teachers in a face-to-face situation. In this talk, however, I am mainly concerned with the deliberate application of mechanical or electronic media, and particularly television, to the learning process.

Now there is strong evidence that where they exist, educational media are generally underused, and when they are used, they are not used effectively, especially if we consider the effort and costs involved in setting up and running educational media systems. I am ready to defend this statement, by quoting evidence from the conventional British universities and teacher training colleges, school closed-circuit systems, institutions overseas, and, in certain aspects, the Open University. There's no point though in using a sledgehammer to crack a nut. All of us here who are concerned with using media in education will probably admit that all is not well. Does this mean though that media are just a gimmick, and don't really have a genuine role to play in education? No. I think not. The problem is that we don't know **enough** about media, and how to use them, in an educational context. We are **ignorant**, and worse, very often afraid to admit it. Alternatively, the **wrong** criteria are applied to judging the value of the programmes. For instance, a number of my colleagues in the BBC judge the worth of the OU programmes by the smoothness and imagination of the production. While these may well be **pre-requisites** for learning to take place, there are **other** factors which also have to be considered, such as whether the students have **understood** what the programme was attempting to do. The depth of our ignorance can be judged from enquiries my colleague, Margaret Gallagher, made of the former 'high-activity centres' in British universities. We were wanting to see whether some of the problems we were encountering at the Open University in the use of media were being shared or over-come in these institutions. Everyone was most co-operative, but basic information regarding costs, evaluation, utilization, even output, were all lacking. There was **no way** in which these institutions themselves could judge their own effectiveness.

Now where does our ignorance lie? To try and answer this, I am going to draw on experience from two quite different areas — the Open University, which I hope won't need any further description, and my work on a UNESCO team advising the government of Thailand on the set-ting up of a national educational media system. Although both the en-vironment and the intended usage of media are quite different, some of the problems encountered are remarkably similar.

Ignorance I would suggest lies primarily in five areas:

(1) We don't know how to get institutions to define **overall** objectives or **policy** for the use of media; and we don't know the most suitable **functions** of media at a programme level, particularly when several media are being used at the same time in an integrated way.

(2) We don't know how programmes **affect** students, or how students can **integrate** programmes fully into their other modes of learning.

(3) We don't know the best — or even adequate — ways of **organizing** institutions so that the best use can be made of media.

(4) We don't know how much money and resources are **appropriate** for a given media system, nor the **proportion** of money and resources that needs to be devoted to various aspects of a media system.

(5) We don't have a relevant methodology for evaluation and research into educational media systems.

Let's take the first of these areas of ignorance — of knowing the best way to **use** media in an educational system. Educational media systems are usually set up for a variety of reasons. One institution may want one because a **neighbouring** institution has one. Individuals or groups within — or even outside — an institution may see the introduction of a media system as bringing power or career benefits to themselves. Another institution may choose a media system because such a system has appeared to be successful — or at least have high potential — in another setting. Or a media system may be introduced — as often happens unfortunately in developing countries — simply because the finance for such a system is available in the form of loans or grants. These motives should not be underestimated. They are very powerful, if not legitimate. Even after a system is set up, it can exist without substantial educational justification. It will have developed its own in-built inertia — 'conservative dynamism' is I believe the jargon. People are in posts with positions and resources to defend. Particularly in higher education establishments in this country, and generally in developing countries, there is a 'laissez-faire' attitude of non-interference. The fact therefore that the existence of educational media systems is widespread is no indication in itself that such systems are needed. This is **not** because there **are** no good reasons for introducing media. It is because, despite a lot of experience now, we still don't know yet how to identify clearly what we expect the introduction of media to do for an educational system. We tend, for a start, to confuse the objectives of the education system as a **whole** with possible objectives for the **media** system.

Let me given an illustration. In Thailand, there are a number of high-level objectives set by the Ministry of Education for the educational system — to increase the sense of Thai-ness, to teach respect for authority and discipline, to help adults and children to solve or cope with problems in their environment, and so on. It would be easy to assume that a media system should be introduced to reinforce these objectives, or at least make the teaching in these areas more effective. However, such an idea takes no account of the **limitations** of media. There are some things it can do much better than others. Also, some of the objectives set for the Thai education system in general were being quite well achieved already. It was decided therefore to examine whether media could help in those areas where it appeared there were weaknesses in achieving high-priority objectives. In particular, a major area of weakness, receiving high priority in Thailand after the October revolution, was in the preparation of children and adults for living in a democratic society. The question we had to ask ourselves was: could media help, and if so, in what way? There are two points I want to make here.  First of all, I think it was a major advance to examine how media might help to tackle a specific problem (or rather a range of problems, as this was not the only one), rather than to devise a blanket system for educational media.  Secondly, do we know enough about the characteristics of each of the various educational media to be able to answer such a question?  Now we **did** in fact think that media could play a major part in this process, particularly in introducing methods of teaching encouraging rational and critical thinking, both directly through media, and through using media for inservice teacher training.  I believe though that to use media **specifically** to achieve such an objective — to prepare adults and children for living in a democratic society — would be a unique decision.  Certainly, it's a gamble, because as far as I know, there is no evidence to suggest that such an approach to using media has worked in the past.  Frankly, we still do not know in what ways media can be more effective than other methods of teaching.  I have suggested that a first step in introducing a media system should be the definition of the overall aims of an educational system, and an analysis of the existing weaknesses.  In other words, what are we **not** doing that we want to do, and can media help us to do it more effectively?  The real difficulty with this exercise though is not in actually carrying it out, but in deciding **who** should carry it out.  Usually, it is extremely difficult to get people with responsibility, authority **and** the requisite expertise to participate together in this kind of exercise, but I will come back to this problem later.

I have been talking about defining **overall** policy regarding the use of media.  However, once a system has been set up, objectives and policy are likely to change over a period of time.  We must therefore know as much as possible about differences in the potential of different media, so that appropriate uses for media, and appropriate combinations of media can be **chosen** to meet the changing needs of the system that media are serving.  Basically, this means finding out what each medium can do that **can't** be done in other ways more economically or effectively.  Do we know this?  We have got some ideas from Open University experience;  for instance, preliminary research has so far identified 25 functions which appear to be particularly appropriate to television in the Open University situation.  These were identified by applying the following criteria: these functions would be **difficult** or **impossible** to achieve in any other way available to us;  or these functions are more **economically** achieved through television, either in terms of student time or cost to the institution.  Examples of such functions are:

(1)  To increase the students' source of belonging to the University, through making the teaching less impersonal, by identification of course designers, giving information at the University, etc.

18

(2) to demonstrate experiments or experimental situations where equipment or phenomena to be observed are large, expensive, inaccessible or difficult to observe without special equipment.

(3) to change student attitudes towards a particular subject area by presenting material in a novel manner or from an unfamiliar viewpoint.

(4) to illustrate principles involving two, three, or n-dimensional space.

(5) to demonstrate, through performance, methods or techniques of dramatic production, or interpretation of dramatic works.

These need much further development, and validating, though, and may well be specific to the Open University situation. We haven't been able to **start** yet on radio. It also appears from Open University experience that the mere availability of media can in fact lead to **new** teaching objectives. With more certainty, we **do** know that using media requires a fundamentally different approach to teaching and learning (another point I wish to take up later). Now there is a tremendous amount of **experience** in the use of television and radio in education, and many people will be prepared to offer advice — but is this advice general or specific; subjective or objective? How can I, as an academic aspiring to teach through television, judge whether the advice is valid or not? And just how much experience is there of integrated multi-media teaching, and how this affects the way that television and face-to-face teaching are used? How much of this experience is codified, validated and communicated to others? Or does everyone have to re-invent the wheel each time? (I am of course talking about the **educational** uses of media, and **not** the technical processes of programme making, which are already well codified.) Until we know a lot more about the most appropriate **functions** of media in a teaching system, it will be impossible to devise any **policy** for media use. At a programme level the current ad hoc system of 'Why don't we do this?...' and 'Can you get me out of this difficulty with your camera...' will prevail, and even more seriously, at a policy level the 'band-wagon' effect of every situation — or even every department — wanting its own media system is likely to continue.

As well as not knowing enough about the appropriate uses to which we can put media, we are also pretty ignorant of their **effects**, and how to **integrate** media into the rest of the teaching. I was going to say that this was particularly true when the student is studying independently, without a teacher, but we have evidence that there are even more problems when an intermediate teacher — that is, one who has **not** been directly involved in the programme — is present. At the Open University, we have begun examining how students make use of our programmes. We keep discovering problems that were unanticipated. We don't know how **many** students have the same difficulties, and we don't know how many more **problems** there remain to be dug up. We do know though that much more research needs to be done into the problems encountered by students in learning from media.

I wish to demonstrate some of these problems from Open University experience. I want to make it clear that the examples I use are both, in my opinion, excellent uses of television, in that they bring to students important and relevant experiences which would have been difficult to achieve in any other way in the Open University situation. It is not the programmes that are at fault, but our ignorance of how to use them properly.

Perhaps the most difficult kind of programme for the Open University student to deal with is the 'case-study' or 'real-life' situation — what Richard Hooper has called 'primary source' material. This kind of programme is very popular with course teams, particularly in the Social Sciences and Educational Studies. Case-studies make 'interesting' programmes, since they usually have a strong story line, and bring the 'real' world to the course. It must be admitted however that far too often, our course teams themselves are not too clear about what students are supposed to do with case-study material. Let me give you an example. I'm going to show you an extract from a programme for a second level course, 'Urban Development'. This programme — 25 minutes in length — has no commentary. It portrays a day in the Chicago Business District.

**(Extract from DT201/TV7 (Videotape) shown at this point.)**

Showing extracts from programmes can be very misleading, but you yourselves may be wondering what the point of that excerpt was. It was intended to show how the nature of the shops and buildings change — in accordance with the theory expounded in the accompanying correspondence text — as we neared the centre of the business district. This theme was just one of several contained in the programme. In such programmes, the student might be expected to assess the case-study material as evidence for — or against — arguments set out elsewhere in the course material. These arguments in fact may be spread throughout the course, since case-studies are 'messy', in that they involve many concepts at one time. Students may also be expected to bring together for the first time, principles or skills developed through the course, in order to analyse or explain the case-study material. But for the students to be able to do any of these things, they must be **helped.** It's just not good enough to show such a programme and expect the student to **know** what to do. Broadcast notes that explain the function of the broadcast, and give the student guidance in what to look for, are needed, at least for the first few times of presenting such programmes. In other words, students must be **taught** how to use such programmes, if they are to benefit fully from them. This programme I've just shown was in fact originally put out with accompanying notes, but these did **not** advise the students on how to **approach** the programme. Subsequently, we are experimenting with notes which more openly tell students what to look for, to see whether this helps them. It was interesting however that of all the programmes on this course, students found this the 'easiest'. We reckon that this is because case-studies can be approached by the student at different levels. A case-study may well be seen as just an interesting story — a nice trip through Chicago — without the student attempting to analyse it in the ways just suggested. A further problem associated with case-study material is that since they draw on real-life situations, they sometimes contain evidence which not only **can't** be explained by the course as far as it has developed, but can in fact produce evidence which **confuses** or even **contradicts** the theories and concepts being expounded in the correspondence text. I know of at least two instances when, working in fact with Richard Hooper, we came across the situation where all the material we collected, no matter how hard we tried, refuted what our academic colleagues were arguing.

I mentioned earlier that intermediate tutors can in fact cause more, rather than less, problems for students, if they are not trained to use media themselves. I want to show you another extract from what I think was an excellent programme, from a BBC Further Education series 'Man in Society'.

**(Extract from 'Man in Society' — shown at this point)**

The producer showed this programme before the course began to a meeting of about 50 tutors running evening classes in conjunction with the course, as an example of the kind of programme being made. Instead however of discussing how programmes such as this could be used in a course of social psychology (as they were repeatedly asked to do by the producer), the tutors engaged in a long and heated discussion about the rights and wrongs of student demonstrations. i.e. the point the programme was trying to make was completely missed.

This example is revealing, in a number of ways. It does demonstrate that we are all, academics, students, and tutors alike, susceptible to distraction by powerful illustrative material. (One of the reasons why it is sometimes difficult to discover the relevance between programme and correspondence text at the Open University is because the selection of material by academic and producer has been more influenced by its dramatic quality than by its relevance).

I have time to show you only these two examples of the kinds of programme which appear to cause students and tutors difficulties. I could have shown many more instances — I do have other examples on the tape. I hope I've done enough though to indicate just how little we know about how to use television, and how to support students in their use of television. We don't even yet have a suitable means of **classifying** different kinds of programmes, a necessary first stage to communicating with each other about student difficulties and their possible resolution.

Even so, these problems do appear to be open to examination and experiment. We can at least try out various programme formats, and see what happens. Far less amenable to experiment is the fundamental problem of how we should **organize** an educational system, so that we can make the best use of media **within** the system. The trouble with media, such as television, and now computers, is that they are late-comers. To cope with them, it might seem a natural thing to create new departments or divisions, responsible for their development and management. But if media facilities are organized **too** autonomously or **too** independently of subject disciplines, they become like ivy without a tower to cling to (if you will forgive the expression). At the same time, I think it has been a fundamental mistake to consider audio-visual media **merely** as a service to subject disciplines. At its extreme, this has led to audio-visual departments sitting back and waiting for patients, who tend to come only when their sickness is in its terminal stages. A separate audio-visual department is, in my view, only tenable as an **administrative convenience**, an efficient way of organizing production, grouping staff and administering money. **Policy** for the overall use of media, and the content of individual productions and their relationship to the rest of the teaching being experienced by students, should evolve from a **partnership** between academics with responsibility for subject specialisms and colleagues of equal status with responsibility for the production and organization of communication media — of which, inci-dentally, I believe face-to-face teaching and books should be considered as integral parts. This means that the **design** of degree courses or any other systematic programme of teaching should take into account from the very beginning the existence of available media facilities. The great mistake has been to see television, or tape-slides, or overhead projectors, or face-to-face teaching, as being **alternatives**, in competi-tion with each other. When used in **conjunction**, though, a whole new range of teaching objectives and methods is opened. What was impos-sible before, now becomes possible. Media are being mis-used when we try to do the same thing as before, but only better. Media used in conjunction allow us to do **different** things. But now we run into another area of ignorance. What? Again, it is difficult to answer, because experience is very limited of designing courses from the very beginning with a range of media in mind, and, as already mentioned, we still don't know enough about the teaching characteristics of media used together. We are seeing at the Open University though, new kinds of courses and parts of courses — not many and not always successfully designed— which do suggest that a breakthrough, even a revolution, in teaching is possible. Courses such as War and Society, which relies partly on archive film as a historical source, and The History of Design and Architecture, relying heavily on a combination of audio tape and extensive colour illustrations, could only have been possible through the use of new media. The media are to some extent determining what is taught, and how it is taught at the Open University.

Some may feel that this is putting the cart before the horse, making media take precedence over subject matter. It is not. If we had no books, we would teach in a different way — by word of mouth, by dialogue. But we do have books, so both methods we use, and indeed, the areas we choose to teach, are different. Most University teaching is founded on the existence of books. But if we consider media to be primarily means of distributing information, then books and television have a functional equivalence, even if their characteristics are different. If courses are designed from the beginning with media in mind, it still leaves us free to reject their use. But knowledge is not finite. The methods available for teaching will inevitably influence what is taught.

Now if what I have said is correct, this has fundamental consequences for the organization of teaching. The mere attachment of a separate audio-visual department to an existing institution is not enough. Radical changes are also required in the rest of the system, to bring together people to work as a team, so that specialists in media can advise subject specialists in the potential of media in their subject areas. This coming together will not happen universally without radical changes on the structure of the institution. This means creating some kind of organizational method which will bring together, naturally, as part of the ongoing teaching process, producers and academics, who work **through** a course together.

This is perhaps the greatest strength — the most important innovation — of the Open University. It's impossible for an academic to teach at the Open University without making use of its media services — and not just television and radio, but print media services, such as diagrams, photographs, layout, etc. The course team system ensures that courses are designed from the beginning with the potential of media in mind. The effect of this can be seen by the demand for broadcasting resources from the academics. Course team chairmen — who are always subject specialists, not media producers — have requested more than 400 programmes a year (television and radio) since the University began, yet our maximum production and transmission load is 300 programmes a year. Because of the demand from academics — or at least from course team chairmen — we are having to broadcast before 7. 00 in the morning and from next year after 12. 00 at night. The course team structure ensures that producers are available to sit in on the planning of every course, right from the beginning. It's interesting to note that a number of conventional universities are beginning to move towards the course team idea, including audio-visual production staff in their teams, to design new or restructured courses.

It's not enough though to get just the **teaching** structure right. The introduction of media requires not only the organization of teaching to be radically altered, but also the organization for overall **policy-making** within the institution to be changed, to reflect the changes in teaching method. This is, I would argue, a major failing in the Open University. Its main policy-making boards are dominated by representatives of two power groups: the six faculties and the 13 regions. Faculties were set up **after** the first foundation course teams had been appointed. They bring together academics with similar interests from various course teams. The division into faculties of course is artificial, and mainly an administrative and management convenience. It allows academics — subject specialists — within very broadly similar subject areas, to have their views represented, usually by the Dean, within the management committees of the University. Similarly, despite their crucial role within the University, the regions are mainly an administrative device for organizing students and part-time staff. But neither faculties nor regions actually design and produce courses. Students do not enrol in a faculty, at the Open University, nor for a region, but for **courses**, and we have evidence that they are enrolling for courses which suit their needs, **across** the faculty structure. Furthermore, academics are appointed initially not to faculties or regions, but to course teams. It is the **course-team**, which is the 'prime mover' — the powerhouse — of the Open University.

I see the recent acrimonious squabbling over resources, and the more frightening long-term proposals for an unrealistic number of courses, (which would have crippled the University, and have now fortunately been modified) to be a direct result of this mis-match between the teaching structure and the policy-making structure in the Open University. The problem is that faculties and regions, as interest groups, **cannot** see the interests of the University as a whole. Until the policy-making structure reflects more directly the influence of the course team structure, the University will not fulfil its potential. Let me give an example – the allocation of broadcast resources....

Introducing into a new institution such as the Open University radical changes in structure is difficult enough. Trying to do the same in well-established, conventional institutions is even more formidable. Such changes will obviously have to come about gradually. But how can this be done? Fortunately, I don't have to answer that question. It is a question which **needs** to be answered though before further resources are committed to new media in such institutions. In particular, it is necessary to involve the **whole** of the system as much as possible in overall policy decisions for the use of media.

If my analysis is correct, and our ignorance is widespread, then it may be thought that research and evaluation in particular has failed. Certainly, there are a number of radical weaknesses in many of the media research and evaluation methods commonly used. Basically, research designs and evaluation techniques used for studying educational media are either wrong, or insufficient in themselves. For instance, questionnaire techniques **can** provide essential **minimal** information about viewing figures, student reactions, and so on. But they are not sufficient on their **own** to tell us **why** different uses of media have failed or succeeded. Students in particular are a weak source of possible improvements since, as I have already mentioned, they are not usually able to judge for themselves the relevance of the programme material, nor do they usually know enough about the subject matter to suggest appropriate alternative methods of teaching.

The greatest weakness though has been the concentration, particularly in America, on comparative studies, that is, comparing teaching by one medium with the teaching — usually of the same material — by another medium. A typical example for instance — carried out by perhaps the most famous name in media research — is the comparison of two groups of school-children in Thailand, one group of schools receiving schools radio programmes, and another not. Not surprisingly, no significant difference was found between the two groups. But even if differences **had** been found, the research would have proved nothing, and been totally useless. There are several weaknesses in research of this kind. First of all, in order to control all variables as much as possible, the content taught, and even the method or style of teaching, must be similar, so that differences can be attributed to one medium, and not to these other factors. But I have already argued that if media are available, this will to some extent influence the actual content chosen, and it will **certainly** influence the style or method of presentation. So, in order to keep the experimental situation controlled, we remove from media all its potential advantages. It's like cutting off two legs of a horse to see whether it can run faster than a man. Secondly, the amount of **exposure** to media in the total context of a students' learning is usually minimal. It is consequently extremely difficult to measure the impact of media separately from all the other influences working on the learner. In fact, it is impossible to control all the variables, or weight them accurately, in most situations. The main weakness though of comparative studies is that they don't help producers or teachers one iota to improve themselves. Comparative studies don't tell us what is wrong, nor even more important, what can be done about it.

Evaluators of media in fact have placed far too much emphasis on performance testing. The main reason for this is the confusion between the **educational** objectives which media are serving — what the students are expected to learn or to do — and what I would call the **institutional** objectives of media — what you need to do to a programme to make it an effective teaching device. Performance testing measures always the **educational** objectives served by media. However, as already mentioned, media are best used in conjunction with each other, and with other modes of teaching, in particular the teacher. In such a situation, it is almost impossible to separate the effect of say television, when used in conjunction with books, face-to-face teaching and discussion between students. Again, apart from giving clues as to which content areas may need reinforcement by media — which may not be the best way of using them — performance testing does not suggest how programmes — or even other methods of teaching — can be improved. Now some of you may feel that this is too narrow a view of evaluation: evaluation should be concerned with whether students learn or not. That's all very well, unless you are concerned — as I am — with learning how to improve teaching methods, how to improve the use of media, and so on. In that case, evaluation of student performance is not enough.

I would argue that there needs to be much greater emphasis in evaluation on media or institutional objectives. By this I mean finding out what are the most appropriate teaching functions for television, what we need to do to support student utilization, what the range of programme format is, how the provision of various facilities affects format, how much money we should allocate between various media, and how we should allocate production and distribution facilities between different subject areas — in other words, on the kinds of question that producers and managers of teaching media are likely to ask. These require different kinds of research from mere performance testing and questionnaires — content analysis of programmes, participant observation of how decisions are made about uses of media, and of how students react to media, and of extreme importance, accurate accountancy and record-keeping, so that realistic costs can be allocated to different media and uses of media, and realistic utilization figures collected, so that effectiveness studies can be carried out. Furthermore, much of this will not be just the responsibility of people labelled 'evaluators' or 'researchers', although their specialist skills will be required. There is a **general** responsibility for evaluation on **all** those responsible for producing educational media.

There are several **reasons** why research and evaluation of educational media have been so ineffective. Most research has been done **outside** of educational media production centres. It has been primarily an academic exercise, carried out in Departments of Education, Departments of Mass Communications or Psychology, usually for individual masters or doctorate theses. Indeed, Universities are not providing adequate backgrounds in their teaching for the kind of research that I feel is desirable, although there is evidence that some Polytechnics are showing more interest. The main reason though for the weaknesses of research and evaluation is the lack of money set aside for evaluation or research by **all** institutions producing educational media. Hardly any University audio-visual department now has its own research or evaluation unit. One that did, recently sacked a researcher to use the money for two technicians. The Open University spends £2 million on broadcasting — and £10,000 (0.5%) on media research and evaluation. The BBC has never been interested in anything other than research into audience figures. For an activity which bristles with difficulties and unresolved arguments, and is still very much in the development stage, the lack of money for research and evaluation is nothing short of scandalous.

Now I realize that I have been trying to prove a negative — that we know very little in fact about how to use communication media properly for teaching. Proving a negative is always a risky enterprise, and in fact I hope during the conference — and in question time — people **will** stand up, and tell me I'm wrong, and that we know, without any dispute, the solutions to the problems I mentioned. To recap, these were:

1. the most appropriate functions for media,
2. student learning difficulties,
3. methods of organizing institutions,
4. finance, and
5. appropriate research methods.

But if I'm correct, and we are ignorant, I wouldn't like to see this used as an argument for not using media in teaching. For a start, we are talking about an extremely difficult activity. Certainly, I believe there are many problems in the use of media to which we don't yet know the answer. But the more I have researched into the use of media at the Open University, the more I have become convinced that we still haven't fully grasped the enormous potential of media. This is mainly because we haven't given them a real chance yet, because we don't know how to use them, or how to organize for teaching through media. So even at the risk of cutting down the level of productions to pay for this, I think we must devote much more in the way of resources to experimenting with new organizational structures, new methods of course design, new uses of media, new methods of teaching with media. To some extent, this is already happening. But we are **not** learning from it. It is not being done systematically, and any learning taking place is local, and not being communicated or shared. So, as a researcher, I take it as axiomatic that these endeavours must be supported by a reasonably funded and relevant programme of research and evaluation, based within the centres producing educational media. The funding bodies such as the UGC and research foundations could do much more to help in these activities by insisting on alterations to the structure of institutions who want to introduce or expand new media, and also insisting on adequate facilities and resources being set aside for research and evaluation. Otherwise, we will not learn and improve on our use of communications media for teaching, and television in particular will remain — just medium.

# Applications and limitations of radio in schools

R. W. JONES, Radio Merseyside

**Abstract:** The paper considers the relative merits of radio compared with other media such as television in the classroom learning situation. The flexibility and availability of radio is analysed, especially the ways in which the teacher can adapt the medium to the specific needs of the pupils by selecting only the relevant parts of any programme. It is argued that the technical simplicity of this adaptation process applies more to radio than to television. The need for a greater critical appraisal of any medium is stressed, especially in considering which is the best medium to use in any given learning situation; for example, which is best to communicate broad concepts, which to convey factual information and which to stimulate the imaginative response etc. Stress is put on the responsibility teachers have for improving their pupils' capacity to concentrate on audio-visual material. The present day misuse of resources, especially radio, is discussed in the paper. There is an analysis of the organization of resources not only at school level but also at local authority level, with the object of ensuring a positive policy towards providing the most efficient service. Finally, the paper suggests that the effective use of resources will come about only when teachers change their attitude towards audio-visual education, a change which will involve greater training at Colleges of Education and, at the in-service level, making the production of materials by teachers for their own specific use a priority.

## ADVANTAGES OF THE USE OF RADIO IN THE SCHOOL SITUATION

### FLEXIBILITY

The advantages of using radio in schools involve such considerations as cost and flexibility. Other forms of providing instruction and enrichment through the communications media such as television impose certain restrictions. Apart from the immense cost of producing the initial television programme — a cost which affects the extent of the coverage — there are also restrictions on the use of these programmes within the classroom situation. For example, it is more likely that a school will be equipped with a tape recorder than with a video tape recorder; video tape recorders are the exception. The availability of hardware is all-important to the effective use of radio, and television, in schools.

29

The advantage of recording a programme for later use is obvious. Teachers have the opportunity of becoming fully acquainted with the contents of the programmes before using them. Furthermore, this practice allows the teacher to select relevant support material, to localize and amplify the programme contents according to the specific needs of the pupils.

For centuries teachers have prepared their lessons from textbooks. What needs to happen is for a similar approach to be taken with tape material. Sadly, it very often happens that, despite thorough notes available to the teacher, the programme is simply used as a 'memorable experience'; the teacher takes the material at the time of transmission without really exploiting the possibilities of such a valuable stimulus.

The use of radio and television demands a great change in the teachers' attitudes towards these media resources and the relevant processes of curriculum development. Any programme, whether television or radio, is only as good as the teacher who handles it, and this handling demands certain skills both in realizing the interpretation and in instituting flexible classroom management. This flexibility is essential because it eliminates unnecessary barriers which inhibit teachers from using resources, especially when there may be a natural suspicion of using them. Given all these organizational factors, at the moment it is clear that, because of its special flexibility, radio seems to have the advantage over television.

**Radio and Television**

It has often been asserted that television is a more effective medium than radio. This assumption is based on the fact that more young people have grown up in a world where television has been the major source of communication and entertainment. An aphorism generally accepted is that one picture is worth a thousand words. One should not fall into the trap of assuming this to be universally true, even as far as educational broadcasting is concerned. The moving picture certainly achieves a seeming reality but this reality, as with any medium, is selective, according to the taste and programme judgement of the producer. There is a danger, therefore, that an over-exposure to the purely audio-visual media may dull the mind into a non-discriminating acceptance of what is being communicated. Often it is likely that an educational programme may be judged, in the mind of young viewers, with the same conditioned attitude as that operating when they enjoy light entertainment. This factor has been observed with Open University students who have needed to reconsider their viewing response to instructional television programmes, having been accustomed for so long to accepting the viewing situation in a non-demanding and non-discriminating way.

30

## The Need for Critical Appraisal of any Media

It is important for the teacher to be critical of any medium in a specific learning situation. In some cases television may well be the best medium to use, and in other cases it may be radio or radio-vision that is the best. For example, there is no doubt that a geography lesson would be enriched by showing actual moving pictures of a foreign country, even taking into account the inevitable selectivity of the producer making the film. The experience will certainly give a valuable approximate view of a country, which a textbook can achieve only in a limited way. Television works equally well in the case of the natural sciences, in which the camera, waiting patiently for a rare phenomenon to happen, can capture the event in stark reality. In both these cases what the teacher does is to use a medium to convey broad concepts about some thing or some place which is outside the direct experience, and indeed the possible direct experience, of the pupil. It is in this context that television has its particular strength.

However, when the teacher wishes to impart hard facts, it may be that radio vision is a more effective medium. This is because the visual image can be arrested, allowing the relevant factual information to be fed into the learning situation.

Television is not as successful in conveying detailed concepts based on facts such as mathematical or scientific formulae. The reason for this is that although such formulae can be made interesting by the use of animations the picture is constantly moving and this distracts the viewer. Even if the formula is kept on the screen for a certain length of time, no television producer can be certain that the length of time he has allowed for the audience to absorb the detail will be long enough for every person in a group situation. In this respect, radio vision is more flexible because the image can be held to suit the individual capacity to understand.

When it comes to radio, there are, similarly, areas for which the medium is not suited. For example, science is extremely difficult to convey on radio, although not impossible. Subtle use of sounds can create the reality of a scientific process taking place in a factory, so long as the commentator uses rich imagery to capture the scene; but, generally speaking, television is far more successful in this respect.

One conclusion may be drawn from what has been said. Just as the producer of a programme has to be aware of the strengths and weaknesses of the medium in which he is working, so the teacher must be equally discriminating as to the effectiveness of any programme for the needs of the pupils. One should never make broad statements about any medium. Producers are constantly trying out new techniques, and the success of the presentation often cannot be assessed until the programme has actually been made. It is therefore important for the teacher to have some knowledge of the nature of the various media before selecting the appropriate one to convey the body of knowledge which is to be communicated. This is especially important if teachers produce their own materials, which is becoming more and more usual with the expanding facilities in teachers' centres and with the building up of resources in some schools.

## The Strength of Radio

No programme can ever meet every teacher's requirements. The producer of a programme inevitably has to make a programme with a mass audience in mind. The producer may be aware of the cultural differences between various parts of the country but there is very little he can do to make his programme specifically relevant to all areas at the same time. In consequence he is left with no alternative to making a programme of general interest to everybody. The mark of a good teacher is his capacity to capitalize on the cultural and environmental background of the pupils by placing concepts in their right context. An example of this occurs most frequently in the difference in attitudes between country and urban children. It is the teacher who has to adapt audio and visual material to the specific needs of his pupils. Ideally, a teacher should select his own material. This may mean extracting the most relevant parts of existing resources and building the lesson around his own interpretation, and presentation. In order to achieve this ideal, two things have to be done. Firstly the teacher has to acquire skills not normally associated with traditional teaching — editing tape, photography, offset litho printing, display design etc. Secondly, the teacher must have readily available to him, at teachers' resource centres, machines to produce the material he needs. It is in this respect that radio is the medium most adaptable to classrooms; it is cheap, easily set up, and flexible, as opposed to television, which is technically unwieldy and, in terms of production, highly specialized. It is possible for one teacher on his own to make a radio programme, using very simple equipment. In many schools nowadays, even the pupils themselves are making their own programmes. The possibilities of radio are endless. Its skills are easily acquired with the growth of such agencies as Teachers' Resources Centres and BBC Local Radio Secondment Schemes.

## Developing the Imagination

Radio never reveals all. It can never capture absolute actuality, which television sometimes succeeds in doing. This is a major strength when it comes to stimulating imaginative responses. Subtle use of sounds and music used to enhance the spoken word can reveal endless dimensions in the mind of each individual. This unpredictable quality makes radio adaptable. It is particularly valuable as a stimulus for emotional experience. In the teaching of creative writing, for example, it is vital that the stimulus should not be too structured. If the stimulus is too structured, then the pupils all receive the same motivation. The result is a stereotyped response showing a lack of originality. If sound is used effectively, and if instructions are kept to a minimum, then it is possible to devise a programme which will stimulate individual responses. The creative writing which emerges from this non-directed experience is liable to be more original.

### Radio and the Learning Situation

The advantages that radio has in the classroom will depend on the readiness of the pupils to listen. Many teachers have observed that pupils find it difficult to concentrate for long periods on radio programmes. There are two possible reasons for this. Firstly, the predominance of television has conditioned young people to be more receptive to an audiovisual stimulus than to a purely audio one. Secondly, the role radio has played over the last ten years has been to provide a constant stream of inconsequential entertainment demanding no concentration. Consequently, for radio to be effective in the classroom the teacher has to virtually retrain his pupils to listen in a discriminating way. No individual teacher can bring about this change. It must be the policy of the school to encourage the capacity to listen. Just as every teacher is a teacher of reading, so every teacher should be a teacher of concentration.

### Mass Media Presentation

The mass audience has grown to admire and accept professional presentation of radio and television. Information, entertainment and opinion are expressed smoothly and quickly. This quality is often called 'slickness' by the critics of the mass media. However, the mass media have become such a powerful force in the national culture that teachers cannot afford to ignore their professionalism. When audio-visual resources are used in the classroom, teachers are competing to some extent with radio and television. As the pace of life has increased so has the rate at which information is presented. Similarly, people nowadays tend to communicate more by speaking than by writing. These factors must be recognized by the teacher in the classroom and he must attempt to meet the professionalism of the mass media and to acquire new skills and use his resources more selectively.

### Limitation of Radio

So far this paper has analysed the strengths of radio and also the few areas in which radio has limitations. The main point in radio's favour is that it is adaptable and cheap. This aspect, however, is only part of the operation. To achieve the undoubted potential of radio as a resource, the necessary policies and organization must be set up on two levels. Firstly, every school should have the equipment for recording programmes off air, and portable tape recorders and editing facilities for the adaptation of radio programmes and their supplementation with local material gathered by teacher and pupils. The availability of this hardware is a management problem which can be solved only by the Head Teacher and his staff, working out an agreed policy towards the efficient use of resources. Secondly, the organization and provision of equipment must be tackled on an Authority level. Local Education Authorities should have a positive overall policy towards resources. The best Authorities have been doing this already but there are still too many Authorities who have little or no policy, with the result that the provision of resources is very much a muddling-through process.

## The Clwyd Project

Evans, K. and Simpson, B. (1973), outlined the provision needed to support teachers with resources, not just with radio but with other resources as well. Three important aspects of the Centre's work are:

(a) Acquisition, maintenance and retrieval of many kinds of resources.

(b) Production and reproduction of resources.

(c) Professional development and training.

The overall policy underlying the Clwyd Project bears the mark of constructive thought. It departs from the usual attitude towards audio-visual education, which goes no further than the first objective listed here, namely the maintenance of machinery supplied to schools. To provide facilities for the three objectives to operate, a great deal of thought has gone into designing a purpose-built centre in Mold, which includes a television studio, a resource media library, and equipment for producing graphics etc. When the Centre opens, teachers will be able to come there to attend courses, be trained in a variety of techniques, and eventually make their own material. The Centre will be fully staffed by technicians and producers whose task it will be to help teachers translate their ideas into professionally produced material for the classroom.

## Resources Management

The limitation of radio, as with any other resource, is not so much the limitation of the medium itself as of its use. Radio has been used in schools in Britain for over forty years yet only recently have teachers progressed from the stage of passively listening to programmes at the time of transmission. Teachers are now beginning to realize that radio is a source of information which has to be adapted and augmented by the teacher for classroom use.

## Training

The importance of audio-visual education at Colleges of Education, and as part of in-service, is now a necessity, as the Clwyd Education Authority has realized. The BBC, through its local radio stations, has been leading the field over the past five years in training teachers in radio techniques. All twenty local radio stations have trained seconded teachers. In the case of one station, Radio Merseyside, thirty-four teachers were seconded between 1970 and 1973. In this period the Education Producer at BBC Radio Merseyside supervised two seconded teachers every month. Teachers were invited to apply for secondment, they were not selected for application. Of the thirty-four teachers, 77 per cent were under forty years of age. 54 per cent were under thirty. The oldest teacher was sixty-four and the youngest twenty-three. 40 per cent were female, evenly spread over the whole age range. It was noted how quickly the secondees picked up the skills of radio production. Each teacher was initially taught the mechanical skills; for example, the use of the mixer, playing records, using a pre-fade mechanism to line up subsequent sequences, editing, and using more than one tape recorder either to feed in inserts or to copy tape. The aim was to teach these skills in the first week of the four week training period. During the first week each secondee was given a programme title to think about and told that that programme had to be completed within the month. During the second week the secondees continued to practise the mechanical skills but writing skills were also introduced. The first thing to be learned was that a radio style must be adapted to the audience the programme is aimed at. For example, the difference between reporting a news item and writing a story for radio is vast. Furthermore, in educational broadcasting a programme-maker must use language suitable for different age groups. In the third week secondees were introduced to other production techniques such as the use of music, sound effects, dramatic inserts, interviews pre-recorded on a portable tape recorder etc. By the final week, the seconded teacher possessed the skills to put a programme together.

The training programme for the second, third and fourth weeks of secondment was flexible at Radio Merseyside. Secondees progressed to their next stage according to how they were getting on. One overall pattern emerged. Generally speaking, the secondees under the age of forty acquired the skills, especially the mechanical skills, far quicker than the teachers over forty. Some young teachers managed to produce two programmes and also contribute to the broadcast output during their month of secondment, whereas a high proportion of the older secondees were still making basic mechanical errors in their final week and found the completion of their programme a strain. Those teachers who were particularly successful have become regular contributors to the

Education Service after completing their secondment. There are two reasons for their selection as contributors. First, they possess skill and talent. Second, they are suitably motivated. This must be true of all contributors to an education broadcasting service. At Radio Merseyside 53 per cent of the secondees under forty still contribute regularly whereas only 25 per cent of those over forty have visited the studio since their training period. These figures suggest that in the field of educational technology there is a gap in motivation between the younger and older teachers. There are several reasons for this:

(a) The older teacher may be physically less dexterous and therefore more easily discouraged.

(b) The younger teacher has been brought up on gadgets and is more ready to accept technology as part of his everyday culture.

(c) The older teacher is higher up the ladder of promotion, being usually Deputy Head Teacher or Head Teacher. He is consequently less keen on being taught new techniques by younger people. Often he is reluctant to listen and seems half-hearted; there was evidence of this among older Radio Merseyside secondees.

Those who derived most benefit from Radio Merseyside's secondment scheme were those who became completely absorbed in radio. Unfortunately this enthusiasm is rare in audio-visual courses run by most colleges and Education Authorities. Often such courses do not go beyond the understanding of the working of the machines. For teachers to become resources-minded they must become involved in the production of material themselves. Radio Merseyside's secondment scheme provides just such a task-orientated training.

## The Future of Radio in Schools

Given that radio is cheap and flexible, it is clear that a great deal of re-thinking needs to be done in respect of improving the provision of resources. The management of resources both at Authority and school level needs to be considered carefully. Most important of all, teachers will never take resources seriously until they have acquired the skills to make their own. Training is a must. The disadvantage of radio is simply the way it is used at present. As Evans and Simpson, (op. cit.) quoted, 'The new contribution of educational technology is that it is problem-based and not gadget-orientated, and the significance of this for the Educational Technology Centre is clear.'

REFERENCE

Evans, K. and Simpson, B. (1973) Educational Technology Centre, Flintshire, North Wales. Programmed Learning and Educational Technology **10**, 3, 186.

# Practical teaching, the media and the Open University

G. D. MOSS, R. MASKILL, A. MORGAN, The Open University

**Abstract:** The Open University is teaching conventional science courses in an unconventional way. One part is the teaching of practical work. That practical work should be taught as an essential part of the repertoire of scientists is accepted. An analysis of 'practical work' into its cognitive and manipulative components and the Open University's ability to adequately teach these separate components has not been attempted.

The objectives of conventional practical courses will be examined along with the objectives of the existing Open University courses. These objectives will then be analysed for the type of learning involved.

The criteria for choosing a particular medium for teaching specific skills will be investigated and from these criteria the particular parts of a multi-media teaching system most appropriate to teaching practical work will be discussed.

The Open University relies almost entirely on the media for teaching practical work, because of its lack of conventional laboratory teaching facilities.

Using the evaluation of practical objectives and of the appropriate teaching media it is hoped to investigate the extent to which the Open University can hope to teach practical work. The implications of these findings on the stated aims of the science courses of the Open University will be discussed.

## INTRODUCTION

Undergraduate study at university is traditionally concerned more with the scholarly pursuit of knowledge within a subject than with the acquisition of practical skills. However, first-hand experience of the methods by which the subject advances is considered desirable, particularly for students going on to do research. In the natural sciences such experience usually takes the form of compulsory laboratory work which may account for up to 60 per cent of the course (Moss, G. D. and Aspden, P. 1973). The bulk of this paper will, therefore, be concerned with the practical aspect of science teaching. The questions it poses are:

(1) What are the objectives of practical work?

(2) How important are these objectives in relation to other teaching objectives in science?

(3) What are the best ways of teaching students to achieve these objectives?

(4) What criteria are used to select media more appropriate to the achievement of these objectives?

(5) How does the Open University try to get its remote students to achieve these objectives?

(6) How is the attainment of these objectives measured?

The first two questions can only be answered by considering the role of practical work within the overall philosophy of science. Figure 1 shows a simplified view of the activity known as science (Popper, K. R. 1963; Kuhn, T. S. 1962; Lakatos, I. and Musgrave, A. 1970). It shows how the body of scientific knowledge is related to a problem and how the problem-solving approach can contribute to, and possibly modify, the central core of knowledge.

A large amount of science teaching involves the transmission to the student of that part of the knowledge core which has withstood considerable testing. The student's attainment and comprehension of this knowledge is measured by tests of recall and comprehension. In Figure 1 we can see that this transmission of information is only part of the scientific approach. In order to achieve the whole approach, the teaching objectives must move from simple knowledge and comprehension (Bloom, B. S. 1956), into areas of application, analysis, synthesis and evaluation. It becomes clear that for the scientists the higher levels of cognitive activity involve a type of thinking that is a direct consequence of experimentation. It is also apparent that the process of experimentation is a useful vehicle for teaching these higher level objectives.

The tendency of most university practical courses (particularly at first and second year levels) is to set the student a series of exercises designed either to illustrate or verify his body of knowledge, or to give a brief experience of some of the practical tasks of science. These courses often occupy a large proportion of student time without appearing to reflect the empirical nature of science. Let us examine the objectives which might be associated with the process of experimentation:

(1) Knowledge of apparatus,

(2) Knowledge of procedures,

(3) Ability to handle apparatus,

(4) Ability to carry out procedures

(5) Ability to select appropriate procedures (Experimental design),

(6) Ability to devise new apparatus,

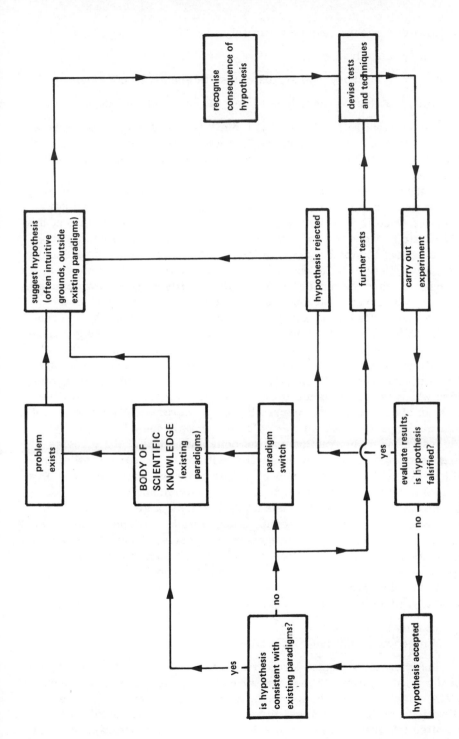

Figure 1: The process of science

39

(7)  Ability to record results accurately,

(8)  Ability to analyse data,

(9)  Ability to interpret and evaluate results and analyses,   and

(10) Ability to relate conclusions to central body of knowledge.

The interesting feature is that from this list of general objectives we can select only three (numbers 3, 4 and 6) which actually require the student to be in a laboratory (i. e. these objectives include manipulative components).

In theory then it should be possible to achieve the cognitive objectives without the student actually entering a laboratory.  The situation which the Open University finds itself in is one in which the student has only limited access to laboratories (to a summer school forming about 10 per cent of his total course, in fact).  Therefore the Science Faculty at the Open University is under great pressure to use other media at its disposal to teach the higher level cognitive skills related to experimentation which conventional universities **might** teach in a laboratory.

The difficulty for the Open University lies in teaching the psychomotor skills.  These can be sub-divided into two types.  Firstly, those which are of a constant nature (such as the operation of a machine which will always respond in the same way to a particular set of operations, e. g. a microscope, a single pan balance, a burette, etc. , and secondly, those which are not constant in this way (such as general preparative skills in chemistry, e. g. recrystallization, chromatography, etc. ).  The cognitive aspects of the former category of skill could be taught by demonstration or instruction and the constant nature of the machine response would allow the manipulative actions to be learned relatively effectively by the student following either a demonstration (on TV) or a programmed set of pictures with a written commentary.

However, this lack of constancy in the area of generalized skills (e. g. dissection) makes the acquisition of this latter type of skill very difficult, without practice, personalized supervision and assistance. It would seem that the Open University is not in a position to teach this type of skill effectively except at its summer schools.

If we therefore return to the kinds of skills associated with experimentation which it is believed **can** be taught at a distance, we have:

(a)  cognitive skills
(b)  simple and repetitive psychomotor skills

Unfortunately, no standard criteria have been established for selecting the most appropriate medium through which to teach experimental skills.  The media available to the Open University are written texts, television, radio, audiotapes, discs, and home experimental kits. These are often integrated in order to achieve a set of selected experimental objectives. For example, TV is very useful in demonstrating the manipulative skills of an experiment, while printed texts may discuss the cognitive aspects of the experimental situations both before and after doing the experiment, using the home experimental kit. Audiotapes have been used to give verbal instructions to students who are busy with apparatus, thus removing the need to refer to a book. Audiotapes have replaced radio in this situation since the student has constant access to them. Unfortunately, this is not the case with transmitted television and this imposes a constraint on the use of TV for demonstration purposes since the student must pace his work to TV transmissions in order to obtain the full benefit of the system. One can visualize the benefits of a video-cassette playback device or a film-loop machine in a conventional teaching laboratory.

As you can see, the major concerns tend to be the **constraints** imposed by the different media rather than their relative teaching **effectiveness.**

## Assessment of Objective Attainment

If we return to our classification of experimental objective, we have:

(a)  Cognitive objectives (e. g. experimental design)

(b)  Simple psychomotor objectives

(c)  Complex psychomotor objectives

Almost by definition, if the complex psychomotor skill cannot be taught except by personal contact, then it cannot be assessed except in the same way, i. e. by observation of the skill being performed in a laboratory. The measurement of attainment of the simple psychomotor skills is a little easier since direct observation is not essential. The student can be asked to **use an oscilloscope** to measure output characteristics of a given circuit (whose characteristics are known). The correct result implies an attainment of psychomotor skill. It is easy to imagine similar tests in Chemistry and Biology. This means that the test need not be carried out in a laboratory but can be done at a distance from the tutor (as is the case specifically in the Open University Electronics course).

The cognitive skills related to experimentation can be measured either by a tutor carrying out observations and interviewing students or it can also be carried out by written tests specifically designed for experimental objectives. It is interesting to note that an experiment carried out last summer (Morgan, A. R. and Moss, G. D. 1973) revealed that in the Science Foundation Course, the results of a written objective test of cognitive experimental skills correlated highly with a subjective tutor assessment (carried out in the laboratory) of cognitive **and psycho-**

41

**motor** skills. It is impossible to say how much emphasis the tutors placed on the psychomotor skills in relation to the cognitive skills in this case and one really needs to establish laboratory based tests specific to psychomotor skills in order to measure the attainment of such skill-based objectives.

## CONCLUSION

The teaching of practical or experimental skills should be regarded in the context of teaching science as a whole. Some of the cognitive skills, particularly those at a high level, are not restricted to being taught in a laboratory. There are, however, some kinds of psychomotor skills which appear to be difficult to teach, except in a laboratory situation. In relation to the scientific method as stated, these form a very small part of the whole.

REFERENCES

Bloom, B.S. (Ed.) (1956) Taxonomy of Educational Objectives Handbook I. The Cognitive Domain. New York: McKay.

Kuhn, T.S. (1962) The Structure of Scientific Revolutions. Chicago: Chicago University Press (2nd edn. 1970).

Lakatos, I. and Musgrave, A. (Eds.) (1970) Criticism and the Growth of Knowledge. London: Cambridge University Press.

Morgan, A.R. and Moss, G.D. (1973) Unpublished data.

Moss, G.D. and Aspden, P. (1973) Teaching Practical Skills: The Open University Approach. Paper presented to the Nuffield Conference on Practical Teaching.

Popper, K.R. (1963) Conjectures and Reputations. London: Routledge and Kegan Paul.

# Communicating by instructional film:
# a presentation strategy

H. MARCHANT, University of Liverpool

'You cannot teach a man anything — you can only help him to learn'

GALILEO (1564-1642)

**Abstract:**  The content and pace of many existing instructional films tend to over-estimate the learning capacities of an audience. The design of instructional facilities in many instances ends with the establishment of a physical environment. Little consideration is given to the type of learning that is to take place and arranging for the presentation to facilitate such learning.

The traditional 16 mm film presentation method may not necessarily be the best one for showing instructional films. In the present study, a clear written statement during intervals in a film showing, of the most important items of information to be learnt, led to a significant post-test performance on these items. The use of rear screen projection facilitated this approach and appeared to motivate the audience to pay closer attention to the film.

It is suggested that attention to the way in which instructional films are used could lead to the improved exploitation of many existing instructional films. Such an approach involves planning for both the activity of learning and the instructional situation itself.

## INTRODUCTION

One way of classifying educational films is on the basis of the functional operations of such films. May and Lumsdaine (1958) identified three main classes of film:  1) Instructional — leading to gains in knowledge, 2) Motivational — designed to affect or restructure attitudes and personal values, and 3) Demonstrational — leading to changes in skill performance. Such a film classification today would have to be extended to include the 'concept' film. Such films were originally designed as short limited units making contributions to concept formation in specific subject areas. A new 8 mm film format and specialized equipment have been developed to utilize such films. In practice these 8 mm 'loop' films have many functional applications. These include the production

43

of changes in perceptual-motor skills or performance, and the creation of open-ended situations for subsequent discussion and analysis. Whatever film taxonomy is adopted the effectiveness of films is dependent on 1) their structure and content (film variables), 2) the manner in which they are used (utilization variables), and 3) the students to whom they are addressed (audience variables).

Learning itself takes place within the learner, largely as a result of his activity. But something must drive this activity and direct it towards the goal of achieving objectives. Research into learning from film shows the importance of proper task analysis and the integration of such an analysis with the pertinent learning variables (Davies, 1972). This need for developmental or formative field research whereby objectives are first clearly defined, and systematic audience tests are then carried out during the actual course of a programme's production, is of paramount importance. A successful adherent to this approach is shown by the award winning film produced by the Royal Navy, entitled 'Programmed Learning' (1970) Ministry of Defence. James and Leytham (1971) provided a useful discussion on the use of videotape recordings as preliminaries to the production and evaluation of film. Formative field research is, however, a long term solution and it does not lead to the improved exploitation of the many existing instructional films.

Previous work in film research has been largely directed to the examination of production variables. The trend towards the individualization of instruction has recently given impetus to an examination of audience variables. As yet there appears to be very little research attempting to determine the most effective method of presenting instructional films. The design of instructional facilities in most instances ends with the establishment of a physical environment. Few references have been made in designing film presentation to the kinds of learning or behavioural changes that are the consequence of film operations. There are many different classifications of learning types and one that has been widely used by programmers of learning is that developed by Gagné (1965). In his review of instructional film research, Carpenter (1971) indicated the need to integrate learning theory and media research. When using instructional film one must not only plan for the activity of learning but design the presentation to facilitate such learning. The aim of the present investigation was to compare the traditional 16 mm instructional film presentation method with a novel presentation strategy in relation to facilitating student achievement of specific educational objectives.

REVIEW

Existing instructional films usually contain a complex set of learning materials. An initial assessment of the film content must be made in order to discover what elements are appropriate to the task in hand.

The use of inferred objectives from existing instructional films is not new and has been widely implemented by advocates of the Keller Plan (1968), users of introductory biology programmes (Meleca, 1973) and other workers (Smith, 1973).

It would appear that when using instructional film  1) the material should be selected with reference to educational objectives (Anderson, 1956),  2) the students should be motivated to attend the presentation (Allan, 1955), and  3) the film should be presented in such a way as to optimize activity of learning (Parker, 1970 and Marchant, 1971).

Recently research work has shown that a clear written statement, during intervals in a film showing, of the most important items of information to be learnt leads to a significant increase in post-test performance on these items (Teather and Marchant, 1974).  In a comparison of three projection methods (front, rear and c. c. t. v. ) post-test scores indicated that the amount students learnt varied with the projection method, rear screen projection being the most effective (Marchant, 1974).

It was hypothesized that the combination of the two utilization variables, i. e. 'programmed' film with written statement and film presentation by rear screen projection would lead to significant increases in post-test film scores.

PROCEDURE

Teachers in training are expected to become familiar with the concepts and implications of educational technology, and postgraduate Certificate in Education students at Liverpool are no exception.  Usually a component of most workshops in educational technology is concerned with the use of television in the classroom — a familiar item of equipment in many local schools (Matheson, 1971).  Such a course component run by the author had the following objectives :   1) to understand the uses of television in education,  2) to be able to identify and operate the various controls on a television receiver, and  3) to be able to make suitable preparations for the most effective classroom viewing of television programmes.

An instructional film entitled 'The use of television in the classroom' (CETO Training Film, 1971), was selected as the most appropriate teaching strategy to achieve the objectives in the time available for this part of the course.  Such a film would not only provide the students with an information base relevant to subsequent practical work, but also serve as an example of how the 'systems approach' to course structure can be applied (Vernon, 1969).  The film was in black and white and had a running time of 21 minutes.

In this investigation the relative effectiveness of two methods of presenting the film was assessed.  These methods were :

(1)  A continuous presentation under traditional viewing conditions, i. e. a large screen, front projection and darkened room, and

(2)  An interrupted presentation in which the same film was shown in five parts, the projector being switched off for 30 seconds between sections, whilst students read through the statements which were relevant to that section, in a prepared booklet.  Projection was by means of a small rear projection screen in daylight conditions.  The viewing arrangements were as set out in figure 1.

The student groups, apart from physical education, had been arranged on the basis of the degree subject(s) they had previously studied. Members were randomly assigned to either the front or rear projection group.  Care was taken to ensure that the physical viewing conditions, as well as the lighting and film sound accompaniment were of optimum values (Ash and Jaspen, 1953 and Bowler, 1974).  These conditions were kept as uniform as possible for all the student groups.

To assess the students' learning, tests on the film content were administered before (pre-test) and after (post-test) the film showing. The test items involved both the recall of factual information and the general comprehension of such material.  Responses were of the short answer type and the maximum test score was twenty.  Identical pre- and post-tests were given to each group.

RESULTS

The results show that the use of the rear projection plus statement (RPS) presentation method enabled students to obtain higher learning gains than the front projection (F) method.  The differences in post-test scores was significant for all the individual groups (Table 1, page 52).  A further analysis of the presentation methods for the combined groupings showed these to be highly significant in favour of the RPS method.  There were no significant differences between male and female response patterns (Table 2, page 53).

Despite the technical content of the film, results showed the same trend in all groups irrespective of the background knowledge of the students.  Thus the short term objectives of the film presentation has been achieved.  The students who viewed the film by the RPS method had learnt half as much again as did the students who had viewed the film by the F method.

The RPS method of film presentation was well received, and there was no evidence that any individual learning styles had been upset by this approach.  Participants personally communicated that their attention was attracted and held by this form of presentation.  The students felt that the review strategy, by means of the prepared booklet, counteracted any propensity to forget the information presented.

# PLAN OF REAR PROJECTION PRESENTATION

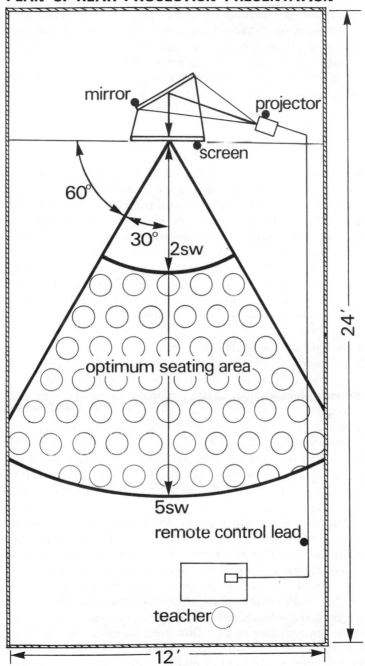

Figure 1

## DISCUSSION OF RESULTS

One generalization from the extensive work of the Pennsylvania Film Research Programme (1947-55) was that depending on how they were used, films varied greatly in their effectiveness. One way in which the amount learnt from film can be increased is by a repeat showing. Although this may in some cases as much as double the amount learnt (McTavish, 1954) it might prove to be excessively time consuming and monotonous. Any event that multiplies learning opportunities might be expected to increase learning (Travers, 1964, 1966). The danger exists that instructional films are viewed with a non-demanding attitude as that operating when viewing feature films. Over the years a fixed format for film utilization by front projection systems has developed, i. e. prepare (introduce film), present (show film) and follow-up (questions on film). The present study suggests this formula to be inadequate given our present day equipment resources and knowledge concerning learning. The adoption of a strategy that promoted the interaction between the 'principles' of learning theory and presentation technique, resulted in a method that improved learning from an instructional film. Such an approach gives impetus to the development of an instructional systems design (i. e. open system) to replace the previous generalized formula (i. e. closed system) that has been employed in learning from films.

Gagné (1968) stated that few instructional materials in existence today have been deliberately prepared on the basis of 'principles' of learning. Students do learn from instructional films (Allen, 1971) but most film research has ignored questions relating to the conditions under which learning takes place. Film presentation needs to be linked with the particular types of learning involved. The necessity to keep in mind the objectives of the learning system was stressed by Salmon and Snow (1968). Having selected a film in harmony with objectives a teacher can still do much to improve the students' learning. The teacher must analyse the events of instruction. These include 1) gaining and controlling attention, 2) arranging for recall and remembering, and 3) guiding and cueing the learner.

McDonald (1961) stated that for communication to be effective required the recipients to be attentive, which is a motivational problem. The concept of attention will have a direct relationship to the length of a film. An analysis of the British National Film Catalogue (1963-72) revealed a trend in reducing the length of films from the 21-30 minute range to the 11-20 minute range. (The film shown in the present study was 21 minutes). Any method of film presentation ensures that attention is initially concentrated on it. This characteristic is due to the psychological response of the individual who will always look for preference at the brightest part of his field of vision. Modern 16 mm projectors are so efficient that films can be used without blacking-out, making daylight viewing of films very effective. Marchant (1974) postulated that the increased screen brightness, rather than the size of screen, may have accounted for the success of the rear screen presentation compared with the front projection and television presentations. Several writers (Berlyne, 1960) have pointed out that some of the effects of novel stimuli are apparently not at their strongest with maximum novelty. They seem to operate most strongly with an intermediate degree of novelty, i. e. in a situation that is rather like something well known but just distinct enough for it to be 'interesting'. The use of a 16 mm projector in the rear projection mode might appear sufficiently distinct from the usual projection method for students to find the situation interesting. The combined factors of screen brightness and novelty of presentation in the present study might have helped to motivate the students to attend more closely the rear projection film screening.

Active involvement in a learning situation is effective in stimulating both motivation and response. Michael and Macoby (1953) have shown significantly better results from response whether overt or covert, when compared with a group making no response at all. The type of response must be considered in relation to both the material being taught and the criterion behaviour required. Arresting the film presentation permits 'pertinent' information to be introduced into the learning situation. The statements in the film booklet provided a review strategy for earlier relevant material. They also acted as a means of reinforcement as stated by Skinner (1954). Remembering through repetition is more likely to succeed if written statements reinforce earlier audio-visual perceptions.

Recent work by Hartley (1973) has shown that researchers are divided as to the effects of pre-tests on subsequent learning and on post-tests. In the majority of studies, however, pre-test effects have not been discernable. Whatever the causes of pre-test effects, the important variables appear to be a) the length and quality of instruction, b) the relevance of the pre-test, and c) the age, ability and experience of the students involved. In the present study, where the subjects might think they already know some of the material, the pre-test could serve to alert the students to their own deficiencies, i. e. give some guidance as to what they are expected to learn from the film.

CONCLUSIONS

The present investigation has outlined a presentation strategy to ensure that an instructional film message has both been optimumly received and understood. The previous emphasis on producing and showing films without reference to conditions of learning has gone. The time to change from the 'cook-book' mode of audio-visual instruction to a communications system approach has arrived. The presentation strategy employed imposes no more constraints than does the more conventional front projection system and offers so many advantages. Results, however, have to be accepted with caution as variables such as the viewers' familiarity with the material and the amount of detail required in recall must be involved. Further research is necessary to replicate the strategy employed with different age groups and film content.

## Acknowledgements

I am indebted to the postgraduate education students for their co-operation. For help in administering the experiments, I thank Mr. M. J. Coombs, and for the figure, Miss R. Smithies.

I also thank Guild Sound and Vision Ltd. , who gave their permission for the film used in the investigation to be copied on to videotape.

REFERENCES

Allen, W.H. (1971) Instructional media research: past, present and future. Audio-Visual Communication Review Vol. **19**, 1, 5.

Ash, P. and Jaspen, N. (1953) Optimum physical viewing conditions for a rear projection daylight screen. Pennsylvania State College, Pennsylvania. Technical Report — SPECDEVCEN 269-7-37.

Berlyne, D.E. (1960) Conflict, Arousal and Curiosity. New York: McGraw-Hill.

Bowler, J.W. (1974) Films and their projection. Audio-Visual, February No. 26, 22. McClaren Group Publication

British National Film Catalogue (1963-72) An Analysis and History of the B.N.F.C. British Film Institute, 81 Dean Street, London

Carpenter, C.R. (1971) Instructional film research — a brief overview. British Journal of Educational Technology **3**, 2, 229-246.

Centre of Educational Development Overseas, Film (1971). The use of Television in the Classroom. Guild Sound and Vision, Peterborough, Lincolnshire.

Davies, I.K. (1972) Presentation Stragegies in Hartley J. (Ed.) Strategies for Programmed Instruction: An Educational Technology. London: Butterworths, 82-132.

Gagné, R.M. (1965) The Conditions of Learning. New York: Holt, Rinehart and Winston.

Gagné, R.M. (1968) Media and the learning process. Paper presented to the DAVI Conference Houston, March 25th. Abstracted in Audio-Visual Communication Review (1969), Vol. **17** No. 3, 351.

Hartley, J. (1973) The effect of pre-testing on post-test performance. Research in Education No. **10**, 56. Manchester University Press.

Instructional Film Research (1947-55). U.S. Naval Training Special Devices Centre. Technical Reports No. 1-65. National Technical Information Service. U.S. Department of Commerce, Port Royal Road, Springfield, U.S.A.

James, P.E. and Leytham, G.W.H. (1971) Videotape to film transfer: an aid to the construction of a graphic teaching programme. Medical and Biological Illustration **21**, 239-242.

Keller, F.S. (1968) Goodbye, Teacher.... Journal of Applied Behavioural Analysis **1**, 79.

McDonald, F.J. (1961) Motivation and the communication process. Audio-visual Communication Review Vol. **9**, No. 5, 57.

McTavish, C.L. (1954) Effect of repetitive film showings on learning. U.S. Naval Training Special Devices Centre. Technical Report No. S.D.C. 269-7-12. National Technical Information Service, U.S. Department of Commerce, Port Royal Road, Springfield, U.S.A.

Marchant, H. (1971) Improving the use of an instructional film. Visual Education. November. 46-47.

Marchant, H. (1974) Film presentation: a case for the wider use of rear screen projection. Educational Media International (in the press)

Matheson, D.L. (1971) Audio-visual Aids in Primary Schools. Advanced Diploma in Education Dissertation, University of Liverpool.

May, M.A. and Lumsdaine, A.A. (1958) Learning From Films. New Haven, Yale University Press.

Meleca, C.B. (1973) Ohio State University Bio-Learning Center uses the A.T. method. The American Biology Teacher 35, 4, 192-197.

Ministry of Defence Film (1970) Programmed Learning. A R.N. Instructional Film (serial No. A2262). Naval Personnel Services and Training Department, Whitehall.

Salmon, G. and Snow, R.E. (1968) Specification of film attributes. Audio-Visual Communication Review Vol. 16, No. 3, 225.

Skinner, B.F. (1954) The science of learning and the art of teaching. Harvard Educational Review 24, 86-97.

Smith, P.E., Roberts, K.C. and Taylor, C.L. (1973) The Use of Inferred Objectives with Instructional Films. ACET Convention, Las Vegas. ERIC Clearing House on Media and Technology, Stanford University, California.

Teather, D.C.B. and Marchant, H. (1974) Learning from film with particular reference to the effects of cueing, questioning and knowledge of results. Programmed Learning and Educational Technology. (in the press)

Travers, R.M.W. (1964, 1966) Research and Theory Related to Audio-Visual Information Transmission. Bureau of Educational Research, University of Utah, Salt Lake City, U.S.A.

Vernon, P.J. (Ed.) (1969) The systems approach and education. A.V. Media, Vol. 3, No. 3, Pergamon Press.

## Table 1

Film Utilization: A comparison between front projection (F) and rear projection plus statement (RPS) presentation methods – individual groups

| GROUP | Physical Education | | Chemistry | | Maths | | Mod. Lang. | | History | | Applied Sc. and Physics | | Geography | | Biology | |
|---|---|---|---|---|---|---|---|---|---|---|---|---|---|---|---|---|
| METHOD | F (N=5) | RPS (N=4) | F (N=5) | RPS (N=6) | F (N=11) | RPS (N=9) | F (N=4) | RPS (N=5) | F (N=7) | RPS (N=8) | F (N=7) | RPS (N=6) | F (N=6) | RPS (N=7) | F (N=6) | RPS (N=6) |
| **(A) Pre-Test** | | | | | | | | | | | | | | | | |
| Mean | 3.30 | 2.75 | 5.20 | 4.50 | 3.73 | 2.22 | 4.75 | 4.60 | 3.43 | 2.87 | 6.07 | 5.16 | 4.00 | 4.44 | 3.66 | 3.34 |
| Standard Deviation | 1.32 | 1.91 | 1.60 | 2.87 | 1.86 | 1.88 | 0.82 | 1.20 | 1.59 | 1.05 | 1.52 | 2.26 | 1.52 | 2.47 | 2.35 | 2.69 |
| **(B) Post-Test** | | | | | | | | | | | | | | | | |
| Mean | 14.50 | 18.00 | 13.40 | 18.50 | 14.81 | 19.55 | 14.50 | 18.60 | 14.28 | 18.50 | 15.28 | 19.41 | 16.33 | 19.18 | 12.84 | 19.01 |
| Standard Deviation | 2.60 | 1.00 | 1.85 | 1.25 | 3.09 | 0.50 | 2.17 | 1.78 | 1.74 | 2.17 | 2.18 | 0.49 | 1.24 | 0.77 | 1.61 | 0.46 |
| **(C) Percentage Gain** | | | | | | | | | | | | | | | | |
| Mean | 66.38 | 88.50 | 55.56 | 90.06 | 67.53 | 97.59 | 63.66 | 91.76 | 65.20 | 90.95 | 66.33 | 96.25 | 76.30 | 99.60 | 56.73 | 94.60 |
| Standard Deviation | 17.51 | 5.55 | 13.25 | 8.58 | 21.17 | 2.76 | 14.23 | 10.51 | 9.28 | 13.41 | 14.29 | 2.99 | 9.74 | 0.97 | 7.62 | 4.08 |
| 't' (A) | 0.448 | | 0.443 | | 1.701 | | 0.190 | | 0.756 | | 0.600 | | 0.347 | | 0.199 | |
| 't' (B) | 2.145 | | 4.543 | | 4.309 | | 2.907 | | 3.814 | | 4.183 | | 4.190 | | 8.186 | |
| 't' (C) | 2.248 | | 4.705 | | 4.511 | | 3.206 | | 3.967 | | 4.628 | | 5.602 | | 8.319 | |
| 'p' (A) | N.S. | | N.S. | | N.S. | | N.S. | | N.S. | | N.S. | | N.S. | | N.S. | |
| 'p' (B) | .10 | | .01 | | .001 | | .05 | | .01 | | .01 | | .001 | | .001 | |
| 'p' (C) | .10 | | .01 | | .001 | | .02 | | .01 | | .001 | | .001 | | .001 | |

Table 2

Film Utilization: a comparison between front projection (F) and
rear projection plus statement (RPS) presentation methods — all
groups and male/female analysis

| GROUP | All groups | | Male | | Female | |
|---|---|---|---|---|---|---|
| METHOD | F (N=51) | RPS (N=51) | F (N=23) | RPS (N=29) | F (N=28) | RPS (N=22) |
| **(A) Pre-Test** | | | | | | |
| Mean | 4.21 | 3.65 | 4.30 | 4.43 | 4.14 | 3.09 |
| Standard Deviation | 1.91 | 2.34 | 1.70 | 2.24 | 2.08 | 2.32 |
| **(B) Post-Test** | | | | | | |
| Mean | 14.56 | 19.02 | 13.86 | 19.12 | 14.96 | 18.91 |
| Standard Deviation | 2.43 | 1.36 | 3.19 | 1.03 | 2.00 | 1.69 |
| **(C) Percentage Gain** | | | | | | |
| Mean | 65.22 | 92.29 | 61.57 | 94.52 | 68.21 | 93.67 |
| Standard Deviation | 16.03 | 8.54 | 19.05 | 6.48 | 12.27 | 10.33 |
| 't' (A) | 1.310 | | 0.225 | | 1.574 | |
| 't' (B) | 10.531 | | 8.228 | | 7.338 | |
| 't' (C) | 11.300 | | 8.528 | | 7.638 | |
| 'p' (A) | N.S. | | N.S. | | N.S. | |
| 'p' (B) | .001 | | .001 | | .001 | |
| 'p' (C) | .001 | | .001 | | .001 | |

APPENDIX: Part of the film booklet used in the investigation
(* denotes the start of a new page)

## THE USE OF TELEVISION IN THE CLASSROOM

This booklet is designed to help you learn certain things from the film you are about to see.

The film, which is about 20 minutes long, is divided into <u>five sections.</u> These correspond to the five sections in this booklet.

<u>After viewing each section</u> of the film, please read through the statements which are relevant to <u>that section.</u>

---

<u>Do not turn to the next page</u> until you have viewed the first section of the film.

---

\*                               <u>Section 1</u>

<u>After you have viewed the first section</u> of the film, read through these statements.

1.    Radio-vision is the use of a <u>radio or tape-recorder</u> in conjunction with a <u>filmstrip or slide projector.</u>

2.    The standard film format for educational films in the past has been <u>16 mm.</u>

3.    <u>8mm film</u> is now widely used in education especially as silent film in loop projectors.

---

<u>Do not turn to the next page</u> until you have viewed the second section of the film.

---

\*                               <u>Section 2</u>

<u>After you have viewed the second section</u> of the film, read through these statements.

4.    Before screening a TV programme to a class, ensure that:
      a) the aerial lead is attached
      b) the mains lead is plugged in, and
      c) the electricity supply is switched on.

5.    The volume control of a television receiver should be turned on approximately one third of a full turn <u>before</u> a class arrives.

6.    <u>Readjustment of the volume control</u> of a television receiver to give the correct listening level for a class takes place <u>after</u> the class has arrived, i. e. immediately the television programme has started.

---

<u>Do not turn to the next page</u> until you have viewed the third section of the film.

---

# The differential effects of voice-over, superimposition and combined review treatments as production stratagies for ETV programming

G. O. COLDEVIN, Sir George Williams University, Montreal

**Abstract:**  While a considerable amount of research in ETV has been devoted to medium comparative effectiveness studies, the differential examination of production techniques as they relate to information acquisition and attitude change is relatively limited.  The primary focus of the present research was to examine the comparative effects of structuring review segments with voice-over, graphic superimposition and combined voice-over-superimposition treatments on information acquisition derived from a television programme.

Three television programmes were produced centering around the theme of forest fires. Each programme was divided into three conceptual units, each of which was supported by one of the three review treatments under investigation. Review treatments were rotated in each programme to control for the influence of placement and content. An additional programme referred to as a 'simple treatment' was produced consisting of identical elements of the three treatment programmes with the elimination of review segments. All four programmes were tested against a control group.

The sample consisted of 500 grade seven students with 100 students each being randomly assigned to one of the four treatment testing blocks and the control group. Viewing and testing conditions were uniform for all treatment groups.

A one-way analysis of variance and mean comparison test revealed that only the superimposition and combined treatments produced significant differences on information acquisition when compared to the simple treatment. No significant differences were noted between the latter two variables. The results support the conclusion that the voice-over review treatment when used singularly does not add significantly to information acquisition.  The type of sensory modality review strategy employed appears to play a significant role in satisfying ETV behavioural objectives.

While a considerable amount of research in educational television has been devoted to media comparative effectiveness studies (Briggs et al, 1967; Chu and Schramm, 1967), the manipulation of message design has garnered relatively limited attention. Indeed, after over two decades of educational television, the general rule concerning the efficacy of commonly employed production techniques is that they are a product of producer intuition based on custom and past experience. Schramm (1971) underscores this point when he notes, 'In contrast to the hundreds of experimental comparisons of ITV with conventional classroom teaching, there are at most a few scores of studies specifically on the content and strategies of ITV'. While television has been adequately demonstrated to be as effective as other media and conventional teaching in imparting information, little effort has been given to the differential examination of production techniques and their effect on learning and attitude change derived from a specific programme or series.

The question more simply stated revolves around one of, 'what can the producer do **within** the programme to enable a target audience to more effectively incorporate the criterion goals?' The approach is one of an internal examination and manipulation of the medium to discover what elements are most beneficial in increasing the level of information acquisition and/or attitude change from a specific production. An empirical framework of this nature may be deemed essential to ETV planners and producers operating in the natural situation. Production decisions based upon research evidence may be far more meaningful as a consequence of such endeavours.

A production variable within the present context may be characterized as a definitive process, method or technique of television production. Shepard (1967) has isolated seven broad categories of production variables, namely:

(1) Camera factors
(2) Lighting
(3) Setting
(4) Graphic devices
(5) Audio factors
(6) Performer variables
(7) Opening-closing format

The present research is concerned with the effects of audio factors, graphic devices and a combination of the two variables in providing redundant or review segments appropriate to a given unit of subject material. The study is thus primarily concerned with the comparative effectiveness of the three reinforcing formats in multiplying the learning opportunities in a given ETV production.

RATIONALE

The limited amount of research presently generated on TV production variables has investigated the influence of colour, camera angles, eye contact, lighting, speed of presentation, music and student-media interaction. The results of these studies are for the most part inconclusive and provide few guidelines for practical production. There are virtually no studies specifically investigating the television production variables under present consideration.

Although a strong theoretical tradition supports the dominance of aural-visual combinations, the empirical research is inconclusive in

this regard. Nevertheless, the more prevalent form of television presentation, particularly among commercial advertizers remains with a
graphic superimposition supported by voice-over dialogue. The logical,
although untested guideline here is that the audio-visual combination
serves as a double reinforcing variable.

Much of the research in audio-visual communication stems from the
Broadbent (1958) theory of perception which suggests that only one main
channel carries auditory and visual signals from the sense organs to
the higher centres of the brain. Inputs are stored briefly in a short
term memory until a channel becomes free. The implication of this
theory is that one would not expect multi-channel input of redundant information to facilitate learning. Severin's (1967) cue summation theory
on the other hand predicts that learning is increased as the number of
available cues or stimuli is increased. The theory also suggests, however, that multi-channel communications which combine words in two
channels (words aurally and in print) will not result in significantly
greater gains than a single channel communication since the added
channel does not provide additional cues.

The work of Travers (1964, 1966) for the most part supports
Broadbent's theory in the finding of no significant differences between a
combined audio-visual treatment and visual alone. Both treatments
were more effective, however, than an auditory mode alone. These
studies therefore suggest that no advantage may be derived through the
use of two channels over the visual channel alone. It should be noted
however, that these results may have only limited application to television production since   1) the studies were concerned with nonsense
syllables, and   2) the material was presented through a synchronized
film strip-tape recorder, both of which made the experiments easier to
control but less applicable to reality. The present study attempts to
verify the effectiveness of these variables in a **meaningful** situation.

Although a considerable amount of research has been conducted in
the area of instructional films, for the most part the results, because
of dubious experimental design and haphazard control of variables, are
non-generalizable to ETV. As Hoban and Van Ormer (1950) point out,
in some experiments auditory presentation has been consistently better
than visual whereas in other studies the opposite results hold. Little
usable residue from these studies appear to offer appropriate guidelines for television production.

Only one study reviewed has direct application to the present
research. Schwarzwalder (1960) examined two levels of visual reinforcement as they affected mastery learning scores in fifth grade science.
The first level used 'supered graphics' in a television production while
the second level presented no redundancy in this format. The results,
although not significant (p $<$ .10) indicated a trend of superior learning

when superimpositions of reinforcing terms were added to the production. The study does not suggest, however, which type of redundancy format is the most effective for mastery learning.

After an exhaustive review of the literature, Anderson (1972) recommends that in

> '.... future research in media communication techniques, it is to be hoped that the relationships of visual communication techniques to theoretical models of perception and learning should be investigated more thoroughly than in the past. There should be a conscious attempt to link production techniques to specific roles they might play in aiding particular types of learning with specific types of behavioural objectives. '

With these perspectives in mind, the present study was undertaken to:

(1)  Assess the comparative effects of inserting review segments as opposed to no review segments, at selected intervals within a television production, on behavioural objectives of the programme;

(2)  Isolate the differential effects of voice-over, graphic superimposition and combined voice-over and superimposition review treatments on cognitive acquisition;

(3)  Identify possible relationships between production review strategies and attitude shifts toward the central themes in the programme.

METHODOLOGY

**Production Techniques**

Three television programmes of 20 minutes duration each were produced, centering around the theme of forest fires.  The subject was deliberately chosen to present novel material in a documentary presentation format appropriate for testing with a wide variety of educational level audiences. Each programme was composed of three broad conceptual units[1]  of approximately six minutes each with a one minute 'intro' and 'extro'. Each of the three conceptual units were further divided into five subunits in each programme.  The three conceptual units in each programme were then supported by either a voice-over, superimposition or combination review treatment.  Review production strategies were rotated in each programme to control for the possible influence of placement and content.

---

[1] The three units were centred around the following themes:  1) The damage and destruction caused by forest fires;  2) the beneficical nature of most lightning set forest fires;  3) the necessity for controlled burning (i. e. , deliberately set fires under prescribed conditions).

All production review treatments were inserted at the end of each of the five sub-units, i. e. , placed **within** the conceptual unit itself. Each sub-unit was then supported with three review statements (a total of 15 statements for each conceptual unit). The voice-over treatment referred to the programme narrator's voice heard over a slide being shown on the television screen. Super-imposition referred to a visual graphic of the three review statements appropriate to a given sub-unit superimposed over a slide on the television screen. The combination treatment employed both the voice-over and graphic superimposition simultaneously. All production techniques, the narrator and narration were held constant for each programme. The only variation in each section of the programmes was the introduction of the experimental review strategies under consideration.

|  | PROGRAMME 1 | PROGRAMME II | PROGRAMME III | PROGRAMME IV |
|---|---|---|---|---|
| CONCEPTUAL UNIT I | Superimposition Treatment | Voice-over Treatment | Combination Treatment | Simple Treatment |
| CONCEPTUAL UNIT II | Voice-over Treatment | Combination Treatment | Superimposition Treatment | Simple Treatment |
| CONCEPTUAL UNIT III | Combination Treatment | Superimposition Treatment | Voice-over Treatment | Simple Treatment |

**NOTE:** Each conceptual unit for Programmes I - III was supported by 15 review statements. Review segments were deleted from Programme IV.

Figure 1: ETV Production Design

In order to test for the comparative effectiveness of the review treatment per se, an additional programme was produced consisting of identical elements of the three experimental review programmes with the exception of any review segments. For the purposes of discussion and analysis this programme was referred to as a 'simple treatment' (see figure 1). Additionally, all four programmes were tested against a classic control group undergoing the same testing procedures as the four experimental groups with the exception of viewing one of the programmes.

## Instrumentation and Testing Design

Cognitive acquisition was assessed by means of a 27 item multiple choice questionnaire and attitude shift through a negative-positive, 15 item Likert type attitude scale. The cognitive portion of the instrument was equally divided into nine knowledge recall questions and the attitude scales into five statements for each conceptual unit. The experimental

59

subjects were first administered the negative attitude pre-test and immediately after viewing one of the four programmes, the cognitive test and positive attitude post-test. The same procedure was employed for the control group with the exception of the programme viewing condition. All programmes were transmitted through 23 inch monitors mounted on standard four foot stands. Care was taken to ensure that the maximum horizontal viewing angle was less than 30 degrees for students nearest the receiver (Gordon, 1970) and that proper viewing distances were preserved. Viewing and lighting conditions for all classrooms were kept as uniform as possible.

The forms employed by the two testing designs are illustrated below.

COGNITIVE ACQUISITION (Post-Test Only Design)

R   X1   01   Experimental Programme I
R   X2   02   Experimental Programme II
R   X3   03   Experimental Programme III
R   X4   04   Experimental Programme IV
R        05   Control Group

ATTITUDE SHIFT (Pre-Post Test Design)

R   01   X1   02    Experimental Programme I
R   03   X2   04    Experimental Programme II
R   05   X3   06    Experimental Programme III
R   07   X4   08    Experimental Programme IV
R   09        010   Control Group

**Note:**   R denotes randomized grouping of subjects
            X represents experimental treatment
            0 indicates appropriate treatment testing

All instruments were pre-tested and subjected to psychometric property tests of item discrimination, item difficulty and reliability. The content validity of the cognitive acquisition tests was assured since all questions were derived from the television programme content. The cognitive test reliability was reported at .84 (Kuder-Richardson reliability test) with a split-half reliability of .97 (Pearson Product Moment Correlation corrected by Spearman-Brown) for the attitude scales.

## Subjects

The sample consisted of 20 grade seven classes drawn from two schools in suburban Montreal. This educational level was chosen since it represented a mid-range of appropriate target audiences for the subject matter content of the television programme. Four classes each were randomly assigned to one of the three review strategy treatments, the simple treatment and the control group. Individual randomization in this circumstance was precluded through original random assignment of students to classes. All subjects were tested during one normal class period. The final assignment of questionnaires for statistical analysis totalled 100 for each treatment (all questionnaires randomly reduced to lowest common denominator, N = 500).

The average age of the sample was 12 years with 40 per cent coming from professional homes, 29 per cent from white collar and 29 per cent from blue collar home backgrounds. Background information was not forthcoming on this variable for two per cent of the sample. The sex distribution was 56 per cent male and 44 per cent female. Virtually all (99.6 per cent) of the subjects had at least one television set in their home.

## Statistical Procedures

A one-way analysis of variance with five independent variable levels was employed to test for main effects of inserting review segments on cognitive acquisition. Similarly, the differential effects of the review strategies were tested with a one-way ANOVA with the appropriate three treatment levels. In both analyses, the Newman-Keuls test was applied to examination of significant mean comparisons. Significant mean attitude shifts between pre and post tests for production review treatments were analysed by means of t test. Significant differences are reported at the .05 level of confidence.

## RESULTS

The data (Table I) reveal a highly significant difference among the generated means for the five treatments under consideration. In applying the mean comparison test (Table II), all four programmes indicate significantly superior mean cognitive acquisition gains when compared with the control group. When the three review strategy treatments are compared with the simple treatment, however, only the superimposition and combined treatment means are significantly greater. The logical conclusion which emerges from this analysis is that the efficacy of review treatments per se are to a large extent dependent upon the type of review production strategy employed. The voice-over review strategy appears to be no more effective than the straightforward simple treatment.

Although the analysis of variance comparing the differential effects of the three review strategies did not quite reach the desired level of confidence (p $<$ .08) the mean comparison test indicated a superior trend in comparing the effects of the combined treatment with the voice-

61

Table I

One way analysis of variance of cognitive acquisition means for five treatment levels

| Source | Sum of squares | df | Mean squares | F |
|---|---|---|---|---|
| Between groups | 3548.67 | 4 | 887.17 | 60.88* |
| Within groups | 7213.92 | 495 | 14.57 | |
| Total | 10762.59 | 499 | | |

* $p < .001$

Table II

Application of Newman-Keuls Test to differences between five cognitive acquisition treatment means

| Treatment | Means | $\overline{X}5$ | $\overline{X}4$ | $\overline{X}1$ | $\overline{X}2$ | $\overline{X}3$ |
|---|---|---|---|---|---|---|
| Control | $\overline{X}5 = 7.94$ | – | 5.40* | 6.18* | 6.92* | 7.32* |
| Simple | $\overline{X}4 = 13.34$ | | – | 0.78 | 1.52** | 1.92* |
| Voice-over | $\overline{X}1 = 14.12$ | | | – | 0.74 | 1.14 |
| Superimposition | $\overline{X}2 = 14.86$ | | | | – | 0.40 |
| Combination | $\overline{X}3 = 15.26$ | | | | | – |
| | | Wr (.05) = 1.05 | 1.26 | 1.38 | 1.47 | |
| | | Wr (.01) = 1.38 | 1.57 | 1.67 | 1.75 | |

** $p < .05$
* $p < .01$

over ($p < .06$) and superimposition with the voice-over ($p < .09$). No superior trend was detected in the comparison of the combined and super-imposition treatments. The power of the visual factor in television production review strategies is thus adequately demonstrated by these combined results. The voice-over treatment when employed singularly in the present study, appears to be ineffectual in significantly strenthening a television production.

62

In all samples, no significant differences were found between male and female response patterns on both cognitive and attitude scores. The same condition held for the influence of socio-economic home backgrounds.

No significant differences were detected in mean gains in pre-post test attitude shifts between the three production strategies and the simple treatment. Two possible reasons may be forwarded for this lack of significant discrimination: 1) the production itself, being directed primarily at information dissemination may not have been sufficiently dynamic to generate significant attitude shifts and/or 2) none of the review production strategies may have been intrinsically powerful enough to induce significant discrimination among attitude shifts. Entirely different types of review strategies may be requisite to producing significant changes in this affective domain when the main thrust of a production is one of imparting critical information.

DISCUSSION

The primary generalization emerging from this study is that in planning review strategies for a general information television production, producers would be ill advised to use only a voice-over treatment. For purposes of efficiency, the superimposition treatment appears to be the more suitable strategy. This is not meant to imply that the combined treatment under normal professional production conditions should be waived in favour of the superimposition treatment alone. The superiority of the combined treatment throughout the cognitive portion of the study suggests that a safety factor may be operating when the voice-over is combined with a superimposition which may accommodate a variety of 'attending to the message' proclivities. The reinforcement effect from the auditory modality in the combined treatment, however, does not appear to be of sufficient magnitude to produce a significant change in information acquisition as opposed to the impact of the visual modality alone in normally populated classroom situations.

The results reported in the present research, even though conducted under highly differing circumstances, support the conclusions of Travers in finding the auditory review mode less efficient than either the audiovisual or the visual but no significant difference between the latter two. It cannot be concluded, however, that as Travers proposes, any event which multiplies learning opportunities may be expected to increase learning. Rather, the type of strategy employed appears to play a significant role in satisfying desired behavioural objectives.

The present study, being largely one of an investigatory nature indicates several avenues for further research. Replication of the methodology with varying age groupings and subject matter contents would appear as a minimal requisite. Since the present research was solely concerned with information acquisition measured at the knowledge level of the cognitive domain, different levels of questioning would validate the efficacy of the treatments in stimulating more complex learning processes. Perhaps most importantly, the amount of single and/or multi-channel reinforcement necessary to produce significant change bears closer investigation. Baggaley (1973) points to similar directions when he suggests, 'The extent to which parallel information may be presented for educational benefit through the auditory and visual channels of the human system before it is overloaded should certainly be investigated.' Research of this nature would add valuable dimensions to the complex relationship between television production and learning processes.

In summary, the methods investigated in the present research are among a host of required validated techniques if a taxonomy of television production variable effectiveness is to be made operational. Hopefully this area which has been largely circumvented with ETV comparative effectiveness studies in the past may henceforth receive the critical attention it warrants.

REFERENCES

Anderson, C.M. (1972) In search of a visual rhetoric for instructional television. Audio-Visual Communication Review **20**, 60

Baggaley, J. (1973) Analysing TV presentation techniques for educational effectiveness. Educational Broadcasting International **6**, 20

Briggs, L.J. et al. (1967) Instructional Media: A Procedure for the Design of Multi-Media Instruction. Pittsburg: U.S. Office of Education.

Broadbent, D.E. (1958) Perception and Communication. New York: Pergamon Press.

Chu, D.E. and Schramm, W. (1967) Learning from Television: What the Research Says. Washington: NAEB

Gordon, G.N. (1970) Classroom Television. New York: Hastings House. 190.

Hoban, C.F. and Van Ormer, E.B. (1950) Instructional Film Research. New York: Arno Press.

Schramm, W. (1971) The Research on Content Variables in ITV. Stanford: Institute for Communication Research.

Scharzwalder, J.C. (1960) An Investigation of the Relative Effectiveness of Certain Specific TV Techniques on Learning. ERIC, ED014 913.

Severin, W. (1967) The effectiveness of relevant pictures in multi-channel communications. Audio-Visual Communication Review **15**.

Shepard, J.R. (1967) A Comparative Analysis of Production Techniques found in Randomly Selected Commercial and Educational Programs. ERIC ED022 360.

Travers, R.M.W. (1964, 1966) Research and Theory Related to Audio-Visual Information Transmission. Bureau of Educational Research, University of Utah, Salt Lake City.

# Psychology and textbook design: a research critique

P. BURNHILL, Stafford College of Further Education
J. HARTLEY, University of Keele

**Abstract:**   The aims of this paper are threefold: (i) to present a list of useful guidelines culled from over fifty years of research on typography and matters related to textbook design; (ii) to provide a critique of the research that produced these guidelines, and (iii) to indicate more appropriate directions for future research in this field.

Thirty-one guidelines for textbook design are presented in three groups: (i) those provided by Spencer, (ii) those provided by the authors, and (iii) those concerned with the comprehension of sentences provided by Davies.

The research which provided the guidelines is criticized on four main interrelated grounds: (i) much of the research may be considered invalid because of the experimental context in which it has taken place and because of the unreliability of measuring instruments; (ii) much of the research has used an inappropriate research strategy, in which variables have been isolated and tested in a piecemeal fashion divorced from natural reading situations; (iii) current typographical conventions have been uncritically accepted; and (iv) there has been no organizing theory to the research.

It is argued that structural clarity at all levels – letters, words and word groupings – is a function of space as the primary variable on a page size of known dimensions. Future research should be focussed on assessing the effectiveness of formats which do not inhibit the rational disposition in space of the component parts that make up text, paragraphs, tables, lists, matrices, mathematical statements etc. Interest in the logical order of the parts and the design of the whole communication must come before any testing of the parts, and parts should not be tested in isolation.

## WHAT GUIDELINES DOES RESEARCH OFFER FOR TEXTBOOK DESIGN?

A considerable amount of research has been conducted in areas that are related to the problem of textbook design. Spencer's (1969) text, The Visible Word, provides a recent and a comprehensive survey, and contains a bibliography with over 400 entries. This book is mainly concerned with research on typographical variables. The more recent bibliography of Hartley et al. (1974a) updates the coverage of these variables, and extends the area of content into other aspects relevant to the production of instructional materials. This bibliography, which does not aim to be as comprehensive as that of Spencer, nevertheless contains over 130

65

entries. A third bibliography (obtained after the preparation of this paper) which covers this field even more widely is that by MacDonald-Ross and Smith (1973).

In this section of this paper we wish first to reproduce Spencer's own guidelines to the research that he describes; we wish then to introduce similar guidelines to the additional research covered in the Hartley, et al. bibliography; and finally we wish to reproduce research conclusions related to the understanding of sentences, for such conclusions have instructional implications. It is necessary, of course, to realize from the outset that such guidelines represent gross over-simplifications of complex issues. Instructional designers and educational technologists are recommended to refer to the original sources for more detailed exposition on these issues. The interaction between theory, experiment and real-life decision making is illustrated in an article on journal design (Poulton et al. 1970).

Spencer's (1969) summary of research on typographical variables is as follows:

"Words set entirely in capitals are considerably less legible than words in lower case. Italics reduce legibility but, provided the counters of the letters are open, bold face does not. Semi-bold types are preferred by many readers. For people with poor vision, semi-bold type is essential.

Excessively long lines cause a sharp increase in the number of regressions. Short lines, on the other hand, increase the number of fixation pauses.

Leading (i. e. the interline space) permits line length to be extended without loss of legibility.

There is no appreciable loss of legibility when type is printed in black ink on tinted paper provided this is of 70 per cent reflectance or more.

Black print on white is more legible than white on black.

Legibility is not significantly affected by the use of paper of high or low gloss but well diffused illumination is important.

Unjustified setting (i. e. equal word spacing, producing a ragged right hand edge) does not decrease legibility.

Reading efficiency is severely reduced by any departure from the horizontal, and by departure from the 90° angle in reading.

A number of non-optimum factors combined, though not strictly cumulative, may drastically reduce reading efficiency. "

66

From the research listed in the Hartley, et al. bibliography we are able to produce a similar set of items with instructional implications. These are:

A preview or summary before instruction can help the reader organize his learning (Ausubel, 1969).

Headings and subheadings can help the reader organize his reading, but they are likely to be more effective if they are presented in the form of questions (Robinson, 1961).

Questions about the ensuing content placed before paragraphs tend to lead to specific learning: the same questions placed after paragraphs tend to lead to more generalized learning — although there is some debate about this conclusion (Boyd, 1973; Bull, 1973; Ladas, 1973).

A pre-test before instruction often has no effect upon subsequent post-test performance after instruction, but there are several instances of where such pre-tests have been shown to aid subsequent learning (Hartley, 1973).

There is no evidence to support the idea that underlining helps understanding (Christensen & Stordhal, 1955), but in these studies the underlining has been done in advance by the experimenters, not by the readers whilst reading.

The role of illustrations is complex. Illustrations can vary from simple to complex, from realistic to abstract, and can be presented with and without colour. Often simple line drawings have been found to be more effective than illustrations containing a great deal of information, but the age, ability and experience of the readers are important, and so too is the function of the illustration (Dwyer, 1972).

Bar graphs are a superior form of presentation for providing accurate information compared with other types of graphs and tables (Feliciano, et al. 1963), although Schutz (1961) found the line graph superior to the bar graph.

Pie charts, and bar graphs are better methods of presentation than are two dimensional representations of three dimensional objects, such as spheres, cubes and columns, when the task is to estimate percentages and quantities (Dickinson, 1973).

In the presentation of complex graphical material, with the task being to read a specific value, there is no difference between performance on a single graph with multiple lines, or on multiple graphs, each with single lines. However, if the task requires the comparison of values the former presentation is superior (Schutz, 1961).

A summary table is better than a detailed table for the recall of specific values (Washburne, 1927), and for accuracy of information retrieval (Carter, 1947; Feliciano, et al. 1963), although a detailed table is superior for accuracy and speed when interpretation is required for the answers (Carter, 1947).

Many types of table (and graphs) are incomprehensible to large numbers of the population. There needs to be a full and direct presentation of all the information the user will need. Items need to be grouped (horizontally and vertically in units of not more than five items) and typographic cues can be used to differentiate different kinds of item (Wright and Fox, 1972).

When displaying tabular or list structures it is helpful to have:

(a) items arranged so that they are scanned vertically rather than horizontally;

(b) typographic distinctions between different units in the table (rather than using conventional abbreviations after each item);

(c) appropriate spacing within and between columns (i. e. with related pairs closer than unrelated pairs). (Wright, 1968).

Performance on both tables and graphs is improved when relevant prose accompanies the material (Vernon, 1953).

When the material is complex, and information about the outcomes of complex conjunctive and disjunctive contingencies must be presented (e. g. in technical manuals or 'government prose') then the use of a flow chart, a logical tree or a decision table is more effective than prose. The optimal format depends on conditions of use (Wright and Reid, 1973).

Maps as information displays are so much more complicated than other displays that it is not clear how any of the above recommendations concerning legibility are at all applicable (Hopkin, 1973).

Finally, in this section, it may be useful to present some of the findings from research on the comprehension of sentences. These findings have been summarized by Davies (1972) as follows:

Simple sentences – which are affirmative, active and declarative — are more rapidly identified and processed than are more complex sentences built upon the simple ones.

Each grammatical complication (e. g. negatives, passives, and queries) when added to the simple sentence, creates an increment of difficulty which delays correct identification and processing.

Semantic and pragmatic factors in language, relating to the way in which logical connectives are ordinarily used, interact with syntactic factors so as to inhibit or facilitate understanding.

Negative qualifiers, except in simple instructions, can appreciably affect the efficiency of understanding.

In the absence of context, responses to negative statements are slower than to affirmative ones, even when the amounts of information conveyed by the statements are equal.

It takes longer to match sentences expressed in the active voice with correlative sentences in the passive voice.

Connectives, such as 'except', 'or', 'if', and 'unless' — which are difficult to avoid in continuous prose — can appreciably affect the efficiency of understanding.

The time taken to evaluate the truth of a sentence is affected more by its syntax (affirmative or negative) than by its truth value (true or false).

## WHAT ARE THE LIMITATIONS OF THIS RESEARCH ?

Apart from the obvious, and previously made statement, that the above guidelines represent simplifications of complex issues, there are a number of points that can be made concerning the research which has produced the guidelines listed. (The research on sentence comprehension is excluded from these comments.) In this paper we wish to point out that most of this research is weak on four separate but interrelated grounds: it is weak (i) because of problems with the validity and the reliability of the measures used; (ii) because an inappropriate research strategy has been adopted; (iii) because there has been an uncritical acceptance of existing typographical conventions, and (iv) because there is no organizing theory to the research.

### (i) In What Ways is Much of the Research Invalid?

The validity — and thus the value — of many of the research findings can be questioned because most of the research has been carried out in experimental laboratories which are divorced from real-life situations. Experiments have shown, for instance, that the reading speed of children can be markedly reduced by simply making them aware of the fact that they are going to be tested on their comprehension of the passage when they have completed reading it (Hartley, et al. 1974b). Other experiments have shown that comprehension varies if the reading is timed or untimed (Preston and Botel, 1951). Yet in real-life our reading is rarely timed or tested. This objection is not one which, having been raised, can now be resolved. It applies to all experimentation. In some situations in psychology measurement can take place without disturbing the situation, but most typographical research is not like this. In order to assess the effects of variables which affect the complex cognitive behaviours being studied it is necessary to set up controlled situations and to develop as far as possible valid and reliable measures. Unfortunately, however, many of the measures used in typographic research are invalid and unreliable. (e. g. is counting the number of words read in a given period of time measuring the legibility of the print? the skill of the reader? or both? or something else in addition?) In our research on the reliability of measures (Hartley, et al. 1974b) we have found test-retest reliability coefficients ranging from +0. 97 to -0. 24, and, in addition, we have reported on sex differences not often commented on in the previous research. The problem of typographic research is that, in order to replace subjective opinion with factual evidence, measurement must take place. Yet the need to gain evidence must be balanced against the possibility that the method of gaining it renders the evidence invalid.

### (ii) Why is the Typical Research Strategy Inappropriate?

Different psychologists have different strategies for doing research, and it is perhaps invidious of us to label 'inappropriate' the one strategy which has been widely used in other contexts. This is the strategy of simplification or of being 'scientific'. It involves the control and isolation of the crucial issues away from their real-life context in order to experiment more precisely on them, and to assume — or to test later — the validity of the obtained findings in the real world. In other areas of psychology, for instance, this approach is quite respectable. Aronson (1972), for example, a distinguished social psychologist, writes:

> "This (...) reflects two of my own biases — biases that I cherish. The first is that the experimental method is the best way to understand a complex phenomenon. It is a truism of science that the only way to really know the world is to reconstruct it: that is, in order to truly understand what causes what, we must do more than simply observe — rather we must be responsible for **producing** the first 'what' so that we can be sure that it really causes the second 'what'. My second bias is that the only way to be **certain** that the causal relations uncovered in experiments are valid is to bring them out of the laboratory and into the real world. "

Our argument here, however, is that this approach is inappropriate in typography because a sign can never be out of context. This 'scientific' strategy leads to the piecemeal testing of issues in isolation from the context in which they more normally appear. All that has happened in

70

fact is that the context has been changed. The problem posed in experiments for the reader is how to interpret the sign(s) in the new context, and this interpretation may be different in the experimental situation from that obtained in the natural one to which the experimenter is hoping to generalize. It is thus inappropriate, for example, in our view to test the efficiency of different column widths and interline spaces without taking into account the page-size involved, the nature of the material, and whether or not the layout of the subject matter is interrupted by tables, diagrams or graphs. Much of the early research summarized by Spencer (1969) has been concerned with a tendency to examine isolated features of layout without reference to dimensional constraints. Much legibility research, involving tachistoscopic displays of different letters, type sizes, type faces etc. is typical of research of this kind. It is our contention that many of the guidelines generated from this kind of research have not been tested in the context of a full page of print. Indeed little typographic research of which we are aware, except our own, specifies the page sizes on which the materials are printed.

It is because we believe this overall dimensional context to be so crucial that we consider such a research strategy to be inappropriate, or, putting it more charitably, to be a less fruitful way of going about things.

### (iii) What is Wrong with Accepting Uncritically Current Typographical Conventions ?

Turning to our next point, we maintain, in addition, that much of the research is weak because there has been an uncritical acceptance by the researchers of existing typographical conventions. What seems to have happened in much research (without naming names — and we have also sinned in this respect ourselves) is that researchers have accepted uncritically the form of anything that happens to be printed, they have designed another way of doing it (e. g. two columns instead of one) and then they have tested readers' reactions to this material with as many measures as could be mustered — in the hope that at least one statistically significant difference between layouts will pop up of its own volition. Present day trends in printing could, however, force us to move away from this kind of research. The development of computer-assisted programs for the control of typographical composition should mean that new questions can be asked concerning layout structures. Unfortunately, however, it appears that the present tendency is to design computer systems which are tied to today's conventions, these being still those developed by the renaissance printers (e. g. centred headings, justified lines, balanced pages) and thus to impose a straitjacket on the structure of printed information which, in content and usage, is quite unlike that of half a millenium ago.

71

## (iv) Empiricism Versus Theory ?

Foster (1973), in a recent survey, categorized legibility research (which he defined as the ergonomic study of visually presented information displays) into twenty different cells. His classification scheme is shown in Table 1.

Table 1

|  | Independent variable | | | |
|---|---|---|---|---|
|  | Text | Alphanumeric | Non-verbal | Environment |
| Detection |  |  |  |  |
| Discrimination |  |  |  |  |
| Identification |  |  |  |  |
| Interpretation of meaning |  |  |  |  |
| Aesthetic interpretation |  |  |  |  |

In principle one should be able to locate any piece of legibility research within the cells of this table.   It is not our purpose here to quibble with the meaning of the terms on the vertical and horizontal axes of this table, but merely to point out, as Foster does himself, that legibility, or typographical research is empirical in origin and lacks a theoretical framework.  Foster writes,  'One of the most prominent gaps in the area of legibility research occurs where the **theory** should be. ...  When such a theory is developed it may be that the structure of legibility research will alter:  however one suspects and hopes that research will be very closely linked to practical problems and their solution. '  With statements such as these we concur, and it is to theory that we now turn.

## TOWARDS A THEORETICAL APPROACH TO TYPOGRAPHICAL DESIGN

We wish to suggest that a shift of emphasis is needed in typographical research to take into account not only the response of the reader to printed information but also the rationality of the design of the stimulus material itself.  At present, the development of a theoretical framework through which to view problems in the construction of a text tends to be inhibited by the notion that 'display' is something we add to an otherwise adequate statement in order to produce an 'interesting' or 'artistic' effect.  This kind of misunderstanding is illustrated by the following passage from the preface to a text on commercial typewriting:

72

'Recent pronouncements by the Decimal Currency Board have dictated that in columns of figures which include the decimal point and the two digits for new pence, the libra sign (£) should be positioned at the top of the column over the **units of the pound.** The style of this book is that the libra sign should always appear over the **decimal point,** and in all typewritten work this practice would seem preferable from a 'balance' and display point of view. The latest preferences of individual examining bodies should be ascertained by all examination candidates. '

Similar examples could be quoted from textbooks in which design is discussed in terms drawn from various periods in the history of the language of art criticism. On the other hand, practising designers who think and work in the rationalist tradition would point to control of the dimensions of linguistic patterning as a matter of prime concern, and to an analysis of the systems of construction and the typographical conventions which have evolved in response to this need. Designers of this disposition would also argue that concern for media per se is not meaningful without reference to sensori-motor control factors in the design and the use of aids to learning. It is not difficult to show that the comprehension of symbolic language is dependent on the co-ordination of abstract relations in two-dimensional space.

In the first line of Figure 1 the spatial relations which govern the structure of written language at the level of the standards of the alphabet have been changed arbitrarily on the horizontal axis of the writing space, as have the dimensions of the intervals which isolate letters at the level of the word and words as discrete units at the level of the sentence. The relative positions of elements has not been changed on the vertical axis.

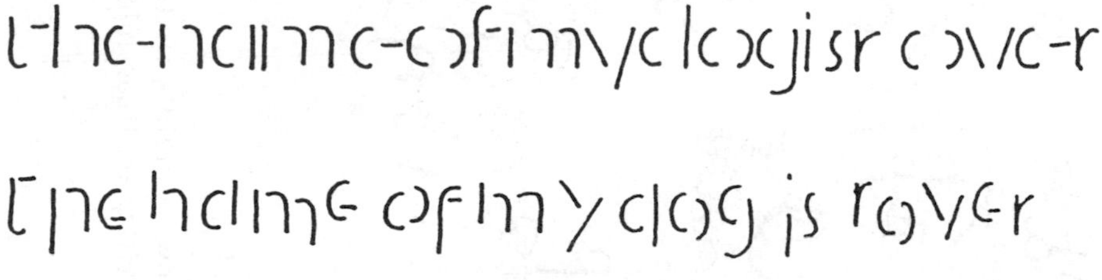

Figure 1

In the second line of Figure 1, the elements have been displaced on the vertical axis of the writing space. (Contrary to the 'common sense' view of writing, the basic and meaningless elements of the system are not the letters of the alphabet. Letters are signs, and signs are meaningful by definition. )

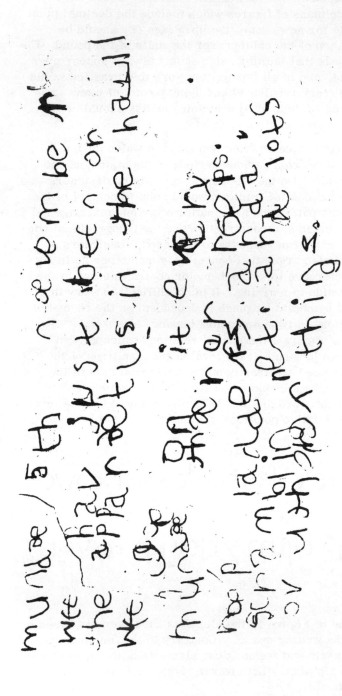

Figure 2a

Figure 2, shows a child's writing when dimensional control has been withdrawn to accord with the notion that writing on lines inhibits freedom of expression.

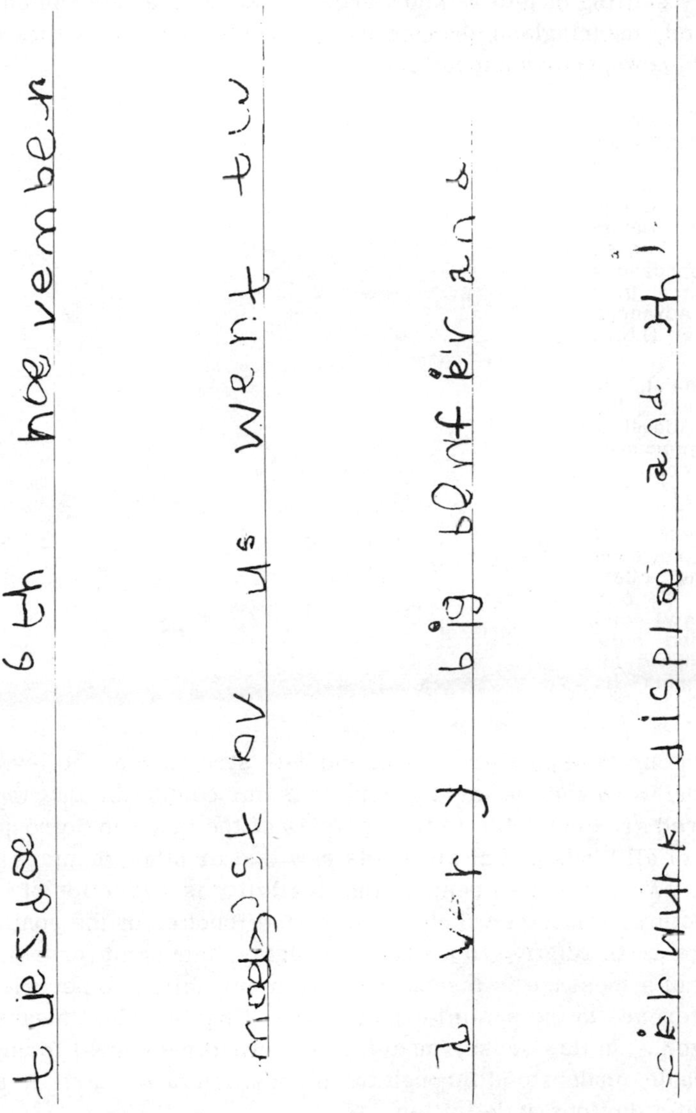

tuesday 6th november

monstrs fir sh went to

I very big bonfire and

firwurk display at Yh.

Figure 2b

75

In Figure 3, the grouping of functionally related events on the horizontal axis of typographic space has been skilfully engineered out of newspaper composition by an irrational obsession for bilateral symmetry. Fortunately for the reader, the system of composition does not permit the arbitrary shifting of letters and words in the vertical dimension. On the other hand, meaningless changes in the line-to-line interval are not uncommon in newspaper composition.

The preferred age is 16/20 years, candidates should hold a minimum of six G.C.E. 'O' levels including Chemistry, Physics, Mathematics and English Language. Applications are also invited from holders of Advanced Level G.C.E. or O.N.C. Chemistry.

The Department is engaged upon the research and development of new processes for the manufacture of speciality synthetic organic chemicals. The job offers interested and varied employment. The Company offers full training, a progressive salary and good promotion prospects. Day release for further education is encouraged.

Figure 3

Although our examples are concerned with structure at the levels of the letter, the word and the word group, it is our contention that the principles involved are applicable to the analysis of the functional grouping of components of all kinds and at all levels of a text or other displays of information. We would also contend that legibility is a function of clearly defined structural relations which are in turn a function of the spatial disposition of parts relative to a whole. Clearly, our comprehension of the meaning of a message is inseparable from our ability to perceive a whole by reference to the spatial organization of parts: 'dog' means 'dog', not 'god'. In this sense, meaning is a two-dimensional form, a perceived whole, understood through the disposition of its parts in space and time, not a dictionary definition.

Fundamental to the problem of making decisions about the dimensional co-ordination of parts relative to their function as elements of a whole statement, is knowledge of the limits of the information field. This is provided by the international standardization of paper sizes to metric dimensions which gives a rationally related set of over-all dimensions for storing information, and thus an opportunity for a more systematic approach to design and specification.

The science of sign systems as a union of elements from the areas of linguistics, social science, and communications technology, has still to achieve autonomy as a discipline. The development of a systematic approach to typographical design and research could contribute to the development of this status. The pollution of the reading environment provides evidence of the urgency of the need.

## Acknowledgements

We are grateful to Susan Fraser, Margrette Young and Ruth Burnhill who assisted with the preparation of this paper, and to the Social Science Research Council who financed our research.

REFERENCES

Aronson, E. (1972) The Social Animal. San Francisco: Freeman & Co.

Ausubel, D.P. (Ed.) (1969) Readings in School Learning. New York: Holt, Rinehart and Winston.

Boyd, W.M. (1973) Repeating questions in prose learning. Journal of Educational Psychology 64, 1, 31-38

Bull, S. (1973) The role of questions in maintaining attention to textual material. Review of Educational Research 43, 1, 83-87

Carter, L.F. (1947) An experiment on the design of tables and graphs used for presenting numerical data. Journal of Applied Psychology 31, 640-650.

Christensen, C.M. and Stordahl, K.E. (1955) The effect of organizational aids on comprehension and retention. Journal of Educational Psychology 46, 2, 65-74.

Davies, I.K. (1972) Presentation Strategies. In Hartley, J. (Ed.) Strategies for Programmed Instruction. London: Butterworths.

Dickinson, G.C. (1973) Statistical Mapping and the Presentation of Statistics. Belfast: University Press.

Dwyer, F.M. (1972) A Guide for Improving Visualised Instruction. State College Pa. Learning Services.

Feliciano, G.D., Powers, R.D. and Kearl, B.E. (1963) The presentation of statistical information. Audio-Visual Communication Review II, 3, 32-39.

Foster, J.J. (1973) Legibility research: the ergonomics of print. Icographic 6, 20-24.

Hartley, J. (1973) The effect of pre-testing on post-test performance. Instructional Science 2, 193-214.

Hartley, J., Fraser, S. and Burnhill, P. (1974a) A selected bibliography of typographical research relevant to the production of instructional materials. Audio-Visual Communication Review (in press).

Hartley, J., Fraser, S. and Burnhill, P. (1974b) The reliability of measures used in typographic research. (Paper available from the authors.)

Hopkin, V.D. (1973) Human factors in the design of maps. In The Visual Presentation of Technical Data. Typography Unit, University of Reading.

Ladas, H. (1973) The mathemagenic effects of factual review questions on the learning of incidental information: a critical review. Review of Educational Research 143, 1, 71-82.

MacDonald-Ross, M. and Smith, E.B. (1973) Bibliography for textual communication. Monograph No. 3. Institute of Educational Technology, The Open University.

Poulton, E.C., Warren, T.R. and Bond, J. (1970) Ergonomics in journal design. Applied Ergonomics 1, 4, 207-209

Preston, R.C. and Botel, M. (1951) Reading comprehension tested under timed and untimed conditions. School and Society, p.71, August 4.

Robinson, F. (1961) Effective Study. New York: Harper and Row.

Schutz, H.G. (1961) An evaluation of formats for graphic trend displays. Human Factors, 99-107 and 108-119.

Spencer, H. (1969) The Visible Word. London: Lund Humphries.

Vernon, M.D. (1953) Presenting information in diagrams. Audio-Visual Communication Review 1, 147-158.

Washburne, J.N. (1927) An experimental study of various graphic, tabular and textural methods of presenting quantitative information. Journal of Educational Psychology 18, 361-376 and 465-476.

Wright, P. (1968) Using tabulated information. Ergonomics 11, 331-343.

Wright, P. and Fox, K. (1972) Explicit and implicit tabulation formats. Ergonomics 15, 175-187.

Wright, P. and Reid, F. (1973) Written information: some alternatives to prose for expressing the outcomes of complex contingencies. Journal of Applied Psychology 57, 2, 160-166.

FURTHER READING

Coleman, E.B. (1962) Improving comprehensibility by shortening sentences. Journal of Applied Psychology 42, 2, 131-134.

Froshaug, A. (1964) Typographic Norms. London: Kynoch Press/DADA.

Goldring, M. (1966) Rational typographic design. Advances in Computer Typesetting. London: Institute of Printing.

Goldring, M. and Hackelsberger, A. (1973) A standard specification system for print production. The Penrose Annual.

Holliday, W. (1973) Critical analysis of pictorial research related to science teaching. Science Education 57, 2, 201-214.

Klare, G.R. (1963) The Measurement of Readability. Iowa State University Press.

Lockwood, A. (1969) Diagrams: A Visual Survey of Graphs, Maps, Charts and Diagrams. London: Studio Vista.

Malter, M. (1947) The ability of children to read a process diagram. Journal of Educational Psychology 38, 290-298.

Malter, M. (1947) The ability of children to read cross sections. Journal of Educational Psychology 38, 157-166.

Martin, B. (1971) Standards and Building. London: RIBA Publications Ltd.

Prince, J.H. (1967) Printing for the visually handicapped. Journal of Typographic Research 1, 1, 31-47.

Smith, F. (1971) Understanding Reading. New York: Holt, Rinehart and Winston.

Smith, F. (Ed.) (1973) Psycholinguistics and Reading. New York: Holt, Rinehart and Winston.

Tinker, M.A. (1960) Legibility of mathematical tables. Journal of Applied Psychology 44, 83-87.

Tinker, M.A. (1964) Legibility of Print. Ames: Iowa State University Press.

Wheatley, D.M. and Unwin, A.W. (1972) The Algorithm Writer's Guide. London: Longmans.

Zachrisson, B. (1965) The Legibility of Printed Text. Stockholm: Almqvist and Wiksell.

# The relevance of instructional systems design to ETV programme production

T. S. ALLAN, Sir George Williams University, Montreal

**Abstract:** The paper poses the question: what has instructional systems design (ISD) to offer the producer of ETV programmes? After outlining a typical ISD fomulation, the paper examines how it works in application to the goal of making a programme for fourteen year olds about the causes of the tides. Analysis of this example is used to show that the steps in ISD are so completely interactive that they must be regarded as abstractions of aspects of a process which is not adequately represented by the ISD. An attempt is made to describe the process more realistically in terms of the tension between creative generation of possibilities on the one hand and selective definition on the other; the empirical and 'hypothetico-deductive' nature of the process is outlined.

Accepting scientific evaluation as one of the most important procedures required by ISD, the paper explores some of the problems in applying such research procedures to ETV production, and suggests two acceptable forms of compromise solution, namely the piloting of representative programmes in a series, and the validation of presentation formulas.

Finally some general points are made: that ISD is most successful where the instructional content can be handled as a closed system in which all the variables are known and quantifiable; that the precise specification of terminal objectives is not always possible, nor desirable, and leads to a purely functional, means-to-an-end view of education which does not adequately represent the reality.

Those of us who work in ETV are acutely aware that one common reason given for its not infrequent ineffectiveness is that the 'software' is just not good enough. Teachers, challenged to be more specific in their criticism, have said things like: 'The programmes are so often irrelevant to the curriculum'; 'A pleasant break from my voice for the class but no more than a desirable extra'; 'Perhaps good in its own way but not in the way we teach the subject here'; 'Have your producers never been inside a classroom?' et cetera. There has been plenty of negative criticism, but not much in the way of positive guidance for the producer except of a very general sort — that programmes should be more closely related to curricular needs and practices, that there should be more direct teaching and not so much enrichment. This kind of advice was common ten years ago and producers, particularly in closed circuit systems which emerged partly as a result of dissatisfaction with existing

ETV, responded with direct teaching series in subjects like mathematics and languages, but there was no real breakthrough and the dissatisfaction continued. In the last few years, however, new voices have been heard from systems analysts and behavioural psychologists asking the producers some very pointed questions: what exactly were the objectives you had in this programme? How much cognitive learning resulted from it? What was your instructional strategy? The producers, recovering from their initial shock, began bringing themselves up-to-date in modern Learning Psychology and Instructional Technology. Here were people claiming that there were rational prescriptions for the design and evaluation of any unit of instruction, a claim which must obviously apply to ETV. Now that the more conscientious producers have had time to catch up on the theory, it is appropriate to take stock and ask how far Instructional Systems Design can really help the ETV producer.

It will be apparent that I approach this difficult question primarily from the producer's point of view. What does ISD offer the producer-teacher, or rather expect of him, if he is to continue to be regarded as a serious educator? He is likely to be dismayed by the extremely formal detail of some of the many descriptions of ISD, and a little confused by the variations in the models and the terminology, but after he has studied a few authors like Banathy (1968), Friesen (1973), Baker and Schutz (1971), Knirk and Childs (1968), I think he might agree that most prescriptions for ISD require the following basic steps:

1. Overall objective (proposal, purpose)

2. Specification of content

3. Specification of learning population

4. Specification of terminal objectives

4a. Criterion test

5. Strategy and tactics

6. Production of instructional system (e.g. ETV programme)

7. Validation of sub-systems or units, and evaluation of system as whole

8. Re-cycling as necessary

Let us take an example to see how the proposed ISD, outlined above, works in application. Suppose I am given the overall objective or proposal: make a programme for fourteen-year olds on the causes of the tides.

(1) Overall objective: the first thing I note is that this proposal already specifies an objective, a learning group, a content, and perhaps also a medium. Without this preliminary specification, which is not necessarily arrived at by ISD, there would be nothing to design.

(2)  Content: a subject has been given — the explanation of tidal action. The possible content is large and the explanation could be given at several possible levels right up to Einstein's General Theory of Relativity. Three things have to be done: 1) exploration of the possible content; 2) selection and definition of the actual content; 3) ordering of the content. But 2) cannot be done except by decisions made about steps 3 and 4 of the ISD.

(3)  Learning population: the population is already specified as fourteen-year olds, but I have to make this much more precise as to nationality, level of intelligence, their place in the school system, etc.  Then I must specify what they already know about the subject.  I consult their teachers and test a sample of the target audience by questionnaire.  I must specify also what they can be expected to learn.  Einstein is out, for their mathematical and conceptual skill is inadequate for any real understanding of Einstein.  How about Newton?  Perhaps, but probably the Newtonian theory of gravitation need only be stated in non-mathematical terms for the purpose of explaining tidal action.  And so on.  I note that the questions all imply decisions about terminal objectives and content.

(4)  Terminal objectives:  What do I expect them to learn?  What do I expect them to be able to do or say which they were not able to do or say before the programme?  I expect them to be able to explain tidal action, but to do this they will have to know certain other things, e. g. the working model of the solar system and the law of gravitation.  I find that in trying to specify terminal objectives I am inevitably specifying content and the characteristics of the learning population.

(4a)  Criterion test:  How will I know that they have achieved the objectives?  By giving them some form of test after the programme.  I could test them on all the objectives, but I can probably devise one question which will be a sufficient test of whether or not they have learned how to explain tidal action, e. g. why are there spring tides twice a month?  I will have to decide what answering behaviour in the form of words or diagrams I will accept as proof of learning.

(5)  Strategy and tactics:  I have already specified some points of strategy and tactics provisionally since I have, for example, envisaged the solar system content in a partly pictorial presentation. I had after all to think of it in some form.  Whoever is planning an instructional system must inevitably plan a series of events in a medium, or, more commonly, in several media, regarding the teacher as a medium for the moment.  There is no disembodied system of instruction which is first planned 'in abstracto' and then expressed in a chosen medium. From the start it is planned in words or pictures or gestures or in a mixture of all three.  It may be translated into another medium later. The ETV producer will naturally plan from the start for his dual medium of sound and vision.  Planning my programme on tidal action I find that

I have already imagined vaguely some parts of the programme and I have arrived already, without knowing it at a rough structure simply by analysing the possible content, working back from the terminal objectives in a logical manner.

The point I am making is a fairly obvious one which would not be disputed by IS designers although their very formal approach tends to suggest that one step follows another in a neat logical series. I am suggesting that all these steps are in fact one complex step which is not adequately represented in the formal model. Terminal objectives cannot be specified without at the same time specifying content, the entering characteristics of the learners, and the main lines of strategy. I think the implication of the completely interactive nature of the ISD steps is that they are abstracted from a process which is not contained in these abstract formulations. The fact that empirical testing is required at almost every step indicates this. If the system was completely known and analysed, then all the variables could be identified and quantified, and testing and evaluation would be the merest formality, like checking that someone had calculated a square root correctly. But it is not so. Validation turns out to be necessary at almost every step, and evaluation of the system as a whole is necessary because the IS designer does not know in advance what the effects of his system will be. He is in an empirical situation in which his basic strategy is 'hypothetico-deductive' (Medawar, 1969), i.e. he collects evidence, makes the most intelligent guess or hypothesis he can, develops instructional material, and tests it. The stress on system gives a false air of strict logical necessity to a process which is inductive, intuitive and hypothetical, a natural process which is only partly understood and only partly teleological.

It is customary when defining the systems concept to distinguish between man-made and natural systems. It is clear that a weapon system is a man-made system, ignoring the fact that it assumes the existence of a natural energy which, however, is completely measurable and under control. The systems concept has been imported into education from its very successful application in such man-made systems, but the instructional process, though man-made in a sense, is not man-made in the same sense as the weapon system. Instruction is a form of communication which is a natural activity of man. In relation to instruction the systems concept is ideal and normative rather than descriptive.

It seems to me that ISD is embedded in a total process which is in tension between two natural, but somewhat opposed, operations of the human mind. The first is creative, inventive, exploratory, generative, expansive; the other is selective, analytic, definitive, normative. ISD has tended to concentrate unduly on the second, taking the first very much for granted. ISD models, in spite of their recognition of feedback, have a simple linear form which fails to do justice to the multilinear simultaneity of the actual process, or to its complete dependence on the creativity of people. Some educational technologists have talked as if conscious system and design were the process instead of being an ideal regularization and systematization of a process which already happens, to a large extent unconsciously, in teaching and learning. I have attempted to produce a more representational model in the appendix to this paper.

I have described the production of an ETV programme up to the point where the producer has developed the main strategy, the macro-structure, of a possible programme. He has still a long way to go before this will be transformed into a linear series of visual images and sounds, which may be called the micro-structure. The final programme has to be precisely specified down to the smallest variable in production. How this is done is frankly not well understood. Throughout the whole of the process the two aspects, the generative and the selective-definitive, continue simultaneously, for the producer-writer must generate a great many possible images and sounds and at the same time select and define which of them he is going to realize in the production and how precisely he will realize them. Can ISD help him at this stage? His problems are now increasingly those of presentation. At an early stage in the planning he has decided, for instance, that he must explain the force of gravity in a simple way, but how exactly is he to do this? Will he use animation? or a 3-D model? or words only? The character-istics of the TV medium do not necessarily dictate the answer. ISD, however, reminds him that one question he must always ask is: will form of presentation 'A' produce more learning in the target audience than form 'B'? ISD tells him that this question can be satisfactorily answered only by validation test, perhaps the most powerful tool in the ISD kit. So two or three versions of this particular part of the pro-gramme must be made and tested on sample audiences and the results analysed according to accepted rules of research procedure and statisti-cal analysis. If one version is found to be significantly better than the others in producing learning, the producer's problem is solved. If, how-ever, the result is no significant difference so far as learning effective-ness is concerned, then he must obviously make his decision on other grounds.

Evaluation makes sense but the research process is slow and complicated, requiring the kind of expertise which comes only from pro-fessional training, and there are many such decisions to be made even in a short programme. Unless the producer is supported by a singularly indulgent production company which does not care how long he takes to make a programme or how much he spends on it, and unless he is trained in research or can call on the help of a research department, this kind of detailed evaluation research does not appear to be a practi-cal proposition. It would slow the rate of production far below any cost-effective level. What is to be done? It may be that previous research already has the answer to the producer's problem, but a study of the literature is unlikely to disclose an investigation of the precise point in question. The weakness of such research from the producer's point of view is that it is seldom safe to generalize from a proven hypothesis to other situations which are not quite the same, and problems in ETV programmes are seldom exactly similar.

Suppose, for example, I have to show the technique of throwing a pot in ceramics. The question of angle of presentation arises. Do I shoot it from the objective or the subjective angle? I look at the research literature and find that no one has researched my particular problem, but I find a report in Chu and Schramm (1967) of an investigation by Roshal into the teaching of knot-tying on film to navy recruits. He found that shooting the operation from the subjective angle was significantly more effective than shooting it from the objective angle. Does this help me to solve my problem? It does not, because the only hypothesis proved by Roshal's research is that if knot-tying from the subjective angle is shown from the subjective angle on film, more learning will result than if it is shown from the objective angle. You cannot generalize from this result to any other superficially similar perceptual-motor skill like tying a knot in someone else's tie or in your own tie by looking in a mirror. Still less will it tell me how best to show throwing a pot. I have no alternative but to conduct experimental research on my own problem. The strength of such research is its precision, but it achieves this at the cost of application to any other situation than the one examined or situations similar to it in every relevant respect.

When there has been a great deal more research of this kind on particular points the producer's chances of finding help from the literature will be increased, but in view of the infinitely large number of possible problems of presentation, the infinite variety of possible educational content for different audiences, and the dangers of extrapolating the findings of any one piece of research, the fundamental problem will remain, namely that the only satisfactory way to select the best mode of presenting a piece of instruction is to make an intelligent guess, test it, re-make, re-test and so on until an effective mode is validated, and this, as we have seen, is so time-consuming that it is not generally a practical solution. Clearly some form of compromise is required which will enable ETV to benefit from research without slowing down the rate of production to an unacceptable level. There are, I think, two types of compromise which go some way towards a solution, though neither is wholly satisfactory.

The first compromise is to neglect most of the presentation detail and simply test a programme as a whole. This piloting procedure has been carried out by ETV producers to a limited extent, but the testing procedures have seldom been rigorous enough to yield a reliable evaluation, and it is too generalized a procedure to isolate specific weaknesses

84

with precision. The method works only because intuition and experience are by no means as unreliable as the scientist is apt to think, and because the results of research into effectiveness for learning are so often inconclusive. Admittedly to do even this piloting for every programme, with the obligation to re-make it if it is found ineffective, would increase the cost and slow the tempo of production. It is essential, however, that at least a reasonable sample of the output should be tested in this way, particularly if the programmes are organized in series as they usually are in ETV.

The other compromise is the Sesame Street solution which is initially very expensive in time and money, but within its self-imposed limits is very successful (Ball, 1970). The Children's Television Workshop spent some eight million dollars in preliminary research and in putting on the first year of Sesame Street. The research, which I cannot describe in any detail here, included a major study of a sample of the projected pre-school audience of under-privileged children, with special reference to skills in the cognitive domain, and with the aim of finding what they could be assumed to know already, how they learned, and how much they could learn at one time. The effectiveness of different forms of presentation was also researched in great detail, e.g. cartoons v. live performers, children v. adult performers, the reaction to puppets, slapstick comedy et cetera. Pilots were made and tested. In addition to this very extensive research and formative evaluation, which continues, summative evaluation was carried out by an outside research group. It may seem absurd to call such a major research operation a compromise solution, but in relation to the enormous output of programmes in the series it is a compromise in one sense. The series is built on a set of presentation formulas and guidelines which have been evaluated as such. If you can establish a general formula as valid, then you know in advance that it will probably be valid for any values you give to the terms of the formula within the defined limits. How far this approach can be applied to learning in older children is another matter. I suspect that the rote-learning of letters and numbers characteristic of the early stages of cognitive learning lends itself to generalized formulation and that this has a lot to do with the astonishing success of Sesame Street. It would be instructive to research the possibility of designing such formulas for ETV at an advanced level. It has to be recognized, however, that the price paid for formula designed programmes is the stereotyping of programmes in the series.

ISD is a system for learning how to instruct, i.e. for **learning** how to promote **learning** in students. ISD itself falls in the problem-solving category of learning, but the learning it promotes may be of any kind from conditioned response to problem-solving. Learning is a natural process of which our knowledge is empirical and incomplete. It has the appearance of being a purposeful system but this is possibly as illusory as the teleological appearance of evolution. Learning takes place, we observe how and when it takes place, and we make some tentative generalizations about if of a causal type. Where we have been successful in hypothesizing stable and repetitive causal patterns of the "if you do 'a' then 'b' will follow" type, then we can teach with definite objectives and apply systems design with success. We do not know, for instance, how men first learned how to boil an egg to produce just the right product, but obviously it was discovered in part by chance and in part by experiment before the correct recipe or system design was finally established. The process is by now completely formulated as a closed system which can be repeated with confidence in its outcome, but learning how to boil eggs as men first had to learn it is a different problem from learning how to instruct people to boil eggs, and learning from the instruction is a different kind of learning from the original learning by experiment. Learning how to instruct people is in fact problem-solving, but where the instructional content consists of variables which are all known and quantified and in a given order, the design of instruction is not very difficult or uncertain. Since education is mostly a matter of learning what has already been learned and completely systematized, it is generally not difficult to systematize the instruction. Instructing a class in Newton's theory of gravitation is a simple matter compared with Newton's own learning, or discovery, of his theory. Suppose, however, that I want to teach people to write poetry or to discuss the individual's responsibility for violence in society (The Last Bus, 1967), I am unable to define my objectives except in very general terms which serve to conceal the fact that I cannot specify the objectives with precision. The reason is that what I wish them to learn in these cases is not a closed system of knowledge, is not a recapitulation of what has already been learned by men, but a new and individual piece of learning, and my degree of success in promoting this kind of learning will be difficult to evaluate in any quantitative way.

The difference between an open-ended programme like The Last Bus and a programme showing how to boil eggs is important for education. In the latter the producer-teacher is the authority who knows all the answers, and his goal, however skilfully disguised, is to lead the students to a pre-determined point of knowledge. In the former the producer-teacher abrogates his authority, admitting by implication that he does not know all the answers, saying in effect: here is a problem, or a starting-point, I do not have the answer nor do I know where exactly this will take us, but let us explore this together. Admittedly this kind of programme occurs mostly in the humanities or in advanced science or philosophy, but the popularity of the discovery method in the cognitive domain indicates a desire to get away from the authoritarian, omniscient attitude even in mathematics and science. More stress is being laid on the process than on the product of learning. ISD, however, tends to lay stress on the product, particularly the product of closed systems of knowledge, no doubt because such products are measurable. Nonetheless even in open-ended programmes with generalized objectives, there is still a product which can be characterized qualitatively though not measured with precision. If a programme, which was intended to spark off discussion, does not lead to anything except a short and desultory expression of opinion this is evidence of its failure; or if the programme to stimulate some creative or research activity is followed by no such activity, the producer had better re-think his programme. ISD certainly can be useful to him in directing his attention to the need to assess the effects of his programme in some way, and also to suggest to him where to look for the causes of failure.

Finally, there are programmes which are not obviously functional, not means to an end, but are simply to be experienced as ends in themselves, like performances of music or drama, the representation of experience in dramatization or film. Such programmes do not have identifiable objectives in the so-called cognitive, affective or psychomotor domains, but are a totality in which perceptual-cognitive, emotional moral and aesthetic elements are inextricably fused. Such programmes produce effects rather than have objectives. Such programmes are needed in education, for the relentless pursuit of terminal objectives becomes a sisyphean labour, the perpetual mastering of means to ends which, when reached, change into means to further ends. The only escape from this treadmill is to make the means an end in itself as well as a means, in other words to enjoy learning for its own sake. It is certainly possible to use something merely as a means, but every means is also the end of some other means, otherwise it would have no existence. Even the most functional tool has a character not entirely determined by its function. This is strikingly so in education in the case of the live teacher who can never be regarded as simply a means or a medium. It is also true of an ETV programme which must always have qualities not wholly definable by ISD.

REFERENCES
Baker, R.L. and Schutz, R.E. (Eds.) (1971) Instructional Product Development, Van Nostrand Reinhold Co.
Ball, S. (1970) The First Year of Sesame Street: An Evaluation. Princeton: Educational Testing Service.
Banathy, B.H. (1968) Instructional Systems. Fearon Publishers.
British Broadcasting Corporation (1967) The Last Bus. ETV Programme.
Chu, G.C. and Schramm, W.L. (1967) Learning from Television: What the Research Says. Washington: NAEB.
Friesen, P.A. (1973) Designing Instruction. Miller Publishing Co.
Knirk, F.G. and Childs, J.W. (Eds.) (1968) Instructional Technology: A Book of Readings. New York: Holt, Rinehart and Winston.
Medawar, P.B. (1969) Induction and Intuition in Scientific Thought. London: Methuen.

# A MODEL FOR E.T.V. PROGRAMME PRODUCTION

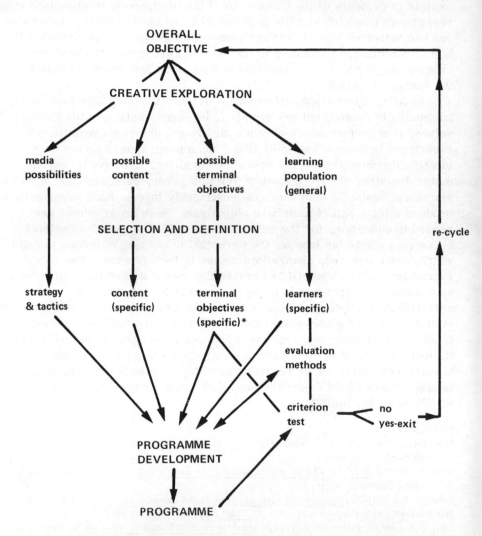

*For some E.T.V. programmes terminal objectives cannot be precisely specified.*

# Computers and sacred cows

R. HOOPER, Director, National Development Programme in Computer Assisted Learnin

**Abstract:** This paper scrutinizes a number of assumptions that have been taken for granted – by the 'converted' educational technologist and/or the 'unconverted' teacher – in the application of communications and educational technology to learning. The author draws examples from the early work of the National Development Programme in Computer Assisted Learning, and from previous experience in the Open University and in the USA.

The assumptions are as follows:

- the live teacher is not a medium

- in educational innovation, development builds upon research

- an educational innovation that is not formally evaluted will not win widespread acceptance

- the essence of evaluation is control group experiments

- the first stage in the design of educational materials is the definition of audience and objectives

- educational communication is a two-way process

The paper suggests that these statements are at best half-truths, and argues that the application of communications and educational technology remains today a highly pragmatic and applied art. The scientific paradigm of proof has been over sold to the detriment of progress.

On the first of January, 1973, anno domini, the bandwaggon of the National Development Programme in Computer Assisted Learning trundled off on its five-year journey. Weighed down by a large chest containing two million pounds, and a stack of research articles dating back fifteen years and running into hundreds of titles, there was some immediate concern as to whether the computers should pull the waggon, or the waggon pull the computers. The latter option was chosen. From the beginning, map-reading was problematic since it was not very clear in which direction to travel. The early part of the route led past a series of impoverished universities, their begging bowls rattling in the winter sunshine. From time to time the journey was held up by sacred cows wandering into the roadway and ruminating. And all the time from the verges came the incessant quacking of — to stretch this rural allegory to its limit and beyond — paraducks. In this paper, it is the paraducks and the sacred cows I want to talk about, drawing mainly upon experiences in the National Programme, but also previous experiences in the Open University, the BBC and the United States.

I would like to begin with the paradoxes. At the start of an undertaking such as the National Programme, there are two contradictory voices talking. One voice is saying that the issues here are very complex with few, if any, simple answers. The other voice is saying, temptingly, that it is all much more clear-cut. For example, the introduction of closed circuit television into American education in the 1950's was seen by many people, both in the funding agencies and in the schools and universities, as a straightforward technological fix to a straightforward problem — shortage of good teachers and need for cost reduction. But as the introduction of CCTV proceeded, people began to realize — in most cases far too late — that it was not so straightforward. For television to be effectively used, courses needed to be altered in subtle ways. Teachers had to be more skilful, not less. Organizational structures had to be modified. Yesterday's graphics for the blackboard was no longer adequate for today's television eye. In some cases, people never did realize the complex nature of the innovation and retired hurt, when TV turned out not to 'revolutionize' education.

One problem is that the simple slogans of the early pioneering years follow the innovation about for ever more — 'television spreads the master teacher to larger audiences'. And it is of course the slogans that get remembered. Many people in Britain still refer to the Open University as 'the University of the Air', even though that notion became obsolete eight years ago.

The issues surrounding technological and curriculum innovation are complex, and it is dangerous to see them as straightforward — for two reasons. Firstly, the straightforward belief swiftly becomes the popular slogan, to hang for ever, albatross-like, round the neck of the innovation. Secondly, it is dangerous because the complexities will erupt — and erupt they will — without any contingency plans being ready for them. Yet, and this is where the first paradox comes in, if there is to be action taken at all in a National **Development** Programme, there must be some simplification. And if there is to be diffusion of the ideas concerning computer assisted learning to the larger, non-specialist audience, there must be some (careful) sloganizing.

Whilst the vast and growing educational technology and curriculum development literature gets yearly cleverer, with ever finer and more powerful distinctions being made, the laymen, and incidentally many of the practitioners too, live on in a much simpler world. Yet, and here comes the second paradox, despite them living in this simpler world, many of these laymen and practitioners have not even partially understood some fairly basic points about educational technology.

The points have probably been distorted anyway during their transition from the specialist group to the wider public. Yet these points are so basic and simple that it can be academic hara-kiri for the specialist himself to spend any time on them. The standard comment on papers given at conferences such as this one is 'There's nothing new there', or 'That's just a rehash of what he wrote a couple of years ago'.

Let me take an example. After many years of educational technology, we still have not succeeded in getting across the very basic and obvious point that the teacher is a medium of communication. One reason for this is that many educational technologists themselves have not got the point, or are still busy arguing the semantics of 'medium', 'mode', 'channel' etc. Articles are still being written by educational technologists, where the word 'medium' is applied only to tapes, film and programmed texts. Quite often, the word 'medium' is not even used to refer to print, for example books. For other educational technologists, the point is so obvious that they tend not to make it, assuming it is understood. As a result we get continuing media apartheid, and little progress. Given that we can get across the simple but I believe powerful notion that the teacher along with books, television, tapes and films is a medium of communication, then quite a lot becomes clearer. People, for example, realize that the teacher in the lecture hall is a profoundly different medium to the teacher in the tutorial setting — for example, as measured by the amount of two-way communication.

But, the teacher is not just a medium of communication. Since education is crucially about relationships with and between human beings, most obviously in the primary and pre-primary school, then the teacher as a human being is both the form and content of education, both means and end.

Coming back to the National Programme, I do not think there are any very obvious solutions to this set of paradoxes. In fact, computer assisted learning seems to raise more problems here than does say, educational television. People generally are very familiar with television — every household has one. People are not only not familiar with the computer but are alienated by, amongst other things, its complexity. It may be difficult to get across basic points about computer assisted learning, because people are distracted by the technological sophistication. On the other hand, the way you are using the computer for teaching or learning **is** constrained often in quite complex ways by the technology, and sooner or later the CAL user has to realize this and get some technological initiation. In trying to avoid the simplified slogan — inherited from American CAI experiences — of 'computerized programmed instruction', it is very easy for the National Programme to get lost in the very abstruse areas of numerical methods, simulation modelling, and partial differential equations.

I would like to turn away now from these paradoxes, and examine some of the sacred cows that the National Programme is encountering — assumptions that people take for granted about educational technology in general, and computer assisted learning in particular. For example, it is quite widely assumed that the National Programme, being a **development** programme, builds on research that has previously been conducted into computer assisted learning. But does it? We have been using print in education for centuries without ever having done sufficient basic research. As Perry (1971) said in his Open University Annual Report: 'There has been some research on the printed word (justified versus unjustified type, length of line, serif versus sans serif, etc.) and some on the construction of diagrams. Though this research provides some useful starting-points, it has not yet provided practical guidelines for the design of texts'.

The point is that development in education has not historically followed research (R & D models are recent phenomena themselves anyway), and any over rigid requirement that it should may be tantamount to killing off many reforming ideas. Even though 90 per cent of the Open University's education is print-based, it would have been somewhat ridiculous to have refused to start the research into print.

The assumption that 'development follows research' is a half-truth. If you examine the history of many of today's everyday household materials, development actually **preceded** research. Vulcanized rubber was invented and developed as a product in the 19th century, long before anyone did, or needed to do, the research into the basic chemical processes. The same story was true of cement, used for hundreds of years before it was 'understood'. In the making of glass bottles, it only became necessary to understand the actual composition of glass when there was a requirement towards the end of the 19th century to mechanize bottle production. The human glass-blower understood how glass worked intuitively, as a result of experience, and could adjust his mixtures of materials accordingly. The industrial revolution in Britain was largely the work of technicians and engineers – the artist/practitioners –, building only sketchily on scientifically validated evidence. I would suggest — as long as the analogy is not considered presumptuous — that educational technology is today in a very similar position to technology in the 18th and 19th century industrial revolution.

In the National Development Programme, for example, we are developing a special computer managed software package, for use in the management of learning in a range of education and training institutions. The ICL systems analyst in charge of designing the specification for the software system has drawn an interesting analogy between such a project and the development of the motor car industry as analysed by Galbraith. In the early years of the car, before mass production got into full swing, variations could be made to the car relatively simply, and needed to be.

In the modern motor car industry, variations may take anything from two to five years' massive investment. Now the application of an educational technology such as computer assisted learning remains uncertain — even where the research has been done, the results are very ambiguous. Thus ease of variation must be built into the computer managed software package. The software must be constructed so that 'quick and dirty' changes can be made, as a result of operational experience, without two to five years' investment.

Educational design remains an iterative process of trial and error. Yet some educational technologists, unduly concerned about their academic respectability quotient, reject the rough and ready models of the practitioner — trial and error — in favour of the more elegant, but so often less workable, predictive models of the theoretician.

Experience in both the Open University and the National Programme would suggest that there is a strong case to be made for research following development in education — as well as vice versa. The Open University provides an ideal test-bed for research into adult learners, for example. For one thing the sample and population sizes are really significant. The computer can, if so programmed, provide a very rich record of student interaction — the conventional tutorial provides no such record of itself. An operational computer managed system can be used to test out a series of hypotheses about learning style, sequence of learning tasks and that old programmed learning chestnut — branching versus linear.

Now the development-follows-research model is closely linked in many people's minds to another major assumption: that the widespread acceptance of an educational innovation depends on formal evaluation as a prerequisite. The easiest way an educational system can fend off — or at least postpone — an innovative idea is to demand of it formal evaluation. We get a curious situation where innovative ideas are subject to formal evaluation but not the conventional methods of instruction. So the innovative idea is handicapped from the start. Of course, and this is the point, in reality educational decision-makers do not depend on formal evaluation (any more than they depend on research findings). The move towards open-plan schooling, the creation of the Open University, have happened largely without much formal evaluation. Educational decisions are more political and serendipitous than is usually believed. The decision of a local education authority to install a CAI system may have more to do with wanting to be first, than wanting to be right. The decision to open plan primary schools may have more to do with cost cutting than educational benefits, though of course it is wise to dress up the decision with references to Piaget, Dewey and Bruner, and other worthies. Educational decision-makers make decisions to do something because they are rather like the cowboy in the film The Magnificent Seven. On being asked why he had jumped into a gorse bush, he replied: 'It seemed like a good idea at the time.'

One of the problems with talking about evaluation is that it is sometimes understood to be synonymous with research. What the SSRC and the Schools' Council call research is often what other people would term 'evaluation'. As Director of the National Development Programme, I have found myself highly ambivalent towards evaluation. On the one hand, independent evaluation of the claims made for computers in education must be a component of any diffusion strategy. On the other hand, some people would wish to see evaluation as the aim of the Programme and are not satisfied with it being just a component of a strategy. And on the third hand, there are times when I feel that computer assisted learning like a new baby needs to be **protected from** evaluation.

Wrigley (1973) head of the Schools' Council research activities, has argued against the evaluation of Schools' Council projects becoming too dominant: 'My view is that the Council **has** put creative curriculum development first, and **has** refused to be constrained and inhibited by the demands that might have been made by careful, cool evaluators.' The aim of the National Programme is to achieve in specified subject areas and in certain parts of the education and training system in this country the 'institutionalization' of computer assisted learning. Now the truth is that 'institutionalization' in some institutions may be actively disrupted by formal evaluation.

This notion of 'disruption by evaluation' is of particular importance if we move on to another assumption — that the essence of evaluation is control group experiments. Such an assumption is widely held in education circles. A chief inspector of schools and a head of a university department of medicine said to me recently that only control group evidence will persuade them — or their masters — to invest in computer assisted learning. CAL must be more cost-effective than other methods if it is to be considered.

On my way to this Liverpool conference I passed a slag heap. On the side of the slag heap there was a grid made up of 16 squares of grass in four lines of four — fenced off. The grass in each of the 16 squares was of a different kind and in each was growing more or less efficiently. That is the classic control group experiment. All the important variables, soil, climate etc., are being kept beautifully constant for all the 16 variants of grass. But, is education a slag heap?

Control group experiments in education leave much to be desired. First and most obvious of all, the holding of variables constant whilst one is varied is all but impossible. Interpersonal communication — between teacher and taught — is full of unknown idiosyncracies. It is highly subjective with each partner to the communication making his own meanings. Secondly, the Hawthorne effect in education remains substantial — particularly with computers around. We are looking in the National Programme at the possibility of a control group experiment to evaluate a project which may use the computer to manage remedial reading. The problem is that if the remedial reader has a feeling that someone is actually bothering about him in a special way, and he'll get that feeling if he is in the experimental group, then his reading will improve anyway. We have even got evidence from a control group experiment to prove it! Lawrence (1973). Thirdly, we always have an ethical problem when we assign children to the experimental or the control group. Fourthly, taking the classic series of over 500 control group studies done in the USA on conventional versus televised teaching, what do they tell us? In most cases, the result is 'no significant difference'. But may not the very design be missing the significant differences.

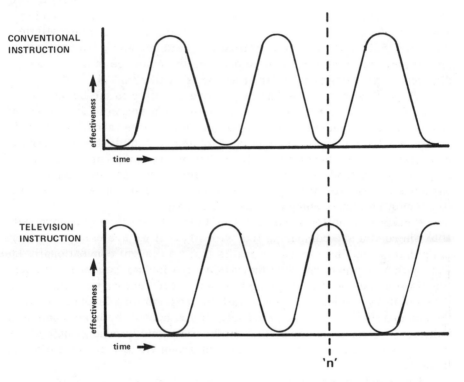

Figure 1

Figure 1 compares in idealized form a conventional lesson lasting thirty minutes with a television lesson. The horizontal axis is time, the vertical axis is educational effectiveness. Now it is possible to hypothesize that at time 'n', the television is being least effective and the conventional teacher most effective. But when we sum the low points and high points of effectiveness at the end of the time period, they of course equal out to no significant difference. And we still do not know what each medium may be most effective at.

95

Now this Figure 1 can be taken to illustrate another point. It can be hypothesized that again at time 'n' the television is not being effective with one individual learner whilst the conventional teacher is being very effective with another individual learner. Again, when we total up, the individual effectivenesses are camouflaged. We do have some common-sense evidence that different learners prefer different media. Some of the adult Open University students, for example, actively dislike the medium of the live tutor at the study centre, and prefer to make their mistakes privately with the correspondence text and radio programme, at home.

But there are other problems with control group experiments. They are enormously disruptive of what would go on naturally in a learning situation. The learning situation becomes more and more unrealistic the more that variables are identified and held constant. Given this unrealism, teachers are likely to dismiss the evidence of significant differences by saying that their situation isn't like that.

Whilst this or that medium may prove effective in the laboratory setting of the control group experiment, its generalization to the rough and ready real environment of the classroom is too often taken for granted. The point of scientific experiments is to reduce complexity in order to establish or refute hypotheses. In education, the moment you reduce complexity you tend to lose credibility. But of course, to return to paradoxes, educational people do not want to be confronted with complexity. Anything that is complex constitutes jargon.

Finally, the notion of control group experiment is only understandable where you are comparing like with like. If we are using computers in primary schools to teach the maths that was taught conventionally last year without computers, then there is a case for comparability studies. But if we are using the computer to teach a different sort of maths, for example using Seymour Papert's child's programming language LOGO, then comparisons are not so obvious. If you accept the basic contention that form influences content, that methods and media change objectives, then comparability studies of the control group variety are of limited usefulness.

The question — does form influence content — is crucial to an analysis of another major assumption that the National Programme, like any other curriculum development/educational technology agency, encounters. According to this assumption, the first stage in the design of educational materials is the definition of audience and objectives. Most educational technologists not only have this assumption, but they are also explicitly aware of it and preach it at all possible opportunities. Yet I would argue that it can be another half-truth. **My** assumption is that form does effect content, methods do influence objectives. Innis (1964) McLuhan's great mentor, wrote 'We can perhaps assume that the use of a medium of communication over a long period will to some extent determine the character of knowledge to be communicated.' The linguist, Sapir (1931), believed this to be true of the medium of language itself — 'Language constitutes a sort of logic, a general frame of reference, and so molds the thought of its habitual users.' A modern example is, of course, computers. Computers were developed during World War Two to solve problems that just could not be solved in any other way — problems in ballistics for example involving extensive calculation. As a result, to quote Levien (1972) concerning computers in higher education for the Carnegie Commission, '...the computer's presence altered the intellectual style of the disciplines.' Bringing the argument further into education, the form-content case is elegantly stated by Bruner (1966) as follows: 'Content cannot be divorced from pedagogy. For it is the pedagogy that leads the child to treat content in critical ways that develop and express his skills and values... For a curriculum is a thing in balance that cannot be developed first for content, then for teaching method, then for visual aids, then for some other particular feature.'

But, of course, the assumption that form influences content is not universally accepted. McClary (1974) on sabbatical from Los Alamos at Glasgow University, has stated in a paper commissioned by the National Programme: 'Developed by physicists, mathematicians and engineers as, primarily, a time compression device, (the digital computer) allowed them to accomplish a greater number of their traditional operations in a given interval of time. Although the computer greatly increased their power and range of investigation, it did little to expand or alter the fundamental concepts of physics, mathematics, engineering or, somewhat later, accounting.'

Any systems approach-oriented educational technologist who talks of first establishing objectives does not accept the notion of form influencing content. Gagné (1971) for example, has asserted: '...most media of communication can readily perform most instructional functions. They can be performed by pictures, by printed language, by auditory language, or by a combination of media. So far as learning is concerned, the medium is not the message. No single medium possesses properties which are uniquely adapted to perform one or a combination of instructional functions. Instead, they all perform some of these functions well, and some not so well.'

Now the debate between these two positions is significant. If one believes that form influences content, there is less place for control group experiments, and doubt is cast on the linear, 'objectives first' model of systems analysis and curriculum development. And the task of educational technology is to orchestrate the media — both human and non-human — in such a way that the special characteristics, in some cases one could say unique characteristics, of each individual medium are exploited. Taking this approach, the National Programme, rather than develop the computer as a surrogate human tutor, would exploit the features of the computer that the human tutor does not share — for example, fast calculation.

Taking the other view, that form does not really influence content, then control groups and objectives-first come naturally. The educational technologist's task now is to choose which of the many media available are best in a cost-effective sense at handling particular objectives, on the basic assumption that all media can, technologically, handle all content. Taking this approach, the National Programme, instead of using the computer as a calculation device is more likely to develop the computer as a surrogate human tutor, to individualize instruction.

But the assumption that the first stage in materials design is the definition of audience and objectives cannot be left there. The definition of audience may not always be a necessary component in the design of good communication at all. The definition of audience may actually inhibit good communication. Did Lewis Carol write <u>Alice in Wonderland for</u> children? Taking other examples from the arts, it is not at all clear that painters like Van Gogh or novelists like Dostoeivski were particularly conscious of an audience.

Similarly, it may not be as obvious as is often assumed by educational technologists that objectives should always be defined. There is a group of curriculum developers in the ascendant who actively are attacking the conventional wisdom of the objectives model of curriculum development. Stenhouse (1971) one of the ringleaders in this country, has written, 'To use the play (Hamlet) as a vehicle for teaching skills is to imply — and students rather readily pick up the implication — that the skills and vocabulary and so forth are the important matter rather than the play... the result... is the use of methods to distort content in order to meet objectives... The objectives model of curriculum design and planning is no doubt a useful one, but it has severe limitations. Accordingly, it is wrong that it should be taken for granted, or advanced as universally applicable.'

In Stenhouse's own Humanities Project, form and content were particularly difficult to differentiate since a crucial aspect of the project was the role of the teacher as neutral chairman — form in some senses was the content of the project.

There is a very respectable if occasionally eccentric school of thought which repudiates the notion of 'knowing what you are doing', of objectives formulation. This school of thought is represented by both philosophers and artists. 'Vagueness' wrote the American composer Ives (1964) 'is at times an indication of nearness to a perfect truth'. Whitehead (1967): 'Adventure rarely reaches its predetermined end. Columbus never reached China. But he discovered America'. Thoreau (1962): 'In view of the future or possible, we should live quite laxly and undefined in front, our outlines dim and misty on that side'.

The point is that over enthusiasm in clarifying what is being or is to be done, in stating objectives and defining audience, may reduce the unpredictability which I believe to be an essential component of education. The famous computer managed system developed at Oakleaf elementary school in Pittsburgh has been bitterly criticized for driving out the original, creative, and unpredictable elements in favour of prepackaged worksheets all hierarchically sequenced with pre-, post- and curriculum-embedded tests. Many elementary and primary school teachers believe that the day's activities should build on what the child brings with him to school that day — by its very nature, not predictable. So many CAI applications have become tedious, mechanistic applications of technology — at the very time when education is moving away from mechanistic models towards Piagetian and Brunerian learning-by-discovery. Thus the sacred cow of 'objectives first' has had a very formative, and too often injurious, influence on educational technology. The worst excesses of CAI and programmed instruction can be traced back to it.

Finally, there is another assumption encountered by the National Programme which, like the assumption 'objectives first', has been very directly responsible for producing some of the mind-less computerized programmed instruction. This assumption states that 'education is a two-way process'. Technically speaking, 'two-wayness' refers to a process of communication between two or more parties where the response from one party actively feeds back into and **changes** the nature of the subsequent response from another party. Education, as a system viewed over a certain time period, is obviously a two-way process. But much educational communication, measured over shorter time periods, for example, the study of a book or the presentation of a lecture, is not really two-way at all. It is ironic that some of the opponents of educational television denigrate its one-wayness without ever admitting that much of the conventional instructional method they use is essentially one-way as well. Clearly there is more two-wayness in the live lecture than the recorded television lecture, but the difference is fairly marginal. The danger lies in the assertion, supported by educational technologists, that effective educational communication can **only** be two-way. This assertion puts pressure on the National Programme in a number of ways. For example, the essentially one-way procedures of batch processing are scorned by computer assisted learning proponents in favour of two-way interactive computing. Many would even go so far as to say that computer assisted learning **only** involves interactive, time-shared applications. Another example concerns graphics terminals. It is claimed that a 16 mm film, demonstrating via a series of moving curves, the performance of a particular mathematical model, cannot be as educationally effective as the use of a graphics terminal which allows the students to sit down and play with the model, altering input values and parameters interactively.

99

Now if the National Programme were to stick too rigidly to the assumption that effective educational communication is only two-way, it would end up with some very expensive applications that no-one would ever have the money to use. The real issue is not one-way versus two-way, but the need for a clever balance in the design of an educational system between both kinds of communication. The point is that one-way methods tend to be cheaper than two-way, just as mass instruction is cheaper than individualized instruction — these two pairs are of course crucially related. Batch is far cheaper, and more reliable, than interactive computing. A 16 mm film, even if computer produced, is much cheaper than graphics terminals costing £2-4,000 a unit, and accommodating usually not more than two learners at one time. If the graphics terminal is hitched to a CCTV system, then of course larger numbers can be covered, but interactive computing is still a more expensive picture-producer than a video cassette recorder.

## CONCLUSION

The sacred cows that I have been investigating — such as two-way communication — are of course related to the paradoxes that I started with. The point is that we come unstuck in educational technology if we use any assumptions as infallible guidelines for action. They are not. Form doesn't influence content, yet it does. Education I would argue, is a highly ambivalent business, with few simple truths and much complexity as one tries to apply communications and educational technology to learning
Much of the problem with educational technology lies in its attempt to ape science and the scientific method. This is the somewhat unfortunate legacy of the behavioural psychologists of the 50s and 60s. An arts perspective may have some things to offer educational technology at the present time. An arts perspective focusses attention on values, where science's attention is on proof. Education is **fundamentally** about values, not about skills and facts. And values, we all know from our philosophy training, can't be proved. No educational technologist with arts training is likely to assert that effective communication is only two-way, since the great literature and art of previous generations is, in a technical sense, one-way. I know of no techniques yet developed to converse interactively with Dostoievski. The independent educational evaluator of the National Programme, Barry MacDonald, who not coincidentally works with Lawrence Stenhouse at the University of East Anglia, suggests that in education we replace the scientific quantitative model of evaluation with more eclectic approaches, drawing upon the methodology of the historian, the anthropologist, **and** the experimental scientist. What is required in educational technology is a sensitive fusion of scientific and arts approaches, of pure and applied, theory and practice. Hubbard (1965) in his book on Wheatstone and Cook's invention of the

electric telegraph, believes that it is this fusion that made the incredible technical advance of telegraphy possible. '...if Wheatstone's design (for the telegraph) was sound and workable, it was Cooke who made and installed it so that it would work'.

I would like to end on a final paradox. The scientific model and the systems engineering model that the educational technologist and psychologist often follow are not the ones that scientists and systems engineers actually use. The simplistic notions of causality, certainty, proof, linearity, are no longer believed in in post-Einsteinian science — if they ever were. 'Modern physics has abandoned the doctrine of Simple Location' Whitehead (op. cit.) Ambiguity is at the centre of modern science — light being both waves and particles is the classic example, or Werner Heisenberg's principle of uncertainty. Heisenberg's contention that the act of observation alters the object being observed, has its obvious analogy in the arts — we call it 'subjectivity'. Popper (1972) and Medawar (1969a) have attacked the established notions of inductive thinking — that scientists derive their theories and hypotheses from empirical observation. Yet inductive thinking is what the non-scientist believes science is all about. Medawar (1969b) in The Art of the Soluble, emphasizes the basic unpredictability of science: 'Unfortunately, it is impossible to predict new ideas — the ideas people are going to have in ten years' or in ten minutes' time — and we are caught in a logical paradox the moment we try to do so. For to predict an idea is to have an idea, and if we have an idea it can no longer be the subject of a prediction.'

Similarly, educational technologists' notions of the systems approach are not the systems engineers' notions. Where educational technologists go on about the need to state objectives as the first step in a systems approach, the systems engineer is specifically involved with feedback — feedback à la Nyquist formula that stabilizes an amplifier system. This emphasis on feedback preempts any obsession with linearity, since feedback is essentially circular and iterative — non-linear.

The assumptions that I have tried to examine in this paper seem to me to be half-truths — and therefore dangerous. They are sired, out of wedlock, by science with systems engineering. The whole truths are much more ambiguous than we allow. As innovators, we are told that too much ambiguity is dangerous, and so the slogans and sacred cows are born. It is about time some of the slogans were rewritten, since we can't do without them, and about time some of the sacred cows were well and truly milked.

REFERENCES

Bruner, S. (1966) Toward a Theory of Instruction. Belknap Press of Harvard University Press.
    p. 164.
Gagné, R. (1971) Learning theory, educational media and individualised instruction, in
    Tickton, S.G. (Ed.) To Improve Learning. Vol. II, Bowker, p. 71.

Hubbard, G. (1965) <u>Cooke and Wheatstone and the Invention of the Electric Telegraph.</u>
London: Routledge and Kegan Paul, p. 149.

Innis, H. (1964) <u>The Bias of Communication</u>. University of Toronto Press (first published 1951),
p. 34.

Ives, C. (1964) <u>Essays Before a Sonata and Other Writings.</u> Norton, p. 22.

Lawrence, D. (1973) <u>Improved Reading Through Counselling.</u> London: Ward Lock Educational.

Levien, R.E. (1972) <u>The Emerging Technology</u>. New York: McGraw-Hill. p.19.

McClary, J.F. (1974) The role of author languages in computer-assisted learning. Paper prepared for National Development Programme in Computer Assisted Learning (unpublished).

Medawar, P.B. (1969a) <u>Induction and Intuition in Scientific Thought.</u> London: Methuen.

Medawar, P.B. (1969b) <u>The Art of the Soluble</u>. Harmondsworth: Pelican, p.111

Perry, W. (1971) <u>The First Teaching Year of the Open University</u>. The Open University, Report
of the Vice-Chancellor, p. 108.

Popper, K.R. (1972) <u>Objective Knowledge</u>. Oxford: Clarendon Press.

Sapir, E. (1931) Conceptual categories of primitive languages. <u>Science</u> **74**, p.378.

Stenhouse, L. (1971) <u>Paedagogica Europaea</u> Vol. **7**, pp. 60 and 62.

Thoreau, H.D. (1962) <u>Thoreau: Walden and Other Writings</u>. London: Bantam Books, p.344.

Whitehead, A.N. (1967a) <u>Adventures of Ideas</u>. London: Free Press, Macmillan, p. 279.

Whitehead, A.N. (1967b) <u>op. cit.</u>, p. 157.

Wrigley, J. (1973) Fools and angels. <u>Dialogue</u>. Schools Council Newsletter **15**, p. 8.

# SECTION B

# Instructional design and techniques

# INTRODUCTION

The second section contains progress reports and reviews of a number of current approaches to instructional design. Applications of the media and the development of course design methodology in various teaching situations are described; and in following those papers in Section A of the book which stressed particular problems of educational technology, the present section may be viewed in terms of the solutions which contemporary approaches can offer.

The first paper, by Elton of the University of Surrey, compares the aims and achievements in recent years of the main self-instructional methods in use in undergraduate science courses: a range of source material is indicated. The particular use of closed-circuit television in physiology teaching at Surrey is discussed by Howland, Midson and Williams: in dealing with the problems of demonstrating practical skills, their work relates to that of Moss et al. reported in the first section. The design, production and use of materials in forces training situations are then discussed in papers by Richardson and O'Hare; and a report on the logistic considerations underlying the installation of resources facilities in a higher education establishment is given by Clarke.

Three papers on course design techniques follow. Applications of Project Network Analysis techniques are indicated by Catlow; while Morton, Bingham and Cowan give an account of an open-ended timetabling system ('free-format') developed at Heriot-Watt University. The problems of creating a truly flexible curriculum are immense, and the latter writers offer valuable guidance in tackling them. In the long-term, such problems are certainly to be eased by the development of computer-assisted techniques, though not before the parameters underlying instructional design have received detailed analysis in themselves, as indicated by Dodd, LeHunte and Sheppard.

The subject of computer assistance in instructional design is pursued by Lawton, who discusses the introduction of conversational interactive design programs using computer graphics into undergraduate courses at the City of Leicester Polytechnic; and by Denis and Lombaerde, who describe the development of computerized student evaluation procedures at Louvain. The discussion of assessment systems in general is taken up by Byrne. The section ends with papers which — as that of Burnhill et al. previously — serve as reminders that educational technology concerns techniques for the transmission of images on the printed page as well as via the other media. Sir James Pitman discusses the use of his well-known initial teaching alphabet in the teaching of English as a foreign language: the beneficial effect of a simplified medium on the motivation to learn is emphasized. The development of a programmed scheme to improve reading skills at primary level is described by Leedham; and the use from 1963 to 1973 of programmed instruction in British industry is surveyed by Ellis, Romiszowski and Howe.

The latter writers' observations of the decreasing rate of conversion to programmed techniques are borne out by those of the present editors: of the sixty papers submitted for APLET's 1974 Conference only four related to programmed instruction per se, and further data bearing on the actual use of programmed library stocks may confirm the view that traditional programmed methods are no longer considered as relevant to the main educational problems as they once appeared.

# An analysis of aims of self instructional methods in undergraduate science courses

L. R. B. ELTON, University of Surrey

**Abstract:** The traditional methods of science teaching — lecture, tutorial and labora-tory — have been increasingly questioned over the past few years, and concern has been expressed that they leave the student too passive in his learning. This has led to much experimentation and innovation in self-instructional methods and the provision of materials suitable for such methods. Some of this work will be discussed in order to illustrate the principles and practices involved, and it is interesting to note that in important instances the original aims of the innovations were significantly different and more restricted from those eventually achieved.

## INTRODUCTION

It is not my purpose to give an exhaustive account of the variety of methods that have been developed over the past decade in order to indi-vidualize students' learning in science. This would be impossible in the time available.[1] What instead I wish to do is to try to analyse what led to this great upsurge of work, what its aims were declared to be and what they appeared to be to the onlooker, which was not necessarily the same. In the process I shall naturally refer to a number of innovations, but this will be for illustrative purposes and I must apologize to all those who will be left unmentioned.

## IN THE BEGINNING

The current upsurge in the development of learning methods in which students work at one remove from the teacher dates back from the early 1960's; the first significant development being almost certainly Postlethwait's audio-tutorial approach to biology teaching at Purdue.[2] This arose initially from a dissatisfaction with existing lecture methods used with very large introductory classes, in which students were not able to actually handle biological materials of even so simple a kind as twigs and leaves. The aim here was quite simple, i.e. to handle simple biological materials, but to achieve it required a total reorganization of the learning situation and this in turn, perhaps not surprisingly, led to a number of unexpected outcomes, mostly judged to be favourable, in particular the advantages of individualized self-paced work. This pattern of an initial specific dissatisfaction leading to quite radical changes designed to overcome it, which in turn led to unexpected beneficial outcomes has been repeated on a number of occasions. I believe that an explanation can be found in the fact that a dissatisfaction is often a rather negative and superficial way of expressing underlying very positive aims which have remained covert and that the subsequent commitment to change leads to massive applications of the Hawthorne effect. As regards the latter point, one should however be aware that the Hawthorne effect has been more often invoked than demonstrated.[3]

The dissatisfactions that led to innovations appear to have been of three kinds :

(a)  Students were not learning well what they were supposed to be learning.

(b)  The student's education was too factual and his assessment was largely on the basis of straight reproduction of material learnt.

(c)  In an age of mass education, students had largely ceased to be in direct contact with their teachers.

It should be noted that these are very different from each other. Thus (a) was mainly concerned with making students perform well in existing rather factual curricula, e.g. in medicine, while (b) was concerned with curricular change and (c) with aspects of university education which are largely independent of the curriculum. To add to the confusion, these dissatisfactions came to the fore at a time when there was still a rather optimistic belief around that mere technological innovation was the answer to many of our problems and much energy and more money was wasted in pouring new technological wind into very old educational bottles. We are slowly beginning to realize that the problems we are facing are both educational and technological.[4]

INNOVATIONS — AN OVERVIEW

If we have not gained as much in wisdom as we might have done over the past ten years, at least we have gained greatly in experience, a necessary pre-requisite for wisdom. We now have a number of significant innovations, which have stood the test of time over at least a few years, and these are now beginning to form a 'bag of tools' from which we can, I hope, start to select the ones most suitable for a given purpose. Let me list a few.

(a)  I have already mentioned the audio-tutorial method,[2] in which a student is provided with study materials and taped or written instructions.

(b)   There is the whole development of programmed learning.  Teaching machines are out, but programmed textbooks have been found very useful, particularly in the teaching of ancillary subjects at the skill and competence level, such as mathematics for engineers.[5]

(c)   The provision of self-tests, often of the objective kind, which enable students to assess their own progress.[6]

(d)   Personalized systems of instruction, based on the principle that a student should achieve mastery of material learnt.  One type of these, also known, after its initiator, as the Keller plan, is perhaps the most rapidly growing sector of the individualized instruction industry.[7]

(e)   Self-service laboratories.  These were originally started at M.I.T. under the title 'Corridor labs';  the idea being that students walking along a corridor would come across exciting experiments and stop and do them before passing on.

(f)   Material suitable for stimulating discussions in groups, such as duplicated hand-outs, in which arguable issues are raised.  These have been found effective even in groups that have worked in the absence of a tutor.[8]

(g)   Recorded material in the form of tape/slide packages as well as audio and video cassettes.[9]

(h)   Computer aided instruction.  This includes such diverse applications as the management of a self-instructional course,[10]  the computer as tutor[11] and the use of the computer on-line to enrich learning.[12]

AN ANALYSIS OF AIMS

The stage has now been set for an analysis of the aims of these and other innovations, an analysis which may not necessarily lead to the same aims as the authors of the innovations themselves professed.[13]   A process aim which appears to be common to all is to make the student more active in his learning and there is little doubt that this aim is in general achieved by all.  However, when it comes to product aims, there are at least three quite different ones that can be perceived, relating directly to the three kinds of dissatisfaction referred to earlier :

(a)   The acquisition of certain knowledge and skills.

(b)   Attitudinal changes relevant to the subject studied.

(c)   Changes in study pattern, particularly those leading to independence of study.

I wish to stress the surely obvious fact that innovations that aim at one of the above do not necessarily also aim at the other two.  What is so interesting is that in the event they often do and in the brief time available I wish to illustrate this through some instances.

(a) **The audio-tutorial method.**   As already mentioned, the original aim here was to provide students with biological materials that they could handle.  By now, the aims associated with individualized instruction and self-pacing have quite overshadowed the original aim, and this is particularly so with regard to the extension of the method to engineering and physics.[14]

(b) **The Keller plan.**   Keller's original aim of mastery of instructional material was derived from experience in the armed forces.[15]   We now have reason to believe that use of the plan can lead to greater independence of learning[16]  and that Keller plan material is likely to transfer more easily to other institutions than any other form of recorded material.[17]

(c) **Self-service laboratories.**   The original 'corridor labs,' were designed to stimulate interest in physics in casual passers by.  Once the pilfering problem had been overcome by putting experiments into vending machines, this worked, but vending machines are a restricting influence on experimental design.  Transferred to a laboratory and designed in terms of specific learning objectives the experiments have become an important instructional aid not only in the teaching of science,[18, 19]   but in helping students to clarify their own objectives in the learning process.[20]

(d) **Computer aided instruction.**   The situation here is somewhat different in that the expense of the medium has led to the realization that an analysis of the worthwhileness of aims and of the likelihood of their achievement is morally imperative.[21]


### CONCLUSION

I have attempted to give you an overview of some of the exciting work that is going on in self-study methods and in particular I have tried to convince you of the over-riding importance of viewing this work in the light of both its declared and its apparent aims.  This is not to say that our 'bag of tools' is complete, and there are likely to be many needs which it will not meet.  Finally, I am very aware of how much I have left unsaid and of how many of my colleagues, both in Great Britain and abroad, I have failed to mention.  I ask for their forgiveness.

REFERENCES

1.  For a critical review with copious references, see :
    Goldschmid, B. and Goldschmid, M.L. (1973) Individualizing instruction in higher education: a review. Higher Education **3**, 1.

2.  Postlethwait, S.N., Novak, J. and Murray, H.T. (Jr.) (1971) The Audio-Tutorial Approach to Learning (second edition). Minneapolis: Burgess Publishing. (A full list of Postlethwait's publications can be found in The Use of Modules in College Biology Teaching (Eds. J.G. Creager and D.L. Murray), (1971) Commission on Undergraduate Education in the Biological Sciences, Publication No. 31, March, p. 169.

3.  Cook, D.L. (1967) The Impact of the Hawthorne Effect in Experimental Designs in Educational Research. U.S. Department of Health, Education and Welfare, Office of Education, Bureau of Research, Project No. 1757, Contract No. OE-3-10-041, June.

4.  Elton, L.R.B. (1971) Problems of innovation in higher education. Times Educational Supplement, 14 May, p. 60.

5.  One of the many examples, but a very good one, is :
    Stroud, K.A. (1970) Engineering Mathematics. London: Macmillan.

6.  Elton, L.R.B.(1970) The use of duplicated lecture notes and self-tests in university teaching. Aspects of Educational Technology (Eds. A.C. Bajpai and J.F. Leedham), Vol. **IV**, p. 366. London: Pitman.

7.  Sherman, J.G. (Ed.) (1974) Personalized System of Instruction. W.A. Benjamin Inc.,

8.  Black, P.J., Griffith, J.A.R. and Powell, W.B. (1974) Skill sessions. Phys. Education **9**, 18.

9.  An unusually comprehensive system is described in :
    Kraemer, J.D. (1973) Individualized education: some implications for media. Prog. Learning and Educ. Tech. **10**, 342.

10. There are many examples of this, particularly in the USA. An interesting European venture is described in :
    Jones, A. (1973) Instructional applications of the computer at the University of Louvain. Int. J. Man-Machine Studies **5**, 397.

11. Blum, R. (Ed.) (1971) Computers in Undergraduate Science Education. Commission on College Physics, College Park, Maryland, Section V, particularly the article by D.L. Bitzer et al., The Plato System and Science Education.

12. The earliest comprehensive system is described in :
    Kennedy, J.G. and Kurtz, T.E. (1968) Dartmouth time-sharing. Science **162**, 223.

13. An investigation which showed how the aims of a given curriculum are differently perceived by different people is :
    Boud, D.J. (1973) The laboratory aims questionnaire -- a new method for course improvement? Higher Education **2**, 81.

14. Lindenlaub, J.C. (1969) Applying Audio-Tutorial Techniques to Laboratory Instruction. I.E.E.E., Transactions on Education, E-12, 92.
    Diederich, Mary E. (1972) An Audio-Tutorial Course in Physics for Engineering and Physics Majors. Report to the AAPT 1972 Summer meeting, Albany, N.Y.

15. Keller, F.S. (1968) Goodbye, Teacher.... J. Appl. Behav. Analysis **1**, 79.

16. Elton, L.R.B., Boud, D.J., Nuttall, J. and Stace, B.C. (1973) The Keller plan − experiment at Surrey. Chemistry in Britain **9**, 164.

17. One of my own courses is at present being used successfully at Strathclyde University and I have had many requests from other universities to use my materials. This is in striking contrast to the experience with video-recorded lectures; see for example :
    Perraton, H.D., Wade, D.A.L. and Fox, J.W.R. (1969) Linking Universities by Technology. National Extension College, Cambridge.

18. Boud, D.J. and O'Connell, S. (1970) Towards an educational technology of laboratory work. Visual Education, December, p. 12.

19. Brandt, D., Ansell, M. and Cryer, N.B. (1974) Minicourses in a first year physics laboratory. Phys. Education 9, 23.

20. O'Connell, S. and Penton, S.J. A Student Designed Self-Service Laboratory, University of Surrey. (in preparation)

21. Taylor, E.F. (1971) History of a failure in computer interactive instruction. In R. Blum (Ed.) Computers in Undergraduate Science Education. Commission on College Physics, College Park, Maryland, p.239.

# Videotapes in laboratory classes: developments in an integrated approach to physiology teaching

R. J. HOWLAND, A. J. MIDSON, R. WILLIAMS, University of Surrey

**Abstract:** At Surrey, Physiology laboratory classes are provided for over one hundred students each week, involving heavy usage of postgraduate demonstrators, who are responsible for demonstrating the experiments, and also for providing the background theory to those experiments, which are repeated ten times in a five week period. The repetition leads to inconsistencies in the teaching from week to week, and it is impossible for academic staff to supervise fully the content and standard of the teaching undertaken by the demonstrators. Therefore a method of presenting recorded introductory material to experiments was sought.

Written material, tape/slide and cine film recordings were rejected, either because they were inappropriate for the simultaneous communication of information in the cognitive/affective and psychomotor domains, or because of production problems. Videotape was selected as being the best available medium for communicating both conceptual material and manual skills. The medium has proved to be acceptable to the great majority of students, and the structured introductions with visually enriched material have contributed to its educational effectiveness. It is intended that, when the Department of Biological Sciences moves shortly into a new building, videotaped introductions to physiology laboratory classes will become near-universal, and the logistics of this provision are discussed. Thus, academic staff will determine in toto the material taught in the laboratory, and students will benefit from having experimental work explained by academic specialists, from the enriched content of the teaching, and from clear, unambiguous and consistent explanations of their laboratory work.

Physiology is studied at Surrey as a major part of three undergraduate disciplines, Human Biology, Nutrition, and Biochemistry. Students from these three disciplines follow a common series of lectures and associated laboratory classes in Physiology, and in any one week more than one hundred students attend the Physiology laboratory. Because of large student numbers, and because of the high cost of physiological equipment, we use a 'circus' system in the teaching laboratories such that five experiments are available in each half of a term. Twice weekly, groups of up to fourteen students work at each experiment, and by rotating around the laboratory complete ten experiments in each term. With five experiments running concurrently, heavy use is necessarily made of postgraduate student demonstrators in laboratory teaching. As the experimental work frequently and unavoidably precedes the treatment of the subject matter in lectures, a considerable extra burden falls on the demonstrators in providing the theoretical framework within which the experimental procedures are carried out. Thus, in addition to simply demonstrating an experiment, the demonstrators are asked to provide a 'lecturette' of some twenty minutes, covering the background to that experiment. Although it is possible for academic staff to maintain a general surveillance of the material presented in the 'lecturettes, detailed supervision of content and mode of presentation is difficult. There are, additionally, two further problems. First, the team of demonstrators is necessarily heterogenous. A demonstrator in his first few terms will be less able to explain an experiment, and deal with problems, than the more experienced demonstrator, leading to variable standards of presentation. Second, the fact that each experiment has to be introduced ten times in each five week period results in a 'tailing off' of the performance towards the end of that period, simply as a result of continued repetition of the same material. Thus, inconsistencies arise in what each group of students receives in the way of theoretical and practical instruction.

In order to obtain a method whereby both the theoretical background and methodology of an experiment could be presented at a consistent standard, and by an academic specialist, we reviewed a number of methods by which properly structured recorded material could be used to introduce experiments. We considered tape/slide, cine film and videotape presentations, and comprehensive written information. These methods were reviewed in relation to the nature of the teaching to be carried out; the transfer of conceptual and factual information as well as the teaching of specific manual skills. Palmer (1971), considering teaching laboratory skills in chemistry, described three domains of educational objectives, the cognitive, the affective, and the psychomotor, and was primarily concerned with the psychomotor domain. In attempting to introduce not only specific manual skills but also theoretical knowledge, our investigations have spanned the cognitive and affective, in addition to the psychomotor domains.

While it would be a simple matter to present factual and conceptual matter in written form, manual skills are not amenable to such presentation. The first level to be achieved in the psychomotor domain is described as 'imitation' (Dave, unpubl.) or 'the initiatory level of expectation' (Alles, 1967), involving, initially, mental imagery of the described procedure followed by overt practice based on that image until the process becomes 'routinized' (Lippincott, 1966) within the student. This method of learning relies primarily upon the translation of the written material into an accurate mental image, is clearly fraught with difficulty, and would have no advantage over the live practical demonstration which itself may not always be ideally shown.

112

Tape/slide introductions were rejected, primarily because psycho-motor skills involve motion as a defining attribute (Palmer, 1971) and as shown by Houser, Houser and Van Mandrans (1970), if the defining attributes of a concept to be learned are not shown in the most accurate representation possible, the resulting skill or knowledge may be in-accurate, incomplete, ambiguous or confused. Tape/slide productions are static and thus cannot be held to communicate the defining attribute of motion. Thus, while providing an adequate medium for the factual framework of an experiment, we considered that it could not adequately convey the associated practical skills.

This left us with the choice of videotape or cine film. From the pro-duction point of view, videotape is more versatile, especially if multiple camera and editing facilities are available, as playback can be immediate and the production process is far less time consuming. The principal attribute of cine film is colour at reasonable cost, but it has been shown, in general terms (Rosenstein and Kanner, 1961; Link, 1961) that there is insufficient evidence to suggest that colour will improve learning. Colour may, of course, make for more favourable attitudes, as sugges-ted by Vander Meer (1954) in relation to cine films. Therefore we elected to use videotape recordings as this gives a number of advantages over the established method of introduction. These advantages may be briefly described as follows. First, academic staff have direct control over what is presented to students, and the responsibility of the demon-strator is then simply to support that which has been explained by an academic specialist on the videotape recording. This ensures that the standard of instruction and factual content of the material is constant from week to week, and close supervision of the demonstrators is no longer necessary. Second, the care and elaboration put into each video-taped introduction is greater in terms of the use of supplementary illus-trations, ranging from simple captions to complex animations, examples of which will be presented later. Also, the demonstration of any tech-nique is guaranteed not to fail or be misleading.

In any single demonstration, there is likely to be some aspect of technique that is overlooked or some unexpected occurence limiting the completion, and hence the value, of the demonstration (Palmer, 1971). By video-recording the demonstration of a technique, the procedure is thoroughly examined, reshaped, refined and rehearsed, and ideal view-points for the observer assured. Third, using the visual effects avail-able in television, such as picture mixing and wiping, split-screen tech-niques and telecine facilities, very convincing, comprehensive and, sub-jectively, easily assimilable illustrations may be effected.

Before actually using video-recordings, however, two questions had first to be answered. Is there anything to suggest that televised material is not at least as effective as face-to-face teaching, and would the transla-tion from face-to-face to television teaching be subjectively acceptable to students?

113

On the first point, Chu and Schramm (1968) surveying the literature, concluded that there is no general area where television cannot be effectively used to teach students. This conclusion was based upon a wide range of disciplines, admittedly largely at pre-university level, where the nearest quoted discipline to Physiology was Science. In assessing effectiveness, the medium itself is not the major factor. What are more important are the circumstances in which it is used, or rather seen to be used, by the students. This leads into the second point, which is that of subjective acceptability, which has been widely reported in the literature as quoted by Chu and Schramm (1968) indicating that, at undergraduate levels, students tend to prefer small discussion classes to television teaching. This, they infer, is because the element of discussion is removed from the teaching process. Furthermore, the degree to which students perceive themselves getting further attention is instrumental in forming attitudes (Mackenzie, Eraut and Jones, 1970). It has been shown (Merrill, 1956; Whiting, 1961) that favourable attitudes are not necessarily correlated with effective learning, and, as Merrill (1956) has stated, the attitudes may reflect one aspect of the teaching and the learning another.

On this basis, we considered that it would be appropriate to introduce videotapes made in the University Television Studio into the teaching laboratories on a pilot basis. This was done initially by introducing one videotape into each of two five-week experimental circuses. The students viewed the tape in a room adjoining the laboratory, the demonstrator being on hand to answer questions afterwards, and the students then moved into the laboratory to carry out the experiment. At the same time, a questionnaire survey was made of the students to obtain some idea of the acceptability of the method. Of the students who completed the questionnaire, 70 per cent favoured the use of videotaped introductions, 17.5 per cent were favourable with some qualifications or were indifferent, and only 12.5 per cent were totally unfavourable. Other comments were elicited from students, and among the more important of these were:

(i)   That videotapes should not take over completely from live explanations

(ii)  Someone should always be available to answer questions afte: viewing the tape. This is in fact the case, the demonstrator always being in attendance.

(iii) The clear demonstrations were greatly appreciated.

(iv) The use of animation and other techniques made many concepts that were previously hard to grasp considerably more comprehensible.

It is worth digressing here to expand this point. We have found the special effects available in the medium very useful in communicating both concepts and practical skills to students, and it is pertinent to give some examples of the use of effects in these contexts.

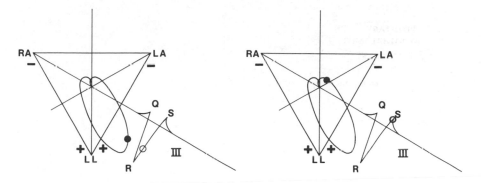

Figure 1: Two stages from an animated sequence, showing the projection of the mean instantaneous cardiac electrical vector on to a standard electrocardiogram lead.

In the primarily cognitive domain, two examples may be quoted. In the study of electrocardiography, the projection of the mean instantaneous electrical vector of the heart on to the standard ECG leads is a concept that is difficult to communicate. We used a three cel animation, showing the vector path, and its projection on to a standard lead (see Fig. 1). This presentation was relatively successful in transferring a difficult concept. Another example in this field is the construction of flow diagrams illustrating regulatory mechanisms. Again, we have used telecine to illustrate the hormonal regulation of reproductive cycles, and a series of sequences in this presentation are shown in Fig. 2.

In the psychomotor domain, we have used special effects, we consider, to great advantage to communicate practical skills. A good example here is a method that we have used to teach students how to estimate blood pressure. It is an oft-quoted statement that medical students frequently complete the preclinical phase of their training having never properly performed a blood pressure estimation. This may be because in this procedure, the senses of sight and hearing require co-ordination, and the auditory component is very difficult to demonstrate adequately, especially to large classes of students. Essentially, the procedure is one of inflating a cuff around the upper arm, and slowly deflating it while watching a manometer connected to the cuff, simultaneously listening with a stethoscope to the sounds of blood flow (the Korotkov sounds) in an artery in the lower arm. Realizing exactly what to listen for is always the major difficulty encountered in learning this technique. Our approach has been to utilize a vertically split screen. On one side of the screen is shown the manometer, on one camera, and on the other side, a caption describing the sounds, using another camera. A microphone is placed over the artery, the sounds being appropriately modulated to provide the acoustic deadness associated with the stethoscope. As the mercury in the manometer falls, the sounds are presented on the audio track, while the

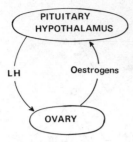

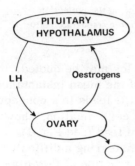

Figure 2: A series of stages from an animated flow diagram used to illustrate the hormonal regulation of reproductive cycles.

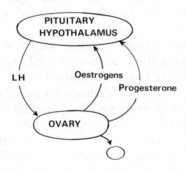

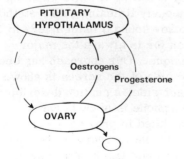

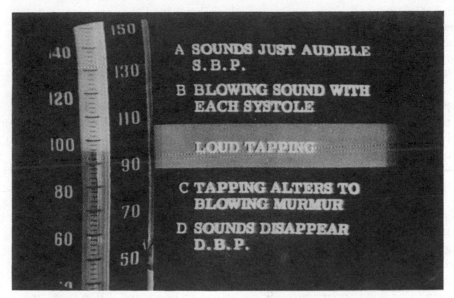

Figure 3: The use of special effects in teaching the technique for blood pressure estimation. The audio track carries the concomitantly heard sounds.

relevant part of the caption is highlighted, giving the student simultaneously the pressure, a lifelike record of the sounds, and a description of what the sound indicates (see Fig. 3). In the experience of the investigators, following the traditional type of demonstration of this technique, students take at least 30 minutes merely to become accustomed to the quality of the sounds, let alone to be able to determine blood pressures. Using the method of presentation described, our students are regularly determining blood pressures both confidently and competently within ten minutes of the demonstration.

Having established that video recorded introductions to laboratory classes are acceptable to the majority of students, their effectiveness must be established. We have approached the evaluation of effectiveness on the basis of validation of the programme per se, rather than by what would be inadequate, unreliable and inappropriate comparison with face-to-face teaching. Effectiveness studies are carried out on the basis of objective tests applied after viewing the video tapes. Apart from indicating the overall effectiveness of the tapes, the feedback from the tests provides diagnostic indication of the less effective areas in the video recordings, which are later revised in the light of the information so obtained. As a result of the feedback obtained with both acceptability questionnaires and with post-tape testing, we are developing an approach to the presentation of video recorded material in laboratory teaching which is giving, at least in our case, a reasonable level of acceptability and effectiveness. Two practices which have lead to increases in both acceptability and effectiveness are, first, the production of structured laboratory schedules to accompany each tape. Such schedules contain all the information given in the tape in a condensed form, together, where possible, with the illustrations used. Also, questions raised in the video recording are given at the same point in the schedule, with space for answering those questions. Secondly, we now give an explicit statement of the objectives of the experiment, both in the opening sequence of the video tape and at the head of the laboratory schedule. Additionally, opinions elicited from students indicated that the preferred duration of the video tape is about thirty minutes, and our tapes now last for approximately that time.

We now consider that we have a tried and tested system, which is both acceptable and effective, providing in a single video tape package all the information required for a student to perform an experiment against an adequate background knowledge. The one potential difficulty with this mode of teaching is the lack of facility for asking questions while viewing tapes. We had considered in-built pauses in the video tapes to provide opportunity for questions to be raised. However, we have found that very few students wish to ask questions, and we consider that this is, in large part, a result of experience on the part of those concerned in making the video tapes, in anticipating specific questions.

We have expanded the innovation so that two in each group of five experiments in each half term over the four terms of the course are now introduced in this way. This, of course, has lead to difficulties with cross-talk between the viewing monitors, and so students are now equipped with headphones, loudspeakers no longer being used. Interestingly, 62 per cent of students reported an increased level of concentration when using headphones.

In the near future, when the Department of Biological Sciences moves into a new building, the Physiology laboratory is to be equipped with a distribution system capable of showing five video tapes simultaneousely, the programmes being routed to eight nine-inch monitors at each of five experimental stations. Two students will use one monitor, each student being provided with a headset with variable volume control (see Fig. 4). Postgraduate demonstrators will be in attendance for the full duration of the classes, but the main part of the actual teaching will be in the hands of those academic staff who make the video tapes. The students will benefit, we feel, in having experiments explained by academic specialists, from the enriched content of the tapes as compared to a face-to-face presentation, and above all from clear and unambiguous and consistent demonstrations of the experiments that they are to perform.

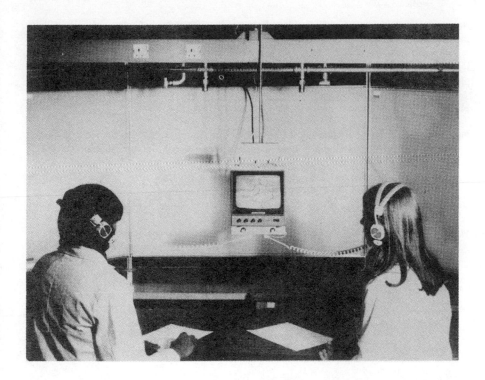

Figure 4: The viewing system as proposed for use in the future. Two students use one Shibaden VM 904K 9" monitor. The headsets house individual volume control.

## ACKNOWLEDGEMENTS

We are indebted to the Teaching and Learning Methods Committee of the University of Surrey for substantial financial support. Professor P.R. Davis, Professor of Human Biology in the University of Surrey, has given us every encouragement and facility, and we wish to record our gratitude to him. Last, but not least, we wish to thank the many students who have been subjected to strange and new procedures in the Physiology laboratories, for their forbearance and co-operation.

REFERENCES

Alles, J. (1967) An outline analysis of psychomotor aspects of behaviour. Restructuring some conceptual frameworks used in curriculum development evaluation, by J. Alles, A. Perara, M. Ranaweera, J. Ratnaike and D. Weerasinghe. Working Paper, Division of Secondary Education, Ministry of Education, Ceylon.

Chu, G.C. and Schramm, W. (1968) Learning from Television: What the Research Says. National Association of Educational Broadcasters, Washington DC. pages 9-10.

Dave (unpublished) Proposed taxonomy in the psychomotor domain. National Foundation for Educational Research and Training, New Delhi, India.

Houser, R.L. Houser, E.J. and Van Mondrans, A.P. (1970) A.V. Comm. Res. **18**, 425

Link, J.D. (1961) A comparison of the effects on learning of viewing film in colour on a screen in black and white over closed circuit television. Ontario Jnl. Educ. Res. **3**, 111.

Lippincott, W.T. (1966) Editorial note in J. Chem. Ed. **43**, 397.

Mackenzie, N., Eraut M. and Jones, H.C. (1970) in Teaching and Learning: An Introduction to New Methods and Resources in Higher Education. UNESCO. Pages 145-146.

Merrill, I.R. (1956) Liking and learning from educational television. A.V. Comm. Res. **4**, 221.

Palmer, C.R. (1971) Videotapes in the teaching of laboratory skills. In Proceedings of Conference on Visual Media in Chemistry. London: British Universities Film Council. Pages 54-62.

Rosenstein, A.J. and Kanner, J.H. (1961) Television in army training: colour vs. black and white. A.V. Comm. Res. **9**, 44.

Vander Meer, A.W. (1954) Colour vs. black and white in instructional films. A.V. Comm. Res. **2**, 121.

Whiting, G.C. (1961) Correlates of achievement, attitude and personality among students taught by closed circuit television. M.A. Thesis, Salt Lake City: University of Utah.

# The design, production and use of ETV learning packages in remedial mathematics

J. C. RICHARDSON, HQ, REME, Bordon, Hants

**Abstract:** Tradesmen and technicians such as Vehicle Mechanics and Armourers in the Royal Electrical and Mechanical Engineers (REME) who want to train as artificers are required to obtain various qualifications first. One requisite is for them to pass a preliminary examination in mathematics. Once selected for artificer training, all students study for a City and Guilds examination at Part I level, and many take Part II as well. This was introduced recently as part of a reorganization of their training. To incorporate the examination without significantly lengthening the training course, the revision content of the mathematics module had to be reduced. This, in turn, led to a reconsideration of the preliminary mathematics syllabus and examination. In preparing the new syllabus a number of learning resource packages were produced, and the paper describes their design and evaluation.

SYLLABUS DESIGN

The City and Guilds mathematics course was analysed lesson by lesson and the prerequisite knowledge listed. A questionnaire was used to find out what previous mathematical background students could be expected to have. Teachers were consulted to find out what the common general weaknesses of students are. Old examination scripts were then used to specify these weaknesses in more detail. From all this information, a new syllabus and examination were devised. Of particular interest is the general area of algebraic manipulation: this is a major part of the new syllabus.

## THE SPECIFIC PROBLEM AREA

Most teachers of mathematics have met the problem of teaching the transposition of formulae. This is a key area of the City and Guilds syllabus. It is also one with which students find a lot of difficulty. The analysis of the errors made showed that students had been tending to learn isolated rules rather than building up a coherent hierarchy of inter-related concepts and principles. This was not unexpected.

The following examples are typical of the errors made:

$$ax + b = c$$

using the rule 'change sides — change signs', they get:

$$ax = c - b$$

they then tend to use the same rule when it does not work and get

$$x = c - b - a$$

Another example is $(x - a)^2 = x^2 - a^2$. This comes from using the distributive law in a situation when it does not apply. Basically they do not 'understand' what they are doing.

It is only fairly recently that a structured approach based on a hierarchy of concepts and principles has been developed, usually in response to students' learning difficulties. Much of the work, is however, at Primary School level. R.R. Skemp in The Psychology of Learning Mathematics builds a hierarchy which extends from what has traditionally been pre-school learning through to GCE 'A' level topics. Such a hierarchy introduces material which is often considered to be the province of modern mathematics. For example, the three basic laws of algebra, viz. the Commutative law, the Associative law and the Distributive law are needed. The concept that adding, subtracting, multiplying, dividing, raising to powers and taking roots are operations is included together with the complex relationships between them.

The resulting syllabus (Annex 'A'), especially in algebra, represents a combination of both modern and traditional material. Unfortunately, this meant that there was neither a single suitable textbook for students nor any programmed materials available.

PROVISION OF LEARNING FACILITIES

For the old syllabus there had been several methods of providing opportunities for potential artificer students to prepare for their mathematics examination. The new syllabus posed problems for each method.

The overall training of a REME Electro-Mechanical tradesman is on a part-progressive basis and involves both on and off-the-job training. There is an initial course of about one year's duration at the School of Electrical and Mechanical Engineering (SEME) followed by several years of on-the-job experience during which they progress from Class III tradesmen to Class II. The next stage is another course at SEME for upgrading from Class II to Class I. Depending upon trade this will last in the region of three months. After further on-the-job experience, those selected return to SEME for artificer training on a course of between eighteen months and two years' duration.

This scheme of training contains only negligible amounts of mathematics prior to the artificer course.

Many potential artificers learn their mathematics in the evenings in the SEME Study Centre whilst they are on their Class II to Class I upgrading course. The Study Centre is manned by trade instructors but the great majority of students are using an assortment of types of programmed learning materials which these instructors organize and administrate. With the new syllabus, particularly the algebraic content, a new method of providing instruction, or rather learning facilities was needed.

About one-third of the candidates each year attend special courses. These are run in Germany at the Higher Education Centre (HEC) and in the UK at the Army School of Education (ASE). Officers from both had been briefed on the new syllabus. The suggestion that learning packages should be made available to cover the new material was welcomed. Within the Army the regular change of personnel on postings makes it unlikely that there will always be a teacher in post who is familiar with both modern and traditional mathematics. Learning packages would help in this situation.

The remaining candidates either study privately in their units with assistance from an artificer or an officer, or where numbers are sufficient to justify it, attend special courses at their local Army Education Centres (AEC).

## Learning Packages

It was thought that integrated audio-visual packages with associated tests, worksheets and precis would form an appropriate resource. Synchronised tape/slide equipment is available in the SEME Study Centre, the HEC in Germany, the ASE and in AECs. This was clearly a suitable media.

It was decided that a series of packages using synchronized tape/ slide presentations would be devised at SEME. These could be tested out in the Study Centre to confirm that they were enabling students to learn and then made available to those other units who would be running courses.

## The Format of the Packages

The format of each package was based on a single pattern. This consists of :

| | | |
|---|---|---|
| a. | A Pre-Test | This was not to be marked at first, but was to serve to focus the students' attention onto the unknown areas of the particular package. It would also serve as a preview for the student and would take about ten minutes to complete. |
| b. | A Group-Paced Tape/Slide Presentation | This was to be used in conjunction with a student response sheet and to follow a repeated pattern of : <br> (1) Presentation of information or demonstration of procedures followed by <br> (2) Student response and <br> (3) Feed back of the correct response. <br> Throughout, the approach would be concerned with drawing ideas out of students' experience rather |

than with telling them about the material. Presentations would last for between twenty and thirty minutes.

c.   A Post-Test      This was to be identical with the pre-test although blue paper replaced green. Up to twenty minutes would be needed for completion.

d.   Answer Sheet     On completion of the post-test the student would receive a pink answer sheet. He would mark both his pre- and post-tests and record the results. This would take about ten minutes.

e.   Precis, Supplementary Questions and Answers     To enable the student to revise the points which he had failed to learn the precis would summarize and extend the presentation material. A set of further practice questions and fully explained answers would complete the package.

## The Design of the Contents

To select the content of the packages subject matter was structured. The area was limited to those parts of the syllabus which contribute to the derivation of formulae from written statements and the transposition of these formulae. From this, a sequence of learning points was derived (Annex 'B'). This was divided into a series of programmes of more or less equivalent size incorporating planned revision and previews of subsequent material.

Because much of the material would be novel to students it was decided that the first package would be explanatory of the series and would be based on students' reactions to the other programmes. Consequently it would have to be the last programme made.

In brief, packages two to five would deal with the derivation of operations and their relationships. Package six would introduce the use of this in the transposition of formulae and demonstrate the importance of the sequence of operations in an expression. Seven and eight would deal with this sequence and then in packages nine and ten basic transpositions would be covered. Using these three blocks, the key packages are five, eight and ten. The distributive law comes under eleven and leads to more complex transpositions in twelve. Algebraic manipulation follows in thirteen to enable answers to be simplified.

Fourteen deals with the multiplication of brackets and leads to fifteen in which quadratics are dealt with. Finally, sixteen, seventeen and eightee use the material learned in previous packages to problem solve. To prove the system, initially, only packages two to five were produced and subsequently six to eight were added. At present nine to fifteen have been designe and are in production but have not yet been used.

## The Production of the Packages

The production of each package followed a fairly routine path. From the learning points, a sequence already existed. Examples were devised to draw out and illustrate the points and to provide for planned practice. The visuals were then drafted. A commentary was recorded live by an experienced instructor using the sequence of visuals as a guide rather than using a written script. Previous experience had suggested this approach because when scripts had been used previously, particularly for television programmes, they tended to lack life or to be a little stilted.

The initial timings of the pauses for students to work were done by the instructor writing out what he would expect the students to write and then allowing an extra 50 per cent. This timing was sometimes modified during validation but mostly it proved to be about correct.

The visuals were then typed on to a set proforma (Annex 'C') and the diagrams added. The photographic process available within the Reproduction Department produced a master from this which was reduced by 40 per cent. This meant that each visual was compatible with a 35 mm slide format. This master was processed through a heat copier to produce a vufoil. The vufoil was cut up and the slides produced mounted in frames. A considerable time was spent investigating different type faces and different vufoil materials. Finally, the 3Ms 888 rainbow pack material was used because it gave the cleanest lines with the least spreading. The reduced size of type face made this an extremely important aspect. The tests, response sheets, answers and precis were then produced.

Once the initial learning sequence had been produced the whole process took remarkably little time. On average, draft visuals took twenty minutes, taped commentaries about forty-five minutes and the drafting, checking and revising of test sheets, response sheets and precis about four hours. The most tedious single job was the cutting up and mounting of the visuals.

## Initial Trials with the Packages

The intention had been to test the packages in the Study Centre, to modify them and then send them out to other users, but with courses being run elsewhere right from the start, the initial forms of the packages were sent out as soon as they were produced. They were sent to the HEC in Germany, to ASE and to a number of Army Education Centres, mostly in the UK. The production of a master for a heat copier saved an enormous amount of trouble in producing several copies of the visuals and was much more convenient than a normal photographic process would be. The validation has been carried out at SEME and modifications devised for the second generation of packages. Some modifications have already been incorporated.

Students go to the Study Centre in the evenings when they have time. They are on training courses during the day and, inevitably, with the pressures of examinations at various stages in their training there are times when they miss an attendance at the Study Centre. This prevents control groups or experimental groups being set up. In practice, data was collected from all students who used a particular package.

The availability of equipment limited the number of separate packages that could be presented in any given session to two. Consequently it was not always feasible to give a student the next package that he needed, and so some students missed out on some packages.

Each package was used in a small group situation — anything from one to twelve at a time. The instructor in charge of administrating the packages watched the students during the various pauses to check that the time allowed for their work was sufficient. If students had not finished he held the pause button on the tape recorder until they had, and noted the extra time needed. New tapes were produced to provide the necessary extra timing.

**The Change from Tape/Slide to ETV**

Each session lasted something over one hour and the programmes were discussed with the students afterwards. As a result of their comments a number of modifications have been made to the wording of questions in the test sheets and to the wording used in the commentaries. However, the main change was the switch to the use of ETV. The tape/slide presentation was shown on to a front projection screen and televised. This then replaced the tape/slide presentation in the package.

All students experienced both methods of presentation and were unanimous in their preference for ETV. Their comments fell into two categories. Firstly they commented that they were no longer distracted by the noise of the projector changing the slides. Secondly it seemed to 'get on with it more': this latter was clarified as meaning that they were less aware of slide change because the screen never went blank. This was something of an accidental effect. During recording the light levels had been relatively low and the camera settings caused the image to persist slightly whilst the slides were changing. This resulted in a sort of cross fading effect.

The ETV form of the package is now used exclusively at SEME and has also been supplied to ASE.

The instructors in the SEME Study Centre also prefer ETV. It is administratively more convenient and less prone to error. The problem with slides is that they can easily slip out of boxes and be replaced incorrectly.

## RESULTS

The results of packages two to eight have been encouraging enough for work on the remainder of the series to be put in hand. The results were assessed in terms of gain ratios. Pre- and post-test scores, marked by the students, were available. From these it was possible to estimate the maximum possible gain, the actual gain, and hence to derive a gain ratio which was then turned into a percentage. These figures are shown in Table 1 (page 128).

The numbers taking the packages varied because many candidates were unable to attend all sessions. In a structured series of packages missing some out is likely to effect results in later packages. Nevertheless, in the preliminary analysis, all available data was considered.

· Item analysis was carried out to determine on which questions students were tending to get wrong answers. In particular packages four, six and seven were scrutinized to find out why the gain ratio was less than 60 per cent which had been considered to be acceptable.

**Programme 4.** The test sheet contains a number of questions in which students translate statements into formulae. They are then required to write down the inverse forms of these formulae. Errors were common in the translation process and so even though the inverse forms produced might have been correct they did not correspond to the answers on the answer sheet. Consequently errors were being penalized twice. The level of difficulty of the translation questions was too high for students at that stage. In particular difficulty was found with questions concerned with powers and roots. The amendment of the programme was considered but it would require an extension of the time taken on the package and this was not acceptable. Instead the test sheet has been modified to ask slightly simpler questions in this field and to avoid the use of follow-up questions. More practice in translation is being added to subsequent programmes.

**Programme 6.** The package introduces students to the principle of transposition using inverse operations. There were no problems with this part of the package. The need to use inverse operations in a particular sequence was previewed and it was lack of knowledge in this area which was resulting in the mistakes. Packages seven and eight work through this material but the aim of this is simply to show students the need for seven and eight. It was decided to leave package six unaltered.

**Programme 7.** This package concentrates on the associative and commutative laws. In one question on the test sheet students are required to use these laws to invent as many alternative forms of given expressions as possible. The limited number of variations produced by most students compared with the numbers possible, prevents students from gaining anything like full marks. A new marking scheme based on the number of

127

Table 1

Preliminary analysis of results

| Outline Contents | Operations Meaning and Relationships | | | | Introduction to Transpositions | Sequence of Operations in an Expression | |
|---|---|---|---|---|---|---|---|
| Package Number | 2 | 3 | 4 | 5 | 6 | 7 | 8 |
| Learning points | a. Operators +, -, x, ÷<br>b. Natural numbers<br>c. ∞<br>d. Inverse operations<br>Words into algebra | a. X as repetitive +<br>b. ÷ as inverse x<br>c. ÷ as repetitive subtraction<br>d. Words into algebra<br>e. ÷ by zero | a. Powers as repetitive X<br>b. Roots as inverse powers<br>c. Table of operations<br>d. Roots as repetitive division<br>e. Factors<br>f. Commutative law<br>g. Words into algebra | a. Integers<br>b. Manipulation of integers<br>c. Rationals<br>d. Irrationals<br>e. Identity elements 0 and 1<br>f. revise previous packages | a. Cancelling effect of inverses<br>b. Principle of transposition<br>c. Role of sequence | a. Brackets and sequence<br>b. Associative law<br>c. Commutative law | a. Table of operators and the conventional sequence<br>b. Omission of brackets<br>c. Sequence of operations in an expression<br>d. Revise previous packages |
| % scores and gain ratio | PRE 30 POST 81 GR 72 | PRE 51 POST 88 GR 75 | PRE 45 POST 73 GR 50 | PRE 27 POST 79 GR 72 | PRE 30 POST 67 GR 53 | PRE 23 POST 70 GR 56 | PRE 38 POST 86 GR 86 |
| Number of students | 54 | 42 | 53 | 50 | 34 | 38 | 32 |

different formats that students normally manage to find will be used in the revised package.

The key packages are five and eight. In both cases the gain ratio comes to more than 70 per cent. Both these packages revise and incorporate the work covered in the previous packages. Good results in these suggest that the system as a whole is producing satisfactory learning.

### Straight-through Group Analysis

A separate analysis was carried out for the first twenty students to complete all seven packages. The results are shown in Table 2.

Table 2

Analysis of results of a batch of 20 students

| Package No. | 2 | | | 3 | | | 4 | | |
|---|---|---|---|---|---|---|---|---|---|
| | PRE | POST | GR | PRE | POST | GR | PRE | POST | GR |
| Mean % and GR of 20 students | 30 | 85 | 79 | 60 | 94 | 85 | 56 | 79 | 53 |

| Package No. | 5 | | | 6 | | | 7 | | | 8 | | |
|---|---|---|---|---|---|---|---|---|---|---|---|---|
| | PRE | POST | GR | PRE | POST | GR | PRE | POST | GR | PRE | POST | GR |
| Mean % and GR of 20 students | 36 | 87 | 80 | 34 | 76 | 64 | 27 | 72 | 62 | 44 | 93 | 88 |

**Note:** The mean score on post-tests overall was 83%

A similar pattern is repeated: four, six and seven are weak but with this group of students who had missed none of the previous programmes all their scores were higher. Indeed, in both programmes six and seven the gain ratio was higher than 60 per cent.

## CONCLUSION

These packages have all been used by students in situations where qualified instructors were not available. Using them, the group has attained mean post-test scores of 83 per cent over all. On this evidence this method of using group paced ETV learning packages is a viable means of providing learning facilities.

(**N.B.** Appendix material giving further details of the syllabus outline and content may be sought from the author.)

# The design of learning packages in the Royal Air Force

B. O'HARE, RAF School of Education, Upwood

**Abstract:** This paper commences with a survey of the development of learning packages at the Royal Air Force School of Education. Several packages produced over the last few years are shown on a continuum which extends from teacher-centred to student-centred. The design of some learning packages is described, and the structure of a booklet written on the design of learning packages within the Royal Air Force is then outlined. Several other packages which utilize the design process set out in the booklet are mentioned. The paper concludes with a report of the results achieved on a continuous flow training course which uses learning packages.

## INTRODUCTION

The Royal Air Force started to take an active interest in learning packages in 1968. Although extensive use was being made of programmed learning at that time, it was felt that it was worthwhile investigating an approach that was possibly cheaper, more flexible and just as effective.

In their first report on package learning for a subject of the Royal Air Force Education Test the Royal Air Force School of Education stated that:

'A properly produced package is based on a "systems" approach: target population and course objectives must first be clearly defined and then the most appropriate teaching methods selected.'

(Research Unit, 1969)

There has never been any doubt that a package would be designed only when the learning objectives had been worked out. However, the major interest in those early days was in investigating the possibilities which were offered by using a variety of learning resources.

## EARLY WORK IN PACKAGE DESIGN

The first package to be designed was on local government which was a module of the Royal Air Force Education Test subject Civics. This Civics package contained, within a foolscap wallet: a guide to the package, sample questions and answers, a set of notes printed on one side of the paper in double spacing (allowing the teacher to add his own notes if he wished), twelve diagrams printed on sheets for reproduction as transparencies and/or student handouts, and thirteen frames cut from a commercial film-strip for mounting as 35 mm slides.

A detailed analysis of the cost of producing this package was made including the comparison of in-house production of slides with the purchase of this material commercially, and of the production of overhead projector transparencies with the provision of transparency masters. As a result of the experience with this first package it was concluded that packaging produced savings in the time and effort required by the teacher to prepare his lesson material, a standardization of the interpretation of a syllabus, and a more effective use of visual aids. (Resources Development Unit, 1970)

## A PACKAGE FOR CONTINUATION TRADE TRAINING

In addition to passing examinations in the requisite education subjects for promotion, airmen are required to demonstrate ability in their trade knowledge and skills. The knowledge element of an airman's trade is tested by written promotion examinations, however, many airmen on shift work or in specialized jobs find it difficult to obtain formal instruction in their trade knowledge. This was the major reason for the development of study guides in continuation trade training.

Alongside this development of basic study guides by Headquarters Training Command, the School of Education was tasked with producing a sample learning package for the theory element of a continuation trade training examination. The purpose of the project was to determine the value of packages as aids to learning in continuation trade training.

A package for trade group 2 (ground radar) was produced in two versions. Each airman taking part in the validation was issued with a student's copy which he was able to take with him to his new station if he was posted during the course. Stations were asked to appoint a supervisor for this validation so that the student's progress would be monitored and assistance given where necessary. Moreover each station was provided with a supervisor's package.

The student's package contained the following:

(1) A guide to the package.

(2) A logbook containing the syllabus cross-referred to appropriate RAF manuals and publications.

(3) Self-assessment tests in short-answer form for each section of the syllabus, together with marking guides.

(4) Two modules from an existing RAF programmed text on electronics.

The supervisor's package contained the following :

(1)  A guide to the use of the package.

(2)  A progress chart.

(3)  Overhead projector transparency originals.

(4)  Four multiple-choice progress tests together with marking guides.

The packages were distributed to 42 stations, and a selection of these stations were visited to obtain first-hand knowledge of how the packages were being used and also to try out, by structured interviews, the questionnaires which would be used for the validation.  A detailed analysis of the validation of both versions of the package has been reported elsewhere (Diffey, 1971).  Nevertheless it is worth repeating that a comparison of students using the package was made with those who did not and the examination results showed a significant difference — a pass rate of 73 per cent compared with 49 per cent for candidates not using the package.  However what was particularly interesting was the success which 'multiple-triers' had had with the package.  Multiple-triers were those candidates who had taken the examination and failed on at least two previous occasions.  The sample taken of these multiple-triers was far too low to draw any firm conclusions; however it indicates an area where package learning might have a great impact.

## A CONTINUUM OF LEARNING PACKAGES

Both the Civics and the Ground Radar packages used a variety of resources for learning;  the former used slides, transparencies and a teacher whereas the latter package used programmed learning, self-assessment tests, a logbook and, only in some cases, a teacher.

These two early packages represent extremes in approaches to learning from packages.  The Civics package was a teacher-orientated one.  On the other hand the ground radar package, which was student-orientated, was constructed primarily as a self-learning package, although teacher involvement was not discouraged.  The provision of an additional package for the supervisor would, it was hoped, positively encourage his involvement.  Nevertheless it should be emphasized that, for many of the airmen, the working conditions did not allow much student-teacher interaction.

If these two packages were to be placed on a continuum of learning packages then they would appear approximately as shown in Figure 1.

This diagram also illustrates several other packages, developed in the Royal Air Force, and these will be discussed later in this paper.  At the student-centred extreme of the continuum the package concept merges with programmed learning.  Indeed both the Driver Training and the Writing Objectives packages are virtually forms of adjunct programming.

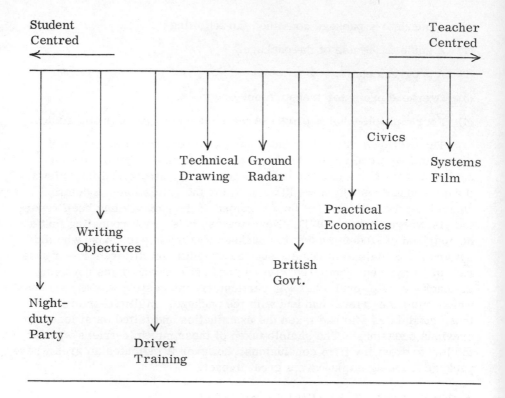

Figure 1: A continuum of RAF learning packages

It might be as well at this stage to give the School of Education's definition of a learning package, so that the essential difference between programmed learning and packaging can be highlighted. A learning package is defined as a collection of resources systematically designed to ensure that the student will achieve the learning objectives.

The word 'collection' illustrates an essential difference between programmed learning and learning packages, although it should be emphasized here that Royal Air Force packages are highly structured compared to many of those developed for schools.

Programmed learning was recently defined by Hartley (1972):

'... as a method of instruction which has measurable objectives, pre-arranged sequences and methods of presenting materials and which is self-correcting.'

The emphasis in Hartley's definition is on structure — the phrase 'pre-arranged sequence' is a far cry from the word 'collection'. Nevertheless it would be pedantic to take this argument any further because obviously there is a point where the two approaches merge and the position taken would appear to depend both on the structure of the subject matter and on the learning environment. Although learning packages generally make use of more varied resources than programmed learning there is no inherent reason for this: perhaps it lies in a lack of imagination on the part of the programme writer or in the constraints such as time and cost.

TEACHER-CENTRED PACKAGES

Over the last two years several more packages have been produced by the Royal Air Force. The experience of designing the first two packages described above was drawn upon in developing a package for Practical Economics, a new subject being introduced into the Royal Air Force Education Test in 1971. This package was intended to be teacher-centred and contained the following items :

(1) Student's log book.
(2) Student's notes.
(3) Teacher's guide.
(4) Progress tests and specimen examination papers.
(5) Miscellaneous aids (e.g. income tax form, computer pay slip).

Two textbooks to be used with the package were not included. All the resources were placed in a box file on the outside of which were affixed specially designed covers to make the container more attractive. The material inside the package was printed by offset-lithography and great care was taken over its appearance and layout.

The logbook of objectives was considered to be an important element in package design; this view emerged from the validation trials of the Ground Radar package. Because Practical Economics was a new subject the complete package could not be validated before its introduction. Nevertheless by enclosing a feedback questionnaire information was obtained both for modifying the existing package and for designing any future packages.

At about this time a film entitled 'The Systems Approach to Training' was being made at the Royal Air Force School of Education and early on it was decided to produce the film as part of a package. This film package contains the film, four overhead projector transparencies, three booklets and once again a feedback questionnaire. Although the film cannot be altered once it has been completed, feedback information can be used both to modify the other contents of the package and also to improve the design of future films.

LEARNING PACKAGE BOOKLET

As a result of the experience in designing these packages a booklet entitled A Guide to the Design of Learning Packages was produced at the School of Education. The target population was identified as 'education officers who may be called upon to design learning packages'.

It was assumed that these education officers would be subject-matter experts and experienced in teaching their subject.

The entry conditions laid down at the front of the booklet are as follows :

(1)  Based on his experience he must be able to:

    a. Identify the problems commonly met by students in studying the subject matter.

    b. Suggest methods of presentation and treatment which will allow these problems to be overcome.

(2)  He must acknowledge the validity and viability of the concept of 'A Systems Approach to Training'.

The steps to be followed in designing a learning package were identified in the first chapter and these are reproduced in Figure 2.

---

Write the Objectives

Arrange Objectives in Logical Sequence

Select Appropriate Tests

Decide on Methods to be Employed

Allocate Learning Resources

Produce the Package

Validate the Package

---

Figure 2:  Steps to follow when designing a learning package

Each of these steps form the subject of subsequent chapters of the booklet.  Moreover every chapter, apart from the first, opens with a statement of its objectives so that readers who already can achieve the objectives have no need to work through the chapter.

OTHER PACKAGES

This booklet has been used when designing most Royal Air Force packages.  Technical Drawing and British Government are two recently-produced packages which utilized the design process outlined in the booklet.

The package in British Government follows fairly closely the pattern of the Practical Economics one.  It uses a teacher-centred approach although allowance has been made for possible adaptation by students working on their own. Again the emphasis is on a logbook of objectives which guides the student through his course.

The Technical Drawing package, on the other hand, has adopted a student-centred approach because of the lack of teachers of this subject in the Royal Air Force. The design of the package is simple but effective. There are a series of exercises carefully structured so that they only gradually increase in difficulty and complexity.

The exercises commence with a partly-drawn diagram which the student has to complete, then a translucent overlay shows him the answer. All 103 exercises have an overlay answer and there are, in addition, a series of tests which can be used as pre- as well as post-tests, if required. An instructor's guide has been included for those stations which can offer formal instruction.

Even more student-centred are the two packages Writing Objectives and Night Duty Party. 'Writing Objectives' was designed by the Training Efficiency Cell at Royal Air Force Strike Command to assist in training instructors who were to be employed in rewriting the syllabuses. It was intended to be used as an integral part of a two day course but in a self-teaching mode (Thomas, Brookes & Hesketh, 1972). The package is made up of three items: a series of enclosures including a glossary, objectives and tests, a collection of notes and a programmed text split into two parts. The student cross-refers to each item as he works through the package which is constructed in the form of an adjunct programme.

The Night Duty Party package was the first one to be designed around job aids. The package arose out of a training survey at one of the Royal Air Force's Equipment Supply Depots. The existing method of learning a specialized procedural job was 'sitting by Nellie'. The task analysis showed that the job could be performed by using algorithmic job aids (Fallon & Easby, 1973). Subsequently a package was constructed which included these job aids and instructions on how to use them, as well as exercises, tests and information about how each job fitted together both in the Depot and in the Royal Air Force.

PACKAGE LEARNING IN FORMAL TRAINING

To complete this survey of packages the Royal Air Force's experience with package learning in one of their formal training courses will be outlined. The Mechanical Transport Driver course at RAF St Athan has been restructured into a continuous-flow training strategy with the theoretical content of the syllabus taught by means of learning packages. Continuous Flow Training can be defined as a way of organizing students so that they flow continuously in and out of the training process (O'Hare, 1972). Learning to drive a vehicle is essentially an individual process, therefore it was only the theoretical content of the syllabus which had previously been taught in groups.

The five packages used are designed in a similar format; a stiff-backed plastic folder contains three parts: students' instructions which include learning objectives and tests, a structured guide written in the form of a linear programme, together with self-marking exercises, and a number of ancillary documents such as books, maps, and forms. As the student works through the package he is advised to examine not only the aids included in the package but also others available in the room, such as film loops, sectioned vehicles, simple teaching machines, wall charts and posters. Each package has a tutor who monitors the progress of the students, helps them with any difficulties they encounter and administers a post-test.

The results achieved by the first 100 Royal Air Force students are summarized in Figure 3. The fastest student took five hours to complete the package and the slowest over 70 hours. The mean total time of 28.9 hours is 22.1 hours better than that obtained under the previous group-classroom strategy (Simpson, 1973).

| Package | Traditional teaching time (in hours) | Mean time for self-study (in hours) | Number passing at first attempt |
|---|---|---|---|
| 1 Safety, Fire and Health Regulations | 4 | 3.9 | 89 |
| 2 Airfield Driving Procedures | 3 | 2.8 | 95 |
| 3 The Highway Code | 10 | 8.5 | 94 |
| 4 MT Operating Procedures | 21 | 10.5 | 80 |
| 5 MT Servicing Procedures | 13 | 7.8 | 96 |
| Mean Total Time | | 28.9 * | |

* The mean total time is less than the sum of the individual package times because some students gained exemption from certain packages in an initial assessment test.

Figure 3: The results achieved by the first 100 RAF MT drivers under training

CONCLUSION

The Royal Air Force's experience with package learning is still fairly limited, however the results achieved so far suggest that packages are both an efficient and an effective way of training. Learning packages have proved flexible and, because they often use existing resources, can be more cost-effective than programmed learning.

Package design for training assumes an acceptance of a systematic approach; in particular, the writing of objectives for the training material has been found essential. Package designers, in practice, have often had to carry out this stage themselves although, in theory, objectives should always be written before the decision is made to package.

REFERENCES

Diffey, K.S. (1971) CTT Learning Packages. RAF Education Bulletin, No. 8.

Fallon, P. and Easby, M. (1973) A Systems Approach to Vocational Training in Maintenance Command. RAF Education Bulletin, No. 10.

Hartley, J. (Ed.) (1972) Strategies for Programmed Instruction: An Educational Technology. London: Butterworth.

O'Hare, B. (1972) Continuous Flow Training -- Why Polarize the Issue? RAF Education Bulletin, No. 9.

Research Unit (1969) Report on an investigation into package learning systems in relation to Part 2 of the Royal Air Force Education Test. RAF School of Education, Upwood.

Resources Development Unit (1970) Final report by the Resources Development Unit of the RAF School of Education into an investigation into package learning systems for Part 2 of the RAF Education Test. RAF School of Education, Upwood.

Resources Development Unit (1971) A guide to the design of learning packages. RAF School of Education, Upwood.

Simpson, D.A. (1973) The use of pre-structured learning packages on the RAF MT Driver Course. RAF Education Bulletin, No. 10.

Thomas, D.B., Brookes, M.W. and Hesketh, P.M. (1972) The Strike Command Training Efficiency Cell. RAF Education Bulletin, No. 9.

# A carrel system for an institution for higher education

J. CLARKE, Dundee College of Education

**Abstract:** To every unit of communication there are four elements: the communicator, the message, the means of communication and the receiver. This paper mainly deals with the means of communication and the needs of a receiver in the context of the Dundee College of Education to be housed in a new building in October 1974, providing accommodation for 1,800 students. The College also has the declared aim of providing about one-fifth of the students' timetabled workload in the form of self-instruction.

Following visits by Mr. Charles Morrison, Principal Lecturer in Education, to the Oral Roberts University in Tulsa, the Oklahoma Christian College and West Harford School (all American institutions housing large highly sophisticated electronic information distribution systems), a view was held in the College that some provision of carrels for individualized study was desirable. However, it was also recognized that funds of a similar order to those granted in the USA were most unlikely to be available to us and therefore the aim should be to retain the desirable elements but to modify, replace or omit the costly facilities. The facility judged to be the most costly compared with the possible educational gain was dial access retrieval. Very tentative enquiries as to the probable level of cost proved it to be, as expected, quite prohibitive, and no further enquiries were made into such a facility after 1971.

## CRITERIA FOR CARREL PROVISION AND BUILT-IN FACILITIES

Once the decision had been made to provide carrels, criteria had to be established which would determine their location, physical shape, type of construction, and the facilities to be contained within the entire installation. At a very early stage in the planning an aim was set that, in time (eventually this was specified as 1978), each student should spend approximately one-fifth of his timetabled time using self-instructional procedures which might require some aural and/or visual aids in their presentation. Some 250 carrels was considered to be about the number required to make this possible and so the feasibility study which I prepared in the autumn of 1971 presented a case for eight additional modules to be added to the Library/Resource Centre being built onto the new College. This addition was in excess of 11, 000 sq. ft. and although by no means the whole of this area will house carrels, without it the provision to be made would most certainly not have been in the Library/Resource Centre. A more or less conventional type library had originally been designed in 1969 to specifications applicable at that time to Colleges of Education which made little if any allowance for carrel installation or the storage of a large stock of non-book materials.

Two basic types of carrel were deemed to be necessary. The first and by far the most numerous would be open and for an individual. The second would be for more than one user or for a situation in which the procedures to be used might be noisy or be spread over a long period of time. In the latter case, security might be a problem, hence the carrel had to be lockable as well as being sound-proofed, but well ventilated, to cater for the use of any noisy piece of machinery such as a typewriter.

We are to provide 212 open carrels and 15 closed carrels. The open carrels have been designed on the premise that students in a College of Education will normally prefer not to be too isolated from their fellows hence three walls only are provided giving a degree of privacy but unlikely to create a boxed-in feeling. They are constructed in line with each alternative position turned through $180^{\circ}$ or in the form of a swastika, with each alternative position turned clockwise through $90^{\circ}$. The closed carrels will effectively be small rooms about six feet square with a suspended ceiling housing the ventilation system. The positioning of these carrels enables them to form divisions or partitions within the Library/Resource Centre which has a total area of 28, 000 square feet and only one permanent internal wall. The Resource Centre is thus designed to be as flexible in layout as possible making it practicable to reposition a large proportion of the whole installation without too much difficulty if this is found to be desirable at some time in the future.

The aim in providing carrels is to make it practicable for any person within the College population (i.e. 2000 all together — 1800 students and 200 lecturers) to use a learning unit of whatever degree of sophistication more or less at will, with ease and above all with reliability. It has therefore been decided to provide the following facilities among the carrels:

(1) Mono. audio replay
(2) High quality stereo audio replay
(3) Unsynchronized tape/slide/filmstrip presentation
(4) Synchronized tape/slide presentation
(5) Individually retrieved monochrome/colour television replay.

## Open Carrel Design

Each carrel position is basically a working surface with a control shelf above, both supported within three walls. Although the prototypes were

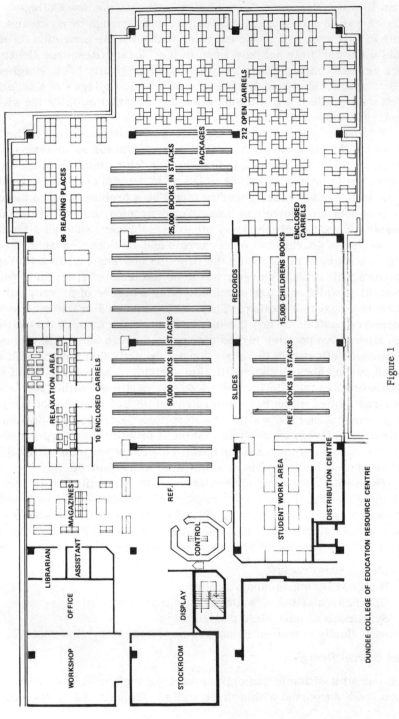

Figure 1

DUNDEE COLLEGE OF EDUCATION RESOURCE CENTRE

96 READING PLACES

PACKAGES

212 OPEN CARRELS

25,000 BOOKS IN STACKS

ENCLOSED CARRELS

15,000 CHILDRENS BOOKS

RECORDS

SLIDES

50,000 BOOKS IN STACKS

RELAXATION AREA

10 ENCLOSED CARRELS

REF.

REF. BOOKS IN STACKS

MAGAZINES

STUDENT WORK AREA

DISTRIBUTION CENTRE

LIBRARIAN

ASSISTANT

OFFICE

CONTROL

WORKSHOP

DISPLAY

STOCKROOM

entirely constructed of timber, the need to make units of four at a realistic cost resulted in a decision to use Handy Tube, 18 mm laminated board and the related fixing accessories. Using these materials each unit of four that is four working surfaces enclosed within three walls, many of which are of course common to two positions, costs about £110 if all the items are bought at the prices quoted by the manufacturers for cut sizes. Each position is 3ft. 6in. wide and the working surface is 2ft. deep. The walls are 4ft. 6in. high and at least 2ft. 5in. from front to back.

Unless the position is to house a projection compartment a working surface made of the laminated board is supported by fillets. This can be lifted out and a projection compartment provided supported on the fillets screwed on at a lower position.

Figure 2:   The Dundee Carrel:   synchronized tape/slide unit and control
shelf within cruciform arrangement of carrels

The projection compartments are of two types. Although the design is basically the same, one houses a Carousel projector used for synchronized tape/slide presentation, the other a filmstrip/slide projector used for hand-loaded, unsynchronized presentation.  Both types of projector can be housed below the working surface as can the screen so making available the whole of the working surface if required. One or two of the units fitted with projection facilities will also have television monitors

143

alongside the projector compartment, the entire facility being available for the presentation of a few very complex multi-media programmes.

Much thought and experiment has been put into the provision of television replays. Our intention has always been to make it possible for a student to control his programme as required. For the better part of two years we have used video cassette machines in carrels. The control has been by the individual student and following our experiences it has been decided that tape lacing and initial setting up of the equipment will be done remotely by an experienced operator but that thereafter control will be passed to the student. The experience on which we based the decision caused us much disappointment as local control of cassette machines seemed to provide the ideal answer to the problem of television retrieval as required. As a result, we have had to increase our planned system of distribution from a central source but the advent of the cartridge players capable of remote control has enabled us to retain the control of the playing of the tape within the carrel.

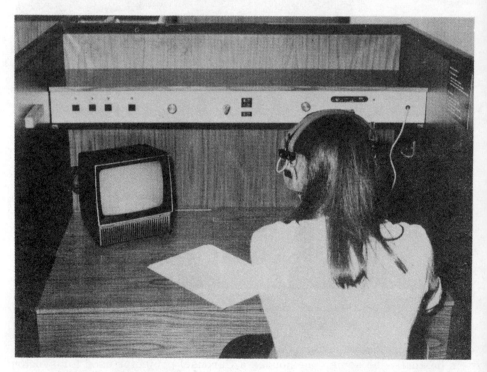

Figure 3: The Dundee Carrel: video presentation from IVC player remotely controlled by four buttons at left of shelf

To use a programme, the student contacts the Distribution Centre by telephone and asks for the tape he requires. The tape is loaded by the operator, run onto the start and control is then transferred to the student.

By using the four control buttons on the fascia of the control shelf the student can view any section of the tape required and can control every function of the machine except the complete unlacing of the tape.  This will be done after the student has indicated to the operator that he has completed his viewing.  Control is then returned to the machine in the Distribution Centre and the tape is unlaced.  If two or more students wish to view the same programme in more than one carrel, or if we wish to play any programme repeatedly, the machines are set to recycle the tape continuously with all control in the Distribution Centre and the remote control facility completely disconnected.

About fifteen carrels will be so linked to the Distribution Centre and a bank of eight cartridge players will provide remotely controlled replays.  Older programmes replayed by open spool machines or off-air broadcasts will also be available but for these there will be no possibility of remote control.

Other modes of presentation available in the carrels with working surfaces only will be of the nature where the aid can be plugged into the power source on the control shelf.  These might be slide viewing desks, microfilm readers, large screen slide viewers or such devices as PIP.  The latter however are probably somewhat noisy for use in an open carrel and will more likely be found in the closed carrels.  A few carrels will also be fitted with high quality stereo players, especially for the benefit of the students taking the major music courses.  Each carrel will house an audio player.  To overcome the problems of reliability and security the players form an integral part of each control shelf. If any player fails the whole shelf can be replaced in seconds as all connections are plugged in and spare shelves of each type required will be held by the librarian in charge of the carrel complex.  The servicing of a faulty unit will be almost equally speedy as the tape decks and home-built amplifiers are also plugged in and can be replaced very quickly indeed for later servicing.  By adopting this policy of modular construction and speedy replacement of faulty elements the system should be able to function for twelve hours each working day with a minimum of highly trained technicians and the probability that at some time no technical assistance whatsoever will be available.  The present plans allow for two trained audio technicians to maintain the College complement of audio tape recorders and players which will number between 400 and 500.  Most of these will be in almost continuous use during term time.

All controls for the synchronized tape/slide facility are provided on the fascia board of the control shelf.  Between forty and sixty carrels will be provided with Mentor players containing circuits discriminating betweeen pulses which provide signals for automatic stops or slide changes.  Many of our programmes have automatic stops built into their presentation but the student can also stop the audio player and, in either event, then retrieve slides for the purpose of revision by using the control buttons on the shelf. A verbatim transcription of the commentary is printed on yellow pages in the student's response sheet. By using this he can find his way into any part of the programme and relate this to the slide from the slide number which appears both in the commentary and on the slide.

Carousel SAV 2000 projectors are installed as standard equipment as the return to zero facility is available. When the student has completed the use of a programme he presses the return to zero button and the slide drum automatically returns to the zero position in which no slide is left in the gate. We can therefore almost guarantee that a full drum of slides is returned to the box in which the learning unit is stored.

Power supplies, television signals and telephone lines to the carrels from the Distribution Centre are carried in a grid covering the whole carrel area with intersections which coincide with the ends of the in-line layout or centres of the swastika type units. Easily removed covers will allow us to supply further services as required.

## Control of the Carrel System

A system to be used daily by a possible population of some 2000 people clearly needs a simple but fool-proof control system. We have adopted the key colour-cap idea to provide the control element for the whole system. A student knowing the learning unit he requires obtains this from the shelf where it will most probably be on open access. The label for the storage box of this unit and the cover of the response sheet within will be of the same colour. The student will then obtain from the librarian in charge, in exchange for his library card, a key with a cap of this colour and a number within the window in the colour cap will indicate the number of the carrel to which the key belongs. The key acts as a switch as it controls the power switch on the carrel. Until the key is turned the power cannot be switched on and no facility in the carrel can be used. Until the power is switched off the key cannot be withdrawn. So in withdrawing the key all equipment must be switched off and unless the student returns the key he will be unable to use the library as he will be without his library card which will be used for the issuing system.

The prototype carrels and the control system have been under development for two years. Feedback received from the students over this time has made evident the fact that we have a proposed installation for the new College which will be appreciated and widely used. Inclusion of some of the facilities has been achieved by compromise in the overall design of individual units but throughout we have been most aware of our principal aim to provide a complex installation which is usable in its entirety with ease and above all reliability even when skilled technical assistance is not available.

# The use of project network analysis in course design

G. R. CATLOW, RAF School of Education, Upwood

**Abstract:** This paper assumes some knowledge of Project Network Analysis techniques and shows how these techniques have been used to plan, schedule and control a project in course design. It shows how the effects of different choices of methods can be determined before the course starts, and it provides a tool for the College Principal, Headmaster or Department Head to control the course design activities of his staff. The network can be used for the allocation of time, staff and other resources, and also for the identification of real and apparent constraints.

## INTRODUCTION

This paper is not an attempt to teach the techniques of Project Network Analysis (PNA). Anybody who is unfamiliar with these techniques, and who is called upon to undertake course design, should first study some of the books and programmes in the reading list which is available. On the other hand, managers of learning, e.g. Principals of Colleges, or Heads of Departments, who are required to make decisions based on network models, as presented by course designers, should find this paper sufficient for their purposes.

Models, such as those produced by PNA, will be used increasingly by those who are asked to plan, schedule and control any time-consuming or costly project. By using a model, management is able to experiment with alternative approaches to a problem, and to determine the likely effects before embarking on the actual project. PNA can produce considerable savings in both time and money by closely simulating most of the actual conditions that will arise during the stages of a project. It is also vital to recognize the differing roles of those who sponsor, control and carry out course design projects, and this paper emphasizes the links which must be forged between learning management and the course design team. In authorizing a training design project those responsible will want to know the answers to the following questions :

(a) What strategies can be employed in the design project?

(b) How long will the design process take?

(c)  What will be the cost of the design?

(d)  What possible methods of teaching and learning are envisaged on the new course?

(e)  How can the work of the project team, and those with whom they must work, be controlled?

(f)  At what stages can the project be examined to see if benefits are likely to result?

Management are most likely to get answers to these questions if they ask for a Project Network Analysis (PNA).

## PART I — DRAWING THE NETWORK

### Introduction

When carrying out project design work the technique of Project Network Analysis may be used for the following phases:

(a)  Planning
(b)  Analysing and Scheduling
(c)  Controlling.

The use of PNA for course design is relatively new and the aim of this section is to give someone with knowledge of the techniques of PNA an indication of how it can be used in course design.  It is also intended to show management how the Network can be used and interpreted to give the maximum information leading to the best possible results.

The distinction between the phases outlined above is not as clearcut as might be thought.  All the activities are actually taking place continuously, with the analysing and scheduling processes assisting in the major activities of planning and controlling.  Figure 1 shows how a planning network is developed in order to provide management with the information to control the project.  We are concerned in this section with the first stage in Figure 1 — the Network Analysis.

### PROJECT CONSTRAINTS

Although it is unlikely that any course design project will have unlimited time and manpower resources, it must be remembered that time and resources are dependent on each other.  A reduction in resources will increase the time required, and similarly, in order to shorten time, an increase in resources might be needed.  This is further complicated by the choice of methods to be used in the course design project.  Certain methods of needs analysis or learning material design will require more time and/or resources than others.  It is taken for granted that any project will be planned within the assumed constraints of minimum resources and

148

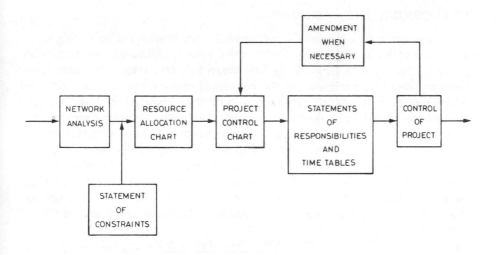

Figure 1:   Development of a planning network

minimum time.   It has already been stated that it might be possible to
reduce time by increasing resources, but we shall see that this does not
necessarily follow, even though we can often reduce the resources required by increasing the time available.   In the early stages of the project decisions will have to be made in this area, but the use of PNA will
at least show management the likely consequences of these decisions
before the project has actually started.

In the early stages of planning it has been found realistic to start
from the premise that resources are limited and time is unlimited.   It is
then possible to decrease the project time by introducing changes in
methods or increases in resources.   However, certain constraints will
most certainly have been imposed by management, and so some decisions
on method and resources will have been made before the network is drawn.
The first of these decisions concerns the method of needs analysis. A full
task analysis (involving an analysis of the behaviour required to carry out
a task, with a view to the identification of areas of difficulty and the appropriate training techniques), although desirable, is usually too expensive
in terms of manpower and time.   Only when a training problem arises
from unsatisfactory performance in an industrial process is permission
for such a full scale investigation likely to be given.   The more common
problems are of reducing course time, reducing learning resources, or
making learning more effective.   In such cases the needs analysis will be
limited to a detailed examination of the present syllabus in order to
identify its components, their importance and relevance.

# NETWORKING THE UNKNOWN

The production of a network for course design is similar to trying to draw a map for a previously uncharted journey. Although the particular journey has never been made before there will be parts of it which have been trodden by people during the course of other journeys. It is the job of the designer to search out the best available knowledge about the procedures and total work involved in needs analysis, objective writing, test design etc., in order to build as complete a picture as possible. Any gaps left outstanding must be filled by intelligent guesses. The great advantage of the network is that, when a guess proves to be inaccurate, the total effect on the project's time and resources can be calculated and decisions made at an early stage. Using the best available information the probable time for each activity can be calculated using the PERT formula.

$$PT = \frac{MO + (4 \times ML) + MP}{6}$$

where

PT is Probable Time
MO is Most Optimistic Time
ML is Most Likely Time
MP is Most Pessimistic Time

Part of a Course Design Network is shown in Figure 2. Activities 25 to 29 are the typing (25-26-27-28) and checking (26-28-29) of the lists of objectives. It is normal to consider such an activity as linear, that is to say that the typing of the lists, checking of stencils and duplicating, all follow in sequence. However, there is usually no good reason to wait for the typist to finish before the originator starts checking the stencils and, if correct, sends them for duplicating.

When the PERT calculation for the typing was carried out it was considered that a good typist working all day would be able to complete the task in the one day, and so the most optimistic time (MO) was given as one However, since it is also possible for the typist to be ill or needed to work on some more urgent matter, the most pessimistic time (MP), including the finding of a replacement typist, was given as five days. The most likely time (ML), which takes account of the usual interruptions for service reasons, was given as three days and so the PERT calculation was

$$PT = \frac{MO + (4 \times ML) + MP}{6}$$

$$= \frac{1 + (4 \times 3) + 5}{6}$$

$$= 3 \text{ days}$$

The most probable time for the typing is thus three days.

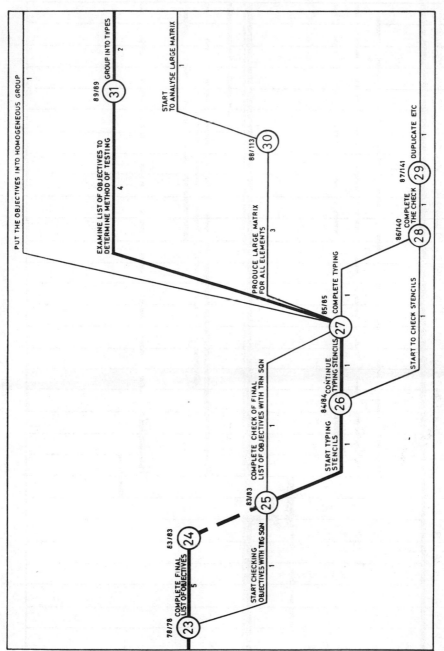

Figure 2: Part of a training design network

151

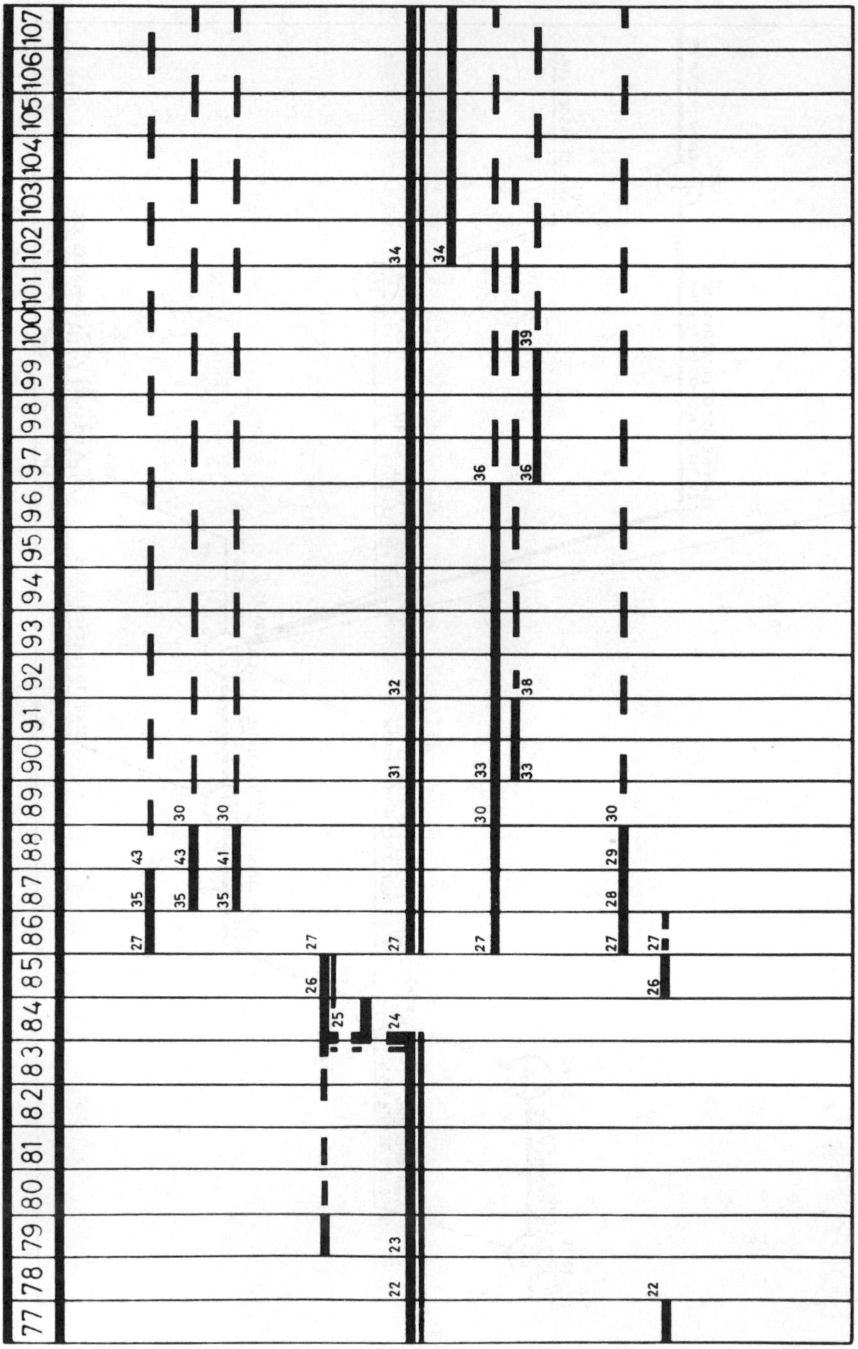

Figure 3: Plotting of activities

152

## SMOOTHING THE RESOURCES

Once the activities have been identified, and their time calculated, they can be plotted on a time-scale of working days (Figure 3). Each activity is shown as starting at the earliest possible time and finishing at the most probable time. From the probable finishing time to the latest acceptable finishing time a dotted line is drawn which indicates 'float', i.e. the extra time available to finish the activity before it becomes critical. Of course the activity on the critical path has no float.

At this stage the resources can be allocated (Figure 4). As the time to be taken for the project is determined by the critical path we cannot, at this stage, reduce the overall time, but we can attempt to use the resources in the most economical manner. For example, in Figure 3 it appears that on day 87 we will need six people; however, all the activities except the critical path activity have float and can start later than day 87. Care must be taken that, in moving the activities within their 'float time' they are still kept in the correct order. However, although the resources have been smoothed as much as possible (Figure 4), it is still sometimes necessary to have extra help.

## SHORTENING THE TIME

If the network designer is asked to shorten the time for the project he must concentrate on the critical path, because this determines the time for the whole project. If the critical activity is typing (as in Figure 2, activities 25-27) it is no use allocating more staff if they cannot type, or getting a second typist if there is only one typewriter.

Although in the particular example given, the time cannot be shortened by the addition of extra resources in the form of training design staff, this is not always the case. It is apparent from the example of the network already given that, unless the critical activity does not involve the course design staff, there will always be one member of staff required for the critical path and one available for some other activity. There may also be a requirement for clerical or typing staff. The network and the resource-smoothing chart must be examined for staff allocations and these should be inserted at the bottom of the chart, as in Figure 4.

The next process, if we are trying to reduce the time, is to examine the activities to see whether the addition of another training designer will help. If the acitivity is a questionnaire which is sent out through the post, completed by the respondents, and returned through the post, it is impossible to shorten the time by the addition of manpower. A probable time of 30 days will remain at about 30 days however many course designers are employed. On the other hand, the probable time for processing is 20 man-days, i.e. 20 days work for one man; two men could do this in 10 days, thus reducing the total time for the design project by 10 days. But

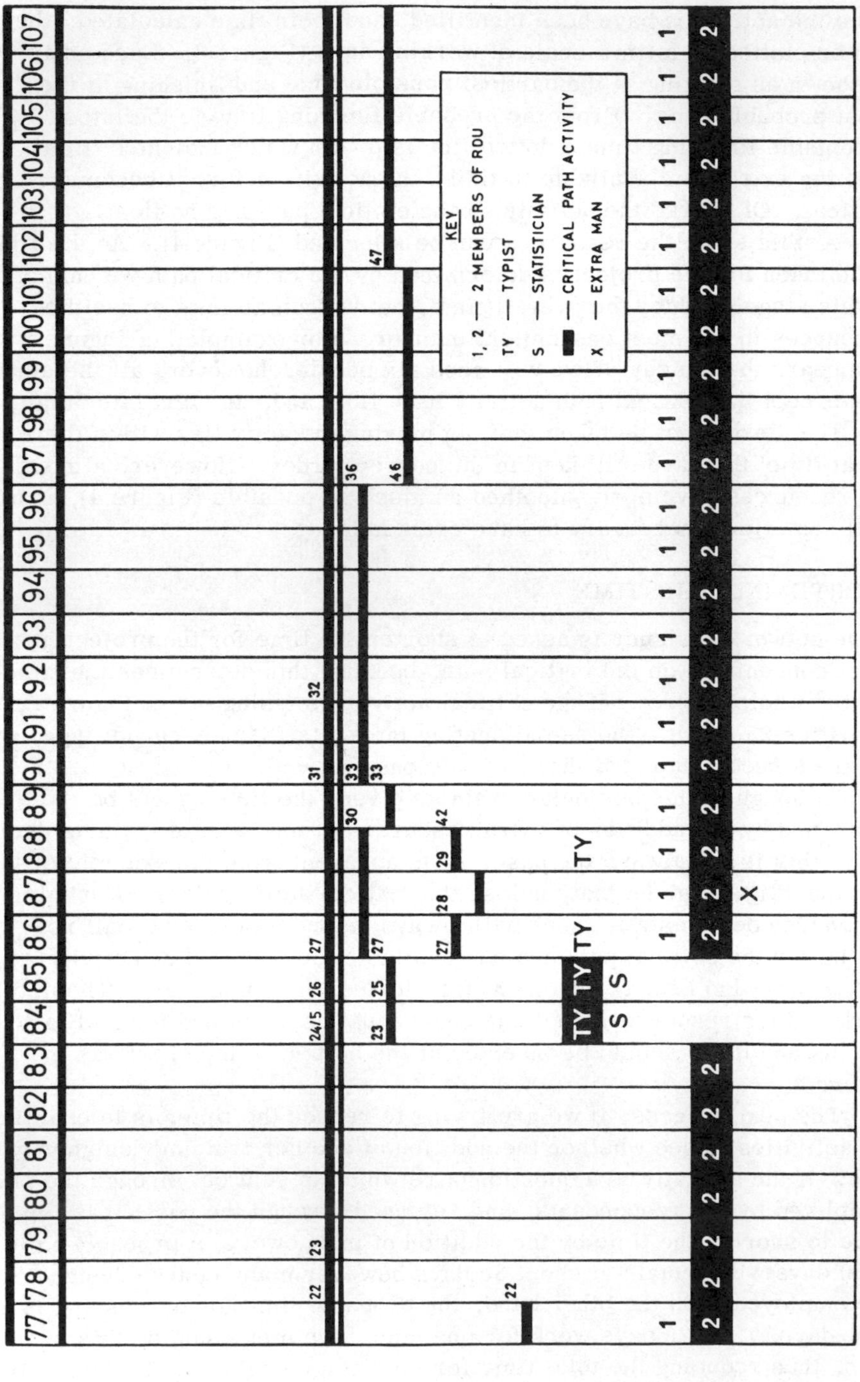

Figure 4: Resource allocation

154

this is only true if the activity is on the critical path; there is no point in allocating more manpower to shorten an activity which already has float available.

The next way to shorten the length of the project time is to examine the methods chosen for the design of learning. For example, it may have been decided to conduct the needs analysis by the use of questionnaires and interviews, the latter intended to include questions about points raised by respondents to the questionnaire. However, in order to save time, the interviews could be carried out while waiting for the questionnaire to be returned. This would save up to 30 days but, without the aid of questions specifically related to respondents' answers to the questionnaire, the results of the job analysis would not be so reliable.

## INFORMATION FROM THE NETWORK

It is possible that the network will have to be amended many times before management is satisfied that a suitable compromise has been reached between time, methods and resources. If the information available to management shows that the course design project is impossible within the constraints, it will be necessary for the network designer to explain to management the effects of changes in the constraints, and it is therefore recommended that the designer has this information to hand when presenting the network.

Once both network and project have been approved the network becomes a control document for the course design team.

## PART II — THE USE OF PROJECT NETWORK ANALYSIS FOR PROJECT CONTROL

### INTRODUCTION

Once the network analysis of a course design has been approved the network draft can be used as a control document for the project. Two further documents should be produced, showing:

(a)  Responsibilities                    (b)  Timetables

Finally, the network charts should be displayed and a simple system (e.g. pins and coloured string) used to compare planned and actual progress.

### ALLOCATION OF REAL TIME

The Resources Allocation Chart, which has been produced in order to analyse the design task, is marked (Figure 4) in whatever number of mandays the project will require. However, it is unlikely that the team will be working for seven days per week, without leave, grant or any other break. As soon as a starting date is given, therefore, and it is known when the

155

members of the design team will be available for work, then 'real' time – i. e. actual dates – can be marked on the chart, as in Figure 5.

There may be times when the nature of the job, or the individual experience of team members, will mean that a member of the team is not allocated on the chart. On the chart an extra man has been allocated to reduce time on the critical path and he is kept on this job, even when man 2 is free, as it does not make sense to switch the extra man 'on' and 'off' the project.

The Chart also shows that two of the working weeks contain only four days because of the Easter Weekend. The 21 days (163-183) allocated at the top of the sheet actually extend over the period 11 April to 11 May, so it is only through the addition of 'real' time that the chart assumes its full significance.

RESPONSIBILITIES

The completion of the network will not only show which jobs have been allocated to people on the team, but the addition of real time also shows the dates on which jobs are expected to start and finish. However, many of these jobs are dependent on decisions by people not directly concerned with course design. An example of this is clerical support. Whoever is responsible for the provision of clerical support can be warned, sometimes a year in advance, on precisely which dates clerical support will be required and for what purpose. Of course it is possible that unforeseen events will subsequently cause the project time to slip, but, again, advance warning can be given. Once the clerical support has been firmly allocated it may be impossible for it to be changed; if such is the case then alternative action – e.g. overtime, more designers, leave changes – can be taken to bring the project back into line with the clerical support.

Where the project is dependent on decisions by higher authority – e.g. Examination Boards – it is possible to warn them well in advance that certain information from the design team (e.g. a draft syllabus) will be available on a certain date, and that their decision will be needed by another fixed date if the project is not to be held up. Higher authority can thus prepare itself by collecting such information as is needed and perhaps calling meetings well in advance if many people need to be consulted.

**Timetable**

Another use for the network chart is in the production of individual timetables or work schedules. Each person who will be working on the project can be given a list of dates for the start and finish of every job. In this way each designer can be held responsible for the planning and execution of particular tasks. Failure to meet target dates can show where

156

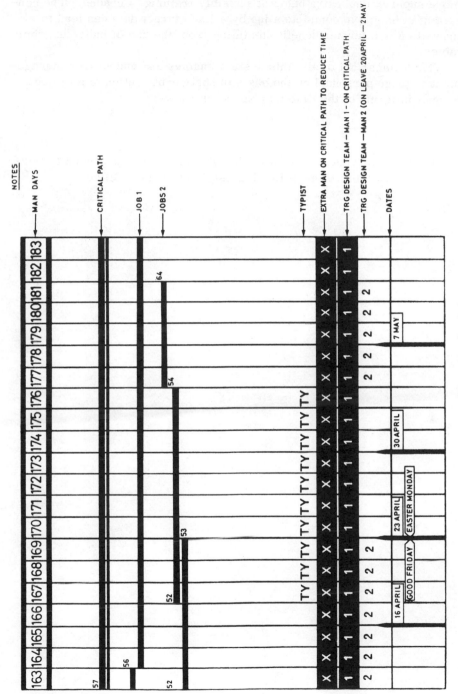

Figure 5: Allocation of real time

more supervision, extra help, or possibly training is needed. The constraint of having to complete a job by a fixed target date can lead to innovation — a further benefit stemming from the use of individual timetables.

Most important of all, this system enables and encourages management to judge personnel on the basis of their contribution to a project, and not in terms of the time they spend on it.

# A free format course based on pre-recorded learning material

J. MORTON, E. BINGHAM, J. COWAN, Heriot-Watt University

**Abstract:** A first year undergraduate course in Theory of Structures was reorganized to enable the instruction to be presented using pre-recorded material. Design projects, drawing office and laboratory work augmented the pre-recorded instruction, to form an integrated basic scheme which complies with the course regulations.

The learning material was partly presented to small groups through tape-overhead and tape-slide sequences; part was also made available through individually paced audio tapes with supporting printed material. Working from supplied objective lists, tutorials and self-marked post-tests, the students monitored their own progress, and used the available remedial instruction at their own discretion. The primary function of the academic staff was to provide individual tuition when particular difficulties arose.

No fixed timetable existed; each student organized his own study pattern, working from a weekly flow chart which detailed the inter-relationship of learning activities. He was free to book for these activities in accordance with his own inclinations, rate of progress and study habits.

The paper mentions the learning facilities and materials and describes the operation of the free format system. The writers then discuss the problems posed, the solutions adopted, and the costing and potential of this mode of organization of a learning situation in higher education.

## INTRODUCTION

The main aim of the Civil Engineering Learning Unit (1) is to use modern teaching methods to obtain an improved learning response from the full spectrum of undergraduates in any class within the Department. Since it was first established in 1971, the Unit has had an increasing departmental teaching commitment (2, 3).

The most recent stage in this development has been the decision to transfer the first year Theory of Structures course from a lecture-orientated presentation to a Learning Unit scheme based on pre-recorded material. The new learning materials were to be offered to the students using a scheme which would permit each undergraduate a fair measure of participation in the planning of his own individual study programme. This arrangement, which will be described here as 'free-format time-tabling', is the main interest in the present paper.

159

The facilities offered by the Unit have already been described elsewhere in some detail (1, 2), brevity precludes a repetition of that information here.

## The Need for Individually Paced Instruction

Any first year class of engineering undergraduates will inevitably contain students whose backgrounds, abilities, experience, training and preferences in study habits vary appreciably. Such diversity introduces considerable problems when planning conventional instruction based on a predetermined study method and study rate. These problems can understandably give rise to discontent within the class group, and for this reason individually paced instruction appeared to offer considerable advantages in the first year of the course.

The arrangement which was proposed would offer each student a 'main line' linear route through the syllabus. The syllabus was logically reorganized to facilitate this sequential approach to tuition, laboratory and drawing office work. Continuity would be ensured by the decision that all main line material was prepared by one lecturer only.

It was hoped that a student with a good background and high ability would be both able and encouraged to move along the main line learning route at a faster pace than his colleagues of average ability; likewise the less gifted student could move at a slower pace. It should thus be easier to pull **out** the good student and pull **up** the below-average student in the same system.

## The Chosen Solution

Whilst the idealized aims had to be married to the practical and economic constraints, the main features of the original concept were retained in the adopted solution. The course could not be presented exclusively as individually paced learning material, since the available facilities did not permit this. In any case, past work with group-paced and individually-paced packages had suggested that the use of group-paced **initial** instruction led to the same learning, in a shorter study time. For these reasons the course material was presented using both group paced and individual presentations, reserving the latter for situations where the problems and needs of each learner were likely to differ markedly.

The individually paced instruction was centred on the learning laboratory, using audio tape cassettes with printed support material; the group paced instruction involved the use of tape/overhead or tape/slide sequences projected without supervision in two small group viewing rooms.

## Timetabling

The free-format timetable was introduced to offer the student the opportunity of working through the syllabus at his own pace, whether individual

or group activities were involved.  No fixed timetable existed; guidance
on the use of the units of learning materials, the average rate of progress expected, and the inter-relationships of the various units of learning material and other activities was made available weekly in the form
of a flow chart (Figure 1).  The student was then free to complete the
requirements according to his own preferences.  Thus some students
preferred to tackle their laboratory and drawing work in the mornings;
others left this type of work until the afternoons, choosing to study new
learning packages in the mornings when they felt fresh.  Some students
even preferred to split up the theoretical work with a sandwich-filling
of an hour in the laboratory, whilst others found continuity of great value.

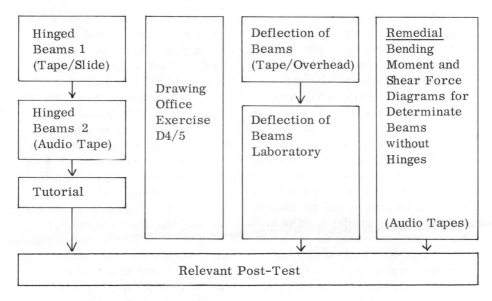

Figure 1: Typical Flow  Chart

A detailed list of objectives was prepared for each topic in the
syllabus and given to the student as an indication of the expected level of
performance.  Hence the use of the free format timetable allowed any
student who felt he could fulfil all the objectives, to bypass the learning
material and attempt the self-marked post-test directly.  If that post-test
was satisfactorily completed, he could then continue immediately, if he
so wished, to the next part of the syllabus.  This formed one of several
paths which were open to the student in the free-format system. If the
results from the post-test were unsatisfactory, he could still join the
rest of his colleagues who had initially accepted that they could not fulfil
the stated objectives.

Whilst every student was encouraged to follow the guidance offered
by the weekly flow charts, each retained the option to spend more than a

week on any part of the course which they found difficult to assimilate —
offsetting this time loss on some other section of the syllabus to which
they could more easily relate.

The student had, on average, 11 available hours within which to
arrange seven hours study and a lunch break. A basic module of an
hour had been adopted — although, to allow time to change rooms, etc.,
it has been found that no unit of pre-recorded learning material should
run for more than 50 minutes, including an allowance for interruptions
and repetitions.

## Booking System

An efficient, cheap and simple booking system, based on an hourly
module, was clearly a crucial requirement if the free format system
was to be successful. The first solution involved the use of two inch
square cards in conjunction with slide boxes. Each student was given
four cards of different colours, with each of which he could book a
place in the learning laboratory, or the two group viewing rooms or the
laboratory. The drawing office and the tutorial room both had enough
capacity to run without booking, and provided a 'cushion' in the timetable. This was a welcome facility, which worked well from the outset.

A master board, positioned near the booking system, indicated the
times at which each learning sequence would be available, and in which
group viewing room it was to be shown. But a booking made for the
learning laboratory left the student free to listen to any piece of instruction which was available on an audio tape, and therefore the master
board made no reference to any specific tapes.

To remove some of the more routine demands for individual tuition,
remedial audio tapes were also made available in the hope that some of
the students who had encountered common difficulties might prefer to
resolve them at their own pace before availing themselves of the tutor.
But individual 'live tuition' would always be available at any time to
deal with outstanding difficulties. The remedial tapes were designed to
fulfil the objectives as listed, and were made by a second lecturer,
using his own style of presentation and approach to the subject, without
reference to the main-line material.

## Progress Boards

Each student recorded his own progress on a large board, indicating
which material he had used, which material he had found unnecessary
and which material he had not yet attempted. This proved valuable to
the students since they could at a glance see how their progress compared with their colleagues. It was even more useful for the authors, as
they could follow trends and were better able to gauge how and at what
speed the material was being used.

## Initial Experiences

The general principles and the particular details were carefully explained to the students on the first day. But they were initially bewildered by the combination of the new teaching methods and the novelty of the free format timetable. This reaction was hardly surprising, and had been anticipated. The two major problems which had to be overcome were, firstly, the lack of familiarity with the new learning methods and with the booking system, and, secondly, the requirement for the student to organize his own study pattern. A full day was devoted to explaining the philosophy behind the course, teaching the students how to use the equipment, and explaining the course regulations. Despite this, the students initially required much gentle nudging along the main line learning route. By week four of the first term the majority of the class were fully familiar with the free-format timetable and the potential it offered, and were also becoming aware of their own individual study preferences. The anti-social personalities had also discovered how to manipulate the system to their own advantage! Booking cards were mysteriously moved to unpopular times, and group viewing rooms were often found to have been overbooked in suspicious circumstances.

To alleviate such problems, the booking system was altered to one in which students made their appointments on a clearly marked sheet, on which alterations had to be countersigned by a staff member. Although less informal than the first scheme, this booking system is still in operation and has been found to be much easier to operate, from a day to day running point of view.

The development of the course and the preparation of the material was costly in terms of staff time. Much of the week's work for one lecturer was devoted to preparing three - four hours of pre-recorded material with the supplementary printed sheets, and to co-ordinating the laboratory work and drawing exercises. The initial effort becomes more attractive when viewed in the long term, and the overall staffing levels during the introductory period have still been consistent with previous experience (2) which has shown pre-recorded instruction to be as cost effective as the conventional mode of instruction.

It was unfortunate that, in this first year of operation, the facility for more able students to move quicker along the main line syllabus was somewhat curtailed because the preparation of material was completed on a weekly basis. But this deliberate policy of obtaining feedback before preparing the next week's material was found to be a powerful advantage for the majority of students, although it impeded the progress of a small group of more capable students.

Feedback of any nature (from students and staff alike), — indeed, every problem arising from the use of the learning material — was recorded, weekly in a file which forms the basis of the first amendment to the course.

The practice of regularly maintaining such a file has been found in past experience to be an invaluable tool in improving and updating such courses.

## Formal Feedback

The entire course was introduced to the students in the first week of the session as a learning system, planned to offer them an improved facility for learning. It was therefore clearly necessary to check the effectiveness of the new learning system by evaluating the student's ability to fulfil the stated objectives, and by measuring his reaction to the new learning approach. Data on the former will be incomplete for some time, but a frank feedback was sought from the class group at the end of the first term. They were asked to complete (anonymously) a questionnaire containing 31 questions on a 5-point scale. The class knew that the results would influence the planning of the second term of the course, and that a reaction against any of the features of the provisional free-format scheme would certainly effect a change.

A 100 per cent return of responses was achieved and a very abbreviated summary of the views they expressed is given below, under the headings used in the questionnaire.

### (a)   Group-paced Instruction

The 50-minute packages tended to be about right or rather fast in pace, with the viewing time, if anything, a little short.

The tapes were stopped occasionally in use, usually to make notes but sometimes to clear up problems. It was felt a considerable advantage in learning to be able to stop the instruction.

### (b)   Individual Audio-Tapes (including Remedials)

This material moved at the correct pace and was of a suitable duration. The ability to stop the instruction was warmly welcomed, and was used to repeat parts which were not understood, to make notes or just to 'leave time to think'.

### (c)   Timetabling and Organization

Over 85 per cent had been glad to take part in planning their own study programme, but less than a third of that number would have wished complete freedom to do so. Only seven per cent would have preferred to have had their timetable determined for them.

The first term experiment was thought 'reasonable' (26 per cent), 'promising' (53 per cent), 'very good' (four per cent) though a few found it to be either 'adversely affected by faults' (14 per cent) or a 'complete fiasco' (three per cent). The access to staff for individual tutorial explanations was strongly commended by all but one student.

164

Asked what system they would prefer in the next term, 83 per cent voted for 'the same again', seven per cent for **more** freedom, seven per cent for more firm bookings and three per cent for a detailed timetable.

### (d)   Group-paced versus Individually-paced Instruction

A tendency to favour more extensive use of individually-paced instruction was revealed.  Opinions on the balance between individually-paced and group-paced material showed that whilst 55 per cent would prefer the present balance to remain, 20 per cent felt that **more** individually-paced instruction would be desirable and 20 per cent of the class suggested that **all** material should be individually-paced.

The writers felt considerably encouraged by this response, which also indicated that the quality of sound reproduction was acceptable or better, although the quality of printed supporting sheets was sometimes criticized.  Transparency or slide visuals were felt to be clear, although occasionally elaborate.

It was decided that the second term arrangements would be unchanged in principle, although effort would be directed to improvements suggested by the questionnaire, within the scope of present facilities and equipment.

### Presentation — the Variable Factors

Even within the constraints presented by the equipment and the room allocations available to this Unit, there are a wide range of possible forms of presentation of learning material.  The main variables to be considered, which are listed in Table 1, can each be adjusted to produce a greater or a lesser influence on the study pattern of each student.  These choices will now be discussed separately, although the interactive effects are also significant.

### Pre-recording

At present the Learning Unit uses pre-recorded instruction for the bulk of the remedial and tutorial work and for almost all its 'first teaching'. Although the endlessly repetitive nature of much teaching laboratory work strongly suggests the need to extend the use of pre-recorded instruction, in some form to this field, this has not yet been done.  Nevertheless it would be fair to comment that pre-recorded instruction, in general, is popular and cost-effective (2) and, for that reason only, no other alternative has been thoroughly examined.

### Alternative Study Paths

The writers have not yet seriously considered the possibility that some students might profit from a sequencing of material other than that shown on the flow charts.  But they are conscious of the fact that even a simple

Table 1.    Variable factors involved in choice of presentation

| Extent<br>Factor | LOW ———————————————→ HIGH | | | |
|---|---|---|---|---|
| Pre-<br>recording | Conventional<br>lecture/<br>tutorial<br>course | Partly pre-<br>recorded<br>and partly<br>'live'<br>instruction | Pre-<br>recorded,<br>plus<br>prescribed<br>reading | Completely<br>pre-<br>recorded |
| Alternative<br>Study Paths | Main line<br>+<br>remedial<br>only | Main line<br>+fast/slow<br>options | Several<br>alternative<br>paths | Free choice<br>of study<br>content |
| Self-pacing | Controlled<br>pacing<br>throughout | Seldom<br>able to<br>stop and<br>relisten | Partly<br>individual-<br>partly group-<br>paced | Entirely<br>individually<br>paced |
| Timetabling<br>Freedom | Pre-<br>determined<br>bookings | Free/<br>fixed<br>format<br>blend | Free format<br>with time<br>constraints<br>on packages | Free format<br>with special<br>fast/slow<br>facilities |

50-minute audio-tutorial tape, and its support sheets, can be used by
various students in many different (even bizarre), and apparently profitable, ways.  If this is so, it is also possible that the same freedom might
usefully be given on a larger scale.  Alternative media could also be
offered by using detailed notes or programmed texts.  Whether motivated
by paternalism, autocratic superiority, or simply fear of the consequences
of failure, the writers prefer not to examine this possibility further
meantime — although they recognize its existence.

## Self-Pacing

The students like individually paced materials;  they find it attractive to
make their mistakes and to listen to a repeated explanation in relative
privacy.  They defend the method strongly **in principle**, and would appear
to favour more use to be made of this facility.  One of the writers, at
least, would also regard an individually-paced study system as the ideal
way to listen to pre-recorded learning material.  Another view stresses
the advantages of a blend of self and group pacing, and the desirability
of group study as a preparation for a professional life in which the interaction of personalities is an important aspect.

The writers are fairly content meantime to accept the blend of self and group pacing which has been described, because they suspect it is a reasonable mixture, and an acceptable (and inevitable) compromise in their current situation.

## Timetabling

At this late stage in the paper 'free-format' timetabling will be defined as the learning process in which, subject to the availability of facilities, each student can book for activities in accordance with the flow chart, but otherwise in accordance with his own inclination, preferences and studying ability. There is little in such a system which could be criticized as undesirable, especially if special arrangements can be made for the faster and slower students; there is much to commend the scheme, which has clearly met with the students' approval.

But it would be equally valid to argue that certain learning experiences should be carried out in a **restricted** time period, even if the student is willing to continue to work long hours inefficiently; and restricting the availability of more complex laboratory equipment is often necessary where heavy demand requires effective utilization. Both situations would suggest that some fixed-format commitments in the form of predetermined appointments may be desirable.

## CONCLUSIONS

The case for free-format timetabling is still best described by the Scottish verdict, 'not proven'. The writers, who each admit to having an independent nature, see this as the system under which they themselves would prefer to study. They have had moderate support for this view from a class of undergraduates, who have only known conventional teaching and the alternative reported in this paper. The writers would add to this their view that an educational system which is to prepare the student for intellectual independence should lead him steadily to that state from the outset.

But all this is not to say that free-format timetabling is the best or the only way to achieve effective higher education. There are still grounds for concern that the student may become unduly dependent on the main-line of study predetermined for him by the system. Nevertheless, the work here presented demonstrates that free-format timetabling can be a viable scheme within an allocation of 11 hours per week. This was not obvious beforehand, nor even in the week the scheme was first attempted! To that extent this paper may be useful to other innovators who feel the urge to offer their students greater freedom, yet have hitherto been inhibited by the absence of reported experience of such an arrangement in tertiary education.

REFERENCES

Cowan, J., Morton, J. and Bolton, A. (1973) An experimental learning unit for structural engineering studies. The Structural Engineer 51, (9), 337-9.

Cowan, J., Morton, J. and Bingham, E. (1973) An intermediate assessment of a developing learning unit. In Aspects of Educational Technology VII, (Eds.) Budgett and Leedham. London: Pitman

Cowan, J. (1972) Student reaction to the use of detailed objectives. In Aspects of Educational Technology VI, (Eds.) Austwick and Harris. London: Pitman.

# Decision making in instructional design

B. T. DODD, Admiralty Research Laboratory
R. J. G. LeHUNTE, Inbucon Learning Systems Ltd.
C. SHEPPARD, Admiralty Research Laboratory

**Abstract:** In recent years there has been increasing emphasis on the application of systematic approaches, and the use of formalized analysis techniques, to satisfy instructional needs. However, this development has been severely handicapped by the fact that the instructional design process itself has not yet been adequately analysed. While some of the practices and techniques are well established, there is a lack of definition of the decision-making structure in instructional design.

This paper describes a research project currently being undertaken by the Admiralty Research Laboratory (Applied Psychology Unit) in conjunction with Inbucon Learning Systems Ltd., to define the relationships between analysis and instruction — the decisions which have to be made, the criteria for decisions, and the rules on which decisions are based. A system has been developed which provides recommendations for some fifty necessary decisions in instructional design. The scale and complexity of the decision making structure has necessitated the use of a computer to process data.

One of the principle long term aims of this project is to provide operational support for instructional designers and evaluators. The designer can feed input data concerning the activities to be learned, the learners, and any constraints on the design of instruction, into a computer terminal, and he will receive a print-out of recommendations. During the project a manual version of the system will also be produced.

## INTRODUCTION

A technology can be said to exist if there is an organized body of know-ledge which is useful to those who are engaged in some practical endeavour in the fields of education and training. In instructional design there is a large body of knowledge available, and there are a number of established practices and techniques. However, we question whether this knowledge constitutes a technology, since it provides hardly any contribution to the decision-making structure in instructional design.

In their report <u>Programmed Instruction in the British Armed Forces</u> (1966), Wallis, Duncan and Knight commented:

'The intensive research on P.I. and its many fields of application has given rise recently to the wider concept of a "technology of training". Some of the component tools of this technology are already well developed. Others are primitive by comparison. We have noted that an adequate realization of the concept entails a taxonomy of training tasks or objectives, and a classification of training techniques, each of them founded upon an acceptable psychological basis. Neither exists at the present time, however, and their construction presents an immediate research requirement.'

This paper describes a research project currently being undertaken by the Admiralty Research Laboratory (Applied Psychology Unit) in conjunction with Inbucon Learning Systems Limited. The aim of this project is to define the relationships between analysis and instruction — encompassing not only the selection of training techniques, but all decisions made in the instructional design process. The basic premise of the project is that the ability to design instructional systems (making best use of human and other resources) is at root a rational activity, so there must be at least one algorithm which expresses this.

In order to define a decision making structure we have adopted the following approach :

(1) Define decisions made in instructional design;

(2) Establish those criteria which influence decisions, including task features, learner characteristics and practical constraints;

(3) Develop rules to link input criteria with recommendations.

A system has been established providing recommendations for some 50 instructional design decisions. The scale and complexity of the decision-making structure has necessitated the use of a computer to process data.

A literature search has been carried out throughout the project. This has revealed that there are many systems of classification in existence for examining task features or ability requirements, and the American Institute for Research project on The Development of a Taxonomy of Human Performance, under Fleishman, provides a great deal of fundamental material towards this end. However, most such classification systems are 'open-ended', without following through to instructional design decisions. There are very few published papers which explicitly recommend algorithms for one or more instructional design decisions, although Davies (1969), and the ITRU publication on CRAMP provide processes for selecting instruction methods on the basis of the task to be learned.

DEFINING INSTRUCTIONAL DESIGN DECISIONS

Many schematic diagrams of the instructional design process have been produced. Their common feature is to show the process as a series, or

170

cycle of neat discrete stages, albeit with feedback between some of the stages. In practice the process consists of a succession of approximations, starting with a gross declaration of intent, and moving through to a precise definition of the instruction requirement.

One fundamental feature which the schematics do not illustrate is that there is a large number of decisions in instructional design. Consider, for the first two stages alone of a schematic, that there are over ten decisions to be made (Figure 1).

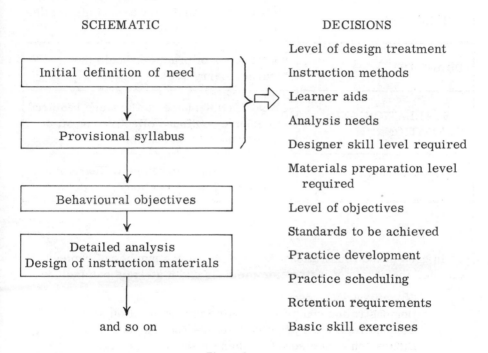

SCHEMATIC

DECISIONS

Initial definition of need

Provisional syllabus

Behavioural objectives

Detailed analysis
Design of instruction materials

and so on

Level of design treatment

Instruction methods

Learner aids

Analysis needs

Designer skill level required

Materials preparation level
   required

Level of objectives

Standards to be achieved

Practice development

Practice scheduling

Retention requirements

Basic skill exercises

Figure 1

In all there are some fifty instructional design decisions. The majority of these decisions are made by the designer, but some may be made by the customer, the designer's supervisor, or the instructor. For example, the decision on instructor : learner ratio is often predetermined to comply with administrative requirements, irrespective of what is desirable for a particular activity to be learned, or a particular type of learner.

Figure 2 shows the main categories of decisions, with illustrations:

171

| DECISION CATEGORY | ILLUSTRATIONS |
|---|---|
| INSTRUCTION OUTPUT | What level of objective action should be achieved through instruction? |
| DESIGN | What depth of design treatment should be undertaken? |
| INSTRUCTION | What instruction methods and materials best meet the need? |
| PRACTICE | What types of practice should the learner carry out? |
| INSTALLATION AND OPERATION | What 'maintenance' actions are required to ensure continued effective operation of the instruction scheme? |
| ORGANIZATION | What is the preferred staff : learner ratio for this instruction? |

Figure 2

In each of the illustrations the designer has a number of choices. For example, the choice of instruction methods and materials can include :

> Objectives with resource access
> Demonstration and practice with learner question sheet
> Demonstration and practice with instruction plan
> Discussion with discussion pointer sheet
> Self-study, information sheets
> Self-study, programmed instruction
> Coaching
> Exposure
> Controlled exposure
> Graduated exercises
> Lecture with guide notes
> Objectives only (conduct of session left to instructor).

This set of choices, together with the choice of practice methods and presentation media, gives a large number of possible permutations. In view of the large choice, and the fact that designers base most of their decisions on 'experience', there is a high risk of poor selection. This risk is compounded by the fact that the person commissioning or attempting to evaluate the instruction scheme may have no reliable yard-sticks with which to assess the suitability of choice.

CRITERIA FOR DECISIONS

Instructional design decisions are based on three types of input factor — task features, learner characteristics, and practical constraints.

During the research project a set of those tasks features which contribute to design decisions has been developed. The initial classification has been based on a study of seaman tasks, and expanded to suit a wider range of task types. Task features include :

**Nature of task:** A short descriptive label, discriminating between body action, hand task, hand tool task, equipment task, symbolic rote task, symbolic task-rules application, etc. This group of descriptions will be expanded to accommodate the widest possible range of activities to be learned.

**Shape of behaviour pattern:** Recognition of the predominant pattern of behaviour to be learned, including the categories chain, discrimination, chain with discriminations, series of discriminations, pyramid of discriminations, etc. This input includes also particular behaviour features like 'stimulus continuum' and 'undefined stimuli'.

**Cueing and feedback:** Separate ratings of the strength of intrinsic cueing and intrinsic feedback in the task.

**Task size:** An accurate count, or estimate of the number of separate responses in chain behaviours, and different stimuli in discriminations.

**Frequency:** A measure of the frequency of occurrence of the task in the 'post-instruction' situation.

**Situation constraints:** Recognition of any constraints on task performance, such as variable quality of task stimuli, variable quality of environmental stimuli, personal hazard.

**Likely complex elements:** Definition, and difficulty rating, of individual task elements which learners are likely to find difficult, such as high work load, need for extraordinary use of senses, consequence interaction of elements, competing behaviours. This list is still being developed and there is a need to define typical difficult elements as comparators for rating.

**Family grouping:** A cross-referencing activity between tasks under scrutiny, and tasks previously learned, to show groupings of like tasks, like sub-skills, like difficult elements, and like generalized behaviours.

At present, the breakdown of task features possibly includes too much detail, since some of the inputs overlap. Also, some of these inputs call for interpretation (e. g. shape of behaviour pattern) or assessment (e. g. difficulty rating of complex elements). These inputs will be refined when a data bank of processed tasks has been developed, and it will be possible to complete the inputs at different levels of detail.

In addition to task features, input information of learner character-istics and practical constraints will include the characteristics shown in Figure 3.

| LEARNER CHARACTERISTICS | Learner motivation<br>Pre-ability range<br>Learning capability range<br>Self-starting ability<br>Responsibility<br>Literacy |
|---|---|
| PRACTICAL CONSTRAINTS | Design time available<br>Job facilities/funds available<br>Numbers to be trained<br>Stability of task<br>Instructor skill level<br>Learner availability<br>Instructor motivation<br>Instruction time available<br>Skill of instructional designers<br>Intended life of instruction scheme |

Figure 3

For the instructional design practitioner it is the practical constraints which usually prove to be the dominant influence in design decisions. For example, the complexity of a particular task may point to a design approach which includes detailed analysis, but this can be overriden if there is a very tight time constraint on design time.

### Decision Making Rationale

A set of rules (translator) has been defined to link input information with decision outputs.

INPUTS         TRANSLATOR         OUTPUTS

Task features    ⟶    Decision        Instructional
Learner characteristics ⟶   rules    ⟹    design
Practical constraints ⟶                recommendations

Rules can take the following forms :

| IF  A  THEN  X |

If task includes skilled     $\longrightarrow$  then   direct response support
motor perceptual action                    (physical assistance or
with two or more                        simulation to control one
dimensions (variables)                 or more dimensions initially)

If learners' learning     $\longrightarrow$  then   incorporate branching or
capability range is wide                   remedial facility in instruc-
                                               tion scheme

| IF  A  AND  B  THEN  X |

If cueing within task is weak
or nil                          $\longrightarrow$  then   include strong overview
AND total number of elements   11         − verbal linkage

If instruction course not                   'spot' visits to successive
'once off'                   $\longrightarrow$  then   courses for maintenance
AND if instructor motivation low      checks

| IF  A  AND  NOT  B  THEN  X |

If total number of elements $< 6$ $\longrightarrow$  then   instruct in task order
AND not stimulus continuum

If behaviour patter 'MIXED
DISCRIMS & CHAINS'
AND frequency less than weekly
AND not repetitive                 $\rbrace$$\rightarrow$then   use algorithm as job/training
AND not high speed requirement             aid
AND not strong cueing

| ALWAYS  X  UNLESS  A  THEN  Y |

Always                       $\longrightarrow$          instruct to task performance
                                         objective

Unless
No job facilities/funds available $\rightarrow$ then   enabling ('knowing how to')
AND no like facilities available         objective

Member of family group of     $\longrightarrow$  then   instruct to task performance
3 or more like tasks                        objective and inter-task trans-
                                           fer level (ability to perform
                                           like tasks through transfer
                                           plus application of basic prin-
               etc.                           ciples)

IF A THEN X OR Y

| If learner responsibility high | then | apply status reward reinforcer |
| AND learner motivation low $\longrightarrow$ | | or material reward reinforcer |
| AND learner initiative low | | |

If task member of family group $\rightarrow$   then   self-study, information sheets
(like task previously learned)
AND no personal hazard               or exposure
AND no high level ( $>$ 7) complex     or controlled exposure
element

IF A THEN CONSIDER X

If nature of task 'symbolic rote'
AND weak/nil cueing                  then    **consider** mediation
AND total number of elements $>$ 6

If technical skill of instructors
is low
AND task includes high/          then    **consider** using closed loop
medium level motor skill                    film or video

From the outset of the project a search of instructional research and design literature has been carried out to provide data for decision rules. In areas where this search has not yielded information, the decision rules have been derived through formal definition of the actions of a team of skilled instructional designers. For some instructional design decisions there is no 'research' evidence available, and research is either not necessary or not feasible. This is true of many decisions which are influenced directly by practical constraints, such as the decision on the depth of design treatment which should be undertaken in each situation.

Most of the decision rules shown in this paper are relatively simple rules, in terms of the number of input factors affecting each decision. Many of the rules in the complete 'translator' system depend on several input factors, like this decision on the depth of design treatment:

If numbers to be instructed $\leqslant$ 30               Then first level
And life of instruction scheme once off or uncertain    instructional
And technical skill of instructors is high            design only. (train-
And training skill of instructors is high or medium    ing spec. +plan, +
And instructor availability is high                  objectives and
And there is no high level personal hazard         exercises + control
And there are no high level complex elements       system)
And there is no high speed requirement
And trainee availability is not a constraint

## APPLYING THE DECISION RULES

A system has been developed, using a computer, to enable instructional designers to apply the decision rules to tasks they are considering. The stages of operating the system are as follows :

COLLECT & CLASSIFY DATA    Information is collected about each task to be learned, the learners, and any practical constraints. An input form is completed for learner characteristics and constraints, while separate task input forms are completed for each task (or for one task out of each family group).

Some of the information is used in its 'raw' form, but certain factors require classification or assessment:

| | |
|---|---|
| Nature of task | – selecting a label from a given list |
| Shape of behaviour pattern | – identifying the shape in accordance with given definitions |
| Likely complex elements | – assessing the difficulty of elements, using a 1 - 10 scale |
| Learner characteristics | – apply a 3 point scale to each characteristic, to show how pronounced it is |
| Practical constraints | – applying a 3 point scale to each constraint, to indicate its severity. |

INPUT TO COMPUTER    The information on input forms is coded and fed into a computer terminal. The computer applies the decision rules, and prints out recommendations.

INTERPRET COMPUTER OUTPUT    The computer prints out a list, showing one or more recommendations under each decision. Figure 4 shows a typical print out extract :

---

|  |  |
|---|---|
| 2.1   PRACTICE METHOD | |
| TASK PRACTICE | RULE 3 |
| COVERT PRACTICE – MENTAL REHEARSAL | RULE 25 |
|    UNLESS LENGTHY PRACTICE TO PERFORMANCE STD. | |
| | |
| 2.2   PRACTICE DEVELOPMENT | |
| WHOLE TASK PRACTICE ONLY | RULE 32 |
| | 127 |
| | |
| 2.3   PRACTICE QUALITY STANDARDS | |
| END PERFORMANCE QUALITY STD. THROUGHOUT | RULE 35 |

---

Figure 4

The print out states :

**Output recommendation :** in this example the recommended form of practice is practice in the task itself, supported by mental rehearsal.

**Recommendation riders :** some recommendations may carry a qualifying statement, like the 'mental rehearsal' rider above. Riders are included wherever there is a limitation or exception in particular circumstances.

**Rule references :** each recommendation includes code references of the rules used, so that the instructional designer can check the rules if he wishes.

## FUTURE DEVELOPMENT PLANS

The system described in this paper is at an early stage of development. It is currently undergoing 'proving' trials, to assess the recommendations for a number of tasks and different training situations. Proposed future developments include :

### 1. Practical Trials
In proving trials the system will be applied to tasks which selected instructional designers are currently considering (or for which instruction already exists). These trials have two aims :

(i)   to build a 'data bank' of tasks, giving body to the system

(ii)  to assess the value and practicality of the system, identifying skills required to use the system and areas of training need for users.

### 2. Extending System Capability
At present the system can accommodate motor perceptual activities and relatively low level cognitive activities. It requires further development to provide complete sets of recommendations for the broadest possible range of tasks (and possibly for 'subject matters' as well).

### 3. Task Classification Development
Within the system classifications are used for :

> Nature of task
> Shape of behaviour pattern
> Likely complex elements

These classifications require expansion and refinement in order to provide comprehensive coverage.

### 4. Producing a Manual Version of the System
A manual version of the decision-making system will be produced, either in full detail or in simplified form. Recommendations will be made for the use of this information in the training of instructional design staff and evaluators.

178

REFERENCES

Many publications, and personal contributions through discussion have acted as sources for the ideas which are now expressed by the rule set of TRANSLATOR 6 (current version of the system). The following list shows key sources and also indicates those which are currently influencing development of the system.

\* These items describe detailed sub-systems which will be built into TRANSLATOR where the need for finer analysis is established.

\*\* These items indicate ways in which the general methodology may be further developed in future work.

\*\*  Annett, J., Duncan, K.D., Stammers, R.B. and Gray, M.J. (1971) Task Analysis. London: HMSO.

Bernstein, B.R., and Gonzalas, B.K. Learning, Retention and Transfer. Minneapolis: Honeywell Inc.

Bloom, B.S. (Ed.) (1956) Taxonomy of Educational Objectives. New York: David McKay.

Carden, G.R. (1970) An Evaluation of the Effects of Repetition of Written Examples. Texas: A & M Univ. Department of Industrial Training

\*\*  Chambers, A.N. (1969) Development of a Taxonomy of Human Performance — a Heuristic Model for the Development of Classification Systems. Pittsburgh: A.I.R.

Chesler, D.J. (1972) Application and Utilization of Training Aids and Devices. San Diego, California: Naval Personnel and Training Research Laboratory.

Clark, M.C. (1972) Aspects of Transfer that Relate to the Development and Design of Instructional Materials. Arizona State University, Instructional Resources Laboratory.

Davies, I.K. (1969) Structure and strategy — instructional decision-making. RAF School of Education Bulletin, No. 6, pp. 48-54, Autumn 1969.

Dodd, B.T. (1965) Teaching/Learning Strategies. Sheffield University: Programmed Instruction Centre for Industry.

Dunn, T.G. and Hansen, D. (1972) Learning by Graphics. Florida State University: CAI Center.

Engel, J.D. (1970) An approach to standardizing human performance assessment. Humrro Professional Paper, 26-70

\*  Farina, A.J. and Wheaton, G.R. (1971) Development of a Taxonomy of Human Performance — a Task Characteristics Approach to Performance Prediction. Pittsburgh: A.I.R.

\*  Foley, J.F. Jr. (1969) Job Performance Aids Research: Summary and Recommendations. Wright-Patterson AFB: AF Human Resources Laboratory.

Gagne, R.M. (1965) The Conditions of Learning. New York: Holt, Rinehart and Winston.

Gilbert, T.F. (1962) Mathetics: The Technology of Education. Reissued London: Longman

Holt, J. (1964) How Children Fail. London: Pelican.

Hunter, H.G. et al. (1969) The process of developing and improving course content for military technical training. Humrro Technical Report, 69-9.

Jeantheau, G.G. (1971) A Study of Training Device Support Materials. Darien, Conn: Dunlap & Associates

\*\*  Martin, E. (1973) Serial Learning Theory. Michigan University: Ann Arbour Human Performance Center.

Miller, E.E. (1963) A Classification of Learning Tasks in Conventional Language. Aerospace Medical Research Laboratories: TDR-63-74.

179

Miller, R.B. (1971) Development of a Taxonomy of Human Performance — A User-oriented Approach to the Development of Task Taxonomies. Pittsburgh: A.I.R.

Norman, D.A. and Lowes, A.L. (1972) Adaptive Training of Manual Control. Fort Worth, Texas: Naval Training Devices Center.

Pearn, M., Belbin, M. and Toye, M. (1972) CRAMP: A Guide to Training Decisions. Cambridge: Industrial Training Research Unit.

** Resnick, L.B. and Wang, M.C. (1969) Approaches to the Validation of Learning Hierarchies. Pittsburgh University: Learning Research and Development Center.

Seidel et al. (1968) A General Systems Approach to the Development and Maintenance of Optimal Learning Conditions. George Washington University. Professional Paper 1 - 68.

Smith, R.G. (1966) The design of instructional systems. Humrro: Technical Report 66-18.

* Smith, R.L. et al. (1972) Job Behaviour Analysis Manual. Los Angeles: Mentec Corporation.

* Smode, A.F. (1971) Human Factors Inputs to the Training Device Design Process. Darien, Conn: Dunlap & Associates.

Stolurow, L.M. (1964) A Taxonomy of Learning Task Characteristics. Aerospace Medical Research Laboratories: TDR-64-2.

Taylor, C.L. (1972) Response Factors and Selective Attention in Learning from Instruction. Arizona State University: AFHRL.

** Teichner, W.H. (1971) Development of a Taxonomy of Human Performance — an Information-theoretic approach. Pittsburgh: A.I.R.

Wallis, D., Duncan, K.D. and Knight, M.A.G. (1966) Programmed Instruction in the British Armed Forces. London: HMSO.

** Wheaton, G.R. and Mirabella, A. (1972) Effects of Task Index Variations on Training Effectiveness Criteria. Orlando, Florida: Naval Training Equipment Center.

* Yagi, K., Bialeck, H.M., Taylor, J.E. and Garman, M. (1971) The design and evaluation of vocational technical job analysis. Humrro: Technical Report 71-15

# Computer assisted learning in technology

P. J. LAWTON, City of Leicester Polytechnic

**Abstract:** This paper examines the use of desk-top calculators and larger computers in the teaching and study of Electronic and Electrical Engineering fundamentals at undergraduate level in a Polytechnic. Particular emphasis is placed on the communication between the author of a computer program and the user so that the user can effectiveley learn from the program. The paper reviews the available equipment and relates experiences with calculators, batch-processing computer systems and on-line computer systems with graphic facilities. It concludes that calculators and on-line computers with conversational programs are very effective aids to teaching and study.

## INTRODUCTION

One of the latest developments in computer systems is the adaptation of a television screen to display numbers, sentences and drawings (even in colour if you can afford the cost). Yet despite the wonder and power of a computer to undertake a vast amount of arithmetic, make decisions, and produce drawings, the old problem of human communication is still with us. Three aspects of the use of calculators and computers are reported:

(1) the advantages and disadvantages of calculators, and experiences with them;

(2) the experiences of using a batch-processing computer system;

(3) the experiences of introducing an on-line conversational computer system.

The equipment in use at the present time is as follows :

Calculators:  a.  to add, subtract, divide and multiply;

b.  as above plus trigometric, logarithms, square root, power, and inverse functions;

c.  as above plus vector algebra and 80 step memory.

Computers:    a.  desk-top with teleprinter;

b.  floor-standing with teleprinters, visual display unit
(television-type screen), discs, graph plotter;

c.  many cubicles, discs, line-printer.

1.  The advantages and disadvantages of calculators are listed as follows:

**Advantages**

- The ability to undertake a vast amount of standard arithmetic which is normally not attempted due to the lack of time.

- The calculator is not as tiring to use as a slide rule and trigometric tables.

- The decimal point is correctly placed.

- The availability of standard routines is essential to Electrical Engineers (e.g. square root, logarithms, $x^Y$, vector algebra).

- Communication via push buttons is normally self-explanatory.

- Standard routines are available to eliminate laborious numerical work thus leaving more time to consider the principles being studied.

**Disadvantages**

- More expensive than slide rule and trigometric tables.

- Standard arithmetic is not mentally practised.

- The arithmetic may not even be understood.

- The solution is often quoted with an excessive number of figures by the user.

- Maintenance is necessary.

- They may be stolen.

The calculators in use are securely fixed to laboratory benches and are available for use whilst the college is open.  Students are often queuing to use them and experience no difficulties in understanding the operation of the labelled push buttons.

## 2. BATCH-PROCESSING COMPUTER SYSTEM

The students use one of the Polytechnic's computers for batch-processing the longer and larger numerical equations using standard programs. Communication with the computer is by punched cards, and with the students is by the written work attempting to describe the application of particular programs and how to use them.  The user of a standard program has to punch cards with the appropriate numerical values, hand these in to the computer centre and wait a day for the results.

Many problems were experienced initially, particularly with the correct punching of data on 80-column cards using the correct format. Eventually a scheme has evolved employing one number per card anywhere in the first twelve columns along with the decimal point. A very serious problem was the delay in obtaining results, especially when the results were not appropriate due to an error in the numerical data. This delay was more serious when programs were being developed as it slowed down the progress of the development. Nowadays, with the reduction in size and cost of computers, the batch-processing of most programs in a single, physically larger computer is unnecessary as a few desk-top computers can be used in an immediate conversational mode.

## 3. ON-LINE CONVERSATIONAL SYSTEMS

The communication with the computer is by means of a typewriter keyboard, and communication with the user is by means of the written word (in fact, sentences) displayed on paper via a teleprinter or via a television screen, both under the control of the computer. The availability of this type of computer system can change the method of teaching and learning. The system can be similar to a programmed learning book with the advantage of immediate evaluation of numerical examples.

An example of teaching program is for Transmission Line Theory. The initial study is undertaken in the classroom where the physical characteristics of electrical conductors are discussed and the formulae developed. The arithmetic involved in the formulae is very laborious, and one hour's work can be done on the computer in one second with **no** mistakes. Thus the program attempts to reinforce the basic features and formulae by restating them at the appropriate stage in the calculations. The students appear to read the statements about names, formulae and features of the transmission line as well as replying, with numbers, to the request for data. The conversation is one-sided, and once started is dictated by the computer.

As well as teaching programs there are lists of standard arithmetic programs (Appendix 1). Again, the communication is via the keyboard and a typical sequence of operations is as follows :

- User selects desired arithmetic from the list

- Types RUN 400 for example

- Operates the RE-TURN key

- Reads the resulting instructions on the paper or screen

- Types the numerical replies

Obtains the desired evaluation and alternatives.

These arithmetic programs are greatly valued by staff and students, especially the permanent paper record of the calculation. The communication via the printed instruction is successful with the majority of users, whilst the speed of calculating enables a range of numbers to be tried out and thus a greater insight to be achieved.

As well as teaching programs and standard arithmetic programs there are interactive design programs with graphics. Very often the operation of a particular piece of equipment is illustrated by a diagram or graph. The appropriate diagram can be displayed on the visual display unit and a permanent copy obtained by means of a direct photograph or copier, or by an X Y plotter as in Figure 1.

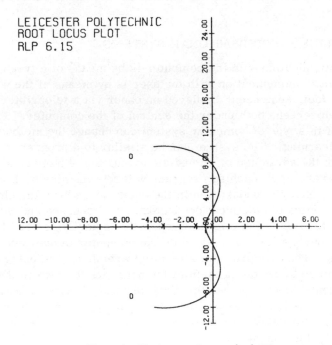

Figure 1. Hardcopy using graph plotter

An example of this type of program is for the design of amplifiers with feedback. During the design stage a single number within a range of numbers might be amended a few times and the effect of the amendment on the appropriate diagram displayed on the screen. These design programs are very useful for teaching purposes as they are attractive to the students and enable the students' numerical suggestions to be immediately tried out.

# CONCLUSIONS

(a)  The teaching and study of the theory of Electronic and Electrical Engineering is easier, more thorough, and more attractive when an on-line conversational computer system is available.

(b)  The use of statements and questions in English (not computer jargon) via the teleprinter or screen ensures that all the necessary numerical values are thought about and obtained.

(c)  The very fast correct evaluation of the formulae enables time to be spent thinking about the meaning of the results.

By restating the basic principles of the theory and restating the formulae, the communication and learning process commenced in the lecture theatre is continued at the computer terminal, provided the statements on the screen are read.  We have already found that after a while the user does become familiar with the statements and tends to read only those which request the typing of a number, which has to be done in order to proceed.  It is planned to undertake tests to determine if any learning of the theory and formulae takes place.

(N.B.  Further details of the program for Transmission Line Theory, and of the options of a typical design program, may be sought from the author.)

## APPENDIX I

### BASIC ARITHMETIC FOR ELECTRICAL ENGINEERS

**List of available programs**

| | |
|---|---|
| RUN 1 | For users own temporary program, statements 2 to 99 ONLY   (See note 1) |
| RUN 100 | Evaluation loop for users own numerical expression (X) (See note 1) |
| RUN 200 | Rectangular to Polar Co-ordinates |
| RUN 300 | Polar to Rectangular Co-ordinates |
| RUN 400 | Complex Division (Rectangular) |
| RUN 500 | Complex Multiplication (Rectangular) |
| RUN 600 | Complex Division (Polar) |
| RUN 700 | Complex Multiplication (Polar) |
| RUN 800 | Impedances in parallel |
| RUN 900 | Impedances in parallel with tolerancies |
| RUN 1000 | Impedance to Admittance |
| RUN 1100 | Admittance to Impedances |
| RUN 1200 | Star to Delta transform |
| RUN 1300 | Delta to Star transform |
| RUN 1400 | Exponential rise or decay $K * (1 + EXP(-t/T))$ or $K * EXP(-t/T)$ |
| RUN 1500 | Resistance, Inductance and Capacitance to Impedance with variable Frequency. |

# Computerized devices for student control: concept learning and heuristic thinking

J. P. DENIS, J. LOMBAERDE, Catholic University of Louvain

**Abstract:** The general purpose of student control by a computerized questionnaire is the evaluation of his concept learning. It is part of a general educational system IMAGO using several media.

First, a general taxonomy of educational objectives is proposed. Then, the computerized questionnaire device is designed: a main sequence of questions the student gets if he always answers correctly, with some branching loops at main questions. The evaluative design attached to an existing questionnaire is considered, and a content analysis of the instructional block preceding the student control performed. For each main item of the questionnaire, the correct problem-solving process is analysed at a pragmatical level. This defines the necessary content/aptitude objectives controlled by the question. So, it becomes possible to give an interpretation in terms of objectives of the path followed by the student. Next the control effectiveness is looked upon and some experimental results mentioned.

Another aspect of the teaching-learning process is heuristic thinking control. This control is closely related to the very act by which the student has access to knowledge. Computer simulation programs, laboratory, manipulations and team work allow learning via guided discovery, and permit greater self-regulation of the student's activity.

When a system has a purpose, a control system (or pilot) is needed to manage, for example, the application of the method, measurement of its effects, comparison with the objectives set up, and the use of this information to improve the method. Two dimensions of a control are particularly important. First, there is the accuracy of the stated objectives and their measurement. This corresponds to the amount of information delivered. Second, there is the use of that information in the improvement of the method for better achievement of the stated objectives. This second dimension is related to the control effectiveness. In addition, there is a third dimension, equally important: the meaning of the stated objectives and their measurement, versus the real purpose of the system. This is the model-building problem which is inherent to each theory.

Let us consider a student who is learning, as a system to be managed. This learner becomes part of an educational system designed and managed by different human beings and by their programs. The learning objectives are stated and a control device is designed. This device is the computerized questionnaire described in this paper.

THE COMPUTERIZED QUESTIONNAIRE

## 1. A General Taxonomy of Educational Objectives

The educational objectives of an instructional system can be classified into :

(a) motivation
(b) knowledge
(c) mental aptitudes: comprehension
application
analysis
synthesis
evaluation
(d) behaviour: task adaptation
critical attitude
communication          (References 1, 2, 3)

This taxonomy is far from being exhaustive and/or mutually exclusive: for example, creativity (4) and expression* aptitudes (5) do not appear in it. At the pragmatical** level of human thinking, it is possible to build a complete taxonomy of human aptitudes (6).

## 2. A Computerized Control Device

The computerized control device discussed here is a questionnaire (7), which the student works through before taking the next instructional module in the sequence. The IMAGO method (Multi-media Computer-Assisted and Computer-Managed Instruction) gives a detailed sequence as in Figure 1.

For some IMAGO courses, there are also remedial programs (8), several for each instructional module content, also creativity stimulation programs (4), and the simulation programs discussed later in this paper.

The computerized questionnaire has a sequence of principal questions 1... N, and at each principal question there may be a series of sub-

---

* Expression aptitude corresponds to being able to utilize several forms of language (formal language, graphical language etc...) and to articulate them.

** Pragmatics considers explicitly the user of a language (which is here human thinking). This is not the case in semantics.

MEDIA                          SEQUENCE

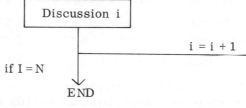

Group meeting with assistant          Introduction

(Small film on TV)              Motivational
                                  block i

Textbook + tape                 Instructional
(+ assistant + slides...)         module i

                                                NO    i = i

Computer (+ assistant)          Questionnaire
                                      i

                                              YES

Group meeting with assistant      Discussion i

                                              i = i + 1

              if I = N

                              END

Figure 1

questions. The student who always answers correctly only goes through
the principal sequence. If he makes an error at a principal question, he
gets one or several subquestions before returning to the principal
sequence (Figure 2).

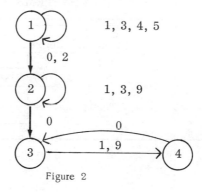

Figure 2

After each response (numerical, alphabetical or formula), the computer
gives some commentary.

189

The structure of the questionnaire makes it impossible to test a whole range of educational objectives. The taxonomy proposed in paragraph 1 above is reduced to:

(a) –
(b) knowledge
(c) mental aptitudes: comprehension
application
analysis
synthesis
–

(d) –

By means of an explicit model of human thinking (in this paper a pragmatical model (6) is used), it is possible to give these elements a precise meaning in terms of content and human aptitudes (see paragraph 3.3).

### 3. Student Control by a Computerized Questionnaire

For the purposes of this paper we shall deal with the analysis of an existing questionnaire (ANSY/2) used in  An Introduction to Systems Analysis.

3.1 Content analysis of the instructional block:

In the instructional block preceding the computerized control two kinds of concepts have to be distinguished: the prerequisite concepts (introduced in previous blocks) and the new concepts (introduced in the present block). Figure 3 shows this distinction for the course element preceding ANSY/2, and Figure 4 shows the schematic structure of the systems analysis concept that the student should learn.

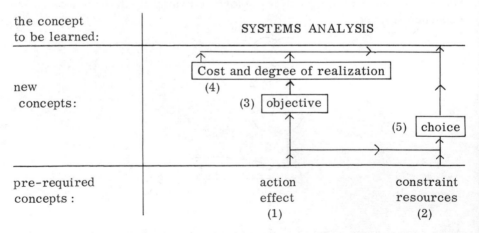

Figure 3

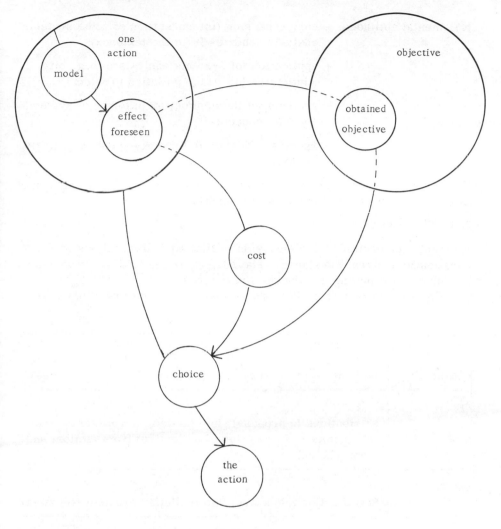

Figure 4

## 3.2 Construction of the taxonomy:

All the new concepts in the content analysis interact as the concept to be learned. These interactions call for certain aptitudes within the learner; and therefore, it is possible to state objectives relating to the new concepts that the questionnaire should control. If we use the reduced taxonomy (above), an example related to the concept Systems Analysis would be:

(a) —

(b) knowledge: (the name of the Systems Analysis concept);

(c)  mental aptitudes: — comprehension (interpretation of some systems analysis schemes from the textbook);

 — application (of systems analysis to e.g. city administration or the pollution problem);

 — analysis (of the application in terms of systems analysis concepts);

 — synthesis (design of a case in systems analysis terms).

Similar taxonomies can be built concerning each new concept.  They are in fact sub objectives of the above taxonomy.

3.3.  The evaluative design:

As mentioned earlier, this discussion is limited to the analysis of a questionnaire already designed.  The purpose of the analysis is to design a method of evaluating the student's responses.

Content analysis of ANSY/2 showed five main concepts (Figure 5).

| Concept / Question | pre-required | | | new | |
|---|---|---|---|---|---|
| | 1 (action) | 2 (resource) | 3 (objective) | 4 (cost) | 5 (choice) |
| Q1 | ! | – | ? | – | ! |
| | Attributions (a proposal) into (action), (proposal choice) into (choice);  Production of (objective) from (action) and from (choice) | | | | |
| Q2 | ! | – | ? | – | ! |
| | Specification (objective) into (pollution problem objective) | | | | |
| Q3 | ! | (') | ! | ' | ? |
| | Production of (cost) from (action) and (choice) | | | | |
| Q4 | ! | (?) | ! | ? | ! |
| | Knowledge of (cost) | | | | |

Figure 5

In each item of the questionnaire, some of these concepts relate to the statement of the question (this is indicated by the symbol !), some refer to an aspect of its solution (?), some are necessary in the problem-solving process ('), and other are not relevant (-).

Looking at the ideal problem-solving process (although only at a pragmatical level), it is possible to attach an evaluation objective to each question. The correct resolution of question 1, for example, gives the graph shown in Figure 6.

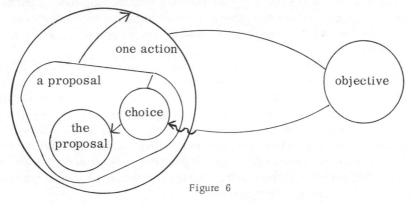

Figure 6

In addition to an awareness of the different concepts (objective) and (choice), the student should be able to grasp their implications: thus each concept (a proposal) implies a concept (action). Then, the concept (action) should produce the concept (choice) by means of the concept (objective), just as learned from the instructional block. The question 1 thus controls the attributions (a proposal) $\subset$ (one action) and (proposal choice) $\subset$ (choice), the structure production (choice) = {objective} (one action) and the concept formation of (objective).

At each question, different answers are analysed by the computer questionnaire program. The format above shows the relationship between the right answer and some necessary content/aptitude-objectives attained by the student. If the answer is not right, these objectives are only attained to a certain extent. One purpose of a branching loop at the principal question is the measurement of this extent. By a more precise analysis of the problem-solving process, it should be possible to define a better value structure for objective achievement than the 1-0 (yes-no) structure exemplified here. The path the student follows in the question-naire can be characterized and evaluated by a sequence {Q1/3, 0); (Q2/1, 0); (Q3/1, 04, 0)} . This sequence then gives a path interpretation in terms of objectives. For example: 'The student knows the systems analysis concepts quite well: he is able to produce and to specify an objective concept from a described situation, but is not able to produce the cost concept'. In fact, the reduced taxonomy may be used here. It is the opinion of the author, however, that at the technique's present state of development there is some danger of misinterpretation in doing this.

## 4. Some Experimental Results

One evaluative study (9) on the questionnaire 'Definite Integrals' shows particularly high success rate: number of students who succeed at a principal question after having gone through a branching loop/number of students going into the branching loop, is higher than 85 per cent. Other important features such as transfer, retention etc... are not yet under study.

Students using the multi-media system learn more quickly. Thirty hour's attendance at the multi-media course were sufficient to produce at the end of the year, a 95 per cent achievement rate in a subject; this would have taken sixty hours by the lecturing system (7). In being a device quite independent of a teacher's competence and reliability, the computerized questionnaire has high reliability. Experimental data relating to several courses have given positive indication of the accuracy and effectiveness of the control device, in terms of single questions as well as the whole questionnaire.

HEURISTIC THINKING

The second part of this paper concerns the teaching/learning of the specific steps to be followed in scientific disciplines — particularly in the experimental sciences: the method used is the modelling approach. Building a model (i. e. the assumed structure of physical reality in, for example, experimental physics) is a fundamental activity in establishing scientific knowledge. Students are instructed in the modelling approach via several learning conditions: practical laboratory applications, simulation programmes and teamwork techniques. The practical applications provide a precise idea of physical reality underlying the concepts; simulation programmes are designed to extend the experimental work, and are useful in the building of a model; teamwork allows the student to acquire an adequate scientific language with which to express the results of experiments, and also permits the team to evaluate the various instructional methods.

### Simulation programmes

In particular we analyse the design and effectiveness of simulation programmes. In physics, simulation programmes must give the best possible impression of reality, and are therefore to be distinguished from a computation programme in the usual sense.

A particular simulation refers to the traction of a steel wire. The candidate selects from four materials and defines their parameters (length of the wire, diameter). To each selected steel wire he systematically applies a weight. The programme gives him the appropriate elongation of the wire. Simulation allows the candidate to go through

194

the different phases of the phenomenon of deformation after traction of a steel wire: elastic deformation (deterministic phenomenon), plastic deformation, breaking of the wire (stochastic phenomenon). There are two ways to become aware of the passage from the elastic deformation phase to the plastic deformation phase: elongation of the wire is no longer proportionate to the weight, and the wire keeps a permanent elongation.

Simulation programmes at present used in Physics cover the following fields: deformation of solids (trials of traction and compression on metal and stone materials, hydrodynamics, and the properties of gases, perfect and imperfect. These programmes have been in use in Physics instruction at the University of Louvain for two years and aim at the acquisition of a modelling approach by the students in the two first grades. The learning conditions used seem effective in enabling the student to build a model of the physical reality under study, and to determine the degree to which the model under construction fits the actual data.

## CONCLUSIONS

1. A conventional approach grounded on guided discovery is largely superior to classic teaching in so far as the student takes a more active part in the development of the course itself. In the new system, the student is led to clearly distinguish:

- the content he has to acquire
- the approach through which he can reach this content
- the guiding maxims relating to the hierarchy and structure of the acquired knowledge.

It emerges that competence acquired in the framework of such a learning process is more permanent and irreversible than competence resulting from classic teaching.

However, teaching through guided discovery assumes the possibility of access, at any time, to vast experimental resources, and it is difficult in practice for timetabling and economic reasons. Computer assisted simulation lessens these problems, enabling the student to have straight access to an experimental universe practically unlimited and extraordinarily meaningful.

2. Participation by teachers in a team gives students the opportunity to find out how a physicist works, and this is essential to his acquisition of the correct approach to the discipline. In particular, the students have become aware of the fact that, although physical effects are numerous, the number of approaches to their discovery are in fact fairly limited. After two lessons in the modelling approach towards physics, the students easily apply these approaches by analogy to phenomena with similar

characteristics. The process saves time and effort, and notably accelerates learning.

3. The very fact that the students are compelled to put across their own discoveries to others, leads them to realize the fundamental importance of an adequate language for the transmission of any scientific result. In classic education, the skills of expression have often been overlooked. The experience acquaints the student, through exercise, with the following problems in the communication of a science:

- on the one hand, with a language other than their natural language though appropriate to modelling processes and to formal scientific operations

- on the other hand, with the skills of communicating their discoveries to others in an explicit form.

(N.B. Appendix material giving further details of the systems analysis and steel traction programs discussed in this paper may be sought from the authors.)

REFERENCES

1. Jones, A. (1972) Multi-media Computer-Assisted and Computer-Managed Instruction. CECD, Tech. Rep. CERI/CT/72.01.

2. De Landsheere, G. (1971) Evaluation Continué et Examens, Précis de Docimologie. Bruxelles, Belgium: Ed. Labor.

3. Denis, J.P. et Martegani, A. (1973) Expérience d'enseignement par découverte guidée. Supports: la simulation par ordinateur et le travail de groupe. Revue Francaise de Pédagogie, No. 23, 48-56.

4. Kaufmann, A., Cools, M. et Dubois, Th. (1973) Stimulation inventive dans un dialogue homme-machine utilisant la méthode des morphologies. IDP-6, Imago Centre, University of Louvain, Belgium.

5. Denis, J.P. (1974) Les systèmes d'enseignement-apprentissage en physique. Imago Centre, University of Louvain, Belgium. (in press)

6. Lombaerde, J. and Jones, A. (1973) A Human Operator Theory: The Pragmatical Model. IDP-4, Imago Centre, University of Louvain, Belgium.

7. Jones, A. (1973) Instructional applications of the computer at the University of Louvain. Int. J. Man-Machine Studies 5, 397-420

8. Centre Imago (1973) La Méthode Imago: Rapport des Journées Mathématiques de Malonne. Imago Centre, University of Louvain, Belgium. (in press)

9. Peteau, M., Cools, M., Dubois, Th. and Jones, A. (1972) Construction de Questionnaires de Contrôle par Ordinateur, basée sur l'étude logique des concepts. IDP-1, Imago Centre, University of Louvain, Belgium.

# Assessment systems and student learning

C. J. BYRNE, The Open University

**Abstract:** The characteristics and influences of many particular student assessment procedures have been studied and there is a large literature on test construction. But apparently there has been little formal theorizing about or investigation of **assessment systems**, i.e., the systematic use of sets of assignments and tests during courses, and their effects on student learning. Yet it would seem that assessment systems play a major part in controlling students' expectations, attitudes, study habits and what is learned. Contrast, for example, how students in a traditional university course might differ in these respects from those in a Keller Plan course.

The paper is essentially a plea for attention to be shifted from individual methods of assessment to total assessment systems. Primary attention is given to summative systems. The **index** is one means of representing the results of summative assessment but an alternative and possibly better way is by means of a **profile**. Both are discussed. The 'continuous assessment' of student learning (i.e., summative assessment systems which span the duration of a course) raises a number of problems in connection with the validity of the results to which these methods give rise. Several alternative procedures are analysed having regard for the nature of the subject matter being learned. Finally, two basic reasons are suggested for the increasingly widespread use of continuous assessment and four important points to be kept in mind in the design of assessment systems are listed.

All of those who are concerned with the design of courses of study must necessarily be involved with the assessment of student learning. But research has focused our attention upon particular aspects of assessment and not upon the assessment system as a whole. Today, however, most carefully designed courses have many assessments and the question naturally arises as to how these should be assembled into a system which functions to desired ends.

Matters of assessment must ultimately come to grips with questions regarding knowledge and the curriculum. But such considerations tend to be space-devouring and, important as they are, they must await a more detailed analysis than this. However, I believe that most of the analysis of assessment systems which I give below is relevant to a wide range of conceptions of knowledge and of curricula (i.e., teaching strategies) which find favour in higher education today. The present paper is essentially an attempt to clarify what I believe to be a topic deserving attention in the hope that others may see fit to conduct theoretical and empirical studies into assessment systems and their relationship to student learning.

## Assessment and Informal Appraisal

The term **assessment** may be used in at least three senses: it may refer to the process by which a student's learning of something is judged to approach a criterion or a set of criteria; to an instrument or procedure used in such a process; or to the result of such a process.

The process of assessment is of two kinds: **formative assessment**, which facilitates the teaching-learning process and that only; and **summative assessment** which, at the end of a course (or program), yields a final appraisal of the student's learning with respect to the course (or program) aims. In practice, therefore, two sub-systems operate in a course: a **formative sub-system** which must necessarily function throughout the duration of the course: and a **summative sub-system** which in part, at least, must necessarily function at the end of the course.

The distinction between the process of formative assessment and that of the informal appraisal of students' learning as it occurs in most interactions between a teacher and his or her students may be regarded as one of degree rather than of kind. A sufficiently able and experienced teacher with sufficiently few students to keep track of might be able to dispense with formative assessment procedures of a formal kind and manage quite successfully on informal appraisals alone. However, as long as we do not possess powerful theories of teaching to enable us to know in advance that our teaching procedures will attain their ends, then appraisal or assessment of some form must accompany the teaching-learning process to ensure that its accomplishments are as desired. And as there are increases in the number of students in a course and in the complexity of what is to be learned, there is also a corresponding increase in the need for assessments of a 'formal' and systematic kind so that both student and teacher can play their respective roles most effectively and efficiently. Of course, we might choose to restrict our talk of formative assessment to those assessments which form a part of a system all the principal features of which can be communicated to the student at the beginning of a course. If so, then we would regard informal appraisal as distinct from formative assessment.

## The Summative Assessment System

The function of the summative assessment system (or sub-system) is to yield a final statement for each student upon completion of a course of study as to what has been learned and how well it has been learned. Such a statement is for use externally to the course and primarily for persons other than the student. For example, the information is required by employers who wish to ensure that their candidates for employment have knowledge appropriate in kind and degree. The award of places in further education and of grants and scholarships are invariably dependent on such information. And within an educational institution, the results of summative assessment enable decisions to be taken as to what subsequent courses a student might most profitably enrol in.

## The Results of Summative Assessment

Upon completion of a program of study in higher education a student invariably has his summative assessment results expressed as a single entity, e.g., as a PASS or FAIL, a class I, II or III, a grade or a grade point average. Moreover, this usually sets the pattern for the component courses of the program.

Such results often have significance on little more than some general good-bad dimension. But it is desirable that they should be capable of a stronger interpretation. A prerequisite for this is a reasonably clear conception and specification of what is to be learned. Given this, however, in what ways can the results of assessment be presented and what interpretations can be made from them? This leads us to examine two concepts the **index** and **profile**.

THE INDEX

The single score (or other entity) which is conventionally used is nearly always an **index** of over-all attainment built from a number of subscores. In the better cases, the index is a weighted sum of subscores where each subscore is known to be unidimensional and where there is some rationale for the weights which are chosen. The rationale is a problem, however. Ideally, we would like the weights to be chosen so that the resulting index correlates highly with an external criterion with which we are concerned. Unfortunately, not only is it difficult in practice to obtain and use a satisfactory external criterion but there are usually many different ones which might be chosen. And this leads to further problems.

As an example, let us suppose that the overall index is built from scores on five dimensions. A decision as to who shall be employed for two jobs may best be made on dimensions one and two for one job but on dimensions three, four and five for the other job. In other words, selection for one job may require an index built quite differently from one which is to be used for selection to another job. And if these indices are lowly correlated, one would be practically useless as a substitute for the other. If such situations were common there could be little doubt that any particular index would be of little value for most purposes. But it is far from certain that such situations are common. It would seem more likely that the majority of decisions would make use of all dimensions but would merely weight them somewhat differently.  If this were so, a suitably chosen index might prove to be reasonably satisfactory for a fairly wide range of decisions.  But this requires investigation.

It should be noted that an index is most clearly satisfactory for those students who score near its extremes.  For example, we can infer from a very high value of an index that a student has performed well on all the dimensions which compose it.  But as we move away from the extremes, the index merely camouflages — for good or bad — the very many variations between students.  Thus, a student who comfortably obtains a traditional first class honours degree in an English university may be assumed to display high ability in all major areas of his studies whereas the many students who obtain lower seconds can be expected to display diverse abilities.  The question as to whether this diversity in the abilities of the latter group is relevant in decision-making calls for an answer.

### The Profile

Whether or not the use of a particular index is satisfactory, the question naturally arises as to whether its defects can be side-stepped by simply assessing the student on each of the more important dimensions from which the index is derived and providing the decision maker with this more detailed information.  The decision maker is then free to select for special attention those dimensions which he has good reason to believe are of primary importance for the decisions which must be made.  Such a set of dimension scores is called a **profile**.

A profile may, or may not, be appropriate for a single course. It would appear that whatever is the conception of knowledge which underlies the course design, what is learned may be either a set of relatively independent parts or a set of inter-dependent parts.  For example, an introductory social science course may be largely concerned with teaching basic concepts and theories. But if there should be a section of it devoted to statistics then the two sections are likely to be largely independent of each other both conceptually and in the kinds of intellectual processes which are drawn upon.  This would be confirmed if correlations between students' performances on a test of this section of the course with their performances on a test of the other section were low.  A case like this would be ideal for the use of a profile of two dimensions, one reflecting a knowledge of social science concepts and theories and the other an ability with statistics.  Yet as we all know, the assessment results on courses of this type nearly always consist of a single score or grade which, far from illuminating most students' strengths and weaknesses, merely camouflages them.  A physics course might consist of separate sections on light, heat and electricity.  If so, then a three dimensional profile would seem to be the most natural way of preserving the information contained in the summative assessments.  Of course, if it could be shown that students' performances on assessments of the separate sections were highly intercorrelated, the use of a composite score or grade would then be justified.  Of if an index based upon the three scores could be justified as widely satisfactory, then it might be deemed preferable to the separate scores.

In both of the above examples, it might be argued that profiles are necessary only because what is administratively a single course is really several courses.  This is true.  But the dimensions of profiles may correspond to aspects of learning which most naturally occur together.  For example, a social science course may be assessed with respect to the following dimensions:

(a)  knowledge of basic concepts, theorics, etc;

(b)  ability to synthesize, to show originality and display insight into the development and use of social science knowledge;

(c)  ability to communicate with clarity complex ideas and procedures in writing;

(d)  ability to plan and execute social science investigations including the collection of data;

(e)  statistical ability.

But these are commonly taught together in a single course.

In the foregoing, I have emphasized the need to have regard for the separate dimensions which underlie assessed knowledge.  In the first two examples, there was a very obvious and practical basis for setting up dimensions.  In the third example, the choice of conceptually distinct dimensions shows more the influence of the psychometric approach.  But in all cases, a set of dimensions may be found to be far from independent statistically, in which case there would be a need to decide whether all of them were justified.

## The Use of Summative Assessment During a Course

Summative assessment has traditionally been performed upon completion of a course and this is natural for it is concerned with a student's terminal knowledge and not with what his knowledge may have been part way through the course.  However, where a course consists of several relatively independent sections which succeed each other, then each section may justifiably have its own summative assessment which occurs upon its completion.

But even where the knowledge to be acquired in a course can be satisfactorily represented on a unidimensional scale, the summative assessment system may span the duration of the course.  For example, the student is assessed at a number of points during a course and the scores obtained are 'conflated' (usually by summing to yield a total). This has become fashionable in recent years under names such as continuous, intermittent or course work assessment. (I am referring to these only insofar as they contribute to summative assessment). In practice, however, there would often seem to be no satisfactory rationale for the systems which are adopted.

Consider, for example, a course of three equal units. The content of each unit, which I shall call topics A, B and C, is tested upon completion of its being taught. Each topic consists of certain interrelated concepts, procedures, etc. and I shall assume that A, B and C are potentially relatable in significant fashion. Let us examine two cases.

If, on the one hand, A, B and C may be both taught and learned independently of each other (i.e., there can be no transfer of learning from one topic to another unless teaching is specifically directed to this end), then either they are taught independently, in which case summing the three assessment scores yields only an index because each score is based on a conceptually distinct topic; or the inter-relationships between the topics are fully taught, in which case the later learning of earlier topics may take place thus tending to invalidate all but the assessment of the last topic.

If, on the other hand, C can be learned only to the extent that B has previously been learned and similarly with B in respect of A, then the situation is quite different. For example, if a student displays on his third assessment that he has mastered C, then he must also by that time have mastered A and B, irrespective of what his level of performance on the earlier assessments may have been. Therefore, to add the scores from the three assessments (even if a differential weighting of the three assessment results were used) would be logically indefensible. But how should the three assessment results be used?

One unsatisfactory proposal is to use the third assessment only. After all, it might be argued, this would assess the student with respect to the ultimate aims of the course. But consider the cases of two students, one of whom performed well in the first two assessments and poorly in the third, whereas the other performed poorly on all three assessments. Using only the third assessment, the students would be judged equal. But surely the results suggest that the first student deserves to receive more credit than the second? Examining of university courses in England in subjects such as mathematics would appear to approximate to this situation where much of the wide variation in results might be lessened if regard were had for earlier assessments in appropriate cases. For example, suppose that A corresponded to the use of certain algebraic techniques, B to an elaboration and extension of these techniques and C to the translation of 'real world' problems into mathematical models to which the techniques could then be applied. If the

202

terminal assessment were to consist of a set of real world problems only and a student had failed to learn the last section of the course, he would necessarily perform poorly on the assessment, no matter how well he had learned sections A and B, for the first stage in solving any of the assessment problems would require knowledge which he did not possess.

A more satisfactory method in principle for dealing with the problem is as follows.

Let a student's scores on the three assessments be $a_1$, $a_2$ and $a_3$. Let $a_{13}$ and $a_{23}$ be estimates from $a_3$ of the minimum scores he would have obtained on the first two assessments if they had been taken at the time of the third assessment. Let $a_{12}$ be an estimate from $a_2$ of the minimum score he would have obtained on the first assessment if it had been taken at the time of the second. Then the student's summative total is defined as :

$$a_3 + \max (a_2, a_{23}) + \max (a_1, a_{13}, a_{12}).$$

This procedure does not give the student the 'benefit of the doubt', but credits him with what he certainly knows. Indeed, it still under-estimates what he knows; for example, if a student improves his knowledge of A or B while studying C but performs poorly on the third assessment, then he gains no credit for this additional learning.

In practice, rarely do either of these types of courses exist in pure form but some mixture is quite common. This, of course, does nothing to simplify matters from a logical standpoint. In view of the complications of such summative assessment systems, one may reasonably ask: Why not confine summative assessment to the end of the course?

There can be little doubt that this is what we should try to do. But in England, the trend is in the opposite direction and the reasons underlying it are worthy of examination. There are, I believe, two main reasons.

Firstly, assessments which take place at the end of a course — such as final examinations — are widely believed to be lacking in validity. Not all the arguments used to support this position are sound, but there is hard empirical evidence that final examination papers which require a small number of essay answers or problem solutions are typically scored quite unreliably and this is of central importance. To most people, it seemed to follow that greater validity would be achieved by abandoning total dependence upon final examinations, increasing the number of assessments, spreading them over time and extending the range of assessment procedures to be used. And so it was natural to have students take additional examinations or tests during a course as well as do projects, long essays and so on, all of which were used for assessment purposes. Substantial pieces of work done by students in their own time not only would appear to contribute to the overall validity of the assessment process but, in students' eyes, they had a face validity in their own right which final examinations, for example, had not.

Secondly, students have commonly faced great uncertainty over the outcomes of their assessments at the end of a course. What they are to be examined upon is rarely well-defined, and a great deal would seem to depend upon luck. Therefore, students have seized upon assessments which are distributed throughout a course because (a) the assessments reveal rather clearly what the aims of the teacher really are; and (b) they allow the student to notch up credit throughout the course, thus relegating the importance of the final assessment.

But the reasons which seem to underlie the present trend towards continuous summative assessment methods, while displaying recognition of important problems, nevertheless suffer from a too-shallow analysis of the various alternatives and of the practical difficulties in the design and implementation of valid continuous summative assessment systems. In short, better solutions to these problems are available than those which are often seen in practice. In particular, the following points should be noted.

Firstly, an assessment system can only yield valid results if those who operate it are reasonably clear about what it is that is to be assessed. This simple and well-worn truism is not taken seriously enough. If it were and if the knowledge of test construction which is available were put into practice, a good many of our more serious assessment problems could be made more manageable. For example, final examinations could be greatly improved in their validity in many instances and this would make them far more acceptable to students, provided only that they were used in conjunction with suitable formative assessment systems.

Secondly, if additional or alternative forms of assessment are to be introduced, great care must be taken to ensure that they are likely to contribute to the validity of the assessment result: merely adding another assessment to those in use does not automatically increase the validity of the procedure and it may well decrease it.

Thirdly, students are not likely to learn purposefully and effectively unless they are reasonably clear as to where they should place emphasis in their studies and how their knowledge will be judged. And although this can and should be communicated as effectively as possible to the student from the outset of the course, it is likely to be in need of continual amplification during the course if it is to be of optimal use. This can best be achieved by means of a well designed formative assessment system.

Fourthly, students need and welcome information on their progress during a course and many welcome a system by which their learning is controlled both in directedness and pacing, such as by a summative system which spans the course. Students who are to face an assessment of consequence after, say, one quarter of a course's duration are more likely to study effectively during that period than otherwise. But to the extent that the system effectively controls the student (strong control would be attained by giving equal credit to assessments which are equally spaced throughout the course), and to the extent that later learning depends upon earlier learning, then the system will yield invalid summative results, as demonstrated earlier. What is needed is, as before, a formative assessment system which is well 'tuned in' to an end-of-course summative system. In this way, much of the reinforcing potential of the replaced summative system is acquired by the formative system and the latter provides much of the same information that the former previously did. The advantages of this approach are that the validity of the summative system is not reduced and students may take risks and make mistakes on formative assessments without consequences for their summative results.

In conclusion, the reader is reminded that considerations of space have necessarily prevented more than a very cursory treatment of a few important features of this topic. I hope, however, that this paper will have contributed a little to shifting some of the attention devoted to particular aspects of assessment to total assessment systems.

# The importance of medium in the generation and maintenance of motivation in the learning of English as a foreign language

SIR JAMES PITMAN, ITA Foundation, London

**Abstract:** My thesis is that if English were made easier to learn — particularly in the earliest stages – motivation would be generated among more intending learners; furthermore, that motivation would be more sustainable among those so initially motivated; that the difficulties imported by the medium play an all-important part in making learning difficult, and may easily – and with no disadvantage – be simplified.

English is, in a number of respects, one of the easiest of all the foreign languages to learn. It is, however, in the medium of its literacy that the great factor of difficulty has been imported. These points were well put by Jakob Grimm:

> 'English may be considered the language of the world out of Europe, and this idiom.... has attained an incomparable degree of fluency, and appears destined by nature more than any other that exists to become the world's language. Did not a whimsical, antiquated orthography stand in the way, the universality of this language would be still more evident...'

'Whimsical' is not a little euphemistic for the difficulties which the medium imposes upon the use of literacy as a concomitant to oracy in the learning of English. Every foreigner knows the difficulties occasioned by our misleading and irrational spelling: many of them — particularly those not used to the three variants of the Roman alphabet — are aware of the difficulty occasioned by the capricious use of our three differing alphabets. Together these two difficulties constitute a formidable barrier to ease of learning which works against both the generation and the maintenance of motive, and indeed deters many from even trying to learn. Very many of those who are not deterred from trying, lose their initial motivation as soon as they discover — which they cannot help doing, so general is the distribution and display of English words in their visual form — the enormous conflict between oracy in English (what their ears and their vocal organs need to learn) and literacy in English (what their eyes and their fingers need to master).

206

Thus motivation widely aborts; and the cause has been — and will continue to be — this conflict and the consequential further handicap, gratuitously accepted, of separating the teaching of literacy from that of oracy. We separate, as will be shown, for an unnecessary reason the learning of literacy with oracy, instead of learning them together, when each could support the other in concordance — in lieu of conflict — about which see paras below. Whereas the learner of Chinese has only one visual form for any one Chinese literate form for each oral form, there is in English no English word that has fewer than three forms: e.g. even A, a or ɑ — the indefinite article!

We need to remember that literacy in English is hard to learn even on the Look-and-Say method. There are so many variant word forms in our literacy.

BAG, Bag, Bag, bag, bɑg,𝒷𝒶𝑔, bɑg, bag, Bag, Bag

Figure 1

Three-letter words have ten or more variant forms (see Figure 1), and FLAG has no less than 16 variant forms. Thus in needing to master three alphabets — the accretions of two millennia — the learner of English finds himself confronted by a considerable variety of forms for what, in oracy, is **only one** form.

The fact that such multitudinous varieties do not impede or cause any hesitation in the reading of English by those of us who have learned and become skilled readers in English is irrelevant, seeing that the issue is the detterence of variety upon those who have no skill in either listening or reading. The fact, however, indicates two points: first, how important is the benefit of context in all language situations; and second, how little we, who have learned to read, realize the inherent difficulties of those less skilled when first learning to read. It is hard for us to appreciate how important are ease and success in the earliest stages of the initial learning process, and how not only in generating motivation, but also in maintaining it, is the expectation and realization of success. We must seek, therefore, a simplification of the learning medium to bring easier and earlier success. After all, just as nothing succeeds like success, nothing fails and deters like failure.

I must make it clear, perhaps, that a simplification of the learning medium involves no reform of the spellings of our 600-year-old form of literacy. The learning period may be initial, remedial, or developmental: in all cases; notwithstanding the use of a simplified initial learning medium (I.L.M.) the learner will in fact be learning to read fluently our traditional orthography (T.O) — even in all its many variant forms, including those 16 of FLAG. The ease and immediacy of the transition once the language has been learned, and once reading in the simplified I.L.M. has been mastered, are now beyond question. The degree of changes in T.O. which will simplify it and make a simple I.L.M. the learning medium need be very small. The only barrier to accepting that change — small though it be — comes from those who have learned literacy in English and suffer apparently an inevitable trauma at 'tampering with our glorious heritage' — from those who attach great significance to each such minor and functionally irrelevant difference.

Those whose emotions are sensitively 'on edge' should rather curb their potential hostility, having first considered that many publications are now, of choice, printed in lower-case characters, and that the proposed systematization of our T.O. for the purpose of teaching English more easily with the characters of the proposed I.L.M., differs from T.O. much less than the characters of our present three alphabets (A, a, $a$ : B, b, $\mathcal{b}$ : etc.) differ from one another, and differs little — and very tolerably — in its spellings. (See Figure 2)

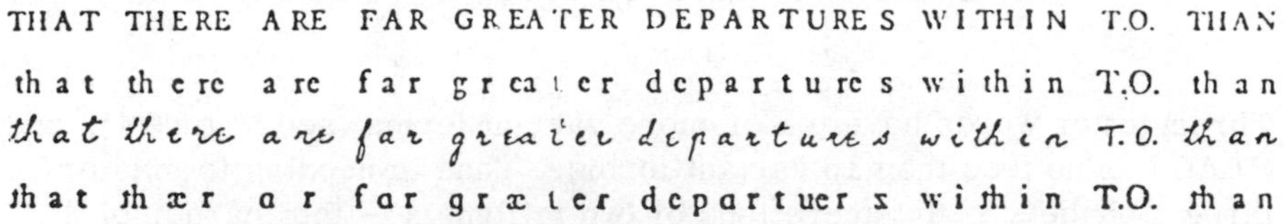

THAT THERE ARE FAR GREATER DEPARTURES WITHIN T.O. THAN

that there are far greater departures within T.O. than

that there are far greater departures within T.O. than

ſhat ſhær a r far græter departuer s wiſhin T.O. ſhan

Figure 2

This is because about 40 per cent of our literacy is already systematically alphabetic in its visual form, and needs no systematization other than the elimination of the upper-case and the cursive variant forms. Of the 22 commonest words, with an aggregate recurrence of 35.4 per cent in a page of continuous matter, eight (e.g. from **and** 4 per cent, **a** and **in** each 2.1 per cent, down to **at** 0.6 per cent) are identical both in T.O. and in any systematization. A further about 40 per cent are digraphic, and so are not dissimilar from the most usual T.O. spellings — that is to say, words incorporating two characters, such as **s** and **h** in **ship,** **n** and **g** in **king,** and the other digraphs which the mediaeval monks were forced to adopt as expedients when translating the Latin Bible and needing to spell, with no more than the 26 letters of our present Roman alphabet, at least 17 sounds of English which had no place in Latin speech, and so no characters in the Roman alphabet.

Here are the 17 + 3 characters (all but two of which are digraphic) which augment the Roman lower-case alphabet and ensure that the second 40 per cent of continuous literacy may be made to appear as, in effect, identical with a generally accepted spelling in T.O.

There are three supererogatory characters ( ᴡh , r and x ), making 20 instead of 17 augmentations to the Roman alphabet. These have been added to make the transition in reading even easier.

| | i.t.a. | T.O. | Example | | i.t.a. | T.O. | Example |
|---|---|---|---|---|---|---|---|
| 1. | ɑ | a | arm | 11. | ω | oo | book |
| 2. | æ | ae | aeroplane | 12. | ω | oo | moon |
| 3. | au | au | autumn | 13. | ɾ | r | her (herring) |
| 4. | ɕh | ch | church | 14. | ʃh | sh | bishop |
| 5. | ɕɛ | ee | feet | 15. | ţh | th | thigh |
| 6. | ic | ie | die | 16. | ʃh | th | thy |
| 7. | ŋ | ng | thing | 17. | uc | ue | due |
| 8. | œ | oe | toe | 18. | wʰ | wh | why |
| 9. | ou | ou | out | 19. | s | s | dogs |
| 10. | oi | oi | oil | 20. | ★ ʒ | s or z | azure |

Figure 3

*This character is in fact that character which is employed, instead of **z**, at the end of the third (i.e. the cursive) alphabet of T.O.

Thus the visual forms of this second 40 per cent are virtually identical in appearance with those they systematize: e.g. ᴄんᴜᴦん , ʃɪᴘ , Wɪʃん, Fᴄᴄ Ⴑ, etc. After all, for learning English there is an important difference between bi**sh**ap and mi**sh**ap; **sh**orthand and nor**th**ern; nor**th**, Sou**th**ampton and **Th**omas. Consequentially the remaining 20 per cent contain those spellings which give the learner of English literacy, and particularly of oracy, the difficulties which Jakob Grimm, and every foreigner since, has immediately found so obstructive to learning oracy in English, and so corrosive of motive. It is only these which need re-spelling to obtain a simplified I.L.M., and even in these the changes may be confined to alternative spellings of that sound which is to be found in T.O., as will be seen from Figure 3.

It is little consolation to the learner to tell him that there are admittedly a number of regular irregularities in the alphabet relationships between literacy and oracy which are so frequent as to become in effect rules, and that these words do not need to be re-spelled because they are only a minor obstruction to learning and motivation. For instance, **ow**, **oa** and **o** are possibly so frequent irregularities as to become virtually regularities and worth retaining in addition to that of **oe** in **toe**. But these are only four out of 37 different spellings of that sound — and anyhow, both **bow** and **row** have heterophonic values; moreover, while **go, no** and **so, home** and **tome** seem to support any such purported rule, **do, to, who,** and **come** and **some** conflict. Thus even these supposed rules are so frequently negatived that Jakob Grimm is seen to have been clearly right after all.

The January 1972 issue of The Incorporated Linguist, in an article entitled Oracy and Literacy, carried a specimen of a medium — Speech i.t.a., the speech-teaching version of the Initial Teaching Alphabet (i.t.a.) (See Figure 4).

209

az every reeder will noe the internaſhonal
fonetic alfabet is wiedly uesd as a meedium
for teeching lisening and speeking, but with soe
græt a departuer from the forms ov
tradiſhonal orthografy (T.O.) that teeching ov
reeding, rieting and particuelarly ov spellig in
T.O. is grætly viſhiæted.

thus the græt advantæj ov speech i.t.a. is
that whiel it mæ bee uesd just as effectivly
as I.P.A. too teech lisening and speeking, it
offers aulsoe a much mor effectiv tool in
teeching reeding, rieting, and cueriusly as
reserch has establiſht, eeven spellig aulsoe.

Figure 4

It is a simplified I.L.M. which systematizes T.O. with no significant
departure from the traditional forms, and has moreover been found in
practice both to achieve more and better successes for the foreign
learner, and so to encourage and sustain motive. Furthermore it involves no difficulty whatever in the 'transition' from literacy in the
I.L.M. to literacy in T.O. The change-over in reading from Speech
i.t.a. to T.O. needs no teaching, and no learning-time or effort. It is
immediate and automatic once skill in the I.L.M. has been achieved.
Admittedly skill in spelling needs teaching — or at any rate effort and
time in learning. It is not, as is the transition in reading, an immediate
and effortless process, any more than it is for the already English-
speaking child. However, for the transition by the foreigner to ortho-
graphic spelling there is already sufficient evidence to confirm for them
and Speech i.t.a. what has been found for the already English-speaking
child and ordinary i.t.a. — that the transition in spelling, though
delayed, is achieved with a higher standard of accuracy. (See 'But will
they ever lern to spel korectly?' Educational Research, Vol. 12, No.3,
June 1972: NFER, Windsor)

The forms of Speech i.t.a. are in essence no different from those in
ordinary i.t.a. (see figure 2 — a random wording comparing T.O. lower
case with i.t.a.). The implication is that while Speech i.t.a. and its

**accompanying tapes** should be used for teaching oracy, ordinary i.t.a. should be used for teaching literacy, and that the two should be used **pari passu** from the beginning (i.e. with no longer any time-lag between the teaching of any passage in oracy and the teaching of it in literacy).

There remain two points. First that language is indivisible, and that therefore, if the purpose be to teach language in the most important form of its manifestations (speech), there is great advantage in enabling the learning of that one skill to be automatically and instantly the learning also of the other three.

Years ago, for the purpose of writing about the teaching of short-hand, I invented my own word, in order that its impact should be undeniably novel, seeing that it had not until then existed. If I now write it — 'Poppollington' — it will no doubt be equally novel. The reader will appreciate that he has instantly learned it, not only as a word to read but also as one to write, one to hear and one to speak. Professor Ritchie Russell, lately Professor of Clinical Neurology, Oxford University, explains this phenomenon by the fact that we have one language centre in our brain, and that a stimulus to that centre — whether a reception by, or an emission from that centre along any of the nerve channels which serve it — produces automatically a companion skill along the other three channels. Indeed, if anyone with the ordinary skills in the English language not only in listening, speaking, reading and writing be also a shorthand writer, a touch typist, a lip reader, a listener and tapper of the Morse code, and a toucher and embosser of Braille, then those seven further language skills would be acquired with no learning effort. It is for this reason that the **pari passu** teaching of the two skills of literacy with the two skills of oracy is so greatly more beneficial when this automatic and instant addition of companionate skills is made possible. Indeed, as Dr. Ritchie Russell has written:

'There is of course a very close anatomical and functional link in the brain between all aspects of language. As man gets more information to his brain through vision than through any other sense, the reading aspect of language may be expected to form a dominant part of the higher uses of language for intelligent thought, etc. It seems likely that for psychological reasons, the visual aspects of language should be developed concurrently with the auditory, and I expect that Russian success in this direction is related to the teaching of Pavlov, who was encouraged 30 years ago, to guide the application of physio-logical knowledge to all aspects of Russian education.'

Where there is conflict instead of harmony in the relationships between literacy and oracy, only oracy is learned when learning oracy, and only literacy when learning literacy — at best two language skills instead of four. For instance, if the inhabitants of this non-existent village were to pronounce that name 'Plumpton' and it were to have been read as

'Poppollington', only the skill of literacy would be acquired, and all occasion for the acquisition of listening, of speaking and of lip reading — all skills related to oracy — would have been missed.

Moreover, because, as Russell points out, the eye is better than the ear in learning language, and thus reading even better than listening, it must surely be helpful to the learner to provide him with the opportunity to use his eye from the beginning as well as his ear, his fingers as well as his vocal organs, so that he may not only learn language more easily but learn it in all four of its skills at any one time. Thus the practice of teaching oracy first and literacy later is doubly wrong — being an imposition occasioned only by the supposition that T.O., with all its conflicts between literacy and oracy, is the best — and only! — initial learning medium which can be used.

The other intriguing point is that we need a new term — a **reading system** as being distinct from a writing system — and to begin thinking in that new term. The specimens at Figure 2 and Figure 4 need no phonetic convention to be determined before they are read. The desired symbol-to-sound conventions will in fact be determined by the speaker's sounds when heard on the tapes. Thus the foreign-speaking learner will listen to that particular version of English speech which had been chosen — and different choices will have been made in the different regions of the English-speaking world, and the print on the pages made to reflect that speech. In the case of ordinary i.t.a. and of the already English-speaking learner of reading, it will be **his** speech habituations — and his alone — which will determine how he pronounces each word he comes to recognize. There can be no supposedly standardized and **single** sound attached to the characters. Indeed, so different is a reading system from a writing system that it is possible to claim that the reading is so perfectly 'phonetic' in its representation of sounds for each and every reader that each of many billions of readers finds his idiosyncratic speech — and unique version of speech — perfectly represented.

There ought not to be, and there cannot be, in the teaching of English as a second language one standard pronunciation of English with its own 'writing system' — as there needs to be (but even then in only an approximation) when the purpose be to print a pronouncing dictionary based, for instance, on the Received Pronunciation — e.g. the dictionary of Daniel Jones. No-one can reasonably suppose that it will be desirable, in teaching English to young Puerto Rican children, to employ tapes spoken with the pronunciations 'most usually heard in everyday speech in the families of Southern English persons who have been educated at the great public boarding schools', as R.P. is defined by Daniel Jones. Good Rooseveltian English is what is needed.

Clearly, therefore, that passage in Speech i.t.a. in Figure 4 will need to be printed and to be pronounced with as many varieties of vowel and even consonant sounds (e.g. m i n o r i t y, m i e n o r i t y: s h e d u e l

212

and s k e d u e l) as there are varieties of 'good' English speech, which
will be desirable for reproduction on the tapes. Moreover since rhythm
and stress are such important factors in those varieties of 'good' English
speech, the tapes, and therefore the print, will need to vary for this
reason also. In other words, just as the tapes must be allowed to vary
for differences in vowels and consonants, so too must they vary in the
incidences of stress and change of vowel, and the printed page made to
vary correspondingly.

There is a wide — indeed general — acceptance by those best qualified to advise on education that the teacher's expectation of the student's
success is of great significance in the success which will be realized by
the student. Moreover the student's own expectations are of equal, if not
of even greater, significance.

There can be no doubt that Jakob Grimm was right: also that a
systematized initial learning medium (I. L. M.) closely related to the
sounds to be both listened to and to be spoken in oracy, is able to eliminate those 'whimsicalities': also that the transition from the I. L. M. to
T. O. is effortless in reading: furthermore that the learning of the ability
to spell orthographically in T. O. (which is particularly difficult in itself —
even more difficult than learning to read) is more easily mastered when
tackled **after** reading skills have been successfully developed through an
I. L. M. rather than while learning to read — which is anyhow difficult.
All of which being granted, the supposition is confidently advanced that
if a simplified I. L. M. be employed, the teacher and student will have an
enhanced expectation of success, and will each of them benefit from a
higher initial motivation: furthermore that each will not only sustain the
higher initial motivation, but even increase it, because they experience
that greater ease in teaching and learning which the simplification affords.

REFERENCES

The following bibliography is relevant to the use of i.t.a. in the teaching of English as a
foreign language. The majority of the items are relevant to teaching literacy through ordinary
i.t.a. Only those four marked with an asterisk are relevant to the teaching of oracy also —
using both tapes supplementing the Speech i.t.a. printed materials for teaching oracy, and
ordinary i.t.a. for teaching literacy. Copies of these items may be obtained from, or studied
at the i.t.a. Foundation.

* Abiri, J. (1969) World Initial Teaching Alphabet **Versus** Traditional Orthography.
   University of Ibadan, Nigeria.
Holmes, J.A. and Rose, I. (1969) Disadvantaged children and the effectiveness of i.t.a.
   The Reading Teacher 22, No. 4.
Larick, J. (1967) The Use of the Initial Teaching Alphabet in Teaching English as a
   Second Language to Speakers of Spanish. Proceedings of the 4th International i.t.a.
   Conference: McGill University, Montreal.

\* Newberry, R.S. (1970) <u>Speech Training in Courses Designed to Prepare Teachers of English as a Second Language for the Use of i.t.a.</u> Proceedings of the 7th International i.t.a. Conference: London University.

Pitman, Sir J. (1965) <u>i.t.a. and Teaching English as a Second Language.</u> Proceedings of the 2nd International i.t.a. Conference: Lehigh University, U.S.A.

Russell, R. and Espir (1961) <u>Traumatic Aphasia.</u> O.U.P.

\* Schmitz op der Beck, F.H. (1969) <u>The Preliminary Use of i.t.a. in the Teaching of English as a Foreign Language in Germany.</u> Proceedings of the 6th International i.t.a. Conference: Vanbrugh College, York University.

Sipes, R. (1968) <u>English as a Second Language to (a) Predominantly Negro Population, and (b) Predominantly Spanish-speaking Population.</u> Unpublished manuscript.

\* Thornhill, J.E.M. (1973) Report of Committee appointed in December 1971 by the Education Department of Gambia to assess the suitability or otherwise of adopting the i.t.a. medium of teaching. Unpublished.

Trepper, T.S. and Robertson, D.J. (1973) The effects of i.t.a. on the reading achievement of Mexican-American children. Unpublished manuscript.

Wilkinson, C.M. (1960) The use of i.t.a. with immigrant children. <u>The i.t.a. Journal,</u> No. 10.

214

# The development of a programmed reading system for primary education

J. LEEDHAM, Loughborough College of Education

Abstract: This paper describes the six year development of a programmed system to improve basic comprehension, reading ability and the expressive skills. Details are given of a three mode programme employing a branching system to take advantage of the vocabulary, linguistic and conceptual steps in a child's development.

From 1966 onwards APLET's successive conference proceedings have quoted experiments in the field of programmed reading, and this paper first reviews these and other approaches towards the application of the principles of programming to the acquisition of reading skills. Widlake's 1967 taxonomy of relevant objectives is used to outline a preliminary definition of a programmed reading scheme applicable and acceptable in 1974. American experience is examined together with details of parallel development at Leicester University.

The paper instances the result of tests on the use of vocabulary by primary authors and examines the motivation of self-marking, self-scoring systems. The process of inter-relating text and visual illustration is described as it proceeded during six years of pre-publication trials. Emphasis is directed to the area of concept development and the use of a skip branching mode on thematic routeways.

Beard, Clarke and Leedham (each, 1967) instance work with slow learners and with primary school children. Widlake (1967) developed a Taxonomy of objectives for reading programmes. Huskinson Packham and Cleary (1969) dealt with skills of discrimination and the Touch Tutor. Gilmore (1972) examined the construction and evaluation of directed oral systems. These are examples of the diversity of approach likely to be encountered in the field of programmed reading schemes.

Widlake (1967) discussed the specific objectives as refined from research reports. He suggested the term 'reading' was non-specific and that the correction of the functional impairment of visual and control mechanisms should be part of operational programming. The concept of 'readiness' might be made more precise by adequate pre-reading programmes. Auditory perception, kinaesthetic approaches could all have prepared objectives. Nevertheless Widlake suggests that 'successful programmes will also take cognizance of the growing knowledge of child development, and not only cognitive development.'

Over the years the definition of a programmed system has widened, Within the definition that such material is previously tested and presented so that self instruction is monitored to ensure progress towards a stated goal, several successful programmes have been published. In Britain the programmed pack to train teachers in the use of i.t.a. (Leedham and Crouch, 1968) employed a mathetical approach, and it has been widely used here and in America. Following the employment of the Reading Master Programme (Leedham, 1965) which involved the first trials in this country with the Language Master, the development of locally inspired programmes has been frequently reported. A carefully detailed programmed reading scheme produced by Cynthia Buchanan in the U.S.A. and published by Sullivan Associates had a less successful introduction in the U.K. This was probably because of its over emphasis on phonic development and dependence on an elaborate teacher's manual.

However, another U.S.A. venture, the Science Research Associates Reading Laboratory proved an early success and has maintained a mounting record of popular acceptance for over five years. Its early material was culturally based on extracts from American publications, and its emphasis was on the provision of readings cards in a graded system. These cards advanced reading skills by the intensive questioning of the read passages and used self-marking and scoring systems together with a 'rate-of-reading' to increase speed. The system had specific aims in terms of extending the attained reading age of participants within a measured time span and has since been amplified by the provision of further boxes of material to cover a wide age range and attainment spectrum. Much material is identified with the U.S.A. system of education and culture.

During this time the development of British trial programmes was under way, first at the Programmed Learning Research Unit at Leicester University and later at the Department of Educational Technology at Loughborough. The first trials had to do with the development of the 'Reading Master Programmes', and with the comparison between the results of instruction in i.t.a. and traditional orthography.

EARLY TRIALS WITH PROGRAMMED READING SCHEMES

This account is from 'Learning to read by programme' in Programmed Learning in the Schools (Leedham and Unwin, 1972).

If we first analyse the attitude of a programme writer considering reading as a skill to be imparted, it would give a fuller meaning to the experiments with machines which we report later.

(a)  First. The programmes are for children who cannot read. This is the target population; the aim is to give them the reading skill. Their age can fairly be considered as any within the span seven to twelve years.

(b) Second. Just what is this skill? It is that skill needed to associate certain symbols with certain sounds in order to create meaning.

(c) Third. What abilities has the child to start with? It is assumed he can hear speech and can speak.

(d) Fourth. How does the skill analyse? Into three divisions:

> Visual recognition of the symbol
> Translation into spoken referent
> Extraction of meaning.

So here we have four points:

(1) A child who cannot read, for various reasons.

(2) The child needs to associate sounds with symbols in order to read.

(3) The child can talk, he can hear the sounds, the symbols mean nothing.

(4) Meaning must be imparted.

The first consideration is to match the sounds to symbols meaningfully. This is easy to say, but depends greatly on the child's pre-reading experience. However, machines should, and in the few cases where they exist, do, link sound to symbol.

If we take a sound we wish to illustrate meaningfully in a programme we would plan something like this : Take the sound 'i' as in PIG. First the child sees a picture of a pig and hears the word PIG from a tape. He repeats PIG. He sees the picture again and says PIG. This time the letters PIG are revealed to him. Next time picture and PIG occur together; subsequently the picture is left out and the word left in. Variations on this ensure that picture or symbols elicit the sound PIG. The same thing is then done for PIN. It might take twenty pictures or frames of each to ensure the correct response. Now comes the question, hotly debated, as to the recognition of the sound 'i'. By omitting the 'i' in P-G or P-N, the child can be called upon to write it 'i', at the same time giving it its sound value. By careful manipulation a vocabulary can be built up so that the child can start reading. This can be done by a simple machine allied to a tape, and this was the pattern of our early programmes.

Work with reading programmes should provide a fruitful field for experimenters. After all, the goals can be defined exactly, and the subjects are known equally exactly; they cannot read. Nevertheless, the labour of organizing programmed schemes is impressive. Here is one account of work under way.

Ten children who had failed to read after two years of attention in school were presented with a programme which started from simple pictures requiring a spoken response into a tape-recorder leading to written response in a step-by-step linear machine. The programme led up to simple sentences illustrated by pictures and then on to a pre-scribed reading scheme. The results for ten children are shown below:

**Daniels and Diacks Test**

| Average chronological age | Average reading age Sept. 1962 | Average reading age March 1963 | Gain in 22 weeks |
|---|---|---|---|
| 7 yrs. 3 mths. | 5 yrs. 1 mth. | 7 yrs. 5 mths | 2 yrs. 2 mths |

For ten other matched children a programmed approach using Sir James Pitman's initial teaching alphabet (a new form of orthography) employed 'listening post' skills. These consist of using taped material broadcast to individual children through headphones and enjoining the use, by the child, of programme cards and programmed responses. The other systems of linear programming such as picture-word response cards were also employed and a typical result is as shown.

**Daniels and Diacks Test**
(using traditional alphabet)

| Average chronological age | Average reading age Sept. 1962 | Average reading age March 1963 | Gain in 22 weeks |
|---|---|---|---|
| 7 yrs. 2 mths. | 5 yrs. 1 mth. | 7 yrs. 10 mths | 2 yrs. 9 mths |

Since this gave a result by i.t.a. programme significantly better than the traditional alphabet result, excellent though this was, concentra-tion has since been directed on i.t.a. Several schools have practised 'listening post' skills and developed their own taped system.

The difficulties of this technique are fairly quick to emerge. The vocabulary can become stiff, the work mechanical. The advantage, of course, lies in the patience and one-to-one ratio of machine and child. It has more time than a teacher — and possibly more patience.

**The Reading Master Scheme**

Such experience led to the development and employment of simplified recording devices which enabled the audio programming to be directly related to the printed symbol. Such a device as illustrated with this text (Figure 1), was first tried in this country at Leicester University by the Programmed Learning Research Unit located there in 1963. The Associated Reading Master Scheme developed a vocabulary which was based on the inter-relation between the frequency of the use of

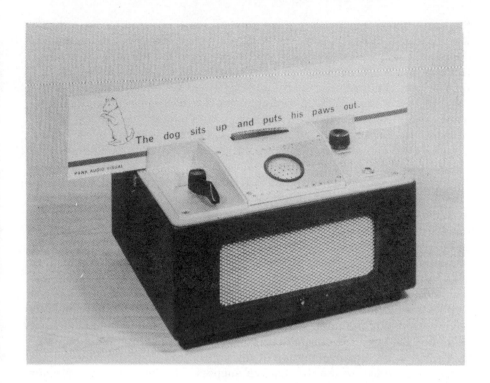

Figure 1

certain words and their phonic development. After considerable trial a
published scheme (The Reading Master Scheme) used booklets, specially
constructed to link illustration and text; in turn these booklets matched
and were supported by the taped cards which carried the spoken words
and illustrations for the child to listen to and repeat for comparison.
One result to emerge was that the cards were more successfully used if
the teacher could record her voice and add illustration and text to suit
local circumstance. The basic vocabulary of 435 words was a useful
acquisition from these experiments and was employed in the parallel
development of the programmed reading scheme, now known as Reading
Routes.

READING ROUTES

The earlier definition of a programmed scheme indicates that 'the
material is previously tested and presented so that self-instruction is
monitored to ensure progress towards a stated goal'.

The Reading Routes scheme observed these precepts in its planning
stages. One hundred and forty titles were scheduled to develop concepts
progressively, and to control the introduction of vocabulary and linguistic
complexity by stages. Trial material was written for twenty topics and

219

the illustrative detail either photographed or illustrated by artists. The three strands of control: vocabulary, language complexity, conceptual development, were specifically written in from the start of the trials. Authors had a limited vocabulary with which to illustrate specified topics, the language complexity was indicated in terms of mood and tense. Illustrations were produced to match the textual requirement. Cards were specially composed to yield progressive questions on text and illustration, on meaning and inference and on some language skills. Topic titles, and subject treatment were specially developed on thematic 'routeways' as explained later.

The finished cards were put to trial but failed to achieve the requisite standard; that each card should be capable of being scored by the child with the minimum of teacher assistance, that the error rate should only occasionally be more than 20 per cent and that the progression through the cards should be sustained. The cards had been prepared by a team of five practising teachers all with authorship experience. It appeared that, as authors we were not yet correctly gauging the skills of our pupils, or that the trials were unrepresentative. The same cards, by now somewhat the worse for wear were tried in another part of the country and with a higher socio-economic group. Much the same result indicated the need for careful revision of our approach. In particular there had to be some relaxation of the vocabulary control and a much more specific use of the illustrative support. In the end, after further trial and error, the following scheme was produced. The vocabulary referred to is the one specially produced for the Reading Routes and derived from experience with the 'Reading Master Programmes' already referred to.

| Folder No. | Colour | Vocabulary | Suggested No. of words | Structure | Approximate reading age |
|---|---|---|---|---|---|
| 1-12 | cherry | basic plus 5% | 200-220 | simple sentence present tense | 7.5 yrs. |
| 13-24 | blue | basic plus 12% | 220-240 | to | 8.0 yrs. |
| 25-36 | red | basic plus 25% | 240-260 | simple and compound, some past tense | 8.5 yrs. |
| 37-48 | gold | basic plus 40% | 260-290 | past tense and more complex sentences | 9.0 yrs. |
| 49-60 | ice | free | 290-330 | tense range complex constructions | 9.5 yrs. |
| 61-72 | orange | free | 330-370 | " | 10.0 yrs. |

| Folder No. | Colour | Vocabulary | Suggested No. of words | Structure | Approximate reading age |
|---|---|---|---|---|---|
| 73-84 | green | free | 370-410 | tense range complex constructions | 10.5 yrs. |
| 85-96 | yellow | free | 410-450 | " | 11.0 yrs. |
| 97-108 | emerald | free | 450-525 | " | 11.5 yrs. |
| 109-120 | lilac | free | 525-700 | " | 12 plus yrs. |

From Leedham (1974)

The illustrative detail was very difficult to arrange. Material had to develop progressively and this needed to be true of both illustration and text, moreover as will be seen later the topics themselves developed sequentially on thematic routeways. Use was made of previous experience reported by Leedham (1968) that sequenced photographs considerably improved performance of a textual programme when employed with younger pupils (ages 8 - 10) and much use was made of photographs taken specifically in support of the text. The inclusion of photographic illustration in addition to line drawing or artist's illustration enabled a more precise and lively use of topic material.

Finally the programme appeared schematically as shown in Figure 2 (see page 222).

Referring to the diagram :

Step 1    The scheme consists of 144 four page folders, they are at ten levels of difficulty, each level differentiated by a colour. Accompanying each folder is its own answer card and project suggestions.

Step 2    The programme breaks into separate compartmented colour codes.

Step 3    Each folder is graded by colour print size, number sequence and the number and difficulty of questions asked.

Step 4    The pupil uses a special work book to write down his answers.

Step 5    The answer card enables the child to score his own work and calculate his percentage result.

Step 6    The percentage result is scored by the child on a special target designed to reveal progress.

Steps 7   The topics are organized to develop pupils creative work and the
and 8     associated projects are also developed sequentially to follow the basic programmed work.

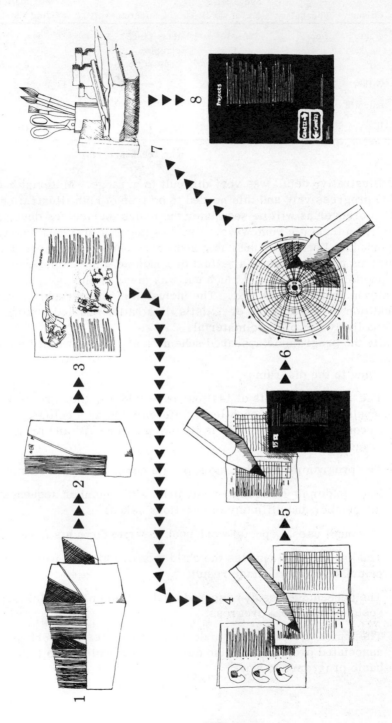

Figure 2

222

From the description thus far it should be clear that the principles of programming set out at the beginning of the paper have been matched in the design of the scheme. The self-marking and scoring systems which are illustrated were the result of much trial to achieve simplicity of operation and to motivate the pupil. To this end it was necessary to keep answers at a very direct level but experience proved that children gained most when given some degree of flexibility in answering. For example it is always required that single word answers are correctly spelled, but answers which occur in sentence form are often marked 'or words which mean this' on the answer card. Nevertheless the importance of the projects in stimulating the child to add to his growing attainment by creative work cannot be overstated. Each project card carries three suggestions and often involve class displays or group work. They are deliberately open ended to encourage individual writing and other forms of creative work.

Pupils can work through the numbered, colour graded scheme, marking their own progress monitored by the teacher, doing some of the associated project work. The grading is small step and the concept development is gradual. There is an alternative way of using Reading Routes which adds variety and quickens the pace at the discretion of the teacher. The Routeways may be likened to a skip branching programme capable of advancing on any one or more of six alternative branches.

| Ordinary and Remarkable | Transport and Inventions | Nature |
| Famous People | Animals | Story and Fables |

Figure 3

These Routeways are alternative ways of proceeding. A child who worked on the animal routeway, for example, would progress on folders 1 to 4, but then if his teacher deemed his ability and determination great enough, he could go on to number 11. The rate of his progress and the necessity to fill in any gaps is easily controlled by inspecting his scoring target. The list of topics for two Routeways is given below and it is expected that the reader can trace the increasing difficulty of the ideas required to be handled by reading through the titles of two of the Routeways.

| Animals | Transport and inventions |
|---|---|
| 1.   Brave Dogs | 5.   Boats |
| 2.   Lions and Tigers | 6.   Trains |
| 3.   Elephants | 7.   Aeroplanes |
| 4.   Ponies in Pits | 12.  Drums |
| 11.  Eagles | 18.  Dancing Dolls |
| 14.  Badgers | 25.  Lighthouses |
| 15.  The Otter | 35.  Finding the Way |
| 22.  Zoo Baby | 39.  Old Tramcars |
| 26.  Fishing | 50.  Coracles |
| 43.  Big Cats, Little Cats | 57.  Marconi and the Radio |
| 49.  Donkeys | 59.  Musical Boxes |
| 56.  Birds of Prey | 69.  Sailing a Boat |
| 73.  The Tiger Hunt | 72.  Edison |
| 78.  Dolphins | 80.  Musical Horns |
| 82.  The St. Bernard | 86.  Icebreakers |
| 83.  Simba | 87.  Airships |
| 84.  Elephants never forget | 96.  Gliding |
| 90.  The Great Auk | 97.  Toys of long ago |
| 93.  The Birds migrate | 98.  The Longest Railway |
| 116. Whale hunt | 104. Atlantic Queens |
| 117. The Hide | 108. The New Motorways |
| 120. Language of Fish | 109. The Hovercraft |
| | 118. The Parafoil |

(At this stage a film record of work in trial schools was presented)

Reading gains measured in reading age are substantial but vary because of the various ways of employing Reading Routes. The entire scheme is now due for widescale use.

REFERENCES

Beard, N. (1967) Programmed Reading: work with slow learners. In Aspects of Educational Technology I. London: Methuen.

Clarke, J. (1967) The development and use of linear programmed instruction in a rural primary school. In Aspects of Educational Technology I. London: Methuen.

Gilmore, S. (1967) The construction and evaluation of a guided oral language system. In Aspects of Educational Technology I. London: Pitman.

Gilmore, S. (1972) The construction and evaluation of a guided oral language situation. In Aspects of Educational Technology VI. London: Pitman.

Greenwood, G. and Widlake, P. (1967) A language scheme for teaching English to Immigrants. In Aspects of Educational Technology I. London: Methuen.

Huskinson, Packham, D. and Cleary, A. (1969) Pre-reading experiments with the Touch Tutor. In Aspects of Educational Technology III. London: Pitman.

Leedham, J. (1965) The Reading Master Scheme. Rank Organization.

Leedham, J. (1967) A summary of research and development since 1964 in Leicestershire. In Aspects of Educational Technology I. London: Methuen.

Leedham, J. (1968) The development and use of multi-media programmes. Ph.D. Thesis: University of Nottingham.

Leedham, J. (Ed.) (1974) Reading Routes. Harlow: Longmans.

Leedham, J. and Crouch (1968) Teachers Programmed Instruction Pack in i.t.a. London: Pitman.

Leedham, J. and Unwin, D. (1972) Learning to read by programme. In Programmed Learning in the Schools, 2nd Edition. Harlow: Longmans.

Widlake, P. (1967) A Taxonomy of Objectives for Reading Programmes. In Proceedings of APLET Conference, Vol. I. University of Birmingham.

# Programmed instruction in British industry: a study of change

P. ELLIS, A. ROMISZOWSKI, A. HOWE, Middlesex Polytechnic

**Abstract:** The growth and development of programmed instruction in British Industry is discussed in some detail. The paper is based on a survey carried out in 1973 and frequent comparisons are drawn with the results of a similar survey carried out in 1966 in order to trace the changes that are taking place.

Programmed instruction now seems to be widely accepted by industry, and use continues to increase, although the early meteoric growth has now dropped off. It is noted how economic and other factors may influence the growth of a training technique. The paper discusses the use made of programmed instruction in terms of categories of trainee, context in course, and presentation media. The sources of programmes used are analysed and a trend for organizations to employ their own programme writers is noted. Consideration is also given to the techniques used in programme writing.

Training by objectives, a technique which involves many of the steps of programmed instruction is finding wide acceptance and the reasons for this are discussed.

There has been a certain amount of confusion in recent years as to the growth taking place in programmed instruction, and the applications being found for the technique. While some claimed that programmed instruction was growing strongly, others held that it had gone into a decline and that use was falling off. The reason for some of this conflict lies in the fact that for the most part any one person could only base his opinions on a few cases of use, or disuse, of the technique in his own experience; what was lacking was data detailing the use of programmed instruction in a large number of settings.

In this paper we attempt to provide such data for the use of programmed instruction in British Industry. In particular by comparing trends found in a survey of use in 1966 (Romiszowski, 1967) with the results of a more recent study using a sample of organizations drawn from the earlier survey (Ellis and Romiszowski, 1973) an attempt is made to specify precisely how programmed instruction **is** developing.

It was found that 52 per cent of the organizations replying to the 1973 survey used programmed instruction. It would be over optimistic to take this as an estimate of the overall usage of programmed instruction, since only organizations with over 500 employees were circulated, (see later note on size and use of P.I.) Also the nature of the sampling could be argued as possibly biasing the return towards organizations using programmed instruction. However, it is notable that with the 50 per cent response rate obtained in the survey, at least one quarter of the organizations circulated were using programmed instruction. It is fair to say therefore, that the use of programmed instruction in larger industrial organizations is now relatively widespread; in fact it was found that less than one quarter of the organizations replying had never used the technique, and had no intentions of using it in the near future. Another point which emerged was that most organizations reporting using programmed instruction make more than minimal use of it, the average number of programmes being twenty.

Two definite relationships emerged between organizational charac-teristics and use of programmed instruction. Firstly, larger oganiza-tions are much more likely to use programmed instruction than smaller ones, the proportions of users in the response ranging from about one quarter of the smaller organizations (less than 1,000 employees) to over two-thirds of the larger organizations (over 5,000 employees). This is not unexpected, and closely follows the trend found in the earlier survey, but with the proportions of users increased. Secondly, organi-zations involved primarily with manufacture are most likely to make use of programmed instruction, while organizations involved primarily in retail and distribution are relatively unlikely to utilize programmed instruction. This result does not seem to be an artifact of the size range that organizations fall into since the pattern of size ranges of responding organizations in the retail and distribution industries is not highly dis-similar to the overall pattern. The question remains open, though, as to why retail and distribution industries so conspicuously lag behind in their use of programmed materials.

Several findings point to the continuing growth in use of programmed instruction. Figure 1 illustrates the numbers of present users of pro-grammed instruction who were users in previous years, as deduced from the number of years of use stated on the questionnaire returns. It seems that although the earlier 'meteoric' growth of programmed instruction (Romiszowski, 1968) has levelled off, it still continues to expand at a decreased rate. It is also noteworthy that of the 133 users found in the present survey, only 58 were users in 1966, the remaining 75 having introduced programmed instruction since the previous survey. The growth in use of programmed instruction is not confined to numbers of users only, evidence emerged to suggest that with continuing use firms increase their utilization of programmed materials both in terms of number of programmes and hours of programmes that they have available.

Some organizations were found who had used programmed instruction, but who had discontinued its use. The proportion was not as high as the more sceptical would have us believe, amounting to only about 23 per cent

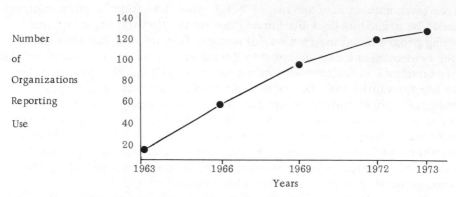

Figure 1   Growth in number of users of programmed instruction

of the organizations known to have used programmed instruction at some time, and many of the organizations in this category indicated either that they had used programmed materials for a specific training need (e. g. decimalization) and that programmed instruction would be used again in the future when appropriate, or that its disuse was due to a general run-down in training effort (e. g. 'no intake of apprentices in last three years'). It is interesting to note that the 1966 usage of programmed instruction of firms who still use the technique, as compared to the data for those who have abandoned it, reveals no clear distinction between groups in commitment to programmed instruction in terms of number of programmes available, or hours of programmes available. On the other hand, it is evident that student hours values were much higher on average for organizations which persevered with programmed instruction than for those which did not. On an individual basis, however, some firms stating only eight or twelve student hours in 1966 are continuing users, so at an individual level 'student hours' is not a reliable predictor of continuing use.

To progress a little from amount of use of programmed instruction we will now consider the types of use made of the technique and how it is used. The survey results indicated that programmed instruction is now well utilized by a wide range of trainees. Technician/apprentice training is still the largest single category of application of programmed instruction, but this tendency is less pronounced than was evident in the 1966 survey. There is some evidence for Whitlock's (1972) claim that there is a shift in the use of programmed instruction from operators, craftsmen and apprentices to clerical and management, but this trend is not strong. The organizations in the present sample are, however, strongly biased toward the manufacturing industries, and it is possible that with a more balanced sample this trend would be more pronounced.

In the context of overall training effort, by far the most common use of programmes is as a standard part of a training course, only infrequently

228

does programmed instruction make up a total course. The frequent use of programmes in a revision/retaining or optional function which was found, indicates that their advantages for remedial work are being realized.

The trend revealed on presentation media is for presentation of programmed instruction by means of a programmed text rather than by a teaching machine. More than three times as many organizations reported that all of their programmed materials were presented by a text as reported that all their programmed materials were machine presented, and overall half as many again reported some use of programmed texts as reported use of teaching machines. Although data is not available to directly compare the 1973 survey results with those of the 1966 survey on this aspect, it seems apparent that teaching machines have lost ground to programmed texts in that time, since in 1966 only slightly more programmes were in the form of a text rather than for presentation by a machine. Even in 1966, however, the student-hours of text usage considerably exceeded the student-hours of teaching machine usage. The trend away from teaching machines found support in data emerging from a different section of the 1973 survey, where the overall trend was for organizations to actually state that their use of teaching machines was decreasing. Audio-visual devices represent a significant minority of the methods of presenting programmed materials, and a small number of organizations use other presentation techniques such as tapes and on-the-job audio.

As in 1966 commercially produced, off-the-shelf programmes predominate, the next most common source being programmes produced by the organizations' own staff. This falls far short of the numbers using commercially produced programmes, however. As in 1966, external consultants seem to be the source of only a small minority of the 'tailor made' programmes used, and a similar number of firms quote a parent company as a programme source. All in all, the picture is largely unchanged from 1966.

A detailed analysis of involvement of the organizations' own staff in programme writing modifies the above picture slightly. As compared to 1966 there is a much greater commitment of organizations' own staff to programme writing. The smaller 1973 survey found slightly fewer users of programmed instruction than the larger 1966 survey, but at the same time found more than twice as many organizations employing their own programme writing staff, and more than twice as many programme writers employed. This supports Whitlock's (1972) comment on the 'upsurge in house produced programmes' although perhaps a term milder than 'upsurge' would be more appropriate.

The trend is for organizations to employ just one programme writer (although larger teams are far from uncommon) and for the programme writing to be on a part-time basis. Again these trends could be noted in 1966, but they have grown noticeably more pronounced in the meantime. An analysis of the techniques used in devising programmed materials shows that skills analysis is by far the most used. Bloom's <u>Taxonomy</u> and Gagné's <u>Hierarchy</u> are virtually unused as bases for programme writing. Ruleg, Algorithms, Mathetics, Structural Communication, Information Mapping and Network Analysis occupy intermediate positions. The predominence of Skills Analysis and the low utilization of Bloom's and Gagné's ideas may in part be due to the bias towards the manufacturing industries in the sample, and the types of job to be trained there. This would emphasize the analysis of manual skills, and play down the training of more intellectual skills. This could not totally account for the finding, however, and we are forced to the conclusion that the work of Bloom and Gagné has found little application in programming for industry.

The general picture of programmed instruction emerges as one of a technique which is still developing and changing to some extent but whose growth is now approaching a state of equilibrium; the claim that it is now in a decline is not upheld by the data available. One fact which clearly emerged was that techniques, such as programmed instruction, cannot be judged totally in isolation, for its application and growth is at least in part controlled by economic and industrial factors which influence the training effort as a whole. This is clearly illustrated by a number of comments by organizations who had abandoned programmed instruction, to the effect that they had not taken in apprentices for several years, or that their training effort had totally ceased. Even so, evidence emerged from other sections of the questionnaire which suggested that programmed instruction, although still increasing in use, was not expanding as fast as the training effort as a whole.

It is interesting to note that even though programmed instruction has ceased its meteoric growth, a technique which incorporates much of the spirit of programmed instruction is now showing one of the fastest growth rates of all training techniques, namely, Training by Objectives.

Rigorous application of T.B.O. involves many of the steps of preparing programmed instruction (apart from the actual construction of teaching 'frames'). Not only is T.B.O. rapidly growing, but it is also already one of the most used training techniques and is considered by industrial trainers to be one of the most important recent innovations. Probably an important factor in the success of T.B.O. is that it is a blanket technique for planning, organizing and evaluating training which can be applied to nearly every training situation, in combination with nearly any other training technique. It has high versatility, unlike case studies or role playing, and so although not used so widely as these techniques as yet, it is much more likely to play a major role in an organization's training effort.

REFERENCES

Ellis, P. and Romiszowski, A.J. (1973) The Use of Programmed Instruction and Educational Technology in British Industry, 1973. Programmed Instruction Centre, Middlesex Polytechnic, Occasional Publication.

Romiszowski, A.J. (1967a) A Survey of the Use of Programmed Learning by Industry, 1966. Programmed Learning and Educational Technology 4, 210-215.

Romiszowski, A.J. (1967b) The Use of Programmed Learning by Industry in England. Programmed Instruction Centre, Enfield College of Technology. Occasional Publication.

Romiszowski, A.J. (1968) The use of programmed instruction in British Industry. Aspects of Educational Technology, Vol. 2, London: Methuen.

Whitlock, Q.A. (1972) Programmed learning and educational technology in industry. APLET Yearbook of Educational and Instructional Technology 1972/1973. London: Kegan Page.

# SECTION C

## Communication concepts and educational technology

# INTRODUCTION

This section draws together a number of papers which have a more obvious bearing on communication. They may be seen to have their origins in communication studies, or they may make direct reference to the communication process — overtly, or covertly by using concepts from communication theory.

The section begins with a paper by Cherry who states quite explicitly that educational technology can be considered to have a wide frame of reference — 'from toys to computers'; he also stresses the importance of gaining emotional acceptance of technical aids to learning, and the need to guard against over-elaboration in equipment. The following paper by Meredith also focuses on the importance of the affective side of instrumentation in learning; the ideas which he generates go well beyond the traditionally accepted boundaries of educational technology, and they open up many new avenues for research and development in this field.

The following three papers by Rowntree, Williams, and Mitchell are more specific. Broadly speaking, they centre on the concept of feedback and its implications for learning. Rowntree emphasizes the value of two-way communication, as distinct from one-way communication, which, he suggests, is more manipulative than facilitative. Williams takes a novel look at the application of telecommunications to education, and he echoes Cherry's point that a particular medium should be acceptable to the user. Mitchell's paper draws a distinction between positive and negative feedback as control mechanisms for learning; he regards the positive feedback model as being less mechanistic than the negative feedback model, and preferable on the grounds that positive feedback places the locus of control within the individual learner.

The section continues with articles by Houlton and Cook who bring an interdisciplinary note to the proceedings. Houlton puts the question, 'What is a medium?' And he attempts to answer it by drawing upon concepts from economic sociology; he further scrutinizes the concepts of medium and channel, and he proposes that an explanation of the difference between these two concepts can best be given at the system-level. Cook's paper provides a perspective of communication and learning from the discipline of ethology; he emphasizes the importance of adaptation, and he suggests that there is a need to initiate assumption-free assessments of the communication/learning process.

The limitations of conventional research styles in education are stressed by Baggaley and Duck, who present three experiments illustrating a more pragmatic approach to the problems educationalists face. In dealing with the psychological effects of particular television production techniques, their work relates to that of Coldevin (Section 1), and indicates that the medium may be used to control learning efficiency in ways hitherto unexploited. The section concludes with papers by Jamieson and Hancock who look at the problem of communication and learning in developing countries. Jamieson gives an example of a specific experiment into functional literacy, and he concludes by outlining the communication problems surrounding field experimentation. Hancock highlights the problem of abstracting a technology designed for a particular cultural milieu and the attempt at transplantation into a different cultural setting; he goes on to deal with the role of international development agencies in applying communication media, disciplines, and techniques to educational development.

234

# Teaching or learning? A critique of educational technology

C. CHERRY, Imperial College, London

**Abstract:** An attempt is made to define a 'teacher' and an 'educated person' in terms such that the values of educational technology (from toys to computers) may be considered. 'Learning' may mean many things, from first learning to speak and so to be aware of one's own personal world-image to learning abstract concepts, social values, skills of all kinds, abilities to reason and persuade and to accept criticism. The vital importance of emotional development is stressed; emotion must precede reason.

Education and technology change the social and physical environment; education should prepare people for change. Change derives from heresy requiring 'courage'. How can 'educational technology' assist?

Technology possesses no power in itself; the power lies in the people's beliefs and these depend upon those person's social conditions and environment (e.g. whether industrialized or not). Reference is made to teaching aids for pre-industrial countries.

The importance of symbolism and imagery is considered, both in intellectual and emotional aspects, together with possible dangers of the technology itself acting symbolically (e.g. 'obsession' with technological gadgets and fears aroused by technology today).

## INTRODUCTION

I must confess at the outset that, when first invited to speak at this Conference, I was somewhat alarmed at the prospect, and rather reluctant. Perhaps it was the title that frightened me: 'The International Conference of Programmed Learning and Educational Technology, 1974'. It led me to imagine an audience wholly expert in computer usage, long experienced in programmed learning and keen to introduce complex modern machines into the classroom. I cannot tell you anything new that has happened in the field of Educational Technology, nor give you results of trials, nor indeed shall I refer to any specific techniques at all, in detail, for this is outside my competence.

You might well be asking what else is there to talk about, at a Conference such as this? So I will start with a short summary of my intentions, and if anyone feels that these are not relevant to his interests, I shall not be offended if they walk out.

Briefly then. I had felt that it might be of interest at a Conference such as this, to stand back for a few moments and to look at the processes we call **education, teaching, learning,** in a rather philosophical way, and also to adopt a particular view of **technology,** in order that discussion of its functions and values may be fruitful. I shall perhaps be rash, by trying to define these terms: education, teaching and learning. As one who has been engaged in the business for 30 years, I feel it a moral duty to do so!

'Learning' may mean many things, from learning to eat and speak to learning to reason, from learning social values to acquiring facts, from learning skills of all kinds to learning how to persuade and how to accept criticism. I shall stress the vital importance of emotional development; for emotion must precede reason.

Both education and technology change the social and physical environment; they are intimately related. Education should prepare people for change of the physical and social environment and this, in turn requires the quality that we call 'courage'. How can educational technology assist?

I shall argue that technology possesses no powers whatever, in itself; the powers lie in its users' beliefs and attitudes and these in turn depend upon the peoples' conditions — e.g. whether industrialized or not, or whether they see purpose in what they are doing. I should like to make some reference to teaching aids for the developing countries too.

Again, I shall mention the great importance of symbolism and imagery, both in their intellectual and emotional aspects, together with some possible dangers of technology itself acting symbolically (that is, 'obsession' with technical gadgets and fears aroused in the public mind by modern technology).

## (1) What Do Teachers Do?

The word 'teaching' means so many things, yet it is frequently used as a blanket-term — and it is 'what teachers do'. It covers so many activities: education, training, instruction, tuition, enlightenment, informing, .... many things. It can even be used in the authoritarian sense of ordering ('I'll teach you to do that again my boy!'), the teaching of obedience. At one end of the scale many questions are raised and controversy can be heated; for example, what is education and how is it distinguished from training? Are our universities for education or for training? Are the Sciences and the Humanities distinct in this respect? At the other end we seem almost powerless to stop the process of learning — say, in the primary skills of learning to walk, or to talk. At all these various levels of activity, technologies have their different values, but I would argue that these values are not for teaching (except in trivial respects); they are essential values for the learning processes.

I would go so far to say that, in a sense, 'teaching' is a bogus activity. This is not meant to be offensive (for I am a teacher myself) and all I mean to say is that teaching is not a positive, direct, activity in the sense 'I to thou'. It is not a matter that I, the teacher, have got something: you, the pupil, want it; so I can pass it to you. Even at the most simple levels of teaching, in the sense of 'informing' about facts, it is not merely a question of these facts being passed from a teacher's head into the pupil's. This function could be served by reference books, data handouts or factual textbooks; the human need not be present. The real human function of the teacher is to persuade the pupil to **value** his acquired facts — to assess them, question them, believe or doubt, and above all to have the courage to question the teacher's validity.

The real, direct, activity is that we call 'learning', rather than teaching. **The real function of the teacher is to create an environment in which learning can proceed.** And any technology that is used forms part of that environment; it is good or bad only in-as-much as it helps or hinders the learning — from the baby's rattle to the modern programmed learning techniques. As we all know, environments can be prepared in which learning can be inhibited, if not made virtually impossible. Desire to learn, at various levels, seems inherent in human beings, but it is a desire that can be suppressed. But desire is emotional, so if any form of educational technology is used its function must be emotional in the first place and perhaps intellectual in the second. Emotion must precede reason; one must **desire,** must **want** to know, and must **like** any new technology involved.

A child survives and develops for long without deep reasoning, at least without verbalized reason and analysis. Intellectual development is usually rapid by adolescence, but we do not regard the younger child as 'stupid'. He or she can deal with their growing personal worlds with a host of mental imagery; they perceive — objects, causes, relations; they speak, they feel, they imagine; they acquire many skills. But they may not be able to rationalize upon all this intense activity as their older brothers and sisters may try to do.

Again, how would we test the hypothesis: 'he is a good teacher' ? Surely by observing the results, the degree of learning. It is learning that we should direct our attention to, as is usually the case, when speaking of 'educational technology'. By so doing we may better ensure that we consider the great importance of its emotional aspects. Such technology will be successful not merely by operating according to rational or logical principles, but only if it does so in ways that are culturally and emotionally acceptable. I want to enlarge upon this point a little later.

As any parent knows, children can be the most outspoken critics. It might be good for many school-teachers to hear what children say about them at home. They will praise some teachers as 'good', whom they like, and others they will damn outright. On what basis of judgement? They know no educational theory and have had little experience of human contacts in variety. It is usually assessed through their feeling of frustration or of release in their desire to learn — and they will usually be right — for feelings are **facts**.

Even at the earliest age, I feel it is wrong to regard the mother/child relation as a direct I-to-thou teaching process. Who teaches whom? It could be argued that it is first the child who teaches the mother — for it is conception and the appearance of the baby that converts the woman into a mother, instills emotional attitudes in her and sets her off into motherhood behaviour. The child learns to babble its own phonetics within about six months, then to speak and to walk, though very few mothers are formally qualified to so instruct. Other skills rapidly follow — writing, scribbling and drawing, making endless things, whilst the child's conceptual and imaginative life develops, its intellect and rationality slowly emerge. All these bodily skills and mental abilities may be greated assisted by that most important type of educational technology, which we call **toys**. I shall refer again later to toys.

In summary, I argue that the primary duty of a teacher is to encourage the desire to learn. Some may inhibit learning, though not necessarily through wrong facts or by irrationality, but more through preventing the pupil emotionally from responding to ideas; at the lowest level by frightening them or by themselves refusing to learn from the pupil. Our question is: how can educational technology assist? So far I have merely argued that it can assist emotionally and perhaps, thereby, intellectually.

Anyone who presumes to speak of educational technology must, assumedly, have his own ideas as to what education is, towards which process he is applying the technology. Otherwise, how can its value be assessed? Or he must have his views as to the product of that process — the educated person. I therefore feel challenged to offer my own opinions, very humbly.

## (2) What is an Educated Person?

I would not presume to offer a formal definition of 'education', for I believe that even education theorists are hesitant. It is as difficult as to define 'intelligence'. Nevertheless, anyone who is engaged in the educational industry must surely have his views upon what it is that he is doing; he must have ideals or some basis of assessing the product. I shall merely attempt a personal description.

For anyone to be judged to be 'educated' it is surely not enough that he knows very many things, nor that he possesses many skills — for then he would merely be 'clever'. His knowledge may become outdated, his skills obsolete; he should be able to continue his learning in ways needed to suit his changing circumstances of age, time and social environment. I would suggest, for our present purpose, that **an educated person is one who is able to adapt to changing circumstances.**

He certainly needs skills, especially verbal skills, but also must understand their relevance, judge his own limitations, be desirous of changing his skills, be willing to accept other peoples' values, be aware of his own value-assumptions and to be prepared to change these, as circumstances change.

Circumstances may change for different reasons. He may travel abroad and mix with other cultures; he would then not make the error of assuming their cultural values, their technologies, or their social institutions to be identical with his own. He might have dealings with other social classes, or other age groups, in his own country, and would need to understand their values, ideas and institutions. But, more relevant to our present theme, he will need to adapt today to a changing society here, in an industrial country — to its changing values, institutions, and ideas. If he cannot effectively change, he will be unable to relate to younger people, unable to adapt to the changing scene, be lost and confused.

How can educational technology assist with education for change? I am not thinking of specialized and advanced technologies, but of all levels, in education of children, adolescents and adults, including toys, school equipment, films, models, radio and television in the home.... what properties can these technologies possess which assist?

It is only a changing society that speaks of 'progress'. Before industrialization, the word **progress** simply meant a 'journey' (as in Bunyan's 'Pilgrims Progress'). But it was the rapid growth of science, the spread of rationalism and, above all, industrialization that changed its meaning to 'journeying forward'. Medieval man saw Heaven behind him and things on earth could only get worse and worse. But the rational processes of science and industrialization were what Max Weber called 'goal directed'. Heaven became placed in front of us, we journey 'forward' now, but never seem to reach there. We expect things to get better and are unhappy when they don't; people in earlier society must have expected things to get worse and occasionally been happy when they did not. Change is essential to any kind of 'progress', however we judge that elusive idea. But change forces us all to adapt, to be somebody different every year and this can be distressing. 'Progress' contains the seeds of discontent, as an inevitable price, and education should be our main protector.

Change comes about by dissent, not by conformity to the status quo. It derives from those people who are dissatisfied, those who have the courage to stand up and say: 'No!', either to oneself, by admitting error, or to others who propose change — by criticizing their proposals, not blindly following them, as the new fashion. Ability to dissent is

239

essential and dissent requires the quality we call **courage**, in the sense
of 'moral courage', or the 'courage of one's convictions'; it is the
essential human quality that gives both adult and child the desire to say:
'Why?' — 'Why should I?', 'Why do you say that?' and not to accept the
answer: 'Because I say so!.' It lies behind the **curiosity** that leads
people, old or young, to want to know why things work, what causes
things to happen.... even the curiosity implicit in scientific enquiry at
all levels. And 'curiosity' requires courage. Education should instil
such courage and, if educational technology is considered, how can it
help? I certainly think that it can, but I do not find it easy to say why
or how. To do so, I must first give my own views on the nature of technology — what it really **is**.

### (3)  On the Nature of Technology — Especially 'Educational Technology

It may be felt by some that, in speaking of emotions and courage, I am
using rather grandiose terms for dealing with such a mundane matter as
technology. To many people, technology merely means **things** — artefacts,
machines, gadgets, contraptions, the products of industry and symbols
of the consumer society. If we regard technology merely as the study of
inanimate objects, however, we might be puzzled as to why it is that so
many people get hot under the collar when criticizing it, deploring the
materialism that it appears to them to symbolize, or when expressing
fear of what they call 'technocrats'.

Technology is indeed an emotional matter, and must be so by its
very nature. Perhaps this is most clearly brought home to us when
something breaks down — when the car engine suddenly stops, when the
electricity supply fails and the lights go out, or when a strike stops all
the trains. We feel frustrated, let down, even angry. This **shouldn't**
happen; something has gone wrong with the world. In brief, a **trust** has
been betrayed.

I would take the existentialist view about technology that was expressed by Martin Heidegger that technology is the mediator between
Man and raw nature. It is essentially a **mediator.** It is the means whereby any human being comes to see his own particular world; the world as
he knows it and his relations to it, his powers, as he feels them, are
those that his technology reveals to him. If your society possesses no
more than bows and arrows, clay pots, wooden ploughs, and fire, you
will see your world through these particular powers of action. If you
possess atom bombs, electric cookers, motor cars and oil-fired central
heating you will see the world and also your own nature, personal powers
and freedoms, very differently. So too, with educational technology; if
I may use that word in its broadest sense, to include everything from a
baby's rattle to an abacus, from books and pictures to films, television
and computers.... the possession of each, acceptance of it and adaptation

to it will change the person's view of the world, and of himself. I would then assess the values of any new educational equipment partly by the extent to which it affects the pupil's view of himself, as a learner, of his power and his responsibilities, as such or, put another way, of what particular ways he would feel frustrated and deprived if the new equipment were removed from his use.

There is always a danger that educational technology can become an obsession, a thing of interest 'for its own sake', like the pleasure that many people derive from tinkering with their cars in the garage. This danger exists in all technology, if it is to be regarded only as **things,** and not as a mediator. The very word **technology** frightens many people and there is quite a strong anti-technology move about us today. This is wrongly-directed; it should not be against technology itself, but rather against some of the specific values embodied in certain examples of it. It is industrialization, or certain economic or political values, our particular priorities, that may call for valid criticism. But technology itself we must have, in some form or other. Have not the anthropologists defined Man as : 'the tool maker and tool user' ?

At the obsessional level, technology can be symbolic only of itself, and not mediate in its intended way between the person and the world. To many, educational technology may conjure up an image of something electronic, modern, complicated, expensive and (to use that awful word), 'sophisticated'. An ideal technology is unobtrusive, even unnoticed.

There is a certain lecture theatre, not a hundred miles from London Airport, that has every seat fitted with closed-circuit television, with radio, with push-button communication, with a bulk of equipment confronting each seated spectator and half concealing him from the speaker. When I spoke there myself recently and when I sat in the audience, I felt that I was in Houston Space Centre. To me, it was almost alarming. But I must be careful not to assume that everyone felt the same! Others might be quite at home and even stimulated. Or there may be specialized uses, for demonstrations, that would not occur to me. There are simply no golden rules.

By contrast, I would mention one use of technology for education that seems to me to be nearly ideal — I refer to the Open University. Here the pupils are necessarily constrained to the home. The television set is a piece of domestic equipment, familiar, acceptable and unobtrusive. It serves to present images in ways and in a situation likely to be emotionally appealing; it brings the face and actions of tutors into the same environment. The annual visits to a college environment for group study and personal tuition encourage pupil's feelings of membership; the images of tutors through the screen and the postal service, their handwritten comments on corrected scripts, etc., become converted into real people, giving human relationships. At headquarters there exists all the complicated and more obtrusive technology — duplicating machines,

241

office equipment, computer and other non-domestic machinery for administrative purposes. I also admire the production of such printed Course material as I have seen, which uses great imagination in some of its imagery. In my opinion it is a very valid use of educational technology, of several forms.

## (4) The Vital Importance of Images and Symbols

It can scarcely be said too often, that the products of technology, the artefacts or machines, possess absolutely no power in themselves. The power exists only by virtue of peoples' beliefs and attitudes towards them; and 'belief' is 'preparation for action'. The powers of educational technology are, initially, rhetorical powers, powers of persuasion, of instilling belief and desire for action. The learner must be stimulated into doing something.

The relation between a person and a machine is what we normally call **design**. The effectiveness of the design, the power of the machine, depend upon the ways in which it can act symbolically. In the case of educational technology, the symbolic values arise not only from the machine itself (its appearance, shape and size, appropriateness to its environment, etc.) but from its use of visual, or aural, or other images for presenting its information to the pupil — as, for example, a television set acts symbolically by its very appearance as a piece of furniture, and also by the programmes it presents.

An idea and its symbol provide an essential unity. Ideas and concepts are revealed or concealed by good or bad imagery. People vary very greatly in their emotional attraction to different styles of image; some like words, some like pictures, others diagrams, others numbers; some respond to personalities more than others, some like mathematical reasoning, some like logical.... It seems to me that designers of educational equipment (and those who consider buying it) can scarcely pay too much attention to the symbolism that it uses. We need continued research into symbols and imagery in education and to the emotional and intellectual responses of different sections of learners, whilst the results could be of profound importance to those concerned with educational technology.

Unfortunately, even with the simple techniques of the past this has been true — chalk and talk. It is not the chalk and the blackboard itself which does anything at all; the powers arise from what is drawn or written on the board. How many pupils have been condemned as stupid merely because the teacher has used an unappealing form of symbolism? Change the image and intelligences may appear to redistribute.

In conclusion, I have argued that educational technology, at all levels, can assist learning first by producing images and symbolism which makes ideas emotionally acceptable to pupils. It is not merely by

242

bringing facts to his attention, or by making ideas more concise, or more logical. Some people are indeed persuaded by logic, more than by beauty, or some may see beauty in logic. The imagery must be **desired.**

## (5) Some Practical Examples. Two Experiments in Cross-cultural Communication

Some people may feel that the way in which I have been speaking is too abstract, or even 'high-fallutin',' so I will end by mentioning two specific examples of research, being carried out in my own section at Imperial College, which illustrate some of my arguments.

However, my own field of study is not educational technology, per se, but communication. Nevertheless, the functions of technology in the learning process are essentially communicative functions. Some of our work here concerns communication with people of other cultures (either people overseas or immigrants) and these examples highlight certain points more strongly. The two programmes I refer to are :

(a) The design of laboratory equipment for teaching elementary science, in Jamaica, India and elsewhere.

(b) Communication of information regarding social rights between a London Borough Council and local residents in such need, e.g. elderly people, immigrants.

In a loose sense, all teacher/learner relations are cross-cultural because, however hard one tries, a teacher is a member of a social group (perhaps seen to be an older age-group, or authoritarian, or of another profession) and the learner is a member of another (the 'student-body', perhaps younger, or coming from a different social class, or ethnic group, or part of the country, etc.) Other cross-cultural relations of a like kind can arise in communication between doctor and patient, or lawyer and client, or local authority and rate-payers, or the police and the public, etc. The problem of communication, perhaps mediated by technical equipment, is that of creating a social membership involving both 'teacher' and 'learner' in common purposeful activity — what I earlier described as 'creating an environment in which learning can proceed'.

The first programme that I mentioned (teaching of elementary science in schools of very poor tropical countries) is being undertaken by Mr. Keith Warren, who has taught science in schools not only in Britain, but also in Jamaica, Bangkok, India and elsewhere. He is working in conjunction with UNICEF, UNESCO and other bodies, with children in primary and lower secondary schools (which is all that most of them ever see). At present UNICEF supplies some hundreds of items of science teaching equipment, which is necessarily brought from Europe or the USA.

Such equipment is essentially based upon the scientific traditions of the Western industrial countries and is designed to be used in laboratories equipped with electrical supplies, with running water, gas supplies, and all the rest. The schools in these poor countries, needless to say, do not have laboratories and indeed are fortunate if they have a cupboard or a table. School work is essentially theoretical, with little or no experimental reinforcement, with little or no constructional work and development of manual skills. UNICEF aim to change this situation and Mr. Warren is assisting by proposing 'kitchen table' experiments, using materials and odds and ends which pupils bring from home, or can find in local stores — things very familiar to them; he then prepares manuals, written specially for pupil teachers, describing how to both construct and operate such domestic equipment. He himself visits and works with them, to learn of the consequences. Advice on repair and on cleaning may also be needed.

Much Western equipment for school laboratories is not only expensive, but wholly out of place — chemical balances, elaborate glassware, large lenses and mirrors, electrical measuring instruments.... These may seem remote and strange things to the young children, bearing no relation to normal life, nor to anything which they have made themselves at home, out of bits of wood, nails, string, cardboard.... nor to their domestic utensils. Again, many concepts of elementary science are based, not upon the real world, but upon an idealized one of perfectly smooth planes, perfect spheres, inelastic cords, exact intervals of time (e.g. stop-watches), uniform motion, etc.

Such concepts are not too difficult for us to grasp, who live surrounded by the products of industry, ruled by the clock, and by elaborate craftsmanship. Nor should we forget something that I mentioned earlier — the fact that most of us possessed toys of many kinds from the earliest age, with which we develop feelings of spacial relationships, of time, causality and other basic scientific concepts. Children in these very poor countries do not have toys in the same sense, but only what they may make with sticks, stones, bits and pieces of scrap. As Mr. Warren urges, the need in their schools is not merely for 'do-it-yourself' classes in elementary science, but also for 'make-it-yourself' activity. And he has found that the children are often far better at this than their teachers (who were taught in an earlier, less practical, tradition).

Figures 1 - 4 illustrate Mr. Warren's suggestions.

Another serious lack of teaching aid in the poor countries is that of **books.** Such books as they may have in their schools are necessarily mostly Western texts, filled with Western images, ideals and even inbuilt political values, and very often written long ago. This is not necessarily due solely to their expensiveness, but often because the countries concerned do not yet have authors writing their own books. This situation is

(A)

(B)

Figure 1: The teaching situation in the schoolroom of this Bengali village (A) looks strange to Western eyes — but not so bizarre as Western-style science teaching apparatus appears to pupils sitting there on the mat on the dung-washed floor (B).

(with acknowledgements to Mr. Keith Warren)

245

Figure 2: The Ubiquitous Bicycle. Virtually the whole of Newtonian Dynamics may be experimentally illustrated by a bicycle, as the main 'laboratory' equipment.

(with acknowledgements to Mr. Keith Warren)

Figure 3: In this experiment a tin has nail holes punched in the sides and contains a little fire of paper, wood and charcoal. If whirled round the head it can fire earthenware ($500^{o}$C) and even melt lead.

(with acknowledgements to Mr. Keith Warren)

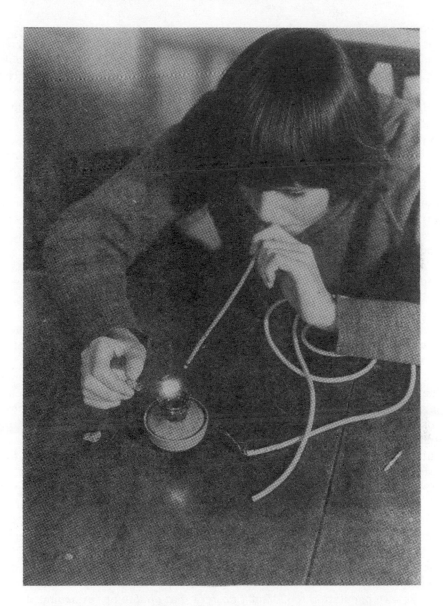

Figure 4: Apparatus for teaching elementary science need not be remote. Imaginative use of local materials can not only lessen the exotic aspect but can widen experience surprisingly and raise the generality of concepts too. This example shows a nine-year-old child using a blowpipe, made of rice straw, with a clay plug at one end having a fine pin hole in it. Blowing through a paraffin lamp can melt thin copper wire (approximately 900$^{\circ}$C).

(with acknowledgements to Mr. Keith Warren)

beginning to change, as native writers appear; again, there are now improved aid plans, such as those of the English Language Book Society which, starting in 1960, has sent out over ten million educational books, under 600 titles, under the advice of people in the developing countries themselves. India is the biggest single user. The subjects cover not only science but law, nursing, accountancy, draughtsmanship, surveying and many other practical matters which are pre-requisites of development.

I will be very brief in describing the second research programme which I have mentioned, because it has not been underway for very long. It is being carried out by Miss Jocelyn Chaplin, for the Camden Borough Council and aims to improve (and to evaluate) communication concerning various social rights, between the Council and certain social groups who would benefit (e.g. elderly people, low-income groups and immigrants such as Pakistani, Greek, Cypriot, Italian, Irish and others).

The traditional modes of communication between Council Offices and local residents has, as we all know, taken the form of officious-looking printed documents, printed in such formal impersonal style, in such pseudo-legal jargon, that they appear perhaps to all of us, as **threats.** They can be far more disturbing to certain social groups however, to whom the 'them-us' division is wider and deeper. If Councils **want** to assist, as they do, alternative techniques must be sought.

Miss Chaplin is experimenting with new forms of image and symbol, including cartoons, films, pictures and words, but avoiding the types of jargon used traditionally by local government which may act to preserve social distance between 'them and us'. Such images and methods of presenting factual information aim to create **trust**, through meaningful cultural communication and the instilling of desires in the minds of those for whom the social benefits are intended.

The illustrations in Figures 5, 6 and 7 are self-explanatory.

In conclusion, I should like to emphasize that, when speaking of simple home-made equipment, or of children's toys, or of creating new forms of image to stimulate emotional response, etc., I am not in any way implying that people of poor countries are 'simple people', nor that their intelligence distribution is necessarily any different from our own. I would apply the same arguments concerning technical aids for education to our own population too. But I do feel that people of, or from, the poorer countries may be handicapped by sudden confrontation by much Western modern technology, without adequate and relevant prior education preparation. Much modern technology does indeed have real validity in the newly-emerging countries; it can create fashions, however, and it can lead people into confusing the symbols of industrial modernization with the thing itself. In the field of education this could be disastrous.

Figure 5: This cartoon has appeared in the 'Neighbourhood Press' and is also used as a poster in shops and elsewhere. It is intended to advise certain residents of the existence of the Housing Aid Centre and of the meaning of a Rent Tribunal.

(with acknowledgements to Miss Jocelyn Chaplin)

249

The Rent Register is for FURNISHED
accomodation. Rents are registered
if a previous tenant has been to
the rent tribunal. If the rent has
been registered the landlord cannot
put it up himself. This is illegal,
and he can be forced to pay back
some of the excess rent. Camden
legal division have already dealt
with many of these cases.
(ADDRESS GIVEN IN COMIC STRIP).

Figure 6:  Local Authority Communication with Local Residents.
This cartoon is one example intended to inform certain social groups of the fact
that a Rent Register exists, about what it is for, and to encourage people to go and
see it, in order to discover their rights regarding rent payments.  It appears in a
'Neighbourhood Press' newspaper, which is locally run and given free through
appropriate letter boxes.    It is particularly directed to young people, and to certain immigrants, living in furnished accommodation.

(with acknowledgements to Miss Jocelyn Chaplin)

Figure 7:   This poster is intended to create an image and concept of 'membership' of the Camden Old Peoples Welfare Association.  It will appear in the local press, shop windows, Luncheon Clubs, Day Centres, etc.

(with acknowledgements to Miss Jocelyn Chaplin)

251

# Instruments and individuals

P. MEREDITH, University of Leeds

**Abstract:** The substance of this paper may be regarded as a sequel to the author's 1958 paper on 'Semantic Matrices' at the Washington International Conference on Scientific Information. Its objective is to go beyond the author's 1966 book Instruments of Communication (Pergamon Press) in order to invite educational technologists to think of themselves as developing 'Instruments of Civilization'. It is almost a platitude to speak of a crisis in technology today. It is not merely an economic crisis. It is a crisis in the minds and hearts of a young adult generation, many already parents, wondering if they have a future. Technology has tacitly accepted a service-role in a master-slave relationship, with no ethical responsibility for its products. The Young see civilization as ugly, frustrating and dangerous. In developing Epistemics over the past thirty years, briefly defined as 'The instrumental study of inter-personal communication', the author has been driven to concentrate on the actual production of media for promoting an educational relation between Aesthetics and Energetics. As technology develops a sense of responsibility it will see the **quality** of energy usage as more important than the quantity of its production.

## INTRODUCTION

The topic which I wish to discuss may be very simply defined as the relation between force and feeling. This definition is simple but its implications are endless. Here I can discuss only those implications which are of uppermost importance at the present time, and, of these, only the ones on which I hope I have something constructive to say.

More academically we can say that the relation between force and feeling is the relation between Energetics and Esthetics. What is currently called 'Energetics' is really a generalization of mechanics and is thus fundamental to all technology. Since the world is worried about a threatened energy shortage (due not to any physical shortage but to the misuse of resources) this is certainly a topic of uppermost current importance. Since the world is also worried about violence and ugliness, directly resulting from misuse of energy, strong feelings are aroused, and since these feelings have a direct effect on decision-making they are just as potent causal agents as fire, water and sunshine.

252

Thus by recognizing feeling as a causal agent I am not introducing subjectivity into science, but actually extending its objectivity by pointing out that objects do not move by Newton's laws alone. The atomic bomb was not produced by Newton's laws. They explain only its acceleration when it was dropped.

Our concept of 'energy', not made explicitly by Newton himself, received an exact definition in terms of Newtonian mechanics. This was a highly rational system of thought whose necessary truth remained unquestioned until the beginning of the present century. Modern energetics takes account of a variety of energy-sources, thermal, chemical, electromagnetic and nuclear which were unknown to Newton. He did not lack the rationality required for this extended view, but the instruments required to detect and measure these forces were not yet invented. When they arrived they revealed faults in the rational structure of classical mechanics. And this is part of my theme.

Nineteenth century science, on which the Industrial Revolution flourished, had become **too** rational. It had forgotten the essential message of Copernicus and Galileo viz. that when observation conflicts with reason it is reason which must give way. What seems rational in one framework, and at one level of observational accuracy, is found to be inadequate in another framework, or at a level of greater accuracy achieved by the invention of instruments which extend human sensitivity beyond the limits of our sense-organs. The telescope and the microscope did more to change our philosophy than all the arguments of philosophers.

I am not saying that we can do without reason. I am saying that reason alone, uncorrected by sensitivity, can lead, at best, to nonsense, and at worst to barbarity. And since sensitivity and feeling are more intimately related than are reason and feeling, we need to take not only a cool look but also a passionate look at the history of science and technology; not only passionate but also compassionate. For, as Copernicus well knew, it is both hard and dangerous to step out of line with one's contemporary orthodox rationality.

This has a direct bearing on current educational problems. For the sacred cows of 'rationality' and 'objectivity' have been the objects of worship in orthodox psychology for the past half-century. As embodied in the I.Q. their effect on educational sensitivity has been almost wholly disastrous. And they have spawned two golden calves viz. the rapidly growing industry of statistical research in psychology and education, and the even more lucrative industry of psychometric test-publication. Being old enough to have nothing to lose I take pot-shots at these thick-skinned cattle whenever opportunity arises.

To score a high I.Q. demands no feeling and only certain specialized kinds of sensitivity, but a considerable reserve of miscellaneous cunning. It is this latter asset which is most highly prized in our educational system because politicians, economic advisers and industrialists need all the cunning at their command in their struggle to keep up with one another in their drive for power.  One might have expected that the world of literature, with Dr. Leavis's slogan of 'sensibility' to inspire it, to have more to say in educating the adult world in the realities of power.  But so obsessed were the Bloomsbury group in overcoming Victorian inhibitions on sex that they largely overlooked the literally lethal preoccupation with power which has dominated our history for centuries.

As I promised to be constructive a word of compassion here is necessary.  Recent events have made us all vividly aware of the perils of power.  Primarily our compassion is for those at the receiving end of bombs and bullets.  But if we look at the realities of technology, whether industrial, military or educational (including the mass media) and ask what sort of lives are led by those who produce, maintain, control or finance this vast exercise in energetics, we see that they are prisoners.  A control engineer in a power station has to spend all his time watching dials, and that's not much of a life.  The more power you have the more vigilant you have to be, and that is equally true for a foreman, shop-steward, manager, banker, police-chief, headmaster, vice-chancellor, or military commander, all the way to the Kremlin and the White House.  All are prisoners of their position.  The more power they have the less free they are to do what they like.  Except, of course, that some of them like nothing else.  They have been so de-sensitized by the upward struggle that all esthetics has departed from their lives.

If educational technology is to be a civilizing influence, and not a mere tool for power-seekers, we have some hard thinking to do. Hard and unpopular.  For whatever innovations we seek to introduce we can be quite sure that the Establishment will attempt to misuse it.  And by the 'Establishment' I mean all the power-groups which have controlled men's destinies, especially in the Western and Westernized world. This is a very broad allegation but it receives daily confirmation on millions of television screens whose nightly message to all our homes is that this is a world of devilry, destruction and death.  The message is not new, only the medium.  The message is as ancient as the Pyramids.  It tells us that all the life-forces in this world are to be dedicated to securing the immortality of power in an ideal **other** world.  The same was the message of Plato to his academy, and of the mediaeval monasteries in which began our educational system of teaching regimented classes to master the mystic symbolism of verbal power, and to keep their hands clean and their collars white.  If they fail they become 'blue-collared' workers with dirty hands building pyramids.  This is the stark dichotomy on which our educational system still works.  What a few people on both sides of the chasm are beginning to appreciate is that clean hands can lead to sterility of thought, and dirty hands can teach us the facts of life.

For dirt is merely the redistribution of the products of life. The one white-collar profession which does appreciate this fact is medicine, and it is no accident that, in the academic world medical schools have been the spearhead of educational technology. It is also the most deeply satisfying of professions because it is dedicated to saving life.

If this sounds like a sermon, well, as Mr. Harold Macmillan recently remarked 'Old men are allowed to preach'. I am not so sure that they should be allowed to **teach**, for events move so fast that their teaching may well be irrelevant to current developments. In any case, I doubt if I have anything to say on technology, as such, which would be news to a gathering of expert educational technologists. However, I can take the liberty of reminding them of certain things which should not be neglected or forgotten. In other words if educational technology is to take our children safely into the 21st century it is as well to look at the 19th century in order to ask why it led to such a bloody awful 20th century. Briefly it was the century in which the widespread application of Newton's laws of motion made possible such a proliferation of machinery that for the first time since the days of the Pharaohs the possibility of the emancipation of slaves became intellectually credible. Two diastrous consequences followed. First the mechanical concept of the universe became a dogma, and scientists began to think of themselves as the prophets of certainty instead of the explorers of uncertainty. Second, because machines were regarded as embodments of certainty the inconvenient facts that they are not only imperfectly designed and manufactured by men but are continually breaking down, requiring continual repair, service and maintenance, were ignored by the philosophers of the Industrial Revolution and by the economists who translated it into the circulation of currency. The result was a massive **expansion** of slavery. Not only are factory-workers tied to the conveyor belt, but executives are tied to their telephones, academics are tied to the examination machine, banks, businesses and research-workers are tied to their computers, politicians are tied to their parliamentary and party machinery, Dr. Kissinger is strapped into his aircraft, and Royal Families will soon have to be handcuffed to their bodyguards.

Now I should like to show that our handling of information can offer an escape from this condition of universal slavery. It is just 24 years since the famous Symposium on Information Theory was held in London in 1950. I have a copy of the transactions of the conference, published in 1953 by the Institute of Radio Engineers, though I was not myself present.

One of the outstanding contributions to that conference was made by Donald MacKay. I can here quote only three brief extracts: (p.10) 'Information Theory is concerned with the making of **representations** — i.e. symbolism in its most general sense.'

255

(p.11) 'The scope of Information Theory thus includes, in principle, three classes of activity:

(1)  Making a representation of some **physical** aspect of experience. This is the problem treated in **Scientific Information-Theory**;

(2)  Making a representation of some non-physical (mental or ideational) aspect of experience. This is at the moment outside our concern, being the problem of the Arts;

(3)  Making a representation in one space **B**, of a representation already present in another space **A**. This is the problem of **Communication Theory**, **B** being termed the **receiving end** and **A** the **transmitting end** of a Communication Channel.'

Finally, one more important definition: (p.13) 'Logon: the unit of structural information, one **logon** is that which enables one new distinguishable group or category to be added to a representation.'

Now Donald MacKay knows well that he and I do not see eye to eye on certain fundamentals. In particular his reference to the Arts reveals an acceptance of the sophistry used in the Gospel to avoid an awkward question. When Christ said 'Render unto Caesar the things which are Caesar's and unto God the things which are God's' he displayed a degree of worldly ingenuity equal to that of Macchiavelli himself. My point is that if God exists then He must co-exist with Caesar and we have to try to survive with **both**, and with whatever relation exists between them. And since each of the three Great Powers regards itself as both God and Caesar, the other two being devils, we ordinary mortals can survive only by a sustained network of inter-personal communication in which we are the masters of our own instruments. Thus Epistemics, in its formal aspect, became essentially a search for a formula for a viable grape-vine. In this formula I had to establish a condition which would make all **logons** in the grape-vine circulation equally available to all. This is the very opposite of a hierarchical structure. The word 'hierarchy' em-bodies in its very etymology the unholy alliance of priests and politicians which has controlled the ideology of the masses since civilization began. The origin of our alphabet in hieroglyphs betokens the priestly cunning by which what is hidden from the multitude remains hidden in the ambiguity of the written word when detached from its context of author-ship and situation.

So let us now examine physics, the one science which has penetrated so deeply into the undercurrents of power that Caesar is now scared stiff, and God Himself may be feeling apprehensive. I take the clue from a 19th century text of Newton's Principia.

Newton's Principia. Sections I, II, III, with notes and illustrations by Percival Frost. Macmillan & Co. 1863 (Cambridge and London).

The following quotation is from Frost's note on Newton's Prop. VI, Theorem V, concerning the determination of the centripetal force acting on a body revolving about a fixed centre of force. The purpose of this quotation is not concerned with the theorem itself but with Frost's corollary dealing with the dimensions of the symbols. For these are fundamentally decisive in giving every communicable concept in physics a precise epistemic structure. The quotation also serves to underline the need to draw a clear distinction between two distinct uses of the word 'dimension', viz. its use in geometry and its use in mechanics. In geometry it is visualized as a straight line. In mechanics it is conceived as an independent variable.

Frost's note is headed 'Homogeneity'. '140. Co. 1, 2. In the expression for F obtained in these corollaries, it is of great importance to observe the dimensions of the symbols.

Thus **h,** being a measure of the rate of description of areas*, is of two dimensions in linear space and of -1 in time.... Hence if the actual areas lines etc. be represented by the symbols, and not the **number** of units.... every term of an equation or of a sum or difference must be homogeneous, or of the same number of dimensions, both in space and time.'

This concept provides the key to all precise physical thinking and to the interpretation of all physical equations. I doubt if its importance is sufficiently stressed in most science teaching. In the pseudo-sciences of psychometrics, sociometrics and econometrics it is completely ignored. It is not itself an empirical concept but rather a bridge between empirical data and mathematical equations. When, for example, we define 'density' as 'mass divided by volume' this is neither an empirical nor a numerical statement. We can abbreviate it as $D = M \div V$. Although this simple concept is as old as Archimedes its conceptual significance is seldom evaluated.

Although this definition is not empirical it cannot be interpreted without reference to perceptual experience. If V is defined as length x breadth x height this applies only to a single shape viz. a rectangular block. But if we apply V to **any** shape we find that we always require three independent linear measurements but their product usually needs to be multiplied by some numerical factor. This latter factor thus provides the clue to the shape. We can say, then, that any volume is 'three-dimensional' in a geometric sense. But all these three dimensions are of the same **type** in a **physical** sense. They are all quantified by space-measurements using a space-instrument viz. the ruler.

---

* As the body moves round the centre of force the radius of its circular path sweeps over a growing area of space. The symbol **h** is defined as 'twice the area described of a unit of time.'

We now come to a point at which very careful thinking is required. The ruler is itself a spatial structure. But so also is the **balance** for determining mass, and the **clock** for determining time. And their scales are spatial. Thus the concept of space is asymmetrical with respect to other physical dimensions. We use space to represent both mass and time and also to represent space itself. To achieve this we cut space up into compartments. These are countable and hence can be represented by numbers.

Speaking of numbers I make no apology for diving into deep waters. My own country is economically in such deep waters that our neighbours are surmising, not without a hint of relish, that we may be drowning. And my diagnosis is that this is attributable to an educational failure in arithmetic. Materially we have far more goods, services, plant and skills than most countries in Asia or Africa but we cannot get our sums right. And this is because children are made to feel that arithmetic is ugly and this feeling lasts through life. So our so-called 'democracy' is glad to hand over the solution of its real problems to statisticians whom it regards equivocally as a cross between high priests and sewage disposal experts. They do their best but they are the victims of a tradition in mathematical education which largely ignores the history of mathematics. Every significant advance in mathematics originates in a moment of insight by some individual personality, and is conditioned by all that has shaped his mind. Thus mathematical publications represent <u>par excellence</u> the instrumentation of inter-personal communication, which is what epistemics is about. Yet it is systematically portrayed as the most in-human of the sciences. And this, more than any other misconception, is responsible for the split between 'the Two Cultures' publicly dramatized some years ago by the eccentric Lord Snow and the egregious Dr. Leavis. For in our universities the faculties whose technology is that of the printed word have grandiosely described their discipline as 'The Humanities'. Yet W.H. Auden himself sadly remarked in his last year that he did not think any of his poems had saved a single victim from Belsen or Buchenwald. But we are all relying on statisticians to save us from drowning, and if they fail to humanize their discipline we shall certainly be sunk. Appropriate to this problem is a remark which I recall from a review of some historical work many years ago in the <u>New Statesman</u>: 'History is an art like any other science'. I will re-phrase this to read 'Mathematics is a history like any other art'. For you need only study the history of the concept of number to see in the simple rhythm of **counting**, and the notations for recording the products of this skill, the pulsations of the brain which have made arithmetic an infinite matrix for the scores of all possible music.

Our mathematical education has gone astray in two respects. First it has ignored the **rhythms**, and so taken the aesthetics out of mathematics by printing its scores in linear arrays of arbitrary symbols containing no

manifest hint of their inner chords and melodies.  And secondly it presents a completely confused picture of the relations between the rational
and the irrational, the real and the imaginary, the finite and the infinitc,
and between quantity and number.  Nowhere is this confusion more
evident than in the misuse of the so-called 'normal distribution curve'
on which psychometrics so devotedly relies.  The equation for this curve,
established by Gauss, contains the symbol for the Greek letter pi.  I
shall therefore describe it as suffering from 'pionic infection'.  It
assumes an infinite population.  Even without birth control thc population
of our planet will always be finite.  I shall now use one of the simplest
bits of educational technology to give a new slant to this problem.  The
favourite media for teaching elementary statistics are coins, cards and
dice.  With a class of, say 50 students, each being asked to shake a
coin in his hands and say 'head' or 'tails', a record is quickly built up,
on the blackboard, of the proportions of H and T over several dozen
throws.  The histogram is a plot of the binomial distribution.  Looked at
fuzzily from a distance it appears as a continuous curve.  Now there are
two contrasting facts about this optical impression.  The first is clearly
brought out in a rather valuable book which I possess viz.  <u>A Treatise
on the Calculus of Finite Differences</u> by George Boole, second edition,
Macmillan & Co. 1872.  Boole was perfectly clear about both the
differences and the analogies between a finite calculus and an infinitesimal
calculus.  'In the differential calculus', he says, $^{du}/dx$ is not a true
fraction, nor have du and dx any distinct meaning as symbols of quantity.
The fractional form is adopted to express the limit to which a true
fraction approaches.  Hence $^{d}/dx$, and not d, there represents a true
operation.  But in the calculus of finite differences $^{Du}x/_{Dx}$ is a truc
fraction.' (I have here romanized the Greek delta used by Boole.)
     Boole later goes on to comment on how much this branch of mathe-
matics 'suffers from its not possessing a clear and independent set of
technical terms.  It is true that by its borrowing terms from the
infinitesimal calculus to supply this want, we are continually reminded
of the strong analogies that exist between the two, but in scientific
language accuracy is of more value than suggestiveness.'
     Now what I want to show by this example is that just as Man has to
learn to co-exist with bacteria, so finite mathematics has to learn to
co-exist with 'pionic infection'.  And this demonstration directly illustrates the power which is in thc hands of every educational technologist
if only he will closely scrutinize **all** his instruments, and especially the
simplest ones — for the others are combinations of these.
     It never occurs to us when tossing a coin that there can be any
answer other than heads or tails.  But the coin is, in fact, not an infinitely thin disc, but a cylinder of finite thickness.  And if the coin is
tossed on a flat table often enough it is not impossible for it to fall,

very occasionally, on its rim.  If this is regarded as perfectly circular there is now no **binary** choice of position but an infinity of positions.

Thus if we are scrupulously true to the technical facts the binomial distribution owes its simplicity to a disregard of real but exceptional cases.  And this may be why education is so fond of this pseudo-normal curve because it does not like exceptional children.  But let us go a step further.  Or rather several steps.  First let us note that just as we would be surprised if a coin did fall on its rim we should be equally surprised if a cylindrical pencil did **not** fall on its round surface.  So as a piece of homework I invite you to construct a range of cylinders of differing proportions, toss them many times, draw the resulting distributions and meditate on the results.  If the curved cylindrical surface were truly circular all these results would exhibit pionic infection.  But now let us look at any one of these visually smooth rims under a microscope.  Preferably an electron microscope.  We now see not a uniform smooth curvature, but nor do we see any sharp, jagged, irregular geometric forms.  We see an irregular distribution of regular molecules.  These form myriads of little surface-groupings, mostly of three, four or five molecules.  The table-surface likewise shows an irregular distribution of regular molecules.  Thus our instruments give us a new epistemic view of probability.  For there is now an enormously large but still finite set of possible contacts compatible with the stability of the coin when it comes to rest.  Each is individually highly improbable but unless the coin goes on oscillating for ever it **must** achieve the certainty of stability.  Thus certainty is composed of a very large number of improbabilities.

Now note that since at this level there are no straight lines all these potential contacts are composed of configurations of curved surfaces.  Each of these is a bacterium of pionic infection.  The cylinder lives with this infection and achieves a healthy stability whenever it falls.  This is an example of what my great friend Warren McCulloch called 'The wisdom of the body'.

There is one further aspect of this example worth noting.  Without using a microscope we might quantify the improbabilities of particular falls on the curved surface by drawing a set of graduations parallel to the axis, perhaps 12 or 50 or several hundred.  With a milled coin we might count the number of little ridges.  If, say, we choose 12, then we have 14 a priori possibilities, of which two, viz. the two flat ends, are sharply different in frequency from the rest.  But the mathematical probability of the rest is entirely arbitrary, being determined by our choice of graduations.  There has been considerable controversy over the difference between so-called 'objective' and 'subjective' probabilities.  What seems to have escaped attention is the number of subjective decisions necessary to define a calculus of so-called 'objective' probabilities.  And since the future does not yet exist, and 'probability' implicitly refers to the future, all our calculations are based either on counting historic events and subjectively assuming that conditions will not change in the future, or on counting artefacts subjectively invented by ourselves.

Finally I come to what is both the most difficult and also the most aesthetic aspect of number. At the time of preparing this paper I could not be sure of how many models and illustrations I could assemble, pack, and transport safely to the point of delivery. This is one of the hazards of educational technology at a distance. So my actual words must be rather general and I put my trust in serendipity to have enough to show the audience that the realities behind the words have a certain mystery and beauty of their own which can run through all our modes of perception. My house is full of numbers of models made by my own inadequate hands. They are thus literally 'digital'. Many of them contain or are made entirely of polystyrene spheres. Thus they have the wisdom of pionic infection. The milennial and futile quest for squaring the circle is seen in a new light. A square is constructed by drawing straight lines with pen or pencil. Their straightness is a visual artefact valid only within the narrow range of sensitivity of our instrument of vision — the human eye. Use a different instrument and the lines become a rubble of atomic spheres. Or measure the stars during an eclipse, as in 1919, and find that the rectilinear propagation of light is merely a human belief derived from our previous insensitivity. Or watch the top of a rigid skyscraper in a gale, through a telescope and see it swaying a foot or two either way. Thus according to the instruments we use rigidity and rectilinearity can dissolve into tiny galaxies of spheres or curved beams of light, or vibrating columns or even into sub-atomic waves, beyond the eye or the ear, but having their own music for which Schrödinger's equation provides a matrix for any number of melodies. Mathematics is potentially as available and as fertile for the blind and the deaf and the deaf-blind as for those with normal sensory equipment, if we can develop the appropriate educational technology for making its rhythms and structures felt, throbbed and handled. This is why we must take up George Boole's hint that 'mathematics suffers from its not possessing a clear and independent set of technical terms'. In an on-going research over many years I have interpreted the word 'independent' as meaning 'free from arbitrary and misleading convention', and the 'technical terms' as meaning tangible forms whose design embodies the relation which I **think** that Wittgenstein was implying in his claim that language is a 'picture' of fact.

The virtue of programmed instruction, which was originated by Euclid, lies in its compulsion on the instructor. It forces him to think clearly on what he has to say, to resolve it into its discriminable atomic propositions, and to arrange these into molecular chains. But if this is then enforced as a program for **learning** in a fixed order the binding relationship which gives the whole theorem its distinctive epistemic significance is seldom glimpsed. For in order to gain mental mastery over a structure we have to pass our hands over its network of relationships many times in order to grasp and ingest its frozen music. This is why I have called this research 'The Handimath Program'. In seeking to implement this project on mathematical perception in terms which would make it educationally available for all I have burnt my fingers very badly, being devoid of commercial sense. But experimental scientists are used to burning their fingers. It is the price we pay for insatiable curiosity.

For the purpose of this occasion I found myself committed to five distinct tasks. I was asked to write a 12,000 words paper for publication in the Proceedings of the Conference. Obviously this could not be read aloud in its entirety at the Conference. So, secondly, I had to prepare an abridged version, in a different style. Thirdly, I learned that the actual presentation was to be filmed. Fourthly, since I wanted to introduce a valid structural investigation of human knowledge I had to find a pragmatic solution, using educational technology, of the problem of giving conrete expression to the abstract concept of 'structure'. And fifthly, since these thoughts have arisen in the course of a 50-year enterprise which I call 'Epistemics', and I was invited to explain this discipline, it is essential to ensure that the medium shall not obscure the message.

A phrase from a recent book-review comes to my rescue. The book is by Iris Murdoch; its title is <u>The Sacred and Profane Love Machine</u> (Chatto and Windus); the reviewer is Paul Bailey in <u>The Guardian</u> March 21, 1974. The particular phrase which arrested me is Bailey's comment on Iris Murdoch's uses of language: 'They have all the resonance of true artifice'.

We at once ask 'how can artifice be true?' and this is like asking how can educational technology ever work? I have not yet read the book but Bailey's phrase gives the answer in a single word 'resonance'. This takes me back to the late '20's when, having taken degrees in mathematical physics and educational psychology, I went to study what was supposed to be scientific psychology under Spearman. I wanted to carry out research on the relation between voice and personality (having had a stammer at school and finding myself with a very woolly voice as a teacher). But for Spearman the only scientific method was that of factor analysis. So I confined that research to my own voice, trying to make it a better instrument of communication. My Ph.D. never got off the ground with Spearman and I only completed it many years later under Hamley, who was interested in my earlier research on the Transfer of Training. By then, however, it was no longer concerned just with acoustics but with the much more general problem of how different persons can share each other's knowledge whether by voice or by any other medium, and in 1944 I gave this study the name 'Epistemics' from the Greek word <u>episteme</u> meaning 'knowledge'.

I do not know if Iris Murdoch's book on the Love-Machine would come under the heading of 'erotic technology', but in addition to this 'resonance' which Bailey detects the book may have a further affinity with epistemics. As a philosopher Iris Murdoch will know a lot about epistemology, the philosophy of knowledge. We all speak of 'subjects' and 'objects'. We divide objects into two kinds viz. those which we perceive for the sake of their intrinsic properties and those which stand as substitutes for something else. The latter include such things as flags and religious emblems, coins, tokens and printed words. The 'something else', which these things stand for, is one of the central problems of philosophy. **How** they do the 'standing' is the **epistemic** problem which confronts educational technology. For these tokens are nothing like what they represent.

Now before we can consider the complementary problem of how we differentiate **subjects** from **subjects**, and the intermediate problem of how we differentiate subjects from **objects**, let us consider two strange phenomena. The first is the human voice. The second is the world of representative art, and of pictures in particular. My voice seems to take something from me to you, but it has more of **me** in it than of **you**, and may, if I am an orator like Lloyd George, have more of subjectivity in it than of subject-matter. On the other hand if I take a photograph of you this has more of **you** in it than of **me**. But both voice and visual representation have in them some degree of subjective influence from both parties, for I adapt my voice to **your** needs and I control the camera to get the picture I want. Also, both being physical media, they have a degree of intrinsic objectivity resulting from the mechanics of sound and the electromagnetism of light.

Perhaps I have said enough to show that educational technologists cannot afford to ignore philosophy. Philosophy can give them no **answers**, but it can force them to ask essential **questions**. One of these questions is how and why we distinguish between 'value' and 'sentiment-ality'? Here again we find a hint from this baffling novelist-philosopher, Iris Murdoch. For though her books are about love they are totally devoid of sentimentality. And when I define epistemics as 'The instrumental study of inter-personal communication' I include such persons as Dr. Goebbels and Galileo, Mohammed and Mao-tse-Tung, Stalin and Spike Milligan, or Charlie Chaplin and Richard Nixon. And I note that 1984 is only ten years ahead. If I am still around I shall be 80, but it cannot be much worse than being 70. I am quite devoid of sentimentality. What I note is that subjects of all kinds use or invent instruments of many kinds to re-distribute the matter and energy in their objective environ-ment. Thus modern ecology is **operational** as well as **observational**. And we need to watch the operators.

Thirty years ago when I was doing research on educational films I spoke of 'The Industrial Revolution in Education. Now industry is mainly concerned with what we call 'the know-how'. It is a curious expression, a noun formed by a definite article, a verb and an adverb — an example of how idiom bends grammar to its purposes. Let us look at this grammar and from it develop a semantic matrix which we can then use as an instrument of thought.

Since all our verbal descriptions will sooner or later have to be coded in symbolic form for purposes of formulation and analysis, we can start by denoting the kinaesthetic experience of three-dimensional body-motion by 'B'. The visual experience of a two-dimensional wave-front of light is 'F'. The tactile experience of drawing a finger over a surface in a one-dimensional digital path is 'D'. And the compression of cycles of acoustic vibration, although proceeding physically from atmospheric space, is a purely temporal sensation subjectively and will be called 'C'. Thus our four modes of communicative sensation are both symbolized and given a dimensional characterization.

As we have seen, these four experiences, which will collectively be called 'E', have four different applications. As real psycho-physical processes in their own right we call them 'R'. As bringing information from material objects and events we call them 'M'. As properties to be used lexically as alternative modes of natural linguistic expression, we call them 'L'. And as characteristics to be used systematically in an artificial notation we call them 'N'. This two-fold classification gives the following table :

| E | C | D | F | B |
|---|---|---|---|---|
| R | RC | RD | RF | RB |
| M | MC | MD | MF | MB |
| L | LC | LD | LF | LB |
| N | NC | ND | NF | NB |

Now as a mere combination of symbols this table does not tell us very much. To give it some flesh we need to give concrete instances of its application. It must be borne in mind that every observer of rapid and complex events has to work very fast to get anything down on paper at all, and a coding system is essential. In any observation of perceptual behaviour we need to know what types of relevant perceptual experiences are happening and what functions they are exerting. Dozens of examples of each of these sixteen types of functional experience could be given, but here we must be content with a single example of each.

264

## Examples of E-variables

1) ERC     (sound as a receptive experience)
       e.g. an audiometric test of a child's acuity of hearing.
2) EMC    (sound as objective information).
       e.g. a child is asked to identify the material source of a
       particular noise.
3) ELC     (sound as a lexical symbol).
       e.g. a child interprets a spoken word.
4) ENC     (sound as a notational symbol).
       e.g. the sound of the formula $H_2O$ used for 'water'.
5) ERD     (touch as a receptive experience).
       e.g. discrimination between rough and smooth, hard and
       soft, rounded and flat, etc.
6) EMD    (touch giving material information).
       e.g. identifying a penknife in one's pocket by hand.
7) ELD     (touch used lexically).
       e.g. digital reading of Braille.
8) END     (touch used notationally).
       e.g. specially shaped knobs for identifying controls in the
       dark.
9) ERF     (light as a receptive experience).
       e.g. colour discrimination.
10) EMF    (light giving material information).
       e.g. visual recognition of objects.
11) ELF     (light used lexically).
       e.g. ordinary reading.
12) ENF     (light used notationally).
       e.g. telling the time from a clock.
13) ERB     (movement as receptive experience).
       e.g. the kinaesthetic experience of dancing.
14) EMB    (movement giving material information)
       e.g. feeling the tremor in a child's hand.
15) ELB     (movement used lexically).
       e.g. gesture language of the deaf-mute.
16) ENB     (movement used notationally).
       e.g. conducting an orchestra.

This matrix is merely a sample of the full system of epistemic notation. It illustrates several points. Epistemics calls in question many popular educational slogans, e.g. that we must proceed from the concrete to the abstract. In many ways the thought of a child is more abstract than that of an adult. Concrete knowledge is achieved by a process of differentiation. Similarly, we cannot always proceed from the simple to the complex. For we live in a complex environment and simplification is a

long and difficult process.  But cognitively we inevitably move from the
**familiar** to the **unfamiliar**.  Indeed this is a tautology.  'Getting to know'
means moving from what is known to what is as yet unknown.

Thus in developing epistemics I work always from familiar experiences, using only the familiar symbols which can be found on an ordinary
typewriter, and only such words as can be found in an English dictionary.
I find I can always make myself understood by children and their parents.
It is only academics who find me baffling.  This is because they project
their own ideology into my words and I am anti-ideological.  For me
ideas are merely instruments to be used as long as they are useful, and
then discarded or re-designed.  I use the ordinary Roman alphabet, the
ordinary decimal arithmetic, the familiar terms of traditional grammar,
and, although the logical structure of knowledge turns out to be non-
Euclidean, I project all these structures on Euclidean planes because
the Industrial Revolution has imprisoned us in familiar Euclidean boxes.
Steam-power was an application of Newtonian mechanics which assumed
that space was Euclidean.  Thus our boxes, buildings and books have
made Euclidean geometry familiar even though it is fallacious when
applied to the Universe.  A matrix is a Euclidean frame consisting of
parallel rows of boxes for holding symbols.  Our interpretation of the
relations between the symbols is constrained by the geometry of the
frame.  By starting from there we can begin to envisage new modes of
thought by successive modifications of the frame.

Five hundred years ago Copernicus dared to envisage a change in
the framework of cosmic geometry.  The result was a revolution not only
in astronomy and mechanics but also in philosophy and theology.  Thus
frameworks are of central importance in every system of knowledge.
Perhaps the most difficult problem in cosmic epistemology arises from
the fact that we can make model frameworks small enough to handle from
the outside, such as a terrestrial globe, and also models large enough
for us to stand inside, such as a planetarium.  We can also walk out of
the planetarium but we cannot walk out of the cosmos.  We can turn over
a sheet of paper, but we cannot turn over the sky.  Some philosophies
seem to assume what must be called a 'theoscopic' viewpoint, in which
the philosopher presumes to stand outside space-time.  There is also a
complementary arrogance into which ontology can easily fall.  This is
the assumption that we can get inside things other than our own bodies.
Any attempt to make a picture of the interior of an atom is an example
of this error.  So is the psychoanalytic attempt to get inside the mind of
another person.  Thus our knowledge is bounded outwardly by the inner
face of the cosmos and inwardly by the outer face of all objects other
than ourselves.  Within this thin shell of cognitive activity we can
resonate to signals from above and below and turn them into pictures or
poems of our own making as far as our imagination can go.  And this is

our zone of known symbolic forms.   Educational technology requires a
grasp of the mutuality of resonance.

THE DEKATRON
(A polyhedral form with ten vertices midway between the octahedron and icosahedron)

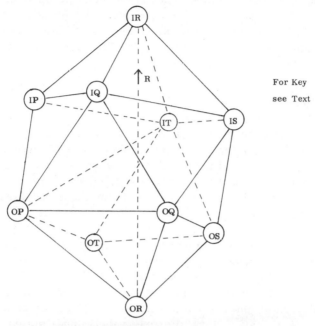

For Key
see Text

Educational programming must allow equal opportunity for all modes of cognition both of
internal states (I) and of objective facts (O).   A 3-D 'matrix' is required to allow equal
spacing of categories.   All ten lie on a sphere.

Figure 1:   Extension of semantic matrices

The matrix shown here in Figure 1 represents only a fragment of
analysis.   It may be regarded as an essay in decimal epistemics for it
has ten cells.   As an example it has the merit that it actually grew out
of empirical research in visual education, in which the need to go beyond
vision became evident.   Also it is instrumental not only in leading to
systematic thought but also in being derived from a study of instruments
of perception.   Many years ago Sir Charles Sherrington, in his <u>Integrative
Action of the Nervous System</u> laid the foundations for our neurophysio-
logical understanding of cognitive processes.

Working with animals Sherrington distinguished three types of
receptor organs, nerves and processes, viz.

1.   Exteroceptors,
     e.g. eyes, ears, etc. bringing information from the outside world.

267

2. Intero-ceptors,
   most of us have no names for these but we experience hunger, comfort, nausea, etc. through internal sense-organs.

3. Proprio-ceptors,
   these lie in the muscles, tendons, joints, the inner ear, etc. and tell the brain how the body is moving and what is its momentary orientation and configuration. This kinaesthetic experience is essential in all skills and must, in Man, contribute fundamentally to his concept of space-time.

Now Man's cortex adds two more processes which bring information even though not localized in specific sense-organs. These are his awareness of his own thoughts and his ability to refer back to past events **via** memory. These, then, are our five instruments of cognition. The instrumentation of science may be regarded as simulations and extensions of these biological necessities. But whilst each of us has all five types of instrument each has direct experience of only his own equipment. Thus when we say that another person is seeing or thinking etc. we are interpreting certain configurations of his body by reference to what we ourselves experience when we adopt similar configurations. For configurations are directly comparable whereas each subjective experience is private. By resonance with our own experience we contrive to achieve a cognition of other people's cognitions. We do not truly share their experience, but this artificial comparison of configurations gives us what Bailey calls 'the resonance of true artifice'. Since most animals, as well as Man, have voices to express their inner states, needs, claims and intentions, the emotive basis of language owes more to the intero-ceptors than to the cortex (hence my early interest in voice and personality). But our awareness of thought and memory must be mainly responsible for Man's rich equipment of vocabulary and grammar as modulations on the basic under-currents of interoceptive needs and proprio-ceptive skills.

These five types of objective equipment with their corresponding distinct categories of subjective experience I have labelled as follows :

1.  OP  :   Performance viewed outwardly
2.  IP  :   Performance viewed inwardly
3.  OQ  :   Quest for information viewed outwardly
4.  IQ  :   Quest for information viewed inwardly
5.  OR  :   Reference to past viewed outwardly
6.  IR  :   Reference to past viewed inwardly
7.  OS  :   Somatic states viewed outwardly
8.  IS  :   Somatic states viewed inwardly
9.  OT  :   Thinking behaviour viewed outwardly
10. IT  :   Thinking behaviour viewed inwardly

Thus our epistemic equipment is here decimalized.

Epistemics comes into conflict with current and enduring educational beliefs and practices most sharply in its treatment of numbers. This is no accident. For there is no inter-personal communication without the co-existence of unique and diverse individuals. Without these we merely have energy flowing from a source to a sink (as in MacKay's 1950 concept of Communication Science). But every state educational system, whatever religious or political camouflage it adopts to conceal its intentions, necessarily exists in order to diminish individuality so as to ensure conformity to a national myth. Paradoxically it achieves this by emphasizing differences. These are numerical differences, obtained by making a totally mathematical use of numbers. Examination marks are treated as units of measurement and are added together to form a ladder of achievement with the educationally subnormal on the bottom rung and the university Ph.D. at the top irrespective of the endless diversity both of personalities and of performances. This scale is closely correlated with a scale of prestige and somewhat less correlated with the price which one can command for one's services. Thus whilst unable entirely to destroy individual differences the system ensures a strong motivation for all to struggle in the same direction. This direction is determined by another numerical myth — the myth of money. By means of this myth (embodied in the slogan 'the pound in your pocket') the great innumerate British Public was recently submitted to a confidence-trick which probably contributed as much to inflation as the Sheiks of Araby. By retaining the name 'penny' whilst upgrading its cash-value to 2.4 old pence, whilst simultaneously reducing its material size to that of an old farthing, the Government put the consumers totally at the mercy of the shopkeepers. The latter had careful training courses in decimalization. The public, whose schooling has ensured that they don't understand decimals anyhow, merely had a few warning captions on television. Being a totally non-political animal I make no comment on the fact that this inflation at-a-stroke happened under a Socialist Government, for the decision to decimalize was taken years earlier, presumably as a step towards Europeanization — though what the continentals make of our strange compromise currency I cannot imagine. My two points are, first, that the training of shopkeepers was by programmed learning, and the deluding of the public was by television, both being forms of educational technology. How much longer will the technologists continue to serve as slaves for State swindling? My second point is, precisely, a **point** viz. the decimal point. 'Those damned dots' as one of our great innumerate statesmen called them. Considering the crucial function performed by this symbol in, e.g. distinguishing between pounds and pence, it is a miserably small sign, easily overlooked. Moreover its position with respect to the base-line differs between different countries and some use a comma instead. How many financial errors result from this tiny bit of symbolic grit in the works is any-one's guess. Its form is almost invisible. Its function to most users is incomprehensible. If technology can spend millions on computers and on re-designing whole cities could we not spare a dime to re-design those damned dots?

It seems to me that there is a bigger challenge to educational technology in the field of numeracy than anywhere else. And the instrumentalism of epistemics indicates the point of attack.

In exploring the relation between energetics and esthetics priority must be given to the earliest and most precisely noted law of psychophysics, attributed to Pythagoras, and still pregnant with unlimited possibilities. It requires objective energy to pluck a tight string. It requires subjective auditory sensitivity to hear the sound emitted. The object-subject relation is a sharp dichotomy between string and person, between energy and experience. If the length and tension of the string are maintained constant the subject experiences a uniform tone. This is a second relation — metric constancy and sensory uniformity. If the string is shortened or tightened a note of higher pitch is heard. This is a third relation, objective inequality giving subjective diversity. The fact that the second note is called 'higher' than the first is a metaphorical use of language. It brings in a third relation. An objective view of length changing from longer to shorter is generally followed by a subjective climb up an imaginary ladder from lower pitch to higher pitch. And the ladder image is translated into a grammatical scale in the comparison of adjectives: lowest, lower, medium, higher, highest. 'Medium' is where language conjoins 'low' (which is highest in the first adjectival scale) with 'high' (which is lowest in the second adjectival scale). This verbal scale, which may be regarded as having five points or seven, as we please, is still today the basis of most subjective evaluations of examination performances. But it is not enough for music. It is an ordinal scale whose intervals bear no numerically defined mutual ratios. Our examination-system is riddled with nonsense by ignoring this fact in using marks obtained by ordinal judgements as additive quantities. Perhaps the student resentment against the stupidity of this system reflects an intuitive commonsense awareness that esthetics is not a philosophical luxury but a necessity not only for enjoyment but for justice in daily life. Esthetics, theology and arithmetic were all conjoined in the mystique of the Pythagorean Brotherhood. Its ethical defect lay in its exclusiveness and secrecy. (The same defect today poisons our social, industrial and international life.)

The fourth psychophysical relation introduces cardinal numbers, and in a remarkable way. If we shorten the length of the string continuously the pitch rises continuously. But if we exactly halve the length of the string the pitch is now heard as having a special relation with the first. This relation is so precise that the subjective judgement of an octave

270

interval can actually be used to correct any slight error in the objective metric division of the string. Herein lies the craft of the piano-tuner, except that he achieves precision by controlling tension instead of length, but the point is that he does it by ear. And 'playing it by ear' has passed into our daily idiom as testimony to the necessity for a precision of sensibility in social situations in which rigid adherence to conventional rules can create inter-personal or even international disasters.

Once we have divided the string in two we can go on to a fifth rela- tion, a whole set of relations, in fact, by dividing it into 3, 4, 5, 6, 7 or any number of divisions compatible with the mechanical limits of the string. And it is through this fifth psychophysical relation that Pythagoras laid the foundations for the whole subsequent development of the theory of musical harmony. For those who are attracted to a physical approach to this fundamental branch of psychophysics I commend The Physics of Musical Sounds by Professor C.A. Taylor (English Universities Press, 1965) which has the good technological sense to include a rise of recorded illustrations.

In a context of education and communication this acoustic approach to esthetics has the virtue of showing the power of a medium which is both non-verbal and non-visual, whilst showing that visual observation can be precisely related to auditory, tactile and verbal sensitivities. But it also puts energetics in a quite different perspective. It is not too much to say that the current world preoccupation with energetics is almost entirely concerned with the use of energy for producing thermal and mechanical **noise.** And it is a sad fact about contemporary youth in seeking to develop novel and often highly original themes, through the technology which makes pop music possible, that in order to shut out the menacing voice of orthodoxy, they obliterate their own themes by so many decibels as permanently to impair their own acoustic sensitivity.

This raises another issue on which epistemics has a direct bearing, too massive for more than a brief reference here. These acoustic casualities of our cultural revolution are but a fraction of the totality of casualities not only of the industrial revolution but of the insensitivity which permits the pollution of our whole environment. The victims of lead and other poisoning, of road accidents, of mismanaged pregnancies and parturitions, of adulterated foods, of industrial and military injuries, quite apart from battered babies and psychological cripples from parental and educational mismanagement, constitute a formidable fraction of the population. All require special individual treatment and technical aids, for the daily efforts both of living and learning. This presents powerful ethical challenge to educational technology. Those of us who are fortun- ate enough to possess our full biological complement of limbs, senses and nerve-cells owe our daily nutrition and comforts to an industrial system which every week deprives hundreds of some vital feature of their make-up. It is a large and ugly fact, in which esthetics, ethics and

271

energetics all meet in an imperative demand to bring academic disciplines to bear on the invention of social remedies. We cannot all attempt everything, but each individual who is sensitive to this imperative may have **some** special gift of intuition, insight and inventiveness whose application and promotion may benefit hundreds of lives.

Thus in speaking of 'Instruments and Individuals' I am tempted to ask for a self-interest in the literal sense. Existentially what am I? What do I know? What can I do? And these questions inevitably lead on to — Whom do I need?, and Who needs me?

'What am I?' is partly answered by the biological instrumentation of heredity, conception and birth. 'What do I know?' is answered by the instrumentation of home and school, which also partly answers 'What can I do?' The questions 'Whom do I need?' and 'Who needs me?' are much more diffusely instrumented, mainly by family, neighbours, occupation and the mass media. They are questions we cannot ask often enough and they are mostly answered when we 'play it by ear', in other words when we develop a sensitivity to the relation between our own needs and those of others.

And finally to something more obviously technical to indicate some of my own individual answers to these questions which everyone needs to ask himself if, at the end of the day, he wants to feel that his life has been, however limited, not entirely wasted.

It started at the age of six. By good fortune Mary Boole, the widow of George Boole (known today through Boolean Algebra) happened to be a friend of my mother's. Being herself interested in mathematics she wrote unorthodox little books on algebra for children. She also developed a kit of sewing-cards with reels of coloured thread. Mathematically these created curves out of tangent lines. With no formulae whatever they enabled children to construct an endless variety of fascinating coloured patterns. In recent times these have been followed by 'Spirograph' and by a still more subtle creative aid known as 'Altair Design'. This was invented by my friend Dr. Ensor Holliday, a medical research director, while recuperating in hospital after a road-accident.

These three, and a few other examples of what is essentially educational technology, have in common the fact that their appeal is aesthetic. They avoid the arid abstraction of formulated mathematics and the crude commercial and industrial utilitarianism of most technical mathematics. Mathematical esthetics does, however, have a very intimate link with physics, as we have seen in the Pythagorean origin of the study of vibrating strings. More recently my friend Dr. Jerry Ravetz (not unknown in environmentalist circles) has shown that vibrating strings still have much mathematical life in them and Dr. Grattan-Guiness has pursued this theme in depth in his 1970 volume on The Development of the Foundations of Mathematical Analysis from Euler to Riemann (M.I.T. Press).

But of course it is not only strings which vibrate but also two-dimensional drums and three dimensional bells; in fact 'the great Globe itself, yea all which it inherit' must compel us to regard harmonic motion as fundamental to physics, and equally, all the way from Pythagoras to Grey Walter, as essential to our mentality and enjoyment. Simple harmonic motion is not only the atom of time responsible for the chemistry of music but, in endlessly varied concords and discords, 'The tides in the affairs of men', an element of reality which puts a numerical constraint on the guesses of historians.

Given our dependence on clocks and calendars, and the innumerable compounds of temporal rhythms on which organized society so intimately depends, the greatest challenge to mathematical education is to find a clear and attractive medium for making multi-dimensional harmonic motion comprehensible.

Since it is a fairly safe prediction that the distribution of energy will present us with serious problems for quite a long time, we need a much better collective understanding of energy. We cannot predict how the problems will develop or what solutions will be attempted, partly because we do not know how long it will take to create a better understanding. What we can say is that the problems cannot be solved by purely quantitative methods. For there is no total shortage of energy. It is its distributions and transformations which create the problems, and these are problems of configuration.

This point may be illustrated by considering what happens when a meteor enters the earth's atmosphere and thus, as a 'shooting star', burns up. As a mechanical mass the meteor has kinetic energy proportional to the square of its velocity, irrespective of its direction in space. The friction of the air reduces this energy, and transforms the difference into thermal energy. If this were all that happened we should simply have a quantitative rise in temperature. But internally the meteor has a molecular structure which can tolerate only a certain rate of internal oscillation and beyond this the configuration breaks up. There is no absolute loss or gain of energy but it is re-distributed and quite different chemical products appear. Now this point is quite elementary but what follows is less so. For what applies to this meteoric transformation is equally true for any energy transformation. It is always both quantitative and configurational. And if the world's energy-problems are decided by men who think in purely quantitative terms, and who have had no training in configurational thinking, their decisions are likely to be disastrous. For the problems involve not only molecular configurations but also industrial, geographical and political configurations.

Since we are dealing with problems of extraction, transport and transformation, the configurations are not merely geometric structures in a spatial sense but patterns of space-time. And I doubt if any educational systems provide the school-population with any systematic and effective discipline in the study of space-time. What they provide merely in arithmetic is inadequate enough, and since many political leaders are quite happy to admit that they are 'innumerate', often in spite of a highly expensive education, the chaos of decimalization and metrication is not surprising. Thus even our purely quantitative collective thinking is grossly inadequate. When we need configurational thinking the muddle is total. It is precisely in this field that educational technology has most to offer. But it is not an easy task. About thirty-five years ago Geoffrey Bell, at the Shell Film Unit, produced a film called 'Transfer of Power'. As a work of art it was very pleasing. But so many transformations were packed into it that it left one's head spinning and gave no clear understanding of space-time relations.

It was through many discussions with people like Geoffrey Bell, John Grierson, Edgar Anstey and other war-time documentary film directors, and also through the writings of Pudovkin and Eisenstein, that I began to grasp the problems of communication. Using a space-time medium to transmit not merely space-time information but, more importantly, qualitative space-time **understanding**, appeared to me as the major problem of visual education. Eisenstein in particular, showed a clear awareness of the need for a logic of relations in determining the precise sequence of film-shots needed to create a pre-decided impression. This preliminary analytical thought may be regarded as an anticipation of some of the principles of programmed instruction.

At that time I carried out an experiment in four Exeter schools. I wanted to determine whether it was possible to obtain a measure of the relative effectiveness of different educational media, such as chalk and talk, still pictures, complete films, and films divided into short segments. Clearly the results would vary from one topic to another, from one group of children to another, from one teacher to another. But above all no comparison at all would be possible if what was called the same 'topic' e.g. hydraulics, was differently conceived and structured on different occasions. It was this challenge which prompted the development of what I called 'Topic Analysis'. Several months before the experiments began I managed to get the teachers from the four schools together once a week at my Visual Education Centre for detailed discussions on the structures of our four topics. The topics chosen were 'Rivers', 'Fruits', 'Hydraulics' and 'Wheatlands', all involving states of matter, space, time, energy, function, value and human intervention. We did not use the word 'program' but essentially we were designing an ordered configuration of items whose content and sequence was collectively decided, instead of being the work of an isolated academic working from a priori principles. This not only ensured that all the teachers were adequately and willingly briefed, so that whichever medium was used, and whichever group of children were being taught, the content and sequence of each topic was invariant. It also enabled the subsequent tests to be rationally designed so as to correspond with the topic structures. Note, of course, that this standardization was a recipe for **research**, not a principle for ordinary teaching.  This is a difference ignored in the cruder forms of programmed learning which give the impression that schools should be run like battery-chicken farms.

Every topic was treated as involving four kinds of items.  There are **performances** in space-time, such as ploughing a field.  There are shapes and qualities to be **observed**, e.g. the parts of a fruit.  There are special **names** for special objects which have to be learnt, such as 'erosion', 'stamen', etc.  And there are the underlying **ideas** by which the topic is held together.  I called these 'P, O, N and I-items' respectively (today they are P, Q, S and T).  There were sixteen experiments in all, each group being taught all four topics but using a different medium for each topic, with four comparable control groups learning the same topics by 'chalk and talk'.  Three principles emerged out of this research, which I call

1.    The principle of Semantic Conservation.
2.    The principle of Matrix Subtraction. *
3.    The principle of Analytical Programming.

The meaning of the third is already, perhaps, sufficiently evident.  The principle of semantic conservation goes completely counter to the accepted methods of educational and psychometric testing, and indeed to most of the orthodox examination procedures, dating back to the Civil Service examinations of ancient China.  For these are all based on semantic destruction in favour of pseudo-metric precision.  They are also based on the belief that the marks gained are entirely a measure of the candidate's ability and have nothing to do with the competence of the teacher or the medium of instruction, or any contingent circumstances. The examination-candidate is treated like, for instance, an isolated piece of metal having a constant electrical conductivity for which a specific instrument is appropriate.

The logic of this reversal of the testing concept led me to a reversal of the scoring method.  Instead of counting how many questions each child got right in the test I counted how many **children** got each **question** right.  This was because the experiment was not designed to measure the abilities of the children but to compare the relative efficacy of the different media.  Thus the resulting charts recorded not the children-scores but the item-successes.  Each item is entered in the chart as a small circle.  In each circle is entered the serial number of the item as it appeared in the test.  Thus these numerals are not scores at all.  They are semantic indicators, showing, by reference to the test content, how

---

* (See Appendix)

the different parts of the topic survived the presentation.  The co-ordinate axes, V and C indicate the numbers of candidates in the visual group and the control group respectively who obtained a mark for each particular question.  This distribution divides the chart into five zones:

1.  Semantic areas very difficult for both groups.
2.  Semantic areas very easy for both groups.
3.  Semantic areas easy for the visual group, hard for the controls.
4.  Vice versa.
5.  Items of medium difficulty for both groups.

Regarded as a matrix, this device, which I call 'The Item Distribution Chart', has a grammar of its own.  As in any matrix there are definable relations between the different cells.  Each position represents a ratio.  It is à ratio of relative efficiencies.  We may regard educational communication as dependent on a quasi-mechanical ratio for each item viz.  Information-load
Instructional-effort

and then translate this into a semantic ratio viz.

Epistemic Type of Message
Epistemic Type of Medium

This latter ratio is not numerical.  But if we now vary the **type** in the denominator by sending the same message through a different medium, using two comparable populations of receivers, their relative successes **do** give a numerical ratio, indicating which is the more efficient medium for that particular message.

Education was psychodelic long before Aldous Huxley persuaded the world of dissatisfied young intellectuals that it was a good idea to expand their consciousness by extracts of mushrooms.  The difference is that the latter makes perceptible the noise already in the brain whereas education pushes into the brain the noise from the outside world.  Either type of noise may be pleasant or unpleasant, and what is discord to one person may be music to another.  What has distorted education is that it requires financing, and he who pays the piper wants to call the tune.  And since most educational systems are controlled by national establishments, and most establishments maintain their power for purposes of defence and aggression, there are martial undertones in most of the tunes they call. Faced with the expectation of being drafted to go and kill Eastern people towards whom they felt no hostility it is not surprising that many young Californians opted to call their own tunes.  And what happens in California today happens all over the world tomorrow, thanks to the power of the mass-media.  What their prophet, Aldous Huxley, overlooked was that it is not only education which is big business but that drugs are sustained by even more insidious big business. It can and does call some pretty diabolical tunes as well as being essential to modern medicine.

276

Thus when we speak of the content of education we are discussing the directions in which the consciousness of children are to be expanded and, as a corollary, the points at which society wants it to be contracted. We cannot avoid value-judgements, and we need to bear in mind that every negation is likely to provoke an unpredictable reaction.

Education is a large-scale industry with thousands of factories all over the world — factories for producing the media, factories for manipulating minds, and factories for the highly profitable business of measurement by means of tests and examinations. In this enormous process of social chemistry the only thread on which any precise analytical research can hope to throw light is defined by the molecular chains used in the design of educational topics. It is here that we see the potential semantic significance of the atomic propositions and logical constants, and the hierarchies of types introduced as instruments of thought by Whitehead and Russell early this century, in the Principia Mathematica. They, of course, could not foresee what would be made of these concepts, or how they would be modified both by application and by further analysis. It was Warren McCulloch, who knew both men well, and whom I counted as my greatest friend, who showed, in the '40's, that the technology of nerve-nets in the brain showed an astonishing correspondence with the constructions of mathematical logic.

But McCulloch was too aware of the necessity of value-judgements to regard the brain as **merely** a system of mathematical technology. When he came to Leeds in 1967 he gave us the interpretation of the reticular formation at the very core of the brain. He harked back to Charles Sanders Peirce who had the foresight to add the concept of 'abduction' to the classical distinction between 'induction' and 'deduction'. By means of this bunch of neurones a mother sleeping soundly through the noise of traffic outside her window, will wake at a tiny cry from her baby. Abduction is concerned not with the quantity of information, nor with logical rigour, but with value-judgements. The word 'value' need not always be interpreted in an emotive sense. Recently Edward de Bono has, I gather, made a very profitable use of the concept of abduction by re-naming it as 'Lateral Thinking'. In 1925, when I was carrying out my first research on transfer of training, I had not heard of Peirce but felt the need for something beyond the stark dichotomy of induction and deduction, and I called it 'transduction'.

The significance of this concept is not simply that our thinking processes need not forever be tied to a linear oscillation between fact and logic, and that we can, in mathematical terms, also move at right angles in the complex plane. This does not tell us why a baby's cry should be more significant than the hoot of a car. The reason why it makes value-judgements possible cannot be found even in two-dimensional mathematical logic, i.e. the logic of matrices. These are still governed by logical constants. What we have lacked hitherto is any well-defined concept of global **semantic** constants.  Since these cannot be arranged along a line the complex plane itself must be rotated to produce a volume. This can then be divided into cells, each cell being the position of a potentail proposition.  If now we can introduce the time-factor into these cells we have the equivalent of what my colleague Eric Cole has recently (in the International Journal of Theoretical Physics) called 'Cellular space-time'.

This is not the occasion to go into the details of this concept, which amounts essentially to a quite new quantization of information.  But there is still one more step required to transform this mathematical structure into a semantic function.  I was still groping for this step in 1958 in my paper Semantic Matrices at the Washington International Conference on Scientific Information.  The message of that paper was (1) that a matrix is simply a two-dimensional array of symbols,  (2) that an algebraic interpretation confers a set of definable relations between the symbols, permitting definable transformations,  (3) that a page of print is formally a matrix,  and if we have a system of **positional rules** governing its interpretation this generates a large number of potential transformations, making the page an instrument of reasoning.  The on-going epistemic research aims to make our rationality more reasonable.

# RESEARCH ON EDUCATIONAL MEDIA (EXETER METHOD)

## THE ITEM DISTRIBUTION CHART (I.D.C.)

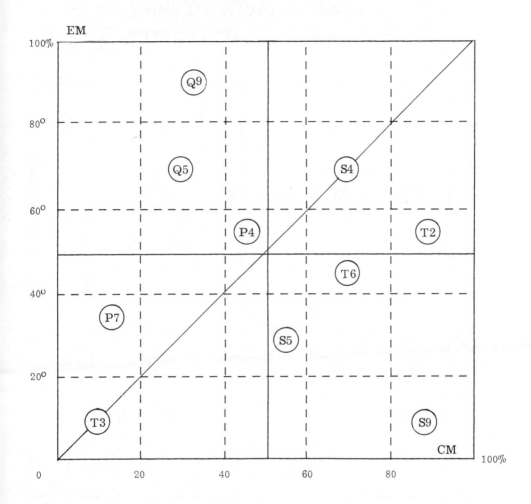

Each item-circle indicates a particular test-item. Co-ordinates of items indicate percentage successes of the two media in delivering the same message — items to two matched groups of candidates. The scores measure the media not the candidates. (Only a sample of items are given here)

Samples are shown from item-scores on a test of 40 items divided into four types: P (Practical), Q (Observational), S (Verbal), T (Theoretical) on a topic taught by an experimental medium EM (here visual) to half the class and by the conventional medium (verbal) to the other half. Each test-item, being classified and numbered, retains its identity in the chart. In the sample shown it is seen that the P and Q types tend to scores above the diagonal, and the S and T types are mainly below the diagonal. T3 was the most difficult item for both groups. Since most school-topics demand a mixture of cognitive moralities this indicates the need for a relation of 'appropriateness' between medium and message, and hence for multi-media resources.

The following chart enables this relation to be experimentally quantified as a 'success-ratio' in comparing the informative value of different media for different types of information.

## RESEARCH ON EDUCATIONAL MEDIA
## ZONES OF SUCCESS-RATIOS OF MEDIA

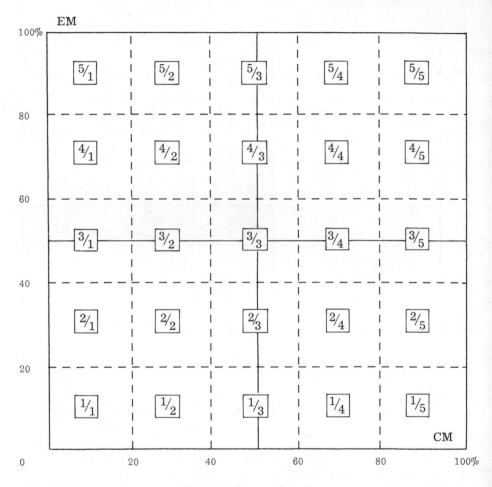

FRAMEWORK CHART for Zones of Relative Success of Media

SRM = Success-ratio of Experimental Medium  EM
                    to Conventional Medium  CM

Zones are marked by dotted lines.
Ratio for each zone is indicated by fraction.

# Two styles of communication and their implications for learning

D. ROWNTREE, The Open University

**Abstract:** The author distinguishes between one-way and two-way communication, suggesting that the former's predominance in education, being manipulative rather than facilitative, is deleterious to learning and that two-way communication should be pursued instead; he indicates how two-way communication depends on feedback being able to assume special potency and he outlines the pedagogic paradigm most likely to allow this; some of the far-reaching implications for choice of learning objectives and strategies and for use of communication media are then examined, the difficulties of implementing a student-directed, individualized education are indicated, and a newly-emerging role for the educational technologist is defined.

Educators generally appear to approve of communication and feel it is something the world needs more of. Yet discussions of communication often rely more heavily on metaphors of persuasion and control than on those of sharing and co-operation. Indeed, some communication deserves being called 'the engineering of consent' — seen at its most blatant in advertising, public relations and party-political propaganda. Against this equivocal background, communication must be seen as **problematic.** Is communication what we assume or would like it to be? If not, what would be the implications for teaching and learning or making it so?

My basic contention is that communication is quite rare in formal education, except in a partial and impoverished form. More than half a century ago, Thorndike pointed out that 'teaching is not telling'. Unfortunately, communication is widely taken to mean 'telling people things'. Effective communication then becomes a matter of telling them so they know they've been told and can make the expected response. Improving the effectiveness of this kind of communication is where many educational technologists came in — along with educational films and tapes, radio and TV, computers and programmed learning. An important paper by Brian Lewis and Jenny Cook (1969) laid the groundwork for a 'theory of telling' as part of, but **not** as a convenient substitute for, a more embracing theory of teaching and learning.

## Beyond Telling

Neither teaching nor communication can be reduced to telling. A teller
is able to operate with only a generalized image of his audience and is
under no compulsion to accommodate his message to the needs of
individuals. Telling implies one-way traffic in ideas (or feelings). One
perceptive analyst has labelled this process **munication** to distinguish it
from the two-way exchange implicit in **co**mmunication. In what follows
I will distinguish between these two kinds of communication by borrowing
the label **munication** for the former and coining the label **co-mmunication**
for the latter kind. According to this convention, lectures, books, radio
and TV programmes, films, gramophone records, etc., count as
**munication** media. Conversely, media allowing **co-mmunication** include
conversations, group discussions, tutorials, encounter groups, and
simulation games. (A phone-in radio programme might be something of
a hybrid — co-mmunication for those phoning-in, munication for those
who simply listen.)

In formal education, munication predominates; and may be highly
effective in encouraging the wrong kind of learning. More precisely, it
may help the student achieve acceptable short-term objectives at the
expense of **more desirable** long-term objectives. By imposing the communicator's definitions of reality, it may hinder the student developing (or
hanging onto) any of his own. Norris Sanders (1966) criticizes textbooks
for what is often equally true of the way other media communicate —
films, TV, lectures, classroom lessons, and all :

> '.... the textbook is weak in that it offers little opportunity for any
> mental activity except remembering. If there is an inference to be
> drawn, the author draws it, and if there is a significant relationship
> to be noted, the author points it out. There are no loose ends or
> incomplete analyses. The textbook is highly refined and as near
> perfection as a human mind is capable of making it — but the author
> does the thinking. The book never gives a clue that the author pon-
> dered (maybe even agonized) over hundreds of decisions. The result
> is that the creative process and the controversy of competing ideas
> are hidden from the students.'

Even in the classroom, research like that of Douglas Barnes (1971)
highlights the tendency among teachers to do most of the talking, to ask
only questions they already know the answers to, to allow only brief
responses, to squash 'digressions', to fail to build on children's out-of-
school interests and experience, and generally to legitimize only a very
limited, teacher-determined range of knowledge. Fantasy and feeling
are deemed especially irrelevant (see Jones, 1972). Much communication, in whatever medium, resembles what my colleague Brian Lewis
calls a 'mention list' — where we mention a number of things to the

student in the hope that, later on, he'll be able to mention them back to us. The long-term alienation effects among students of being treated as passive receivers rather than active creators of knowledge are explored in the growing literature of 'educational pathology' (e.g. Blishen, 1969; Henry, 1971; Holt, 1969; Reimer, 1971; Postman and Weingartner, 1971; etc.), and range from docility and dependence upon 'authoritative others' to cynicism, hostility and drop-out.

I have elsewhere (Rowntree, 1974) made the distinction between **manipulative** learning systems, whose purpose (seen most clearly when elements of indoctrination and training are involved) is to enable learners to fulfil other people's expectations of them, and **facilitative** systems, whose purpose is to help the learner cultivate and fulfil expectations of his own. Munication is essentially manipulative, and co-mmunication is essentially facilitative. We cannot facilitate the student's personal growth and autonomy without co-mmunication — without opening ourselves to **his** perceptions, **his** experience, **his** point of view. In doing so, we risk being changed ourselves. A colleague, Nick Furbank (1973), expects his literature students to be able to 'say something which makes the tutor radically rethink his own conception of an author or literary work'. Graham Holderness (1973), rebuking those teachers who regard students' personal viewpoints and anecdotes as an 'irrelevant' interruption to their teaching, illuminates the process:

> 'Discussing The Rainbow with a group of (Open University) students and hearing the personal responses, the individual contributions of a wide variety of ages and occupations — the "irrelevant anecdotes" of a farmer, an ex-miner, an engineer, a schoolteacher, a single woman, a married.woman, a woman with children — to my mind enriched the reading of that book infinitely. It came to life as I had never seen it before — and I had taught it many times.'

My colleague,Tony Bates, often quotes the showing of a TV film about a violent police-student clash (in an anti-Vietnam War demonstration) to a group of social psychology tutors. They were repeatedly asked to discuss how they would use the film with their classes in order to illustrate selective perception (comparing what police viewers would see in the televised scenes and what student viewers would see). Instead they embarked on a long and heated discussion about the rights and wrongs of student demonstrations as such. Tony Bates (1973) says this indicates:

> '....that we are all .... susceptible to **distraction** by powerful illustrative material .... that **the** function of the broadcast (must) be clearly recognized and held in mind during the transmission.... (and that we must ensure) that discussion and analysis of programmes is **relevant**. (my **accentuation**)

283

But it might also be held to indicate that 'messages' and experiences, especially if dramatic, may have more than one valid meaning and that value-judgements about 'distraction' and 'relevance' are not solely for the teacher to decide. In this case, the 'students' (being actually tutors!) were no longer socialized to submit to other people's definitions of reality and so insisted on exploring their own.

The co-mmunicator will recognize the potential ambiguity of many 'messages' and will neither be able to anticipate all possible meanings himself nor expect 'his' meaning necessarily to prevail. As T.S. Eliot is said to have said to an eager interpreter of The Waste Land: 'If you honestly see those meanings in it, then I suppose they must be there'. Co-mmunication allows room for the **negotiation** of meaning and the prospect of mutual learning through dialogue and discussion.

## From Munication to Co-mmunication

How do we get from munication to co-mmunication? We must extend the idea of **feedback**. One primitive, still popular, model of communication (Figure 1a) envisages a Sender (S) who transmits a message to a Receiver (R). Now S cannot formulate his message without at least some idea of R's characteristics, but it is only when he gets feedback from R — a sign or signal or response — that he can judge the effectiveness of his message and adjust it if necessary. So far, the model is one of munication. R's nod or wink, or comment or repetition of the message ( or even questionnaire responses or audience measurements), merely indicates the quality of the telling.

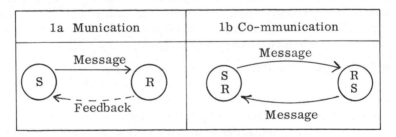

Figure 1   Two communication styles

The breakthrough from munication to co-mmunication occurs only when the feedback becomes so potent and insistent that it has to be recognized as **a message in its own right**. That is, it becomes not merely a response to S's statement but itself a statement which causes S to adjust his perception of reality — in some way to see things differently. In short, R must become S and S must become R (Figure 1b) and this **alternation** of roles must continue throughout the co-mmunicative episode. Such for example, would normally be the dynamics in a conversation, or

284

even in a decision-making conference, among friends and colleagues —
in what Paolo Freire calls the 'convivial dialogue'.

In educational terms, this role-alternation would imply that students
act not simply as receivers and processors of teacher-messages but
also as generators and senders of messages (about themselves, their
ideas, their perceptions, their experiences) which the teacher **values**
and allows to change his personal perspective on the student, the subject
under discussion, his own feelings, or some other feature of the situation. Metaphorically, the difference is between a factory, in which raw
materials (students) are uniformly processed, and a family, in which all
members grow together, in diverse ways, through sharing and enhancing
one another's uniqueness. Unlike the many educational technologists
who seem to be mostly interested in optimizing munication (by operating
on the means of message-transmission between S and R), I believe that
in the interests of full communication we must urgently look also for
ways of facilitating the role-alternation between S and R.

Co-mmunication, and alternation of roles, cannot take place unless
the initial Sender is willing to **accept** a certain feedback as message.
Whether or not he does so is partly a practical question. How far can a
teacher responsible for a large group of students afford to abandon the
convenience of municating to a notionally homogeneous group (in which
individual differences can be glossed as 'noise in the system') in favour
of enabling co-mmunication among diverse individuals? Partly it is a
question of inter-personal politics. How far is the teacher prepared to
share control of the situation, to relinquish some of his power to impose
his own meanings and decide what is to count as worthwhile learning?
Writers like John Holt (1970) and Herbert Kohl (1972) offer insights into
such practicalities and politics.

Above all, the willingess to co-mmunicate must be seen as part of
the teacher's professional world-view, his **pedagogic paradigm.** According to their values and beliefs about education, knowledge, learning, and
the student, different teachers can be seen as taking up different positions
along a continuum whose opposite extremes are hinted at in such dicho-
tomous terms as: authoritarian vs. democratic; closed vs. open
(Bernstein, 1971), teacher-centred vs. student-centred; dominative vs.
integrative (Flanders, 1970); realist vs. idealist (VanderMeer, 1969);
objectivistic, psychometric vs. subjectivistic, phenomenological (Esland,
1972). Very crudely, one end of the continuum tends to attract the
teacher whose first loyalty is to a public corpus of pre-existing knowledge
(which he knows everyone ought to acquire) and the need to 'get it across'
to a succession of students who learn, as far as their finite capacity and
motivation will allow, by absorbing and reproducing the **products** of other
people's experience. The other end of the continuum attracts the teacher
who eschews generalizations about what everyone ought to know and who,
believing people to have unlimited capacity for growth unless 'discouraged',

gives his first loyalty to individual students and encourages them to exercise their own developing motivation and intentionality in the acquisition of cognitive and affective **processes,** making their own meanings and creating new knowledge out of their own ideas and experiences. Of the two paradigms (whose myriad beliefs are merely sampled above), the former is more typical of secondary schools, the latter of infant schools; perhaps, also, the latter paradigm is more typical of arts-based subjects than science-based subjects, and more typical of women than men.

Only those teachers sympathetic to the latter paradigm are likely to strive for communication built on co-mmunication. To do so has a number of far-reaching implications, not least in the procedures for choosing objectives and strategies for learning, in using communication media, and in student assessment. To begin with, co-mmunication requires of the teacher some shift of attitudes from 'Here is what I'm going to teach you and it's your job to learn it' towards 'How can I use my personal interests and expertise to help you enrich your understanding of, and reach out from, whatever you are interested in?' The latter attitude recognizes that some of the most powerful messages emanating from students embody their wish to have some say in what they are learning about. (The pupils quoted by Edward Blishen (1969) in The School That I'd Like offer deeply-felt testimony to that effect.) Thus, the co-mmunicating teacher will put less emphasis on coercive strategies enabling a notional 'typical student' to achieve teacher's objectives and will concentrate on enabling each individual student to identify his own objectives and explore his own best strategies.

## The Negotiation of Objectives

In a very small way, the student who elects to study one course rather than another can be said to be, implicitly, choosing one set of objectives rather than another. However, we know that objectives are often so implicit as to be practically undetectable, and, in any case, students don't always have much choice as to which courses they take. Again, as it happens, different students inevitably get different things from a course; but this often gives rise to anxiety rather than celebration, for only the 'required' learning is legitimized by the system's assessment procedures.

Students quite naturally hope that a course will adapt to their needs rather than expecting them to adapt to its. For example, Open University students, who are committed to pre-packaged courses demanding from them a series of written assignments, ask that at least some of the assignment topics should be individually negotiable between the student and the tutor responsible for assessing his work (rather than being uniformly dictated from the centre for all students alike, regardless

286

of their individual needs and circumstances).  A further extension of this would be student-initiated projects allowing students to take considerable responsibility for their own learning (with guidance from tutors), establishing their own priorities within the course, deciding which parts to explore in greater depth or in different ways than colleagues.  The clash of paradigms is evident in Open University discussions between educators who argue that students' interests will be better served by putting our efforts into perfecting 'student-proof' packages at the centre and those who, believing this to be neither possible nor desirable, argue that the emphasis should go on finding new ways to individualize and make personal the learning through more flexible interaction between students and tutors out in the regions.  In literary studies, for example, one manifestation of this latter emphasis would be to say to students not 'Read **this** book by **this** author (and we'll discuss it)', nor even 'Read **any** book by **this** author', but 'Read **any** book by **any** author (or write your own), and we'll discuss it'.

Transcripts of classroom interactions in college courses given by such educators as Carl Rogers (1951) and Nathaniel Cantor (1972) show how objectives and content can be negotiated through messages from students interpreted by a non-directive co-mmunicating teacher.  An early experiment by Robert Mager (1961) suggested how the potential of student-directed learning could be tapped.  Mager taught electronics by undertaking to answer whatever questions students cared to ask (but only those), discovering in the process that students adopted quite different learning strategies and objectives than those that would normally be imposed by a textbook or classroom teacher. Significantly, both Carl Rogers and Nathaniel Cantor typically began their courses by asking students the reasons why they enrolled, what they hoped to get out of it, and what questions they hoped it might answer.  Postman and Weingartner (1971) give many examples of how students can formulate their own objectives if they are encouraged to learn **through asking and elaborating their own questions rather than hunting for answers to other people's.**  Similarly, Colin and Mog Ball (1971) show how secondary school students can develop their own objectives out of problems they encounter in the local community.

So the teacher who wants to co-mmunicate should open himself to the objectives proposed (explicitly or implicitly) by his students.  In addition, he will identify objectives of his own.  (Though some teachers are rightly suspicious about colleagues who over-elaborate and rigidly pre-plan their objectives, it is also right to be suspicious about some other teachers whose refusal to discuss objectives at all may reflect a municative and potentially manipulative stance.)  Clearly, one of the co-mmunicative teacher's objectives will be that students should learn to formulate their own.  This was dramatically illustrated by Roger Harrison and Richard Hopkins (1967) in their training of Peace Corps volunteers.  Since they wanted to wean recruits from their dependence on experts and enable them to take responsibility for fraught situations on their own, they required students right from the start to take the initiative in **planning their own course.**

Indeed, the teacher needs to be able to make the distinction I have explored elsewhere (Rowntree, 1973 and 1974) between 'process objectives' (that is, methodologies and life-skills) and 'content objectives'. Thus the teacher who holds most important such 'process objectives' as those listed by Postman and Weingartner, and

> '.... measures his success in terms of behavioural changes in students;  the frequency with which they ask questions;  the increase in the relevance and cogency of their questions;  the frequency and conviction of their challenges to assertions made by other students or teachers or textbooks;  the relevance and clarity of the standards on which they base their challenges;  their willingness to suspend judgements when they have insufficient data;  their willingess to modify or otherwise change their position when data warrant such change;  the increase in their skill in observing, classifying, generalizing, etc.;  the increase in their tolerance for diverse answers;  their ability to apply generalizations, attitudes and information to novel situations'

will recognize that they can be rigorously pursued through an infinite variety of investigations (within or cutting across subject 'boundaries'), allowing students plenty of room to achieve their own objectives as well as 'his'.  Furthermore, such objectives contribute to the student's autonomy rather than narrowing his options and manipulating him.  A sense of priorities, and of the one-to-many relationship between process objectives and content objectives, enables the teacher to be opportunistic and acceptant of a wide diversity of student purposes. He will be able to enter into the kind of transaction described by Nicholas Farnes (1973) :

> '.... 'trade-offs' can be made between the child's purposes and the teacher's purposes, so that some from both sources can be incorporated into an activity that has meaning for the child because it is rich in those things he is interested in doing and at the same time fulfils many of the teacher's own purposes. Activities that the teacher considers important and perhaps the 'real' purpose of education are best achieved when the child sees them as a means of achieving purposes that he considers important.'

In practice, a curriculum is a negotiated compromise between what 'the system' requires, what the student wants to learn about, and what the teacher feels capable of teaching.  To resort to Venn diagrams,

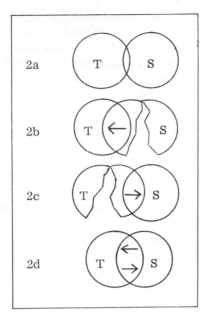

Figure 2

Figure 2a shows what the teacher regards as important (T), what the student regards as important (S), and the area of overlap in which they have common purposes. In 'munication' (Figure 2b) the teacher attempts to drag the student across into his area, fracturing the student's integrity in the process. The reverse procedure (Fig. 2c) rarely happens but would be equally destructive. The truly co-mmunicative way to increase overlap (Figure 2d) is through the mutual trust and respect that enables the teacher to enter into the student's **weltanschauung** to the same degree as he expects the student to enter his.

## Strategies, Media and Assessment

The proposed emphasis on co-mmunication affects our concepts about such strategies as 'individualized learning'. Programmed learning is largely responsible for the myth that individualized learning is necessarily student-centred. That the student is working alone does not mean the work is individualized. Indeed, to achieve his own goals he may need to share his ideas and take counsel with one or two similarly-inclined colleagues or even with a sizeable and diverse discussion group. Most 'individualized learning' (whether or not based on pre-packaged material) is essentially municative. That is, the student is simply being allowed to go at his own pace, and perhaps in his own way, towards someone else's goals.

Related strategies like 'discovery learning' (Shulman and Keislar, 1966) and 'mastery learning' (Bloom, 1971) also need to be looked at again. If the student is asked, in effect, to 'discover your own Newton's Laws of Motion' (that is, where the product is pre-determined), or if the objectives being 'mastered' are not of deep personal concern to the student, then they represent elaborate strategies for telling rather than co-mmunication. Not, of course, that telling is to be proscribed. If the teacher has information or insights the student needs and requests it would be churlish to refuse. And there will often be justification for encouraging the student to investigate questions he hasn't asked, if one is convinced that the relevance of the resulting experience will emerge as he engages in it. It is the teacher's **intention,** and the student's interpretation of it, that determines whether the teacher's 'telling' contributions are manipulative or facilitative.

Many also are the implications for our use of communication media. How far, for example, can learning be both pre-packaged and individualized? Resource materials are sometimes so pre-packaged, pre-structured, and virtually pre-digested (what Edgar Friedenberg calls the 'TV-dinner approach') that the student is left no freedom to use the package his own way and take from it just what he needs. We should be suspicious of monolithic packages that assume all students have the same objectives and the same learning style.

Perhaps the best approach to educational packaging is 'modular' — implying a multiplicity of smaller packages, or units, or sets of learning materials. They may be open-ended and non-prescriptive, or they may be quite specific about the objectives they are most useful for; either way they should impose minimum constraints on teachers and students who wish to choose from among them, and combine them with other resources in personally meaningful ways. This is what David Hawkins (1965) calls 'multiple programmed' materials: 'material that contains written and pictorial guidance of some sort for the student, but which is designed for the greatest possible variety of topics, ordering of topics, etc., so that for almost any given way into a subject that a child may evolve on his own, there is material available which he will recognize as helping him further along that way'.

The teacher must not expect to be able to preview all the rich profusion of learning resources his students should have access to (any more than he could monitor all the media experiences they are exposed to **outside** the school). But he should expect to learn about these experiences from his students and to help them convert experiences into learning and growth. In short, no amount of materials and packages can facilitate co-mmunication unless the student has full access to 'human interaction' media — allowing him to consult and debate with teachers, fellow-students and people from the outside community.

290

Nathaniel Cantor (1972) saw more clearly than most what can be entailed by a truly individualized use of learning resources:

'No two students will learn in the same way. Every individual will take out of the course what he feels he wants or need and will put into it whatever efforts his capacity and willingness to learn allow. The (teacher) who is aware of these differences in learning will permit different students to use him, and the material of the course, in their own unique ways. As long as the student is sincerely trying to do something with himself and struggling to learn, he should be permitted to move at his own speed and on his own level.'

And what of student assessment? When different students within a group are pursuing different objectives through different inquiries at different levels, peer-comparisons become difficult; so marking, scoring and grading become more problematic than ever. Assessment of such student work may need to encompass, through description and interpretation, all that the student is becoming, rather than concentrating merely on his achievement of pre-determined measurable outcomes and ignoring the unanticipated or less-easily quantifiable outcomes. In other words, assessment may need to follow what Malcolm Parlett and David Hamilton (1972) describe, in talking of evaluation, as the 'anthropological' (participant observer) approach rather than the 'agricultural-botany' (treatment-yield) approach. Assessment may also need to be continuous rather than terminal (formative rather than summative), replying heavily on **self**-assessment by students. Significantly, in one of the most fully student-directed courses in British higher education (for the diploma in behavioural science at North London Polytechnic) students have responsibility not only for course-design and organization but also for their own assessment.

## A Role for the Educational Technologist

The progress towards full communication (in which co-mmunication predominates) is not easy, especially if attempted too hurriedly. (See Gross et al (1971) for a case-study of failure in a U.S. primary school and, by contrast, Caton (1972) for an account of success in a British secondary school.) Teachers are not normally given much experience of co-mmunication during their training (but see Hannam et al (1971) for an important exception); pupils may at first appear hostile or inept when asked to abandon their dependence in favour of thinking for themselves; colleagues may be less than sympathetic if they view the emerging paradigm as disruptive of their own professional security; in any case those who wield the power within society may not thank us for presenting it with people who are used to having their view of things taken into account.

How can the educational technologist help the cause of learning through full communication? If he so wishes (and not all will), by continually questioning the aims and objectives of all the communication and learning he is associated with. By asking whether the overall drift is municative or co-mmunicative, manipulative or facilitative, teacher-centred or student-centred. By asking whether 'the system' truly encourages the individuality and developing autonomy of each student. By asking how he can use his insights and heuristics to help the learner cope with problems of learning and not simply the teacher with problems of teaching. Increasingly, and especially if he is the teacher himself, we may hope to find him fulfilling the role described by Everett Reimer (1971) for the designers of 'learning networks' who:

'.... will have to understand knowledge, people and the societies they live in. They will have to be dedicated to the idea of student-directed, individualized education. They will have to understand the barriers to the flow of relevant information and how to reduce them without generating counter-actions which would annul their efforts. They will above all have to be able to resist the eternal temptation of subtly directing the studies of their clients instead of opening ever new and possibly dangerous doors for their investigation.'

REFERENCES

Ball, C. and M. (1973) Education for a Change. London: Penguin.
Barnes, D. (1971) Language and learning in the classroom, in Journal of Curriculum Studies 3, (1) May 1971, pp.36-7.
Bates, A. (1973) Problems of broadcasting, pp. 26-30 in Teaching by Correspondence in the Open University. Milton Keynes: Open University Press.
Bernstein, B.B. (1971) Open schools, open society, in Cosin, B.R. et al. (Eds.) School and Society: A Sociological Reader. London: Routledge and Kegan Paul.
Blishen, E. (Ed.) (1969) The School That I'd Like. London: Penguin.
Bloom, B.S. (1971) Individual Differences in School Achievement: A Vanishing Point? Bloomington, Indiana: Phi Delta Kappa International.
Cantor, N. (1972) Dynamics of Learning. New York: Agathon. (First published 1946)
Caton, B.J. (1972) Transcript, pp. 43-4 and A practical attempt at collaborative learning pp. 49-58, in Esland, G. et al.(1972) (see below).
Esland, G. et al. (1972) The Social Organization of Teaching and Learning, Units 5-8 in Course E282. Bletchley, England: Open University Press.
Farnes, N.C. (1973) Reading Purposes, Comprehension and the Use of Context, Units 3-4 in Course PE261. Bletchley, England: Open University Press.
Flanders, N. (1973) Analysing Teacher Behaviour. London: Addison-Wesley.
Furbank, N. (1973) Personal note to author.
Gross, N. et al. (1971) Implementing Organizational Innovations. New York: Harper and Row.
Hannam, C. et al. (1971) Young Teachers and Reluctant Learners. London: Penguin.
Harrison, R. and Hopkins, R. (1967) The design of cross-cultural training: an alternative to the University model, in Journal of Applied Behavioural Science III, No. 4, pp. 431-440.

Hawkins, D. (1965) Messing about in science, in Science and Children, February 1965. Quoted in Holt, J. (1970) p.145 (see below).

Holderness, G. (1973) Those anecdotes can be relevant. Letter in Open University Newspaper Sesame, Volume 2, No. 4, May 1973.

Holt, J. (1969) How Children Fail. London: Penguin. (First published 1964).

Holt, J. (1970) How Children Learn. London: Penguin (First published 1967).

Jones, R.M. (1972) Fantasy and Feeling in Education. London: Penguin.

Kohl, H. (1972) 36 Children. London: Penguin.

Lewis, B.N. and Cook, J.A. (1969) Towards a theory of telling, in Int. J. Man-Machine Studies (1969) 1, pp. 129-176.

Mager, R.F. (1961) On the sequencing of instructional content, in Psychological Reports, Volume 9, 1961, pp. 405-13.

Parlett, M. and Hamilton, D. (1972) Evaluation as Illumination: A New Approach to the Study of Innovatory Programs. Occasional Paper No. 9, Centre for Research in the Educational Sciences, University of Edinburgh.

Postman, N. and Weingartner, C. (1971) Teaching as a Subversive Activity. London: Penguin.

Reimer, E. (1971) School is Dead: An Essay on Alternatives in Education. London: Penguin.

Rogers, C.R. (1951) Client-Centred Therapy. Boston: Houghton Mifflin.

Rowntree, D. (1973) Which objectives are most worthwhile? in Leedham, J.F. and Budgett, R. (Eds.) (1973) Aspects of Educational Technology VII. London: Pitman.

Rowntree, D. (1974) Educational Technology in Curriculum Development. London: Harper & Row.

Sanders, N.M. (1966) Classroom Questions: What Kinds? New York: Harper and Row.

Shulman, L.S. and Keislar, E.R. (1966) Learning by Discovery: A Critical Appraisal. Chicago: Rand McNally.

VanderMeer, A.W. (1969) Educational philosophies and communication, in Wiman, R.V. and Meierhenry, W.C. (Eds.) Educational Media: Theory into Practice. Columbus, Ohio: Merrill.

# The application of interactive telecommunications systems to education

E. WILLIAMS, University College, London

**Abstract:** While a substantial amount of work into instructional media has been reported little of this research has considered two-way communications media such as the telephone. This is unfortunate since many recent educational theorists have stressed the importance of interaction between student and teacher as opposed to the one-way flow of information in lecturing. In view of the explosion of interest in novel telecommunications media (e.g. videophone, conference TV, graphics media) research attention to the educational applications of two-way media is necessary.

Three pioneering efforts in the use of telecommunications in education will be discussed. These are the Open University experiment on telephone tutorials, the University of Quebec conference system and the University of Wisconsin medical education system. Ways in which such systems could be assessed for their effectiveness in enabling learning and allowing the development of a relationship between students and teachers will be discussed. Extensive reference will be made to the experimental work of the Communications Studies Group, who have by now carried out over 20 laboratory experiments and five field studies, all aimed at assessing the influence of various telecommunications media upon social interaction and upon the outcome of the task in hand.

Recently reading a copy of 'Humpty Dumpty', a magazine produced by a group of radical psychologists and sociologists, I came across a criticism of the Open University as follows :

'If I think of the good things about a university, I think of such things as coming into contact with teachers and other students who are alive and stimulating, being able to ask them questions and put my own point of view and grow through a process of conflict. If I think of the bad things about a university, I think of such things as one-way communication, fixed courses and texts, impersonal paper-work and examinations. The Open University has a lot of the bad things, and precious few of the good ones.'

While I feel the author is perhaps too hasty in rejecting the Open University as an institution (I support it myself to the extent of being a student), he is making a valid point. Most educationalists would now

294

reject as oversimplified the model of a teacher, as information source, transmitting information to the student, the information recipient. Rather they would emphasize that feedback from the student to the teacher is equally important; without such feedback, the teacher has no means of discovering whether his message is understood. Furthermore, involvement in two-way interactive discussions is, as 'Humpty Dumpty' suggests, a more interesting, involving process for the student than merely passively receiving information from the teacher.

Most educational technology, however, is the very negation of interactive learning. Broadcast television or radio, and educational films, tapes, and records are truly one-way: there is no chance of the student questioning the 'teacher' when the latter is preserved on celluloid. Those technologies which do provide feedback do so in an extremely limited way; programmed learning units and computer marked tests give the student no chance to question the 'teacher' or to ask him to elucidate his argument.

Lest you should conclude that I am an educational Luddite, anxious to abandon all technology in favour of the 'good old methods', let me say that I am convinced that, with increased needs and demands for education, particularly higher education, the use of educational technology is inevitable and justifiable. However, we should examine carefully the assumed model of the educational process implicit in the selection of any particular technological system; in other words, we should be aware that to some extent the medium is the message.

There are mechanical aids, old and new, which can help us in our approach to education based on a 'Let's discuss this together' model rather than a 'Be quiet while I am telling you the facts' model. These are primarily the interactive telecommunications media. Even the humble telephone could be used more extensively; many are unaware that conference calls with up to seven people, each at their own telephone, can be arranged. Within a local dialling area, such calls would nearly always be cheaper than bringing the participants together face-to-face. More elaborate systems for 'many-to-many' discussions are the Loud Speaking Telephone, or even more elaborate, the Remote Meeting Table (which has a system of automated speaker identification). All these systems transmit voices only, so, to forestall mutterings about the importance of visual information in education, let me point out that electrowriters, and facsimile machines, both of which can be used over normal telephone lines, can transmit a wide range of written or graphic material. Furthermore, fully visual systems such as the Bell Picturephones and the Post Office's Confravision are now being marketed. These latter systems are, at present, extremely expensive, but costs are expected to fall rapidly.

How, then, could such interactive systems be used in education? To a large extent, the answer depends on the ingenuity of the user, but let me briefly mention three field experiments which may give some indications of the possibilities. Ben Turok, an Open University tutor in North London, has been experimenting with loudspeaking telephones on a conference call hookup to connect several study centres at once. A general discussion between small groups of Open University students and their tutors can take place. Initial reactions seem to have been positive, and the next step, students using their home phones to 'attend' tutorials seems only a short step away. A similar experiment has been underway for three years at the University of Quebec. This university has a 'campus' dispersed across hundreds of miles, and uses teleconferencing for administration and teaching. Tutors at the Institut National de la Récherche Scientifique at Varennes have been teaching physics to students at two or three other locations simultaneously. Loud speaking telephones and electrowriters (since the course has a strong visual component) are used. While there were some criticisms of the system by staff and students, it was satisfactory enough in that particular context to be used regularly. The third experiment is taking place at the University of Alabama School of Medicine. Dr. Klapper, in charge of the project, is interested in continuing medical education for practitioners who have ceased their formal education and are working full-time. A single free-phone number has been set up, and doctors and other health personnel throughout Alabama can phone any time that they have a medical problem. An operator, who has some skill in the medical area channels the calls to members of the University Medical faculty, who can then try their best to help with the problem. The latest figures I have suggest that the system is growing in popularity, with 300 to 400 calls per month.

Clearly telecommunications can play an important part in education. However, before large investment is made into new forms of educational technology, whether one-way or two-way, it does seem prudent to investigate the efficiency of these methods as compared to the more traditional ones. Telecommunications may be easier or cheaper than face-to-face communication, but is it as effective for the tasks in hand? Most of the work of the Communications Studies Group of University College London during the last three years has been aimed at answering this question. The project has been concerned primarily with telecommunications for general office and administrative work, but the studies have been at a sufficient level of generality to be relevant to the educational context.

In any such assessment of effectiveness, it is necessary to ensure sufficient experimental control as to allow one's conclusions to be unsullied by the threat of artefacts. In order to demonstrate our methods for discovering the effectiveness of telecommunications, I shall describe an experiment I carried out at the Communications Studies Group recently. Groups of four people came together and communicated face-to-face, via closed circuit television, or over an audio link for 30 minutes.  There were 15 such groups using each medium.  The ostensible task was to generate ideas about the 'Problems of Travel in Britain'. These ideas were recorded as produced by the 'secretary' of the group, who also noted down who proposed, seconded, and dissented from the ideas.  Analysis of these results showed that there was no effect of the medium of communication on the number of ideas generated, upon the originality of the ideas, or upon the quality of the ideas.  Patterns of agreement or disagreement (coalition formation) were effected by the medium, however, with the split into coalitions in the telecommunications conditions tending to be between the two telecommunications nodes.

About 20 such experiments covering a range of different tasks and situations have now been completed, and we are in a position to make some generalizations about the effects of interactive telecommunications media.  Figure 1 summarizes the tasks or processes which have or have not been found to be affected by medium.

| TASK | MEDIUM EFFECT |
|------|:-------------:|
| Information exchange | X |
| Problem solving | X |
| Generating ideas | X |
| Conflict of objectives | X |
| Risky decision-making | X |
| Attitude change | ✓ |
| Interviewing | ✓ |
| Getting to know a stranger | ✓ |
| Bargaining and negotiation | ✓ |
| Coalition formation | ✓ |

Figure 1:  Tasks and Processes Affected or Not-affected by Communications Medium

From these results it seems possible to generalize:  tasks which involve little interpersonal understanding, where a moment-to-moment comprehension of the other's feelings is unimportant, are unaffected by communications medium.  However, if the task requires a detailed understanding of the other's feelings or reactions (information which is primarily transmitted by non-verbal cues, and is thus excluded by audio media) are media sensitive.  Such highly interactive situations, where the future strategies of each participant are maximally contingent on the reactions of the other, are not carried out equally effectively over telecommunications as face-to-face.  Interestingly, it is not true that face-to-face is always more effective than telecommunications media;  in the attitude change situation, where two people who disagreed each tried to change the other's opinion, there was **more** attitude change over an audio medium than via closed circuit television or face-to-face.

How does this apply to the teaching situation? Clearly quite a large amount of teaching falls into the 'information exchange' and 'co-operative problem solving' categories; media effects here are minimal, so teaching via the telephone would be as effective as face-to-face. It could be argued that an important component of teaching is 'attitude change', which, as we have seen, is affected by medium of communication, but is most efficient over an audio system. The special situation in teaching, where it is often especially important for the teacher to be aware of cues to understanding or boredom, usually expressed non-verbally, from the students, may negate some of these conclusions.

The use of graphics is vital in education: how the various graphics media would match up to the demands of teachers is a question which deserves empirical investigation. A rigorous application of such experimental techniques to the assessment of telecommunications technology in education does seem worthwhile from these initial extrapolations of the Communications Studies Group's experimental findings.

A second line of work pursued by the Communications Studies Group has been an investigation of the acceptability of various telecommunications systems. Even if telecommunication can be shown to be as effective as face-to-face for a given task, it must still be acceptable to the users, who will otherwise ignore or avoid it. The measurement of acceptability can be carried out by means of in-depth interviews or by questionnaires: the Communications Studies Group has used both methods with users of about eight telecommunications systems. Numerous conclusions have flowed from such studies :

(1)  Users generally agree with the findings of the empirical studies mentioned above, i.e. they would be happy to use telecommunications for tasks where no media effects have been found.

(2)  Audio systems particularly, and video systems to a lesser extent, are seen as giving less personal contact than face-to-face. Teleconference meetings are seen as more formal, serious and business-like; less friendly, sociable and pleasant. It is often mentioned that the chit-chat is cut out of teleconference meetings, and that they are, in consequence, shorter and more efficient per unit time.

(3)  Concern is often expressed about the privacy of video telecommunications systems; people are worried about using them for private, personal or confidential matters. Less concern is expressed with audio systems like the telephone or with face-to-face.

(4)  The convenience of telecommunications for busy people is often stressed. The advantages of being able to participate without wasting

hours of travelling time is often sufficient to outweigh other perceived advantages.

It is difficult to assess what the acceptability of telecommunications in the educational context would be without similar field studies, investigating the attitudes of teachers and pupils to the systems in use. The collection of such data would in itself be a justifiable reason for field trials of telecommunications in schools, universities and elsewhere.

In conclusion, may I express my hope that interactive telecommunications media will be amongst the forefront of the technologies considered for introduction into education. With increasing specialization, and with the shortage of specialized staff, it is often vital to augment the teacher by means of technology; but only by remembering that both teachers and students should take an active role, and thus their contact should allow for interaction and mutual influence (to their mutual benefit, we hope), will we ensure that technology augments and improves the teacher-student relationship, rather than replacing the teacher, and turning the student into a passive listening and button-pushing automaton.

REFERENCES

Champness, B.G. (1973) Attitudes towards person-person communications media. Human Factors 15, 427-48.

Chapanis, A., Ochsman, R., Parrish, R. and Weeks, G. (1972) Studies in Interactive Communication: I The effects of four communications modes on the behaviour of the teams during co-operative problem solving. Human Factors 14, 487-509.

Christie, B. (1974) The perceived acceptability of two teleconference systems for six activities. Unpublished paper of the Communications Studies Group No.E/74060/CR.

Klapper, M.S. (1971) The telephone and continuing medical education. Alabama Journal of Medical Science.

Short, J. (1973) A report on the use of the audio conferencing facility in the University of Quebec. Unpublished paper of the Communications Studies Group No. P/73161/SH.

Short, J. (1973) The effects of medium of communication on two person conflicts. Unpublished Ph.D thesis. University College, London.

Void, O. (1973) The Open University works for Enoch Powell. Humpty Dumpty 3, 7-9.

Williams, E. (1974) Brainstorming and coalition formation over telecommunications media. Unpublished paper of the Communications Studies Group No.E/74003/WL.

# The ubiquity of positive feedback in educational cybernetics

P. D. MITCHELL, Sir George Williams University, Montreal

**Abstract:** This paper challenges a construct which underlies much of our thinking about feedback in instructional communications. Instructional technology is outcome and function oriented, and aims to establish and maintain some stipulated behaviour. Usually this is presumed to be a negative feedback process. That is, the instructional system counteracts any deviation from the desired norm by messages intended to reduce the discrepancy between the student's behaviour and the target vector.

It is argued here that the acquisition of new behaviour is viewed more appropriately as a positive feedback process which amplifies deviations from an initial state.

Positive feedback processes are implicit in such notions as knowledge explosion and success breeding success. Unregulated, positive feedback processes result in destructive runaway to maximum (such as a stove whose thermostat calls for more heat as the oven becomes warmer) or to zero (the same stove if the initial impetus produces a cooler oven). Carefully regulated, as in the jet engine, positive feedback can be beneficial.

'Learning' is essentially a transition in the organism from one state (or capability) to another. This transition represents a sequence of one or more deviations of increasing magnitude from the original state. Response differentation, or shaping, typifies this deviation-amplifying positive feedback process. Achievement of some desired new state (but seldom the intervening states) leads to the assertion that learning has occurred. The use of a reinforcer (e.g. food, money or other contingent event) provides augmentative feedback. This supplements the organism's own sensory system which continuously monitors his external and covert environment as he generates activity.

The student demonstrates positive feedback processes when his attention is attracted such that he engages in overt or covert activities that lead to further involvement with the instructional communications. His enhanced attending and responding may be so self-sustaining as to produce a significant increment in his capability. Contingency management procedures facilitate this positive feedback process.

Forgetting is a runaway to zero process in which disuse of capability leads to difficulty in utilizing it. This positive feedback cycle can be broken by monitoring the capability in question and activating a negative feedback process to maintain homeostasis. In designing the student's sensory encompassment, massed and spaced repetition of instructional communications or activities (including recall) may be necessary. But self-regulation by the student will be a major factor in generating and maintaining positive feedback cycles.

# INTRODUCTION

In planning educational systems and products the educational technologist tries to allocate the limited resources available (e.g. materials, money, educators' time and students' time) so as to maximize the likelihood of learning. To do so, he needs a model, however crude, of the potential student and of systems and procedures which seem likely to produce an increment in his capability (i.e. his aggregate knowledge, attitudes and skills). This paper delineates such a model with particular reference to instructional communication and control, i.e. educational cybernetics.

# COMMUNICATIONS AND CONTROL

Communications models are usually designed as either an open or a closed-loop system. In the open system model discrete bits of information are encoded and transmitted by a communicator and, presumably, decoded and experienced by a recipient. Too frequently in practice this model engenders the Hiawatha effect; just as Hiawatha, in Longfellow's poem, 'shot an arrow into the air/It fell to earth I know not where', so the educational communicator cannot even be certain that his message has reached its target.

The second, closed loop (or cybernetic) model elaborates upon the one-way communications model such that the response sent back to the communicator both assures him that his message has been received and allows him to select future messages according to that response. Cybernetic control, as Wiener succinctly expressed it, is 'nothing but the sending of messages which effectively change the behaviour of the recipient' (Wiener, 1954, p. 8). Thus instructional management is outcome and function oriented, and aims to maintain some stipulated student behaviour. It will counteract any deviation from that norm by messages intended to shift the student's behaviour to that target vector — a process known as negative feedback. (It should be noted that sender and receiver, controller and controlled, might be the same person whose messages may be, for example, written or covert reminders.

A major conceptual flaw permeates much of our thinking about the notion of feedback, for the term is applied indiscriminately to positive and negative feedback, as well as to knowledge of results and even rewards and punishments. Popular accounts seldom make the all-important distinction between positive and negative feedback. I will argue, however, that positive, rather than — as commonly assumed — negative, feedback accounts for most significant human learning. But first let us examine the terms involved.

301

# FEEDBACK

## Reciprocal Control

Feedback occurs when two or more systems interact. And where one of these is animate, reciprocal communication and control exist even if one system dominates. Instructional control presumes a dominant instructional system and a responsive student who may be viewed as a 'feedback system which generates its own activities in order to detect and control specific stimulus characteristics of the environment' (Smith and Smith, 1966, p. vii). In fact instructional designs implicitly regard the student as just such a goal-directed **negative** feedback system. What are the implications of this approach?

## Negative Feedback

Recall that the thermostat and governor of a steam-engine, the standard illustrations of deviation-reducing negative feedback, are designed to maintain a steady state. But while such a homeostatic model might be used to describe the maintenance of an acquired habit, or skill, the student who is moving toward a new goal would certainly not fit this model. I would maintain that goals not currently in the student's behaviour repertoire cannot normally be reached by negative feedback.

## Positive Feedback

Positive feedback can be illustrated by a thermostat with reversed connections, which calls for more heat as the chamber becomes increasingly warmer, or an engine governor which drives an engine faster in response to an increase in speed. In both these cases the runaway situation is disastrous. But consider another example: in the turbo-jet increasing thrust increases intake which, in turn, increases thrust; the engine is prevented from destroying itself by someone's monitoring the process and limiting the fuel. Illustrative biosocial processes are preferable to mechanical systems.

Unchecked, positive feedback inevitably results in runaway to maximum or to zero (or some threshold), depending on the initial impetus. Most all-or-none responses and so-called vicious circles are positive feedback systems (e.g. paranoid disorders, neural impulses; cf. Stanley-Jones, 1969). Positive feedback cycles are also implicit in such notions as knowledge explosion, 'success breeding success' and runaway inflation. But a regulatory intervention (sometimes by negative feedback processes) can break the process before the system collapses. Such carefully regulated, beneficial, goal-oriented **amplification** by positive feedback is both possible and desirable.

Compound interest is an example of a regulated positive feedback process, as is educational development at the personal and societal level where newly acquired knowledge and skills make possible further elaboration and integration of aggregate capability, which, in turn, facilitates further acquisition. In this latter, destructive runaway to maximum is prevented by capricious events (lack of resources, hunger, fatigue, distractions) and intentional control. Alas, runaway to zero in the individual (failure begets failure) requires, but does not always receive, drastic intervention.

## POSITIVE FEEDBACK IN EDUCATION

Uncritical acceptance of learning as a negative feedback causal process, coupled with neglect of positve feedback processes, fosters continuing ignorance of positive feedback — a sine qua non of education. Without positive feedback we would be habit-bound; any development, whether it be maturation, accumulation of wealth, urban growth, or thought disorders, requires it. The concept of positive feedback provides the framework for integrating the successive patterns of a student's development — development which allows any seemingly insignificant (and perhaps improbable) deviation from an initial state to be amplified, making further deviation more probable until something intervenes and the person shifts attention to another stream of events.

## LEARNING

Generally defined as a relatively permanent change in capability (not attributable to other phenomena), learning is essentially (i) transition from one state to another (by acquisition, generation, or assimilation) and (ii) maintenance or reproduction of that new state after the passage of time (by recall, utilization or reproduction of the new conceptual, affective or behavioural organization). This is simply illustrated.

Consider a rat newly placed in an operant conditioning box. He has a very low probability of pressing the lever. However, in the process of response differentiation, or shaping, a response of higher probability for example, facing the lever, 'produces' food and a click. Approach and eating behaviour follow, which in turn are followed by ingestion (and ultimately, by digestion, alteration in cell chemistry and therefore of regulatory mechanisms which control food searching behaviour). This natural sequence strengthens the events which preceded it, making lever-oriented behaviour more probable. This in turn makes further differential reinforcement and feeding possible. This deviation-amplifying sequential process takes the organism from its original state (in which lever pressing has a very low probability) through several states to a new state. In this illustration, of course, the positive feedback process is regulated, not only by satiation, but also by the intervening steps and the experimental paradigm of shaping through a reinforcement procedure. It should be noted that although transition state is a positive feedback process, maintenance of lever pressing behaviour — a steady state — can be controlled by the same reinforcement procedure, now part of the negative feedback process.

The reinforcer provides augmented feedback for two disparate processes. Undoubtedly this accounts for some of the existent confusion about feedback. Because infrahuman organisms don't easily yield information about dynamic but covert feedback processes, let us consider learning in man for whom internal processes are both observable and communicable.

Although learning is inferred from external observations of behaviour, the process need not result in immediately overt behaviour (Mitchell, 1972). In addition to monitoring his behaviour, the organism, man, monitors his inner environment. By exercising this capacity for self-reflection, man can apprehend specific events within a wider perspective than an external observer (often yielding a unity otherwise lacking in an experiment). But verbal reports have been used for information about man's covert events, and a plethora of such reports suggests that positive feedback is involved in acquisition of new capability. This evidence suggests the following two examples of positive feedback processes in learning.

STUDY

Having arranged his environment to reduce the probability of distractions, the ideal student scans his plans, sets sub-goals or questions, and expends effort in establishing voluntary attention and in generating enthusiasm for the task at hand. If intrinsic interest develops along with the newly assimilated knowledge, the process is that much easier. Thus he proceeds until this positive feedback process is terminated by reaching his short-term goal or by distracting stimuli.

Conversely the not-so-ideal student gets trapped by a runaway to zero process as he putters about, setting inadequate or no sub-goals and questions, and expending little or no effort in motivating himself or attending. His attention wanders, motivation flags, and little is assimilated even though he may spend as much time as the ideal student.

Probably the average student drifts from one feedback cycle to the other as some feature in the chain of events is altered from these caricatures. Each increment in capability requires positive feedback.

The self-motivated student with successful learning strategies demonstrates qualities of psychological balance which few students approach. However, once these qualities are known (and many **are** known) it should be possible to devise instructional programmes which incorporate activities characteristic of the good student and thus provide for all students the high standards of learning set by the most successful of their number.

Meanwhile some students have acquired a sense of failure which, once established, can be self-sustaining. Instructional communications can be prepared to break this potential runaway to zero process. Rather than incorporate them into a regular programme, propadeutic and prophylactic programmes should prove useful.

In our laboratory we have been investigating the effect on study skills of brief instructional sessions intended to show students successful strategies of self-management. Students with poor study skills were shown how to set and define their own educational objectives; to conduct a task analysis for each; to use simple conceptual models to assist in identifying their goals and tasks within the structure of the subject; to externalize self-monitoring techniques and to use these for reinforcement; and to establish their own procedures for stimulus control and contingency management. A pilot study showed significant improvement in study skills.

INSTRUCTIONAL CONTROL

The planner of educational communications must arrange the student's environment and formulate his instructional messages so that: (1) the participant's attention is attracted and held; (2) the student who exerts the effort of attending and responding to the communications finds the organization of subject matter intelligible and, hopefully, intrinsically motivating; (3) the student engages in overt or covert activities necessary and sufficient to produce a transition in his capability with respect to the content of the programme; and (4) the propensity to forget is counteracted. All four criteria involve the student in interlocking positive feedback processes.

It is critical to establish a positive feedback process that tends to maximum rather than to zero. Since this process **amplifies** deviations it is important to plan the initial impetus to move the student in the right direction. The behavioural engineer offers the producer of audiovisual programmes the contingency management heuristic procedure of shaping which has been singularly successful in fostering a transition state. Thus implicit feedback frequently can be augmented by external (artificial) consequences. (Even broadcast television can do this by, for example, running contests in which viewers submit something stemming from the programme for a prize or some other recognition.) Classroom presentations, of course, are amenable to behavioural engineering procedures; indeed, even with synchronized instruction from the media of mass communication, the teacher can individualize instruction by this means.

INSTRUCTIONAL DESIGN

The positive feedback model of learning predicts that intensive stimulation confined to one subject or problem over several hours, days or

305

weeks may generate a (controlled) runaway to maximum in which the student appropriates capability more and more rapidly. Thus a person who somehow 'discovers' and begins to devour a subject (by reading as much as he can about it, staying up all night, skipping meals, talking about it, etc.) turns himself into what may be called a 'machine for positive feedback'.

A practical application suggests itself. In most educational institutions students spend about an hour on a subject and then shift to another. At home, study patterns reflect a similar need to cope with a varied curriculum. Positive feedback processes are terminated soon after being established. Suppose intensive cramming were designed to occur at the **beginning** of the term (so that the student worked virtually non-stop for several days on one problem or subject). Following this transition process, during which a large-scale increase in capability should occur, a maintenance schedule should begin. This intensive period of acquisition followed by a lengthy period of consolidation to prevent forgetting, to provide practice, and hopefully to lead to new insights, should be more successful in making significant changes in the lives of students than the too frequent end-of-term cramming followed by no sustaining schedule.

Similarly in a short instructional programme it may be beneficial to establish expectancy and information levels which sustain a positive feedback process of high amplification by cramming new information into the first portion of a programme and following up with further instructional control designed to reduce forgetting and promote utilization.

FORGETTING

Research evidence is accumulating which suggests that acquisition of new knowledge or skill occurs in an all-or-none fashion (in a single trial) as does creative insight. Furthermore, it may be that such apprehended experience can be retained relatively permanently under special circumstances (e.g. by using mnemonic tricks). Otherwise it is forgotten fairly rapidly. A problem for instructional design is to arrange the student's sensory encompassment to prevent forgetting.

Since forgetting may be a runaway to zero process (in which disuse of a capability leads to difficulty in utilizing it) it can be prevented by breaking the positive feedback cycle. One approach is for the student or the instructional system to monitor the capability in question and, as it drifts away from homeostasis, to activate a negative feedback process (of recall, utilization or practice, followed by overt or covert reinforcement) to maintain it. Often the instructional communication is repeated for re-acquisition. Although maintenance of homeostasis presumably is a negative feedback process, it is noteworthy that repeated actions become easier with practice, suggestive of positive feedback.

In our laboratory we are currently investigating the effects of varying the number and spacing of messages in instructional television programmes to determine an optimal presentation strategy to counteract the undesirable positive feedback process that produces forgetting. For short-term retention of aural information in television programmes, spaced repetition (interval at least seven seconds) was more effective than massed repetition which, in turn, was superior to single instructional communications (Edwards and Mitchell, 1974).

## CONCLUSION

In thinking about instructional control educational technologists often have been too mechanistic. The student is not analogous to raw material flowing through an assembly line. Rather he is an active self-organizing system in interplay with the instructional system. Although designers of the latter have produced many interesting and useful systems based on the negative feedback model of learning. I have tried to show that positive not negative, feedback processes account for learning and that these reside in, or are controlled in large measure by, the student. Our responsibility is to incorporate in instructional control those elements and processes inherent in successful students' strategies of self-management. In doing so we utilize the propensity of positive feedback to produce and sustain transitions in capability which compose learning.

REFERENCES
Edwards, Ludwika and Mitchell, P.D. (1974) Differential Effects of Spaced and Mass Repetitions in Audio-Visual Presentations. Paper prepared for presentation to the Canadian Society for the Study of Education; June 1974.
Mitchell, P.D. (1972) The sacramental nature of behavioural objectives. In Aspects of Educational Technology VI, (Eds.) K. Austwick and N.D.C. Harris. London: Pitman.
Smith, K.U. and Smith, M.F. (1965) Cybernetic Principles of Learning and Educational Design. New York: Holt, Rinehart and Winston.
Stanley-Jones, D. (1969) Kybernetics of Mind and Brain. Springfield, Illinois: C.C.Thomas.
Wiener, N. (1954) The Human Use of Human Beings. Boston: Houghton Mifflin.

# What is a medium? Reflections on technology, money and economic sociology.

R. HOULTON, University of Liverpool

**Abstract:**  Ten years after the publication of McLuhan's <u>Understanding Media: The Extensions of Man</u>[1] the concept of 'medium' remains unclear, though its adoption by previous non-users, like Colin Cherry, suggests that it is playing some part in the structuring of perceptions and analyses in the field of communication.  Neither Information Theory nor Linguistics have relied on the concept, and the way in which it has been used by sociologists has been ambiguous or confused.

   In economic sociology the concept can be clarified by drawing a system-level distinction between a medium and a channel.  This provides an analytical dimension which has proved valuable in understanding the pattern of development in the motion picture, record, and broadcasting industries in the United States.

   What remains uncertain is whether this formulation can be extended into other areas and other disciplines.  Difficulties which were not evident in the analysis of analog  communication systems emerge when the model is translated into digital systems.  However, this may prove to be one method of extending our understanding of the medium of money.

## INTRODUCTION

It is now ten years since Marshall McLuhan's <u>Understanding Media</u>[1] was published and started what can only be called an extended apotheosis of McLuhan and his 'understandings' by magazines, newspapers, books, television and radio on an international scale.  Then the reaction set in. Three years ago Dr. Jonathan Miller performed an autopsy with fairly blunt instruments and concluded his report in unequivocal terms :

> '.... I can rehabilitate no actual truth from what I have read. Perhaps McLuhan has accomplished the greatest paradox of all, creating the possibility of truth by shocking us all with a gigantic system of lies.' [2]

Today, through the dust of a decade of probes and counterprobes it is evident that McLuhan's central concept of 'medium' has remained immune from analytical development.  Instead, the plural, 'media' has become a semanticly overloaded cult-word with a whole range of in-

group and out-group harmonics. We have had a great deal of controversy of whether a medium was 'hot' or 'cool' but not about what a
medium actually is.

However, the concept has been adopted by previous non-users like
Colin Cherry — which indicates that it is playing **some** part in the structuring of perceptions and analyses in the field of communication.

This paper, in addition to examining this curious non-usage and
one seminal confusion in sociology about the definition of a medium,
attempts to derive a definition from an examination of technology-based
communication systems.

## Usage and Non-usage

Colin Cherry in 1957 wrote his classic, On Human Communication, without using the concept of a medium.[3]   In his opening chapter he raided
the Concise Oxford English Dictionary for fourteen key definitions — and
'medium' is not among them.  It is fascinating to read the opening chapter and observe the way in which it seems the sentences are constructed
to avoid using the word.  Two examples can illustrate the point:

(1)  'But life in the modern world is coming to depend more and more on
**'technical' means** of communication, telephone and telegraph, radio and
printing.'[4]

(2)  'We also have economic **systems for trafficking** not in ideas but in
material goods and services;  the tokens of communication are coins.'[5]

In Cherry's World Communication: Threat or Promise published in 1971
this self-denying ordinance was dropped.[6]  The previous quotations can be
compared to the following passage which amounts to a descriptive definition of a medium:

'.... money is a technical means of communication, the invention
of which permitted totally new forms of social organization.  Its
coins, notes and bills are tokens of exchange, readily convertible
to numbers or words on paper accounts.  **Money, like other media
of communication, telephones, telegraphs, computers, data links,**
offers "power to organize" various forms of social institution.'[7]

Of course, telephones, telegraphs, computers and data links are
Professor Cherry's subject area — telecommunications — but money is
of crucial importance to economists like myself.  So we are looking for
a definition of a medium which can be used with money **and** telecommunications.

It is interesting to note that neither of the two fundamental contributions to the field of communications in the past thirty years — Shannon
and Weaver's A Mathematical Theory of Communications,[8]  and Noam
Chomsky's  transformational-generative  grammar[9] — needed or used

309

the concept of a medium. So one question should be prominent —'if they didn't need it why should we?

## Media and Sociology

Let me begin by looking at a central and fundamental ambiguity about the concepts of medium and channel which can be found in Harold Lasswell's seminal article <u>The Structure and Function of Communication in Society</u>.[10] This is regarded as a permanent reference point in the sociology of communications because it offered a paradigm of the communication act and also outlined the major subdivisions of communications research in 1948. Lasswell suggested that there were five major areas of study: control analysis, content analysis, media analysis, audience analysis, and effect analysis. And media analysis was defined in the following words: 'Those who look primarily at the radio, press, film, and other channels of communication are doing **media analysis.**'[11] From this it would appear:

(a)  radio, press, and films are channels of communication,

(b)  that those who study them are studying media. Therefore, media and channels are interchangeable and represent the same **system level,** OR

(c)  alternatively, media is a class which includes among its members radio, press, film and other channels of communication. Therefore, media represents a higher system level than channel.

The confusion and ambiguity was not dispersed when, in 1957, Lerner published an article, based on Lasswell's original division of the subject area, which incorporated Lasswell's suggestions and a footnote written by Lasswell which explicitly accepted the thesis Lerner was putting forward.[12] Lerner appears in this article to say that a channel can include both 'Media (broadcast)' and 'Oral (point-to-point)'. This can only mean that a channel represents a higher system level than a medium; that all media are members of the class of channel. To be fair, Lasswell and Lerner's circumlutions should be placed in perspective. The concept of media has been marginal to the obsession of may sociologists with the 'mass' aspects of 'mass communications', especially the impact of different 'messages' on audiences and their political consequences. The socio-technical, institutional, and economic foundations of the large-scale public communications systems which have developed in the past 100 years have remained largely unresearched (which no doubt saved some research patrons from a certain amount of embarrassment). However, it is an indication of weakness that the sociology of mass communications cannot offer a clear and useful definition of a medium.

You will have noticed that I've begun talking about systems. So I draw your attention to the general rule that : **Rules and models which** relate to processes, interactions, and change should be specific in terms of system, scale, and level. It is dangerous to transfer or otherwise displace models and rules between systems and levels without care and severe qualification.

Displacing concepts between system levels is an obvious offence against the Theory of Logical Types.[13]   However, when 'displaced concepts' become the basis of policy decisions the results can be socially disastrous.   I will argue later in this paper that it was this kind of error which led many politicians and economists to advocate economic policies which aggravated the Depression of the 1930's.[14]

Lasswell and Lerner's confusions are relatively insignificant beside the blunders in economics.  But it is clear that their system levels are not clear and I want to argue that some distinction is vital in establishing what a medium is.

## A Derived Definition

While the concept of a medium cannot be derived from first principles, it can be developed from an analysis of the way in which modern communications systems have been developed.[14]   As Marx observed the 'technology discloses man's mode of dealing with nature... and thereby also lays bare the mode of formation of his social relations, and of the mental conceptions that flow from them'.[15]

Let us consider television a social communication system.  It can be divided into three constituent parts.  One large group of social arrangements, cameras, studios, microphones, producers, performers, etc., is concerned with **recording** a television image.  Another set of arrangements deal with the **transmission** of the image: either 'direct feed' from the studio, or from VTR's, television machines, there are also landlines, and transmitting towers.  Finally, the system is completed by arrangements for reproducing the image — aerials, power sources, and television receivers.  I want to draw attention to three fairly obvious aspects of this communication system:

(1)  It has to be integrated and stable.  The templates which are the basic design elements for recording, transmission, and reproduction must fit one another.[16]   A change in the template of one subsystem can cause the whole system to malfunction and could destroy its raison d'etre.

---

14.  Briefly, the economic establishment supported cuts in Government expenditure which had the effect of decreasing demand and increasing unemployment.

16.  I prefer the term template rather than 'coding and decoding' because it does not carry the same associations of precision and determinism.

(2)   The templates represent a specific historical point in the development of scientific and technical knowledge.  Science and technology can evolve generations of related yet different templates and this makes it possible for a society to develop a whole series of similar yet incompatible communication systems.  (However, evidence suggests that such a proliferation of competing communication systems can mutually inhibit growth.)

(3)   The system templates have played an important part in determining the social organization of the subsystems (in a similar way as the DNA molecule relates to living systems.)  The templates of monochrome and colour television make it possible for the system to be organized on a **broadcast** basis using a six megacycle signal which would have needed landlines and community viewing theatres.[17]   It seems to me quite conceivable that if television had been developed first in Russia rather than the USA that it would have been organized around viewing theatres rather than placed in people's homes.

Having outlined the basic epistemology of television the question is can hierarchies be detected within this system?  Wittgenstein pointed out that public usage is often a key to understanding and it is clear that an appreciation of system level differences is shown by viewers, television industry workers, and critics.[18]   People refer to the **medium** of television when indicating some phenomenon located within the generality of the system.  And reference is made to a television **channel** when the system offers a choice; in other words, a channel indicates a link-up between specific recording, transmission, and reproduction subsystems.  This usage can be illustrated: for example, a society may decide to adopt the **medium** of television.  However, this choice will be followed in logic, and time, by an additional decision of whether or not to have a multi-channel medium.  This common usage is so well established that it must appear to be a statement of the obvious.  But I have not discovered an explicit medium/channel distinction in the literature so far.  And I think the distinction is important because it clears up some of the ambiguities and confusions surrounding the term medium and channel and provides us with that vital differentiation of system levels.

The argument in this section can be summarized:

**Definition 1.**  A **medium** refers to a general communications system in which images are transferred in a form determined by recording, transmission, and reproduction templates.

---

17.  Perhaps this would have been the outcome if the motion picture industry instead of the broadcasting/electronics industry had directed the research and development programme.

**Definition 2.** A **channel** refers to a specific communications system, an integrated arrangement of recording, transmission, and reproduction sub-systems operating within the framework of a medium. All channels have a media-referent and depend on the templates of that medium.

## The Media Dimension

These definitions, I suggest, can be applied both to technology-based communication systems and money. The 'media dimension' provides us with an important area in the analysis of social change. Any study of the development of the mass entertainment industry in the USA which neglected this media dimension would be deficient. The United States has provided not only the crucial templates, but also models of social organization which other countries have chosen to accept or reject.

The history of the motion picture, broadcasting, and recording industries can only be understood in terms of innovatory and interventory strategies aimed at controlling the development of media templates. With television the monochrome templates were the focus of an inter-corporate and intra-Government power struggle that lasted over a decade.[19] Colour television provoked a tripartite innovatory dispute between the Radio Corporation of America, the Columbia Broadcasting System, and the Federal Communications Commission. Television is sometimes portrayed as a boon to humanity which was produced in quiet laboratories by disinterested scientists. This is far from the truth; in fact, the birth-pangs of television were accompanied by controversy, conflict, corruption and deceit.

Media level conflict has occurred with all the systems: the US broadcasting networks used one interventory strategy after another to prevent the Frequency Modulated (FM) broadcasting medium from being established. A non-compatible colour television medium was used to prevent, or slow down, the development of the monochrome NTSC television. The 45 r.p.m. record medium was a deliberate attempt to prevent the $33\frac{1}{3}$ r.p.m. long playing record medium from being established. Such has been the turbulence of innovatory strategies and countervailing interventions that some have been counter-productive to the long-term interests of the companies sponsoring them.[20]

Deliberately designed incompatibility between related media has been the consequence of uncontrolled innovation and intervention. And,

---

20. The combatants included alliances forged between different sections of the electronics and broadcasting industries. The Federal Communications Commission was enmeshed in the struggles. Other interventory strategies which were being pursued at the same time, over-lapping and reinforcing the struggles over television, brought in the Courts, Congress, and the Presidency.

ultimately, the public has been forced to bear the cost of duplicated stocks and lost economies of scale.

Before moving on to explore the concept of a medium I would like to draw attention to the practical application of what may appear to be a tenuous theoretical discussion. Anyone concerned with the purchase of technical communications equipment should ask himself, his engineers, and any eager salesmen who may be around, three basic questions:

### 1. Why is this Specific Medium Available?

In other words, why has any given set of templates been selected from the social pool of technological knowledge? Has the selection been made to promote planned obsolesence? Will the equipment show high short-term profits to the manufacturer and high long-term costs to the user?... The list of questions that can be raised under the 'medium' heading is endless.

### 2. Are the sub-systems, the equipment, available in a multi-media form — can they be made compatible with other communication systems?

Non-compatibility is a weapon in the competition between firms owning different patent rights and with different vested interests. Where there is easy access into an industry and where a mass-market exists, manufacturers will sometimes produce compatible equipment — a good example is the three-speed record player. But given a situation of low production runs, a limited number of suppliers, and institutional purchasers the pressures for non-compatible equipment are often great.

### 3. How many channels is the equipment designed to carry? In other words, what is the range of choice with the equipment?

Again, the interests of the seller and the buyer may diverge in relation to the channel capacity of equipment. Low capacity equipment may be sold 'at cost' in the knowledge that additional channels must be bought eventually through ancillary equipment which has a high rate of profit.

These three questions define the area of dialogue between the buyer and seller of communication systems. But, for the most part, what should be a dialogue is actually a monologue from manufacturers.

However, I do not want to linger on media analysis and social change — although the subject is fascinating. Instead I want to probe these definitions and develop the model a little further.

### Analog and Digital Communication Systems

Once the definitions of medium and channel are extended beyond technology-based communications systems they become slippery concepts. But it is important to extend them if only because linguists, information

314

theorists, and economists have notions about communication systems even if these are vague and rarely explicit.

The distinction between analog and digital communications systems is familiar in cybernetics, anthropology, psychology and computer science.[21] The broadcasting, recording, and film media of the mass entertainment industry have templates which process an analog image of the sounds and situations which occur before the camera or microphone. It is an analog of these events which is reproduced, with varying degrees of fidelity, in speaker or on the screen.[22] These representational communication systems we can call **analog media**. However, there are digital communication systems. These are not representational: an arbitrary relationship exists between the sign and the object or process it refers to. In a digital system the image has an **indirect** relationship to the form of matter or energy that conveys it. The print of an ink-stained palm can convey the analog image of 'hand' but the pattern of four fingers and a thumb is not revealed in the letters 'h-a-n-d' or 'l-a m-a-i-n'.

Integration is as essential for digital systems as for analog media, and the process of language learning involved the ability to grasp the basis of this integration. Integration brings us back to templates and the nature of digital templates has been the source of considerable speculation in linguistics. As Lyons has pointed out 'Chomsky maintains that it is only by assuming that the child is born with a knowledge of the highly restrictive principles of universal grammar, and the predisposition to make use of them in analysing the utterances he hears about him, that we can make any sense of the process of language learning.[23] Perhaps **part** of the template for spoken digital communication does derive from the neural technology of the human mind. But the question I want to raise is, what kind of medium are we talking about? If we can define a medium we may have a clearer view of the templates. However, certain difficulties arise when a distinction is drawn between

---

21. A more precise form of words may be desired by the critical reader. Analog systems used in mass entertainment process images of general sensory experience which (apart from) the initial cues needed to scan, process and organize the information presented) are directly related to the way in which these images and events are experienced by the individual without the intervening agency of the medium. Of course, the analogic images themselves are the carriers of digital media — the sounds that the radio or television reproduce are 'understood' at another level as English, German, French etc.

This is the appropriate point to acknowledge an intellectual debt to Gregory Bateson and the work he has inspired. cf. G. Bateson (1973) Steps to an Ecology of Mind. St. Albans.

22. Of course, the sounds which are reproduced may be those of a digital communications system — like English or French. But these and other types of signal occur at different levels in the hierarchy of processes within the system.

a medium and a channel in digital communication systems because it is possible to construct two different formulations of a medium.

First, a medium can be formulated out of the **technical** factors involved in the integration of digital systems. The form of the symbols of language can be considered integrals: 'sound' or 'print' carries the language. Oral language and printed language can therefore be considered to be separate media. To understand the images a person must 'tune in' to the different channels of English, French, Russian, etc. Now, this technical formulation is a hybrid — at the media level it has the attributes of an analog system. A page of Chinese characters can be appreciated as an analog of the brush-strokes or type-face which produced it. Children can be taught parrot sounds and which can be appreciated simply as parrot sounds. Digitalization, therefore, takes place within the channels of this medium. This formulation of a medium appears to me to be related to the domain assumptions of information theorists, behavioural psychologists, and some linguistic theorists. And perhaps it provides a clue as to why Cherry, Shannon and Weaver, and Chomsky have not required a concept of media.

Secondly, a medium can be formulated out of the **cognitive** integrals within a digital system; in other words, using the common referent of images within the system. For example, the English language is a communication system in which written, spoken, and sign forms are related to each other through ideas, words, and common grammatical rules. The templates for processing the images are located within the knowledge of populations of people; the system depends on a behavioural technology. Therefore, 'English' is the medium and digitalization takes place at media-level. The alternative forms of presentation — print, longhand, shorthand, the spoken word, and lip-reading — are therefore channels, the alternative source of images within the language.

These two models of digital communications systems relate to different system levels and are, therefore, not necessarily mutually exclusive. They advance our understanding as to why the use of the concepts of channel and medium by sociologists has been accompanied by ambiguity and confusion. Secondly, they provide some pointers as to where the traditional concern of philosophers, the problem of knowledge, may relate to other areas of communication study.[24] Finally, they add weight to the question: what kind of a communication **system** do people think they are studying?

## Economics and the Medium of Money

'We must have a good definition of Money,
For if we do not, then what have we got,
But a Quantity Theory of no-one knows what,
And this would be almost too true to be funny.'[25]

It is well known that economics has been transformed over the past two generations by one man, John Maynard Keynes, who modified and displaced many of the key paradigms of the discipline. Keynes' reputation had many parts, but one of the most important facets was that of a monetary theorist. Before writing the book that started the Keynesian Revolution — The General Theory of Employment, Interest and Money,[26] — Keynes had laboured for several years on his 'masterwork' — the two volume Treatise on Money.[27] In the preface he wrote as a man completely disillusioned with his achievements and compared it to pushing through 'a confused jungle'.[28] He also noted that, 'Now I have emerged from it I see that I might have taken a more direct route...'[29] This has led to an unjustifiable assumption that the Treatise was made redundant by the General Theory — but this is not the case. Any serious student of the medium of money should read both books in their date order.

I want to offer a simplified 'translation' of a certain aspect of the Keynesian Revolution to illustrate how the medium of money was important.[30]

Up to the end of the 1930's conventional wisdom dictated that the response of any Government to an economic depression should be to cut state expenditure. In 1931, in Britain, this caused a political crisis when the Government decided, with the approval of the contemporary financial, industrial, and economic establishment, to cut the welfare benefits to unemployed workers. Nearly all economists now agree that the action of the Government made the depression worse — which was the opposite effect to that intended. Why did they do it? The reason is that conventional economic wisdom for over a century had been based on misconceptions derived from transferring the small-scale system characteristics of (a) a barter-economy, and (b) a household budget to a large-scale national industrialized economy.

To understand this mistake we have to answer two basic questions in political economy in pre-Keynesian terms. First, how does economic activity start — through demand or through supply? In answering this question the 'classical economists' made a disastrous simplification: they banished the medium of money from their economic model and assumed a **barter economy**.[31] They reasoned that a man, before travelling to market, would ensure that he first had something to barter with, and

---

30. This simplification will, no doubt, be considered extreme by economists and dangerous in that it cannot deal with the subtleties or the originality of Keynes' ideas. But this is a transdisciplinary essay — and one cannot make the omelette without cracking a few eggs.

31. The term 'classical economists' has become a shorthand for 'the domain assumptions of orthodox British and American economists in the period 1800-1939'. It is, in fact, an abstraction.

therefore, supply must always precede demand.[32]   The ramifications of
this answer need not detain us other than to note that it became accepted
economic policy that governments faced with a depression must ensure
that the confidence of suppliers, in other words, financiers and industrialists, must be bolstered at all costs.   Once confidence was restored on
the supply side it was felt that economic activity would then inevitably
increase and the level of unemployment would fall.

The second basic question was also deceptively simple:  what should
a prudent Government do when and if tax returns are suddenly and
permanently reduced because of a depression?   Governments and
Chancellors of the Exchequer thought of themselves as prudent house-
wives — 'saving candle-ends' was Gladstone's famous phrase.  A house-
wife should cut her expenditure so that it matched her income.  And
Governments should do the same when 'income' from taxation fell during
a depression.

To appreciate the powerful influence of these two notions and the
models of society they were based upon, it is necessary to understand
that they were complementary.  The barter-market system represented
a **world of resources without money.**  The household balancing its budget,
regardless of whether granny and the children starved to death or the
roof fell in for the want of a nail, represented a **world of money regardless of resources.**

Keynes said, in effect, that the answers to these questions were
wrong.[33]   In the aftermath of the Treaty of Versailles he had attacked
the delusion that money was a form of wealth independent of commodities.
The General Theory spelled out why the characteristics of a modern
national economy with a sophisticated communication system based on
money should not be equated with a barter system or a household budget.
**Demand**, in other words people spending **money**, and not supply, as Say's
Law implied, was the determinant of the level of economic activity.
Governments were not subject to the same restraints as households —
they had control over the economic communication system, the medium
of money.  By increasing the amount of effective demand in a society a
Government could ensure that resources were brought into employment.
Cutting Government expenditure during a crisis, therefore, only made
the depression worse.[34]

There have been a number of consequences of Mr. Keynes.  He
revealed the inadequacy of classical economics in handling concepts and
models which relate to the management of the whole of an economy -- the
level which is now known as macro-economics.  He introduced the

---

32.  This conjecture had the appearance of certainty and was accordingly dignified with the
title of Say's Law after an 18th Century French economist.

34.  It will be appreciated that this outline is highly stylized and simplified.

important concept of money as 'liquidity' — which, interestingly, is a more static concept in communications terms than the 'velocity of money' which was of prime importance to classical economists. The consensus view among neo-Keynesian economists today is that 'money matters only slightly in the short run, and not at all in the long.' [35]

It appears to me that the idea of money as a communication system has not advanced since Keynes' day at the macro-economic level. At the micro-economic level economists are still dependent on ideas of communication which were established by the classical economists.

The advocates of a quantity theory of money, led by Professor M. Friedman, would deny this. But besides the debate between the neo-Keynesians and the Friedmanites — which sometimes has the appearance of being the only game in town — monetary specialists have polarized. As Clower has pointed out, 'they have tended to turn either to econometric study of observed behaviour (measurement with so little theory that it really does not matter), or to consciously academic exercises in the dynamics of monetary growth (theory with so little reality that it does not matter either). [36]

It would be interesting to know what kind of a medium the different factions of monetary specialists think money is.

## Money, the Medium — Some Observations

Just to show that a 'media debate' in monetary circles might be interesting to the spectators, I would like to offer a couple of notes. Marx in the 19th Century noted the strange communication linkages associated with money. [37] When used in buying and selling, money becomes a matching analog of the commodity involved. But once the transaction is concluded, money becomes a digital medium storing the past and future images of economic activity. Over centuries the units of money needed to create an analog image of a commodity have tended to increase (in other words, there has been a process which is crudely termed 'inflation and the falling value of money'). At the same time, because of the continuous process of innovation over the past three centuries the range, and number, of digital images has enormously expanded. [38] Two interesting processes — are they linked? Is innovation and inflation the result of situations where powerful institutions exercise control over both processes in order to serve their self interests?

Within economics there has been a series of debates which fall roughly into the digital area which stretch back to John Locke and David Hume who were, appropriately, two key figures in the development of

---

38. This linkage is important in Schumpeter's conception of economics and society. cf. J.A. Schumpeter (1939) Business Cycles. New York.

'the problem of knowledge'. In the past, the **cognitive** formulation of the medium of money has been represented in the debate. However, in recent times it has been absent.

The last major advocate appeared in the 1920's, Major Douglas, who Keynes, in the concluding chapters of the General Theory, attacked and called 'a private, perhaps, but not a major in the brave army of heretics'. Douglas was the advocate of spending what he called 'social credit', which may have been confused and imprecise but which rested on the view that money was a communication system based on the existing stock of social knowledge.

The monetary debate now appears to be conducted within the paradigm of a digital **technical** formulation of a medium. The major difficulty for professional economists is trying to understand why some members of the public will not forswear their 'primitive' desire for a permanent analog relationship between gold and money. But this is a debate between the discipline and 'outsiders'. A substantial amount of internal argument is concerned with 'technical' questions about the importance and influence of the different channel arrangements within the system.[39] The proposition that the templates for the medium of money are located in the stock of social knowledge would not fit easily into the models of contemporary economics. Yet most economists, as individuals, would accept that if the public's confidence in money collapsed, no amount of legislation or action by the monetary authorities could re-establish the use of the currency.

Let us hope that it does not require a trauma, similar to the inter-war depression, before we engaged in a critical scrutiny and revision of the basic monetary paradigms in economics.

Which finally brings me to this conference. Money is the most potent educational medium in our society — yet we still depend on simplistic notions of how its learning programmes are developed. Societies surely must 'learn from the experience of inflation .... but how and what do they learn?

## 'The Medium and the Message'

Having listened to my paper you may think that the concept of medium should be allowed to drift gently out of the physical and social sciences to ultimately sink under its semantic load. But I don't think this is likely to happen if only because of the importance of the concept in economic sociology.

Now, this essay has asked, 'What is a medium' and noted usage in other disciplines — and it is from these disciplines, as well as from economics, that some authorative answers must eventually come. And if

---

39. Non-economists can find a readable outline of the debate in L.S. Ritter and W.L. Silber (1970) Money. London.

answers are not forthcoming this essay may nevertheless serve to sensitize people to the problems of defining system hierarchies in communications analysis.

REFERENCES

1. McLuhan, Marshall. (1964) Understanding Media: The Extensions of Man. New York
2. Miller, Jonathan. (1971) McLuhan. London.
3. Cherry, Colin. (1957) On Human Communications. Cambridge, Mass.
4. Op. cit. p.5      )
5. Op. cit. pp.4-5 )   emphasis added.
6. Cherry, Colin. (1971) World Communication: Threat or Promise. London.
7. Op. cit. p. x.
8. Shannon, C.E. and Weaver, W. (1949) The Mathematical Theory of Communication. Urbana. Paperback Edition 1964 cf. pp. 6-8 and p.34.
9. Cf. Allen, J.P.B. and van Buren, P. (1971) Chomsky: Selected Readings. London.
10. Lasswell, H. (1948) The structure and function of communication in society. First published in L. Bryson (Ed.) The Communication of Ideas, New York, 1948. Reprinted in W. Schramm (Ed.) Mass Communications. 2nd Edition, Urbana, 1960, pp.117-130.
11. Op. cit. p. 117. Emphasis as in original.
12. Lerner, D. (1957) Communication systems and social systems. Originally published in Behavioural Science, October 1957. Reprinted in W. Schramm, op. cit. pp.131-140.
13. Whitehead, A.N. and Russell, B. (1910) Principa Mathematica. London.
14. Quoted in text as footnote.
15. Marx, K. (1887) Capital Volume 1, London. p.372, fn.3.
16. Quoted in text as footnote.
17. Quoted in text as footnote.
18. Wittgenstein, L.J.J. (1953) Philosophical Investigations. Oxford.
19. For further elaboration cf. Houlton, R. (1973) Innovation, Intervention, and Media Analysis, Ph.D. Thesis (unpublished) University of Leeds, March 1973.
20. Quoted in text as footnote.
21. Quoted in text as footnote.
22. Quoted in text as footnote.
23. Lyons, J. (1970) Chomsky. London, p.106.
24. A diversionary point: does Chomsky's negative review of Skinner's Verbal Behaviour rest on an implied difference in the perception of media?
25. Boulding, K.E., first published in the Michigan Business Review, March 1969. Reprinted in Wilsher, P. The Pound in Your Pocket 1870-1970. London, 1970, p.9.
26. Keynes, J.M. (1936) The General Theory of Employment, Interest and Money. London.
27. Keynes, J.M. (1930) Treatise on Money. London.
28. Op. cit. p. vi.
29. Op. cit. p. vi.
30. Quoted in text as footnote.
31. Quoted in text as footnote.
32. Quoted in text as footnote.
33. Keynes, J.M., General Theory, op. cit.
34. Quoted in text as footnote.
35. Clower, R.W. (Ed.) (1969) Monetary Theory. Harmondsworth. p. 20.
36. Clower, R.W., op. cit. p.21.
37. Marx, K., op. cit. Chapter II and Chapter III.
38. Quoted in text as footnote.
39. Quoted in text as footnote.

# Communication and learning: an ethological approach

R. M. COOK, Université des Sciences et Techniques du Langedoc, Montpellier

**Abstract:** The discipline of ethology, influenced as it has been by the study of evolution, provides a perspective on the problems of Communication and Learning which may inspire new and more heuristic directions for research.

An attempt to illustrate this thesis is made by a consideration of the general principles adopted by ethologists in the study of the behaviour of animals and men; the most important of these is the realization that any aspect of behaviour forms part of an adapted behavioural whole: thus it should not be studied in isolation from other aspects of behaviour.

The consideration of aspects of the phylogeny of communication indicates the kind of evolutionary process which may be at work: this at the same time sets human communication onto the background of adaptive significance and clearly demonstrates the extent to which genetical heterogeneity for different sensory (and therefore communicatory) capacities is important in a population. This highlights the fact that individual differences exist, not just for 'intelligence', but for the relative usage of different sensory modalities.

Finally an ethologically based research scheme is suggested which would endeavour to initiate an assumption-free assessment of the communication/learning process.

## SOME ATTRIBUTES OF ETHOLOGY

In this paper I shall attempt to do three things; the first of these is to give an outline of ethology as an approach to behaviour which could be valuable to those concerned in the assessment of educational communication processes; then an endeavour will be made to pick out some of the broader relevant conclusions to be drawn from the study of animal communication; and finally to suggest some lines of approach to the study of human communication and learning based on ethological ideas.

The development of ethology, parallel in time with that of experimental psychology, has been guided largely by the influence of evolutionary and biological thought, rather than by the philosophical and far more anthropocentric influences on the development of psychology. The study of the educational process, communication and learning, in

322

humans has naturally been under far greater influence from the latter of these two disciplines, often wielding the tool of experimental analysis with equal, if not greater, rigour than ethology. But the theoretical starting points engendered by a **purely** psychological approach can lack meaning, or even seem artificial, when untempered by other approaches, for example ethological, which see all behavioural phenomena on a common biological background; if such a background is not taken, even solely as a starting point in the study of human behaviour, then what other theoretical framework can logically be appropriate?

If a contribution to behavioural science has been made by ethology it is, in stressing the adaptive nature of behaviour; behaviour is seen, not just as something an organism happens to have, but as the raison d'être of the organism's existence and evolution — an adapted entity which cannot be fully understood by considering solely its present state, evolution and ontogeny are essential attributes. Such an approach, if adopted, has the merit of forcing thought to encompass all aspects of behaviour, and implies the impossibility of limiting observation or analysis to one aspect alone. Adaptive significance revealed in one aspect of behaviour, for example a particular mode of feeding, immediately implies a certain type of adaptation in another, for example the locomotor capability of the animal to get into that feeding situation.

Research questions arising with this assumption of the adaptive origin of behaviour will therefore necessarily be directed with a view to elucidating the whole behavioural animal, in as complete an environment as possible. Hence the great advantage of ethology in making initial studies on animals in the field, where research questions can mature in parallel with the observation of animals behaving in their richest and most natural ways.

To illustrate the implications which this approach may have for the study of communication and learning in humans I should like to sketch aspects of communication and learning in animals.

### Evolutionary aspects of communication and learning

In these sections it is evident that the material dictates concentration on 'communication' to the virtual exclusion of 'learning', although the latter aspect has a good documentation (e.g. Thorpe, 1963). The reason is that the word communication can only be completely distinguished from learning at a purely logical level; experimentally the two 'processes' merge so as to be effectively indistinguishable, since no learning can be demonstrated except in the form of further communication by the learner; thus the communication processes 'emission' and 'reception', represent the more important and tractable side of the behavioural process; from the point of view of this conference communication is also by far the most important process to be understood, since what is here being discussed is not the biochemistry of learning, or any other of its physiological properties — these are only implicit substrata whose actions and properties may be influenced at the level of communication; put another way, learning is an intervening variable between communication and re-communication — firstly communication in the form of reception by the learner, and then in the form of emission by him, either as action, or as further specific communication. This of course does not imply that learning is not complex, nor possesses many components; it is the elementary point that learning can only be influenced through communication, using this word in its widest sense.

Much time may easily be spent in exploring and defining the precise connotations of the word communication, and it is not my intention to enter into this here. A scheme advanced by Tavolga (1970), developed from Schneirla's concept of 'levels of integration', provides a basis upon which the interactions of animals with themselves and with their environments may be classified. Since this scheme is relevant to a consideration of the evolution of communication it will briefly be presented: the two most elementary levels of interaction advanced by Tavolga are classified as 'vegetative' and 'tonic'. The former of these simply reflects the fact that by existing an animal or plant emits stimuli of various sorts, which are potential material for interaction with another plant or animal. These stimuli are manifestations of growth and form rather than of behaviour. At the 'tonic' level the effects of on-going processes — chemical outputs, excretion, regular locomotor activity etc., are the emitted signals. At the 'phasic' level broad band width and relatively unspecialized stimuli are emitted; uncomplicated sexual interaction (if such exists) involving simply approach and withdrawal would be classified here.

At the 'signal' level true communicatory behaviour emerges; structures tend to be specialized to produce and receive signals within a relatively narrow band width; acoustic and pheromonal communication in insects would be included here, and perhaps the songs of birds. Within this level Tavolga makes the important distinction between the 'biosocial' and 'psychosocial' levels — largely with reference to the development of behaviour and communication; the former reflects signal communication dominated by organic processes, as for example in social insects, whereas the latter emphasizes the role of learning in behavioural development, which is for example well documented in the mammals.

Beyond these, Tavolga argues for two distinct 'higher' levels, 'symbolic' and 'language'. Few people would now dispute that most primates are capable of some form of symbolic interaction, from simply pointing to symbolic facial expressions which humans also can recognize. The language level is distinct from, but clearly dependent upon the symbolic; Tavolga characterizes it as a level at which symbols are used in a teleological sense.

Clearly it is artificial to try and interpret communication in a framework such as this without realizing that there must be continuous grading between the categories employed: what enables separation into 'levels' is simply distance on a continuum of developing complexity; under such conditions the distinction between qualitative and quantitative difference breaks down.

Furthermore, some of the communicatory equipment of an animal may belong to one level of integration, whereas others are at different ones: thus to create a phylogeny embodying these ideas is effectively impossible. This indicates the important point that different levels of communication can and must occur at the same time in the same animal. The lesson from this at the human level is to examine very carefully the levels of interaction which can possibly occur in communication processes, and try to analyse their inter-dependencies. It is even more important that this should be done on a developmental basis, where shifts in the relative importance of the different levels might be extremely important.

In a slightly different context Jamieson (1973) has recently stressed the respective roles of 'direct' and 'indirect' perception in communication and learning. One can characterize the indirect perception as being one step removed from reality. It seems to me that this is a key process in the evolution of communication in the animal world in general; as a communication process evolves so it becomes less directly anchored to the animals normal physiological functioning, more symbolic, and thus more 'indirect'. There are some interesting classical instances in ethology which serve to illustrate such a contention, and provide some insight into the evolution of higher vertebrate communication.

Clearly, complex communication has evolved where it has adaptive significance. In most vertebrates this adaptive significance is at its highest with respect to two main types of behaviour, which are possibly to some extent interdependent: the first is sexual behaviour, where complex physiological processes need to be co-ordinated between individuals. In land animals there must be communication processes ensuring the temporal and spatial accuracy in the control of behaviour, if the gametes of the two sexes are to be united. The second is in territorial behaviour, the biological functions of which are still badly understood. To maintain territories, which appear to be so essential for so many species, systems of communication are necessary which may even outweigh those of sex in their complexity. To evolve the necessary communicative behaviours in these two situations, which are highly specific to any species considered, almost opportunistic use has been made of pre-existing behaviours which were originally designed for simpler and more down to earth purposes. As morphological change evolves by the gradual modification of existing structures, so can behaviour, welding established components into new tools.

In the case of territorial behaviour, one more complex behaviour which has evolved is the 'threat display', which has been particularly well perfected by birds; this tends to occur when two animals meet at the edge of a territory, one happening to intrude, the other already occupying and therefore prepared to defend his territory: the defender is on his own land and therefore motivated to attack the intruder; but all-out attack is checked by the conflicting motivation of flight, since he is very near someone else's territory: the resulting behaviour, usually very distinctive, is what we call threat. The ethological interpretation, supported by several lines of argument, is that the arousal of these tendencies simultaneously leads to unique combinations of the elements of behaviour originating from each of the basic behavioural systems, which may then, by natural selection, evolve into a co-ordinated display of threat, a concept which to men is an ideal one to employ at the border of one's territory. Such display is communicative in that it signals intention without drastic physical action. (It can turn into attack or flight according to how the other animal behaves). As such it is a regression from reality, and the beginning of symbolic content. This point is given even more significance from the point of view of the evolution of communication when one considers two individuals at the edge of their territories, threatening each other; here is the opportunity for information exchange, intention movements of each animal producing a bilateral communication, rather than the non-communicative situation of chase and flight; as Manning (1972) has stated, threat postures are a primitive form of language.

A similar model to this has been used by ethologists to explain the evolution of highly complex courtship displays found in many animals. The sexually motivated male is in principle subject to other motivations which may be conflicting; aggression towards a second animal on his territory, in this case a female, may only just be balanced by an appeasement display by that female; in this conflict a unique combination of behaviours may be evoked which provide the material for the evolution of a more complex display. But the more important conclusion to be drawn from the study of courtship displays is that communication itself has been one of the most important factors in the formation of new species; the courtship act is one where the sensory equipment of the participating animals may be used in more and more subtle ways to elaborate more specific and more refined modes of communication. Related populations of animals may differ initially only in their modes of courtship communication, but this is enough to separate populations genetically, and create potential new species. The implication of this is that populations of animals carry in them sufficient genetical variability for processes such as this to occur. Individuals must differ genetically in the relative usage of different sensory modalities, and in the degree of refinement of their sensory capacities. Such a process has been demonstrated by research on the courtship behaviour and speciation in fruit flies of the genus Drosophila, (for an example of genetical diversity enabling refinement of a communicatory process see Cook, 1973). Genetical diversity in sensory systems is both encouraged and built upon by evolution.

## Ethology in the study of human communication and learning

Most scientists are very wary of making assertions about human behaviour based on phenomena observed in animals; whereas all must accept without question the history of man as a biological entity, behavioural phenomena observed in non-human species cannot be assumed to be also possessed by, or, as is so often suggested, to be at the roots of behaviour of which he is not conscious. What animal studies may be able to provide, especially in the case of communication and learning, are guides to the kind of behavioural adaptation that may be evolved to deal with specific problems in the environment of the species. The organization of communication and learning systems of different animals varies to such an extent in specificity, flexibility and complexity that all that can be attempted is interspecies comparison rather than direct inference.

Now that the anthropocentric motivation of early workers has worn off, there is one great lesson that has been learnt by behavioural science in the study of animals: the simple one of objectivity. Faced with the alarmingly large social repertories found in primate species, subjective interpretation is effectively impossible. The only way to gain a semblance of order is to systematically describe and apply techniques of discrimination amongst the behaviours so described in order to sort them into communicatively meaningful units — usually implying the action of some underlying motivational system, such as hunger, thirst, territoriality, sex etc., (see Connolly, 1972 for description of ethological techniques).

But the motivational system underlying the type of communication about which this conference is concerned, education, can be seen to be sadly without precedents in the animal world: in general our motivations for complex communication are unique to Homo Sapiens and far less directly tied to physiological constraints. Not only does the content of communication in man, largely through the medium of language, differ from that of any other species, but, more important for the assessment of the efficacy of the communication process, so does the context radically change. How often in the primate, except in the simplest of communicative situations such as the altruistic warning cry, does one individual communicate with all the rest at any one time? This must be rare in primates, but as a phenomenon of human communication forms the basis of this conference. Most information flow in animals is serial, passing from one animal to one or a few others in one interaction; but in humans it must be essentially parallel if informational precision is to be retained, and large numbers of individuals instructed. Educational

327

information flows radially from a relatively few accepted sources (i.e. books or teachers) to a much larger array of receivers (i.e. learners). Whereas over time this involves a serial process (in which knowledge is updated and modified), the actual educating process is essentially parallel.

It is for reasons such as these that one of the main problems of educational research exists: that of the assessment of educational effectiveness. No simple objective criteria for this exist, because no simple biological function is being served by communication: in the absence of such objective criteria of achievement, assessment has been reduced to its more fundamental measurable properties, such as factual reproduction of information and other specific skills of application. As far as the communication media are concerned the former variable is the more important, and thus the tendency in media research is to concentrate upon the manipulation of communication variables which influence this dependent variable of reproduction of learned information. The first point an ethologist should stress is that using variables such as this, and knowing many of the presentation variables which influence it, is only the beginning, and possibly a beginning at the wrong end.

The first reason for this is the old universal difficulty about psychological tests of attainment, and their relationship to subsequent activity of the individual in the real world. Clearly one may rigorously and objectively test retention of material presented by various methods, and thereby assess the effects of certain presentational variables. But the danger may be that the variables found important are specific to the test situation – they may for example lead to easier immediate recall but be less important for subsequent use by the learner in a practical situation because of the narrowness of their context. A pertinent detail may be highlighted by a televisual trick, but is it thereby put into long term store? Such questions are elementary in that they are long standing problems of psychology of which most would-be educators must be aware.

From the ethological point of view the more important criticism about the use simply of questionnaire information and post-test material in the assessment of communicational effectiveness is that such a paradigm may very easily distract from the fact that a behavioural process is, or should be, the material for study and not the test score. One might argue that a test score reflects part of this process. Perhaps it may, but far too small a sample of it, and the orientation is misleading. Baggaley (1973) has recently stressed a heuristic approach to the development of educational media, where the research stratagem does not start in a straight line from one fixed point of assumption, but rather reflects a gradual modification of the measurement and presentation tools available, as they are seen to interact with one another. Such a broad stratagem would clearly be a fruitful approach, but there is an heuristic aspect which Baggaley did not stress: that the stratagem should concentrate on elucidating the gamut of processes which are involved in the act of communication at all possible logical levels. Relying on post-tests and attitude assessments is not heuristic in this way. A really heuristic approach is perhaps only possible once one has escaped from the value laden domination of specific educational achievement.

In this regard every ethologist has an instinct: observation and description precede analysis and interpretation: turn the camera on the animal and see what it actually does before making any conclusions about the relationship between variables: time honoured behavioural variables of the classroom, attention, fidgeting etc. can tell more about communicational effectiveness and the processes underlying it than the conventional test scores, and attitudinal inferences. Is boredom not easier to detect through behavioural observation than through verbal attitude.

Ethology, rather than raising many principles of animal communication directly relevant to man has this approach to offer: to take the educational situation in its widest context, and see what people do in it. Tinbergen (1963) has levelled the criticism that psychology has skipped the preliminary descriptive stage that the natural sciences passed through. Is this also the case for educational research?

When studying animals it is an easy attitude to adopt that every aspect of behaviour must be described; with animals we don't have those subjective grounds for rejecting a behaviour as trivial. But this latter tendency, when allowed to enter the study of man, immediately skews the results in the direction of those acceptable to man. Tinbergen (1963) has stressed the danger of failing to describe behaviours which may seem trivial. Thus **everything** the potential learner does should in principle be described, at least at some level of complexity (i.e. 'hand touched face' rather than description of muscular movements). The fullest ethological study of the communication and learning process would take the widest possible time samples in the learning situation, studying activities before learning and after the educational session, as well as during rest periods; after all, the practical difficulties of gaining and recording data are far less in the 'classroom' than they are in the 'wild'; the possible repertoire of the individual for non-verbal behaviours is to some extent limited, and the camera can easily be made to encompass all the individuals present; the group is truly 'captive', and as such presents an ideal medium for study.

But how many significant components in the process of learning could one expect to be reflected in simple movement and non-verbal terms? Clearly such a question is not answerable at the moment; but one can say with certainty that the processes which are so related will be the most important ones; a task of ethology is to discriminate the trivial behaviours from the 'functional' ones, or as is more likely in the case of human learning, to isolate behaviours that are correlated with certain sub-processes of communication and learning.

REFERENCES

Baggaley, J.P. (1973) Developing an effective educational medium. Programmed Learning 10, 158-167.

Connolly, K.J. (1972) Ethological techniques. In Psychological Assessment of the Mentally Handicapped. P.J. Mittler (Ed.). London: Churchill

Cook, R.M. (1973) Courtship processing in Drosophila Melanogaster, II. An adaptation to selection for receptivity to wingless males. Anim. Behav. 21, 349-358.

Jamieson, G.H. (1973) Visual media in a conceptual framework for the acquisition of knowledge. Programmed Learning 10, 32-39.

Manning, A. (1972) An Introduction to Animal Behaviour. 2nd edn. London: Arnold.

Tavolga, W.N. (1970) Levels of interaction in animal communication. In Development and Evolution of Behaviour. L.R. Aronson, E. Tobach, D.S. Lehrman and J.S. Rosenblatt, (Eds.) San Francisco: Freeman.

Thorpe, W.H. (1963) Learning and Instinct in Animals. 2nd edn. London: Methuen.

Tinbergen, N. (1963) On aims and methods of ethology. Z.f. Tierpsychol. 20, 410-433.

# Communication effectiveness in the educational media: three experiments

J. P. BAGGALEY, University of Liverpool
S. W. DUCK, University of Lancaster

Abstract: Three experiments in televisual presentation are reported in which the following effects were established:

- the 'keyed' insertion of a picture background significantly increased the apparent credibility of the programme presenter;

- the edited insertion of varying audience reaction shots significantly affected a speaker's perceived popularity and interest value, and judgements on her educational ability;

- the re-recording and edited insertion of the interviewer's role in a discussion significantly increased his perceived tension, sincerity, and apparent intelligibility.

   The experiments are examined for their practical implications in the presentation of educational materials, and as exemplars of a predictive style of research likely to provide insight in general problems of media communication effectiveness.

Whenever in educational technology the call for a closer investigation of media effectiveness is heard, the popular plaint is returned that our knowledge of the learning process remains too scanty for useful conclusions to be drawn. Educational technology has developed little in its initial stage, and continues, with jingoistic fervour, to offer the men, the machines and the money before defining the conditions of their use. The shortage of appropriate theoretical bases in media research is at once a substantial reason for this lack of direction, and a convenient excuse for accepting the situation. However, a technology claiming to offer educational benefits, while unable to draw conclusions about the problems involved, has need of critical examination, preferably from within before others match its present achievements against the original promise and draw their own conclusions.

   A recent verdict that 'educational technology is consolidating more than advancing' (APLET International Conference, 1973) offers little hope of new impetus for change from within the field. And the principal means of progress at the theoretical level may prove to be a gradual infusion of ideas regarding communication and learning processes from other disciplines.  Unfortunately, the problems educational technologists face in the need to demonstrate the value of their role are immediate, and the evolution of general principles of communication effectiveness becomes a matter of urgency.  In previous discussion of the research strategies likely to aid the design of effective techniques for media use (Baggaley, 1973), it was suggested that investigators should strive for insights into the problems of teacher-student communication in specific situations rather than a comprehensive theory of learning for all seasons at once.  Practical solutions within the educational system, it was argued, are reached by the accumulation of guidelines for teaching and learning skills via a pragmatic approach.

In illustration of this position, three experiments are reported which examine the effects on a student audience of television production techniques in common usage.  The data are examined for their immediate relevance to the problems facing media production specialists at a practical level, and as a basis for speculation regarding future research into communication effectiveness generally.  In all three of the experiments the subjects were 25 members of a postgraduate Certificate in Education course (9 females and 16 males).  The class was divided into two groups — half the males and four females in one group, half the males and five females in the other.  The experiments ran consecutively.

EXPERIMENT I

**Purpose.**  In the straightforward TV reportage situation, where for lack of more appropriate visual information, the lecturer or studio presenter features in vision as well as sound, the producer has the choice of setting him against either a blank or a decorative background.  The modern electronic process of 'keying' permits the producer to combine the image of the presenter with the image from a second camera looking at, for example a photograph or slide:  the illusion is created that the presenter is set against a background, while problems of studio set construction are avoided.  The benefits of such a technique are wide-ranging, and since the advent of colour TV its use has greatly increased owing to the greater ease with which effects can be created.

Yet production staff must guard against adverse effects — such as the distracting influence of an irrelevant or abstract background — which in educational television particularly could seriously undermine the presentation's impact.  While the latter is a simple effect to predict — and one of which any producer would be aware — the scope for misuse of such techniques in unknown, since to the writers' knowledge the precise effects of an added context on, for example, viewers' attitudes to a presentation have never been investigated.  In tackling this question the present experiment sought to determine whether the insertion of a background image has the potential for more subtle effects than might commonly be supposed.

**Procedure.**   A news-type item reporting an archaeological dig by members of Liverpool University was scripted by a professional TV newswriter, and two televised versions of the item were prepared. The two recordings were made simultaneously using two cameras immediately adjacent, and separate recording circuits. The image, of a 'head and shoulders' close-up on the presenter, remained constant throughout the recording; the presenter read his script from a cueing device between the two camera lenses and appeared to address each of them directly. The two camera angles were indistinguishable, and the two recorded versions differed perceptibly in only one respect: that on one the presenter was seen against a plain grey background, while on the other he appeared to be in front of a large-scale studio photograph of the archaeological site in question, effectively inserted by the keying process despite the problems of keying in monochrome. The recorded item lasted 70 seconds.

The two versions of the item were presented one to each group of subjects, who were then asked to indicate their impression of the televised presenter on the set of 7-point adjectival scales (semantic differential) given in Table 1 (page 334). The scales related to qualities of personal attractiveness and expertise.

**Results.**   The significant differences in response between the two student groups (Table 1) indicate that when the presenter appeared against the keyed background he was judged to be more honest, profound, reliable and fair than when seen against the plain background. On the other hand he was not regarded as significantly more informed or expert, and the overall ratings of his interest value on the two tapes were virtually identical. The insertion of the picture background seems to have had less influence on the impact of the speakers' message than on his level of personal credibility — a totally unpredictable effect upon the amount of trust which the two groups were prepared to invest in him. Reasons for this are offered in the overall discussion of results below.


EXPERIMENT II

**Purpose.**   In a situation where the lecturer or presenter is addressing a televised audience, the possible influences on the viewing audience of background and general context are more complex than those of a simple picture background alone. The perceived attitudes of a studio audience may not only affect the viewers' assessment of the lecturer but also the performance of the lecturer himself. In order to determine whether viewers' perceptions of a lecturer's performance may be affected solely by the type of audience reactions shown — i.e. regardless of the type of performance actually given — the effects of inserting various prerecorded audience reaction shots into a standard lecture presentation

TABLE 1. Mean ratings of a TV presenter set against (+) a picture background and (o) a plain background.

| | 1 | 2 | 3 | 4 | 5 | 6 | 7 | t | P < |
|---|---|---|---|---|---|---|---|---|---|
| Unpleasant | | | | | o+ | | Pleasant | 0.390 | |
| Informed | | | o - - + | | | | Uninformed | 0.671 | |
| Strong | | | + o | | | | Weak | 0.397 | |
| Honest | | + - - - - - o | | | | | Dishonest | 2.134 | 0.025 |
| Sceptical | | | | | o - - - + | | Believing | 1.082 | |
| Shallow | | | o - - - - - - - + | | | | Profound | 2.228 | 0.025 |
| Confusing | | | | + - - - - - o | | | Straightforward | 1.497 | |
| Reliable | | | + - - - - - - - o | | | | Unreliable | 1.845 | 0.05 |
| Direct | | + - - - o | | | | | Evasive | 1.190 | |
| Interesting | | | | o - + | | | Uninteresting | 0.281 | |
| Fair | | | + - - - - o | | | | Unfair | 1.930 | 0.05 |
| Expert | | | + - - - - + | | | | Inexpert | 1.004 | |
| Insincere | | | | + - o | | | Sincere | 0.557 | |

(N.B. At df = 23, $t_{0.05}$ = 1.714)

334

were estimated by the procedure used in Experiment I.  In order to increase its general entertainment value, producers commonly add pre-recorded audience applause or laughter to the sound-track of a presentation similarly; though visual shots of an audience are usually presented for reasons of production variety rather than in the more deliberate attempt to bias the viewers' specific reaction to a performer. Nonetheless, effects of audience reactions upon the perceived interest value and popularity of a speaker are to be predicted.

**Procedure.**  A three and a half minute extract from a televised lecture in Welfare Economics was selected during which the lecturer (female) was seen in medium close-up at a lectern, and in near and long shots at the blackboard.  The detail was varied using a single camera with zoom lens.  The extract was copied onto two videotapes.  At the same point in each of the two recordings, shots of an audience were presented, prepared independently with the help of a group of student actors, and edited into the lecture to give the illusion that lecturer and audience had been together at the time of recording.  No audience sound was presented, and, while audience reactions were seen, the sound-track of the lecture continued uninterrupted.

The actors obeyed instructions to portray the following stereotypic reactions (positive vs. negative) :

(a)  Leaning forward agog, vs.  Leaning forward head in hands;
(b)  Two people showing interest in lecture, vs. Two people talking;
(c)  Person scribbling eager notes, vs. Person doodling;
(d)  Person with hand to chin (intense), vs. Person with hand to chin (yawning).

The same actor, or couple of actors was shown in each contrasting pair, and the length of reaction shots ranged from 7 to 16 seconds.  The positive reactions were edited into one tape, negative reactions into the other. Though the audience 'reacted' to an imaginary lecturer, and the lecturer, in addressing an imaginary audience, was in effect acting also, the realism of their performance and the credibility of the total edited effect was verified during the debriefing of subjects and subsequent analysis. In both conditions, the audio-visual presentation of the lecturer herself was identical, only the reaction shots being varied.

Each of the two versions was presented to one of the two student groups as in Experiment I and their reactions to the lecturer invited on the scales given in Table 2 (page 336).  No subject was familar with the lecture content.

**Results.**  Highly significant effects of the manipulation on the speaker's perceived popularity and interest value occurred as predicted (Table 2).

TABLE 2.    Mean ratings of a TV lecturer given (+) positive and (o) negative audience reactions.

| | 1 | 2 | 3 | 4 | 5 | 6 | 7 | | t | P < |
|---|---|---|---|---|---|---|---|---|---|---|
| Confusing | | o | - - - - | + | | | | Straightforward | 2.740 | 0.01 |
| Strong | | | | | + - - - o | | | Weak | 1.001 | |
| Honest | | | o - + | | | | | Dishonest | 0.626 | |
| Shallow | | | o - - - | + | | | | Profound | 2.001 | 0.05 |
| Ruthless | | | | o - + | | | | Humane | 0.479 | |
| Insignificant | | | o - - - | + | | | | Important | 1.489 | |
| Reliable | | | | +o | | | | Unreliable | 0.071 | |
| Interesting | | | | + - - - - - | o | | | Uninteresting | 2.771 | 0.01 |
| Popular | | | | + - - - - - - - | | o | | Unpopular | 4.350 | 0.001 |
| Nervous | | | o - - + | | | | | Not nervous | 0.841 | |
| Fair | | | | +o | | | | Unfair | 0.246 | |
| Humorous | | | | | | +o | | Not humorous | 0.062 | |
| Expert | | | | + - - - - - | o | | | Inexpert | 1.927 | 0.05 |
| Inferior | | | | o - + | | | | Superior | 1.005 | |
| Unpleasant | | | | | o + | | | Pleasant | 0.569 | |
| Sincere | | | o + | | | | | Insincere | 0.127 | |

(N.B. At df = 23, $t_{0.05}$ = 1.714)

336

As in Experiment I, however, other significant effects were less predictable, in this case revealing the apparent influence of the editing procedure on the impact of the speaker's message. For in the negative condition she was seen as significantly more confusing, more shallow and less expert than in the positive condition; and it should here be re-emphasized that in both conditions the lecturer's performance was held constant, only the reaction shots being varied.

EXPERIMENT III

**Purpose.** Much illusion in the visual media is created by one or another form of editing procedure as in the second experiment. However, when the need for editing arises for reasons beyond the producer's control, either due to faulty camera work or limitations in working conditions, then the edited effects may be less than completely satisfactory. In location filming, shots are typically recorded out of sequence for convenience and edited together subsequently. In situations where only a single camera is used, the illusion of a multi-camera situation may be created, even within the presentation of, for example, a continuous interview, by (a) training the camera on the interviewee throughout the recording session, (b) re-recording the interviewer's questions and facial reactions when the interview is over, and (c) editing the sound and vision together in a manner that maintains the continuity as best possible. To the viewer unaware of this technique, the illusion of continuity may be effective enough, though the occasional inappropriate nod or smirk on the interviewer's part may cause certain bewilderment. Accordingly, the third experiment was conducted to see whether effects of the viewers' unconscious reaction to this technique might be measured.

**Procedure.** A three and a half minute extract from a televised interview was selected. The interviewee, a poet, was seen answering questions about his work from a colleague well-versed in the subject, and able to maintain a continuous and easy flow of conversation. The two sat in opposing armchairs, each one permanently fixated by a camera. While the interviewee was seen in a variety of close and long shots, shots of the interviewer were fixed at medium close-up from head to waist-level. As in the previous experiments, two versions of the presentation were prepared. The first was straight and unedited. By an editing process, however, all shots of the interviewer were replaced in the second version by material recorded after the actual interview was over, in which he repeated his questions and gave reactions to imaginary replies. Differing from the first version solely in the presentation of the interviewer, the second was thus effectively prepared according to the technique described above, in which a single camera is used and yet the impression of several created. The continuity and developing logic of the interview was care-

337

TABLE 3. Mean ratings of a TV interviewer seen (+) in actual interaction and (o) in simulated interaction with the interviewee.

| | 1 | 2 | 3 | 4 | 5 | 6 | 7 | t | P |
|---|---|---|---|---|---|---|---|---|---|
| Sincere | | | | o - - - - - + | | | Insincere | 2.194 | 0.025 |
| Pleasant | | | + - - - - o | | | | Unpleasant | 1.195 | |
| Honest | | | | o - - - - + | | | Dishonest | 1.206 | |
| Shallow | | | + - - o | | | | Profound | 0.919 | |
| Tense | | o - - - - - - - - - - - + | | | | | Relaxed | 2.738 | 0.01 |
| Ruthless | | | | | o+ | | Humane | 0.171 | |
| Believing | | | | o - + | | | Sceptical | 0.537 | |
| Hostile | | | | | | o - + | Friendly | 0.963 | |
| Inferior | | | o+ | | | | Superior | 0.126 | |
| Reliable | | | | o - + | | | Unreliable | 1.009 | |
| Direct | | | | o - - - + | | | Evasive | 1.221 | |
| Straightforward | | | | o - - - - - - - + | o + | | Confusing | 2.090 | 0.025 |
| Expert | | | | | o + | | Inexpert | 0.249 | |
| Nervous | | o - + | | | | | Not nervous | 0.863 | |
| Fair | | | o + | | | | Unfair | 0.561 | |
| Stable | | | | | o+ | | Unstable | 0.258 | |

(N.B. At df = 23, $t_{0.05} = 1.714$)

fully preserved. At no stage during the recording session was the interviewer aware of the experiment's purpose: the re-recording of his
questions and reactions was described to him as a routine procedure
providing material for use if the interview should need editing for technical reasons.

Viewers impressions of the interviewer were sought by the procedure of the previous two experiments, and differences in their reaction
to the two versions are indicated in Table 3.

**Results.** In the edited version of the recording, the interviewer was
seen as significantly more tense, not surprising in view of the instruction given him to pose his questions and to simulate interviewer reactions
in vacuo. The significant increase in his apparent sincerity in this condition may derive from his successful effort to perform the role realistically. More interesting in the present context is the finding that in the
unedited version the interviewer was seen as significantly less straightforward (more confusing) than in the edited version, again an apparent
effect on the impact of his message.

In the following section, the three experiments are discussed
jointly.

DISCUSSION

In each of the experiments, it will be recalled that the experimental manipulation concerned a single aspect of conventional production technique,
while all other characteristics of the presentation were held constant
between the two experimental groups in order that any significant differences in the effect of the total material might be directly attributable to
the manipulation itself. Since the experimental comparison was made
between different audiences of the same type rather than between scores
derived from the same audience at different times, possibilities for subject bias were avoided in favour of the lesser problems encountered in
the selection of comparable groups. The use of attitude scores as the
experimental index was thus directly inferential rather than merely
descriptive, permitting a review of the main findings, and certain conclusions regarding techniques likely to increase the educational effectiveness
of media production in specific situations.

The specific findings may be summarized as follows :

**(I)  The 'keyed' insertion of a picture background increased the speaker's
personal credibility rather than the impact of his message.**

The effect on this particular speaker's personal qualities may be explained
by hindsight. Considered separately, his visual appearance and vocal
manner in the recording conflicted; and it is felt that his voice was the
main mediator of his construed image as honest, profound, reliable and

339

fair, while his visual appearance was less favourable — probably in view of his steely reliance on the cueing device which he was required to fixate throughout the recording. Whether or not a cueing device is available in the studio, the additional value of a desk script is indicated. And unless the speaker may be assumed by his audience to be an expert — which the conventional television reporter is not — his need to refer to notes in this way will be expected in any case.

While further data is needed in order to confirm the interpretation placed upon this effect previous findings regarding the separate processing capacities of eye and ear discussed most notably by Broadbent (1958), certainly indicate that the auditory and visual content of a communication must be carefully matched in order to prevent the receiver's attention from shifting between them and favouring one at the expense of the other. If decorative rather than informative, the insertion of keyed visual detail may serve to distract an audience's attention from the speaker's visual presentation, leaving his auditory channel as the main communicator. Of course, when an educational producer is compelled to use an expert presenter who has difficulty in projecting a favourable visual image, this technique may be used to good effect. For by an effect on the presentation's arousal potential, the presence of background detail in such a situation may improve its value even when irrelevant to the subject under discussion.

The natural response to a situation such as this should of course be to question whether the chosen medium is necessarily the most appropriate: in certain situations a televisual presentation conveys nothing that the audiotape and/or visual slide projection media do not convey more economically. However, in presentations where a televisual technique is necessary for some of the time though not all, the use of keying for purely decorative purposes may be valuable despite the fact that the auditory channel carries the actual information for learning.

**(II) The edited insertion of varying audience reaction shots affected the impact of the speaker's message as well as more personal qualities of popularity and interest value.**

The powerful persuasibility of this technique is clearly evident, suggesting that the insertion of favourable audience reactions may enhance the motivational value of a recorded lecture even when the reactions are simulated as here. Though the insertion of negative reactions would naturally be unacceptable on ethical grounds, the improvement of a lecturer's perceived expertise, profundity and clarity in this manner would be no less ethical than by any of the other techniques which producers employ to increase the effectiveness of their presentation. Editing, dubbing, keying and superimposition techniques, for example, all aim at illusion similarly; and a pre-recorded selection of standard audience

reaction shots would prove a valuable addition to the educational producer's stockpile.

In view of these findings, producers should certainly guard against
the random use of audience shots selected solely in order to vary the
content and pace of presentation. The possible negative influences on
the viewers' reaction to a speaker may certainly outweigh any benefits
to be derived.

(III)   **The re-recording and edited insertion of the interviewer's role in
a discussion increased his perceived tension and sincerity as well
as his apparent intelligibility.**

Clearly, the effects on audience reaction to a single person in this way
may be as varied as the shots of him selected; and further investigation
of reactions to the relationship between two discussants, and to each of
them given variation of the shots of the other, might yield interesting
differences of a more subtle nature than observed here. Certain inferences regarding the effective use of this particular editing technique in
the educational media are nonetheless possible.

The need for care in preserving continuity in the use of the technique
has been indicated above. For the interviewer the main problem in re-
recording his role is to preserve a natural manner even in the absence
of normal feedback from the interviewee. In the present experiment,
every effort was made to avoid the customary pitfalls of the technique and
to create the edited illusion of continuity effectively. None of the negative
effects that may arise from hasty editing were observed; and the increase
in the interviewer's apparent tension in the edited version is the only
effect which on its own might be considered adverse. However, in view of
the accompanying increase in his perceived sincerity, it may be concluded
that when carefully used the technique has general potential for enhancing
a presentation's impact. The unforeseen role of the technique in heighten-
ing the interviewer's apparent intelligibility (as measured from 'straightforward' to 'confusing') indicates several positive production guidelines.
One may question, for example, the value of using two cameras and the
necessary peripheral apparatus in situations where the use of a single
camera and simple editing techniques may be shown to produce a more
powerful educational format. In view of the programmed learning tenet
that educational material should be organized in a logically developing
sequence of recognizable steps, the straight transmission of an unscripted
interview or discussion situation may not necessarily be an effective educational strategy at all. If the interviewee alone is seen the effect is
naturally monotonous. If two cameras are used, however, in the effort
to cover both participants, the director cannot always predict the moment
at which to transfer from one to the other; and when he is only fraction-
ally late in switching to the participant now speaking, the auditory and

visual presentations may conflict. Even momentary confusions of this sort may be argued to weaken the logical structure of the production: and when more than two cameras are used the problems multiply.

By use of the one-camera technique to ensure that the auditory and visual detail in a presentation are at all times complementary, dangers of confusion in the system might be avoided. The opportunity for a producer to add structure to an initially unstructured situation — indeed, for the interviewer to rephrase his questions more succinctly — may improve the logic of the material, and recalls recommendations for the application of programmed learning principles in educational media production, reviewed by Leytham and James (1973).

POSTLUDE

In each of the present three experiments, the unintentional effects of production strategy that were isolated suggest the subtlety of the medium's control in the formation of a viewer's most basic attitudes to the communication and in the direction and efficiency of his attention during its transmission. The implications of such effects are immediate. On the one hand, the attractions of conventional production techniques for varying the detail in a display must clearly be examined in relation to their power to distract viewers from the educational content of a communication; and on the other, the need, so easily overlooked in educational situations, for deliberate effort to control the learner's attention to material, should be recognized. The subtlety of the effects observed indicates the scope for deliberate control over the communication and learning processes to be achieved as the practical effects of presentation techniques in educational usage become known.

Other investigators may attempt to replicate the precise effects observed here: they are unlikely to do so. Findings from much research in the educational media are certainly dependent on the materials used and to a large extent on the subjects to whom they are shown. In seeking evidence for the value of a production by measurement of the information derived from it, differences in ability between subjects may be countered by pre-test/post-test comparison. The effects of pre-testing on post-test performance, however, may in turn conceal the more pertinent effects of interim presentation under study. Where learning gain is the sole index of presentation effect, an inadequate knowledge of the intervening variables will reduce the likelihood of replication further. And in the comparison of presentation effectiveness between media, or between strategies in the use of a single medium, the inferential value of a set of data is thus restricted not only by its dependence on the experimental situation but by the shortcomings of conventional techniques for experimental measurement.

The scope for inference in media research may be increased by the investigation of more stable research measures. In all educational situations communication and learning are mediated by attitude, and the investigation of an intervening level of information such as this provides a more fundamental basis for studies of the communication and learning processes than is derived from studies of educational gain in isolation. In seeking support for the conclusions drawn from attitudinal data, the relationships between attitude and educational gain may be explored, and attempts made to reproduce the findings at one level in the other's terms. But in the pursuit of questions such as these it is easy to lose sight of the more practical problems which prompted the research originally. As long as the conclusions drawn from a set of data are supported by reasonable theory, the immediate need in educational research is to justify them at a practical level wherever possible. By testing the inferences from experimental data, rather than by merely attempting to replicate the precise findings in an equivalent form, more comprehensive and valuable insights into the processes concerned may be obtained. Further testing of practical guidelines for communication effectiveness, however they are derived, is likely to be of more immediate value in the development of an effective educational technology than attempts to further prove the validity of their original basis.

By the gradual infusion of theory from existing disciplines such as psychology, sociology and engineering, guidelines for communication effectiveness derived in the pragmatic fashion illustrated here may be supplemented and refined. The possibilities of a particular media production technique in various situations may be assessed, for example, in relation to the principles of communication apparent to ethologists:

'At least two types of communication display may be distinguished in animals: those which attract attention and simultaneously convey a message, and those which attract attention prior to the transmission of a message.'

(Cook, 1974)

In accordance with Cook's first display type, certain televisual procedures — as the use of different camera angles for purposes of pace and variety — may serve usefully to control attention throughout an educational presentation. Techniques such as the use of background detail or sound-track music, however, when used during the transmission of information, may aid learning by certain members of an audience though distract others: such techniques may only prove maximally effective from an educational point of view when used prior to the delivery of information as in Cook's second display type.

In developing communication effectiveness in the educational media, very little practical research has yet been attempted. That the viability of research conclusions varies, both in theory and practice, according to specific situations is an unfortunate limitation of educational research in general. For applied benefits, this constraint should be accepted and tolerated. No realistic scheme for research in the educational media is likely to lead to fully generalizable conclusions about the processes of communication and learning in all situations, though the continual inference of practical guidelines may be sufficient to meet specific situational problems as they arise. To the cynical observer, the present shortage of presentation guidelines, and the consequent inability of educational technologists to define specific applications of the media they recommend, must smack of charlatanism. According to the Concise Oxford Dictionary, strict empiricism, the reliance on observation and experiment to the exclusion of theory as in much of educational technology at present, implies quackery also. However, in a discipline based on pragmatism, theory and practice combine, and general principles of communication effectiveness evolve in response to the actual learning problems encountered. Once the specific values of the media in given situations can be demonstrated, the evolution of a more mature technological discipline will have been accomplished.

## ACKNOWLEDGEMENTS

The writers are grateful to Miss Sheila Smith, Messrs. K. Duck, B. Rollinson, N. Shrimpton and J. Thompson, to the technical staff of Liverpool University's Audio-Visual Aids Unit, and to members of the University Drama Society, for their help in preparing the experimental materials.

REFERENCES

APLET International Conference Proceedings (1973) Programmed Learning and Educational Technology **10**, 381-382.

Baggaley, J.P. (1973) Developing an effective educational medium. Programmed Learning and Educational Technology **10**, 158-169.

Broadbent, D.E. (1958) Perception and Communication. London: Pergamon.

Cook, R.M. (1974) Personal communication.

Leytham, G.W.H. and James, P.E. (1973) Programmed learning in the presentation of video-taped recordings. Programmed Learning and Educational Technology **10**, 136-143.

# Instructional innovation: a field study in functional literacy

G. H. JAMIESON, University of Liverpool

**Abstract:** Innovation in educational practice can take the form of new procedures, new technical aids, or a combination of both. However, innovation in one place may be 'old hat' in another. In this article, an account is given of an experimental educational research project which evaluated the effectiveness of traditional/ expository teaching and programmed instruction, which represented the innovatory aspect of the study. The project was concerned with the teaching of basic literacy to village communities in central Iran. The article demonstrates the significant advantages of the programmed method, but it ends by highlighting the problems of communication which were faced during the experiment. It is suggested that communication problems may be assessed in physical terms (road, transport, etc.) or in conceptual terms (differences in interpretation of a message): it goes on to suggest that the latter problem increases in intensity as messages (instructions) pass through the various agencies standing between the researcher and his subjects when the experiment is carried out in the field.

## INTRODUCTION

Innovation in teaching and learning is usually concerned with the application of new technologies or procedural changes. But the ultimate effectiveness of any form of innovation in pedagogical practice will depend as much upon its acceptance as upon its intrinsic properties. The innovator can be seen to be facing two problems of communication — (a) communication of the desirability or need for change; and (b) maintenance of the fidelity of his message as it passes through the various agencies engaged in its transmission.

In particular, field experimentation is extremely susceptible to this kind of problem. Although attempts at scientific rigour may produce controls over some variables and statistical procedures may be enlisted to partial-out or minimize certain interaction effects, the field experimenter can rarely achieve optimal control over all possible effects.

This article traces the steps in the implementation of an experimental study into the effectiveness of programmed instruction in a functional literacy project (Jamieson, 1974). It concludes by drawing out the communication problems which existed in the implementation of the field experiments.

## PROBLEM

One of the major problems facing developing countries is the establishment of literacy throughout entire populations. Illiteracy, aside from personal impoverishment, may hinder economic growth, particularly when such growth is based on industrialization which requires the employment of workers with at least minimal literacy. Further, illiteracy is a barrier to the spread of new ideas which require to be transmitted by the medium of print.

In furtherance of the aims of the 'Experimental World Programme in Literacy', UNESCO (1970, 1972) set up a number of functional literacy projects. Functional literacy, to quote the UNESCO (1970) report, 'should be taken to mean any literacy operation conceived as a component of economic and social development.... It is distinct from so called traditional literacy work in that it is no longer an isolated or distinct operation, .... a functional literacy project is related to precise collective and individual needs.... differentiated according to the environment and to specific economic and social objectives.'

This article takes a look at a single functional literacy project which was set up by UNESCO in collaboration with the Iranian Government at Isfahan. The problem was to construct programmed instructional materials for use in the project and to evaluate their effectiveness. The work was carried out by an international team working in collaboration with Iranian nationals who had the task of translating the didactic materials into the vernacular, Farsi.

## PROCEDURE

### (a) Preparation of programmed guides

Guides were prepared for use by instructors. These guides were planned in a linear format which presented factual information in parallel with associated suggestions about teaching procedures. The objectives of the guides was that they could be used by people with no teaching experience and an average standard of literacy. The following notes, which were included as a preface to the guides, give some indication of their contents.

1. This guide gives you factual information and advice on how to proceed with your teaching. You do not have to keep to the exact words used in the programme, but it is important that the sequence is followed and the facts adhered to.

2. The sequences have been divided into sessions, so you will have to decide yourself when to bring a session to an end.

346

3. Each sequence begins with a page setting out the contents of the sequence and the objectives to be obtained.

4. You will find that each page in the sequence is divided into two parts, on one side you will find factual information, and on the other side you will find suggestions about teaching procedures.

5. Throughout the guide you will find answers to questions. These answers have been provided to help you in your teaching, in case you are not familar with the teaching material.

These guides were planned for use within an experimental project; but it was considered that if they proved to be successful, they could be used as exemplars for other functional literacy projects.

## (b) Content of the programmed guides

The contents of the guides fell into five interrelated components : technical; scientific; socio-economic; mathematical; literacy. They dealt with the growth and marketing of sugar beet; a crop which is being introduced for intensive agriculture in the region of Isfahan.

The following list illustrates the range of work covered during the four weeks of instruction available in the guides.

### Technical

(i)  Recognition of optimal growth in the sugar beet plant.
(ii)  The qualitative requirements of the factory receiving the product.
(iii)  Harvesting and preparation of the plant for dispatch.
(iv)  Construction of silos.

### Scientific

(i)  The formation of sugar in the plant.
(ii)  Analysis of sugar content.
(iii)  Distribution of sugar in the plant.
(iv)  Microbiological causes of plant decomposition.
(v)  Methods of plant preservation.

### Socio-Economic

(i)  Value of agricultural research.
(ii)  Advice available through agricultural agencies.
(iii)  Place of co-operatives.
(iv)  Hygiene.

### Elementary Mathematics

(i)  Percentages.
(ii)  Multiplication and division.
(iii)  Metric measurement.
(iv)  Estimation of length.

347

## Literacy

Words were drawn from each of the above four areas, thus providing the functional literacy element. For example, when the instructor was discussing the sugar beet plant he would be required to draw upon specific words from the guide.

### (c) Preparation of test material

A test was constructed which was later used for the dual purpose of pre-testing and post-testing the participants on information sampled from the instructor guide. In addition to this test, weekly tests were administered. The objective of these tests was to find out whether information from the various concept areas in the programme was being learnt to the same standard.

### (d) Field experimentation

All the experimentation took place in villages within a distance of 15-55 km from Isfahan. Access to the villages was on unmade tracks which could accommodate motor transport.

Village classrooms were set up. These constituted a single room in each village with simple seats and a blackboard. Lighting was provided by oil pressure lamps.

### (e) Experimental design

The experiment was designed to appraise two factors :

(i)   Status of the instructors.
(ii)  Effect of the instructional material.

Recruitment of instructors, all of whom were male, was made from qualified teachers and literate farmers. They were randomly assigned to two conditions of instruction: programmed (involving the use of the new instructional guides); traditional/expository. In this 2 x 2 design it was proposed to have ten instructors in each cell, with twenty-five subjects assigned to each instructor; owing to fluctuations in attendance, poor record keeping, and occasional dishonesty, reliable data was only available in an attenuated form. This was not entirely unexpected, considering the nature of field experimentation involving peasant communities. The results of the experiment are based on the following numbers :

Programmed instruction:

| | | | |
|---|---|---|---|
| Farmer instructors | N = 6 | Teacher trained instructors | N = 5 |
| Subjects | N = 63 | Subjects | N = 61 |

348

Traditional/expository instruction:

Farmer instructors    $N = 6$    Teacher trained instructors    $N = 2$

Subjects              $N = 56$   Subjects                       $N = 28$

## RESULTS

The pre/post test was scutinized for test items which, on the basis of the course procedure and content, could be considered to be capable of being answered whether the participants had been in the programmed or expository instruction groups.

Percentage gain scores between the pre- and post-tests were computed. The group mean percentage gains were as follows:

| | |
|---|---|
| Farmer instructors (Traditional/expository) | 34% |
| Teacher trained instructors (Traditional/expository) | 24% |
| Farmer instructors (Programmed instruction) | 59% |
| Teacher trained instructors (Programmed instruction) | 54% |

Tests of proportions (Z) were calculated for each of the possible inter-group comparisons.

The Z coefficients and probabilities are given below:

1.  T.E. teachers v. T.E. farmers
       $Z = 1.0$,  $p < 0.15$

2.  T.E. farmers v. P.I. farmers
       $Z = 2.891$, $p < 0.001$ *

3.  T.E. teachers v. P.I. farmers
       $Z = 3.617$, $p < 0.001$ *

4.  P.I. farmers v. P.I. teachers
       $Z = 0.481$, $p < 0.315$

5.  All T.E. v. All P.I.
       $Z = 5.0$,  $p < 0.001$ *

* Significant beyond the 0.1% level. In each case the significance in favour of the P.I. group.

### Summary of weekly tests

The weekly tests were item analysed for correctness of response or lack of response. Table 1 (page 350) gives the percentage scores of the combined programmed groups on each weekly test; the means for the whole period is also given.

Table 1. Three-way classification of responses to questions in the weekly tests

| Week | Literacy | | | Maths | | | Concepts | | |
|---|---|---|---|---|---|---|---|---|---|
| | Right | Wrong | No Response | Right | Wrong | No Response | Right | Wrong | No Response |
| 1 | 84% | 9% | 7% | 64% | 20% | 16% | 49% | 46% | 5% |
| 2 | 51% | 39% | 10% | Not tested | | | 22% | 30% | 48% |
| 3 | 56% | 7% | 37% | 61% | 29% | 10% | 37% | 28% | 35% |
| 4 | 63% | 29% | 8% | 59% | 31% | 10% | 64% | 24% | 12% |
| Grand Mean | 64% | 21% | 15% | 61% | 27% | 12% | 43% | 32% | 25% |

## Instructors' questionnaire

Six weeks after the completion of the experiment, a questionnaire was administered to all the instructors, farmers and trained teachers, who had taken part in the P.I. groups. They were asked to respond on a five-point scale to a series of questions relating to the use of the new didactic materials and to give their subjective judgement on the value of this particular type of instruction. In all but two instances the mean group response scores were either neutral or in a negative direction.

## DISCUSSION OF RESULTS

What stands out clearly from these results is that the programmed method of instruction was markedly superior to the traditional/expository method. Statistically speaking the programmed method achieved significance, irrespective of the status of the instructors. In effect the programmed guides made up for the deficiency in professional competence of the farmers. This finding is illuminating when judged against the subjective evaluations of all the instructors who used the programmed guides, because their evaluations were not, in general, in favour of the new method.

The findings from the weekly tests reveal that the literacy and mathematical components were learnt more efficiently than the components from the concept areas belonging to the technical, scientific and socio-economic components; this may reflect the specificity of the learners' interests or intentions within the learning situation. Such a finding does not discredit the implied functional orientation; but it does suggest that the learning of concepts requires either a wider contextual involvement, or greater emphasis within the existing programmes.

From the obtained results it is possible to conject that the potential of P.I. material would be enhanced even further when instructors, who are more sympathetic about its application, are employed. This leads to the obvious suggestion that careful familiarization with new material is an essential precursor of its introduction. Such familiarization should go beyond the point of 'just coping' to a position of self assurance gained through competence. However, in practice, when the recruitment of instructors is made from peasant village communities, particularly communities which are not easily accessible to central training agencies, it may not be logistically possible to arrange extensive courses of familiarization.

## PROBLEMS OF FIELD EXPERIMENTATION

Field experimentation in situations involving peasant communities is problematic in a number of ways. But if research into human learning is to go beyond the banal it must face up to a variety of 'real-life' situations. In fact the important strides made by the late Sir F.C. Bartlett owed much to his acceptance of complexity in carrying out psychological research.

In terms of this particular study, the main problems encountered were :

(i)   Problems of group homogeneity.
(ii)  Irregularity of attendance.
(iii) Personal honesty.
(iv)  Acceptance of change.
(v)   Problem of message de-naturation — that is, loss of fidelity of the purpose and content of the innovatory programme as it passes through the various agencies standing in line between the initiator and the recipients.

Point (v) can be extended into a communication problem with two facets :

(a)  Physical distance — the lines of communication between the central agency and the villages.

(b)  Conceptualization distance — this refers to the difference between the various agencies in their conceptualized understanding of the aims, objectives and procedures of the experiment.

Figure 1 illustrates schematically some of the communication problems which field experimenters encounter in functional literacy research. It also indicates the need for research to be undertaken in the reverse direction, from the consumer to the planner. Such research might suggest answers to the question of what innovations are likely to be acceptable and the best methods of achieving their acceptance.

351

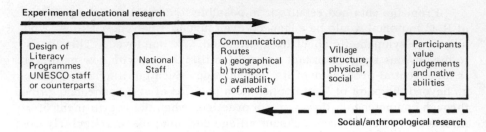

Figure 1

## ACKNOWLEDGEMENTS

Thanks are due to UNESCO who commissioned this study. In particular, appreciation is made to Mr. P. Henquet; to Dr. L.A. Biran who was responsible for most of the early work in programme preparation; to Mr. M. Verron who devised the instructors' questionnaire; to Mrs. A. Klein who supervised the technical content of the programmes; to the Iranian staff, who were many in number, for translating the didactic material, arranging the printing, and supervising the field experiments.

REFERENCES

Jamieson, G.H. (1974) Functional literacy: a field study of instructor and instructional
     variables. Inter. Rev. of Applied Psychology, (in press).
UNESCO (1970) Functional Literacy: Why and How. Paris: UNESCO.
UNESCO (1972) Guide Pratique d'Alphabétisation Fonctionnelle. Paris: UNESCO.

# Communication and learning applications to the development process

A. HANCOCK, UNESCO, Paris

**Abstract:** The author is concerned with international aspects of the theme of 'communication and learning', with the creation of communication models, agencies and institutions in the developing world, and above all with the transfer of experience and expertise at the international level.

The paper begins by pinpointing the role of development agencies, both multilateral and bilateral, in applying the communication media, disciplines and techniques to educational development and to the learning process. It considers, specifically, the work of Unesco, and makes special reference to the Communication Sector and to the Department of Free Flow of Information and Development of Communication. Particular emphasis is laid upon the systematic development of media, both mass and interpersonal.

The work of the department is of various kinds. Certain activities are descriptive, research based or normative, attempting to evolve generally valid theories of communication, and to offer case study material for analysis and guidance. Others are experimental: creating pilot programmes and experimental models, designed and evaluated under controlled conditions, for later extension. A major part is operational — planning and implementing communication services, agencies and institutions, and providing the necessary expertise and training environment.

Examples and case studies are drawn from both developed and developing country situations, and particular attention is paid to the countries of Asia.

## INTRODUCTION

I should begin by describing what I shall **not** be talking about today. I am not a psychologist, and I shall not be discussing the learning process. Nor am I a sociologist, and any references which I make to diffusion theory will be based upon experience, not upon professional research. What I am, at present, is an international civil servant, reasonably well versed in the developing countries of Asia, and with a professional background in educational media planning and production. My role here, as I see it, is to broaden the discussion base by taking account of international models, especially as these affect the development process. I shall therefore be talking mostly about **transfer**. Not the technical transfer implicit in all communication transactions, but the transfer of models which takes place whenever technology is abstracted from one environment and implanted in another. In other words, the application of communication knowledge, techniques and experience to the development process. Within Unesco, this is our principal business; culling from the accumulated experience of many countries models which have the potential to affect other situations, where social and educational development depend upon rapid but controlled innovation.

I shall also be making some a priori assumptions. I am first of all taking communication to cover not only mass media forms, but the whole complex of channels, audiences and messages which we now recognize to be interlocked in the communication process.

Similarly, I take the term 'learning' to imply something as broad as the changes in human behaviour which are the result of experience; in our work, which concerns changes in attitude and social motivation (for example, in the family planning communication programme), we are engaged on more than the acquisition of skills, knowledge or techniques.

I have certainly no title to discuss how learning takes place, or to suggest methods of accelerating learning processes. But whether learning occurs in a disciplined instructional context, or in the wider world of 'lifelong' education, I also take it as understood that a diffusion process, of some kind, is involved. This diffusion process has been described in many ways, ranging from audience-centred descriptors (the breakdown of learning and attitudinal change into steps of awareness; interest; evaluation, trial and adoption, to name one approach) to functional descriptors (the identification of different kinds of 'measure' which change circumstances, methods, perceptions, goals and values). No doubt the debate will continue. The task of the communicator, in all of this, is to translate a consensus of research findings into practical action — identifying suitable organs, media, channels, messages and environments to allow diffusion to take place.

## ITEMS AND STRUCTURES

I shall therefore be talking mostly about the rather neglected field (as far as communication research goes) of **implementation**. In other words, I am not simply discussing themes and models, but the structures which are required to make these operational.

This is not so problematic in the simplest forms of transfer. At the individual level, if we want to communicate or learn, we use language or we refer to compilations of experience; the structures involved (whether they are psychological or social) are understood. At the level of formal education, the structures are also, by now, classic; we have all reached our present positions by following through an educational system. Thus, if we question its satisfactoriness as a system, we do so within common frames of reference.

354

The position is rather different when we begin to devise models for new forms of communication. In a simple design for an educational media system, for example, we probably begin with something like the following:

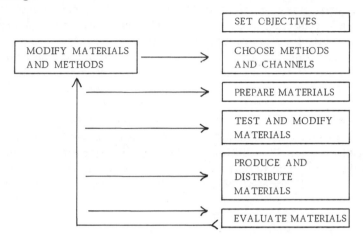

In this model, we have begun to mix concept with implementation. We acknowledge the importance of the political or organizational framework within which materials are prepared, tested, evaluated. We recognize that the quality of our model will in practice be dependent upon the means which we find to make it a reality.

Yet even here, we are mostly dealing with adaptations of existing structures — a production agency, a school system. In other areas still (non-formal adult education, for example, or development work) there may be nothing to fall back on. We may have to invent a framework within which to operate, and devise completely new approaches to extension activities, media co-ordination and so on. I shall be coming back to this point later, but even this glancing reference should be enough to show that, in some contexts, the structural aspects of the model are quite as important as the thematic or conceptual.

We might expand this situation diagrammatically as follows:

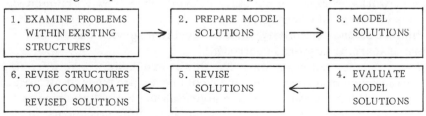

Closing the loop is the major difficulty. It is the reluctance of the originating structure to modify itself which may finally impede progress —

reluctance with a weight of investment behind it.  Problems and model
solutions are not thrown up in a vacuum;  an agency is created with a
declared responsibility to identify problem areas.  This agency may be
a media service, a Schools' Council, an Open University, a Unesco.
It identifies problems according to its stated terms of reference, then
devises model solutions, which it tests and evaluates.  It is subsequently
charged with putting its solutions into practice.  It creates a complex
and often expensive machinery for the purpose, including sub-systems
to produce, test, distribute, interpret and utilize materials.  But it is
after this stage that difficulties often begin.  In practice, the model
solutions may prove to be not so ideal after all.  Problems change, or
are partly resolved;  new problems emerge;  new solutions are proposed.
What happens when these demand the modification of the whole apparatus?
When a production or distribution system, a cable network, a complex of
transmitters, are found to be no longer integral to the new situation?
How easy is it to change a structure to which so much investment has
been attached, which now has so many resources, and on which the live-
lihood and professional reputation of so many people depend?  The problem exists at many levels (certainly not only at the international) and
deserves some special attention in research.  It seems to me that the
most recalcitrant task in the United States has been to devise paths for
the development of educational media which make a realistic allowance
for present media structures.  Educational television and public television have had to weave their way around an alien, and usually hostile,
network of commercial programming;  the formula for 'Sesame Street',
for example, was based upon coming to grips with commercialism, and
devising a model which could be successful on more than one plane.  In
the United Kingdom, the debate over the future of educational broadcasting largely concerns the extent to which existing interests — of both
broadcasters and educators — can be accommodated — this is surely
what the discussions on the Fourth Channel, the possible creation of a
separate educational broadcasting corporation, are all about?  At a
lesser level, are there not universities, both in the United States and in
the United Kingdom, which have a long-term commitment to cable distribution networks, which may not suit, in every case, newly articulated
demands of users?  In London, is there not a concern to bring together
two distinct strands of activity, in the television service and in the
pattern of learning resource centres?

I am certainly not suggesting that this is avoidable;  if we were to
wait for new demands to emerge, we would never progress at all.  But I
would suggest that the most sensible approach to original planning is to
take account of this dilemma, and to make supporting structures as
flexible as possible, capable of sustaining, even encouraging, change.
Rigid structures will inhibit progress, where progress demands the
modification of the overall system.

This is certainly not the principle upon which our own approach is based, within the Communication Sector of Unesco. We have also, in the past, seen the difficulties which random, weighty and rigid structures have produced. We are now anxious to set up forms which do not inhibit in this way; though we are bound to make assessments of the most important trends, and of the best models to contain and promote them, we prefer to construct a framework which will not automatically become useless if we are wrong.

It may often seem to the outsider that there is little coherence in the communication activities of an agency such as Unesco. It is indeed true that, as with most international agencies, our programme often reflects a compromise, representing the balance of national interests on which the organization is founded. Structurally, we are often open to misinterpretation — so much so that the way in which we work may be clear only to those who look from within. The area of educational technology is very well a case in point. Because the field is wide, with an impact on many fields of human interest, it is not confined to any particular sector. I am from the Communication, but I cannot claim fully to represent the views of other sectors, or to state a 'Unesco' philosophy. If I can for a moment briefly describe the structure of the organization, I should mention that there are major strands of Education, Science, Social Sciences and Culture, and Communication, apart from the administrative corps. Although communication is essentially an interdisciplinary field, its functions are important and numerous enough to be consolidated in a separate sector (which did not exist at the time of the organization's creation). Yet inevitably, communication activities still enter, to a greater or lesser extent, into the programme of other sectors — of science, culture, and especially of education. For many years, a modus operandi was created between the Education and Communication sectors by assuming that the Education sector would deal with educational technology as it affected in-school audiences, while the Communication sector would devote itself to adult and non-formal education, and to the broad field of general communication. You will appreciate that today the distinction is simply not supportable. A systems approach implies a continuum of activity, as well as a logical deployment of resources, which cannot be reconciled with an arbitrary division into 'in' or 'out-of-school' operations. Similarly, the use of mixed channels, including interpersonal channels, also works against 'traditional' hierarchies — communication is no longer only 'mass communication', and media are no longer only 'mass media'. The Department in which I work was once known as the 'Department of Mass Communication' the title has now been abandoned. As we see new patterns of communication growth, so we have to find new methods of collaboration. I do not think I need labour this point, as many of you must find yourselves in a similar predicament.

### The Communication Sector of Unesco

What I am describing, therefore, when I discuss our work, is in organizational terms a mixture of past, present and future.

Within the Communication sector, the Department which is mostly concerned with media and educational technology is that of the Free Flow of Information and the Development of Communication. It is a long title, and we prefer to know ourselves simply as FDC.

Within 'FDC', there are four substantive divisions. One is concerned with the free flow of information (that is, working internationally to remove obstructions to communication flow, through the promotion of codes of ethics, protocols, the removal of tariffs and other political and physical obstacles to traffic). The second is concerned with book development, and its work is directly related to the outcome of International Book Year. The third is concerned with Communication Research and Planning, in particular with the elaboration of communication policies and communication planning disciplines; and the fourth, with the Development and Application of Communication. These once again reflect some ad hoc organizational decisions, but taken overall, they show that the work of the department has a number of characteristic slants. Some of these are normative and regulatory; much of the work of the Division of the Free Flow of Information falls within this category. Others are concerned with information flow — for example, the development of an international network of mass communication documentation centres, with common cataloguing and retrieval systems, intended to provide quicker and more comprehensive exchanges of information and research materials across the world. Five of these centres have already been identified, in the United Kingdom, France, Scandinavia, Singapore and Ecuador, though the operational lines of the system are still tentative. Others are concerned with the advancement of communication policies and planning — based on the idea that communication is an interdisciplinary activity which calls for integrated action, and requires its own expertise, methodologies and tools, in the same way as education or economic planning.

Operational functions principally identified with the work of my own division — that of the 'Development and Application of Communication'. It is the division which relies most heavily in its work upon extra-budgetary finance (UNESCO's Regular Programme has a coherence of its own, but project development, and widescale expansion, are normally dependent on external funds, coming from such sources as the United Nations Development Programme).

Our work includes, in summary form, the development of infra-structures, experiment and model formulation, professional and institutional development, and the application of communication techniques to a whole variety of special audiences and problem areas. I will give examples of these functions later, but you will see at once that they are interdependent.  They relate to a small sub-system for communication growth which might be expressed as follows :

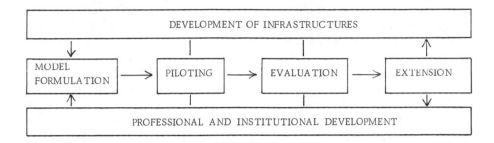

In this diagram, three activity strands have been picked out — the development of infrastructures; model formulation (including the piloting of experimental and innovative forms), and professional and institutional development.  It is their interrelationship which is important.

Model formulation and the 'pilot' project are processes with which we have been engaged for a long time.  It is a well known principle that, under Unesco's Regular Programme, pilot programmes are tried out in limited environments, and then, after evaluation, expanded and extended on a wider base.  The usual approach is that a particular area for experiment is defined (often at the time of a Unesco conference).  The experimental form is planned by a group of consultants, and to a greater or lesser extent evaluated theoretically.  The experiment may be with a particular technique (for example, the use of video equipment), or with a particular problem area (for example, the development of a management model for family planning communication).  The evaluation will be at the very least a scrutiny by specialists;  it may be based upon specially convened workshops or expert meetings, even (though infrequently) on a simulation exercise.

The result of this process is that an operational plan is prepared, in conjunction with whatever country or institution has shown an interest in the experiment.  A 'pilot' project is devised, and the experiment is mounted, with evaluation built in as a constant check on its progress.  On completion, a final evaluation is made, and a decision is made as to whether or not to extend the project on a wider front.

I realize that this account begs many questions — of the satisfactoriness or otherwise of the process of modelling of evaluation procedures, of the theoretical base on which we proceed.  What I am interested to emphasize here, however, are the dangers inherent in treating pilot experiments on their own, without reference to other kinds of activity.

Our experimental programmes have had some successes, and also their quota of failures.  The failures may be attributed to many factors

— inadequate evaluation and research, the reluctance or inability of co-operating Governments to continue with a programme after it has run its term, lack of resources to extend the model. But I would say that a main reason why the success ratio is not higher lies with the unprepared-ness of the country in which the experiment is being conducted to sustain its growth. And it is on this premise that the other functions cited are stressed — the building up of infrastructures in a country to a point when they are capable of nurturing growth; the training of professional personnel; the linking of resources in a co-ordinated programme of experiment across many related problem areas. Again there is nothing very new in these activities — Unesco has been engaged in professional communication training since the nineteen fifties. Any novelty is in the greater coherence of our effort. I must confess that, personally, I am not too much in favour of the 'pilot' approach in the communication field. I can recognize the force of an argument which says — first of all, you must develop and test your model in limited circumstances and get it right: then and only then can you expand. The practical difficulty seems to be that most pilots, after evaluation, do not expand — because the momentum, the availability of resources, the trained cadre of personnel, and above all the political support are simply not there to move the project to its next phase. This is what happened with educational television in Niger, in the Philippines, in India, in Thailand, and until recently in Malaysia and in Singapore. I would not quibble with the need for proper planning and evaluation, but I feel that from the beginning they must be seen in the context of a larger commitment. The model is itself part of a wider system, not something which can be tried out in isolation, and then expected to grow of its own accord.

In practical terms this has led us to organize our activities in a different way — and in particular to reframe our relationships with institutions and projects, at Headquarters, regional and national levels.

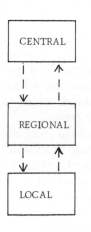

| | |
|---|---|
| CENTRAL | INFORMATION EXCHANGE PLANNING CO-ORDINATION PROGRAMME SUPERVISION MODEL FORMULATION |
| REGIONAL | ADVISORY SERVICES REGIONAL TRAINING OPERATIONAL PLANNING REGIONAL CO-ORDINATION |
| LOCAL | DEVELOPMENT ACTIVITIES PROJECTS TRAINING EVALUATION |

360

The main innovation in this pattern of working is the introduction of a second tier of command, at the regional level. In the past, we have had projects supported by secretariat project officers (based in Paris), and experts attached to projects at the in-country level. This has produced some excellent work, but on a rather sporadic, ad hoc basis, in which generalized lines of development are not too clear. The distance between the secretariat officer and the national expert has been too great; the man in the field could not have a detailed knowledge of overall programmes and policy; at the same time, the Headquarters officer was too remote from field conditions to base his planning on specific needs.

In the new version, executive authority is where possible decentralized. The degree of decentralization is limited by our own resources, but we hope that, with the appointment of regional advisers of a senior status, we have contact points who are close enough to countries to see real needs and trace potential, but who are also close enough to the Secretariat to understand the shape and design of the whole programme.

We are also trying, as far as possible, to base regional advisers on centres of communication development — institutions which we feel have a particular quality and strength, and which can sustain not only national development in a flexible and open fashion, but can also serve as nuclei for inter-country exchange and growth. Our first attempt was in Asia — and I can speak with some confidence of this attempt, as I was the first regional communication adviser to act in this capacity. My main function was to travel widely, and to identify centres, services, institutions, which seemed ready to 'take off'. I was based upon the National Broadcasting Training Centre in Kuala Lumpur, Malaysia, which was not only building up a reputation as a full-time training centre for Malaysian broadcasters, but was also making its premises available for regional training programmes, whenever sponsors could be found. My rôle was therefore catalytic — to plan for the development of the centre, in both its national and regional rôles, while using it as a base from which to identify other initiatives.

This pattern is being continued in other countries and continents — advisers are now being appointed in Africa, Latin America and the Arab States. It is also being adopted in one important area of applied communication — family planning. The decision to base these on existing centres, rather than in regional administration offices, is important; the advisers are expected to have professional as well as administrative skills. The new Unesco representative in Malaysia, for example, is an ex-Head of Staff Training for a major broadcasting company.

Professional and institutional development are natural offshoots of this position. Unless there is a cadre of trained personnel available in the developing world, nothing permanent can come of innovation — and the needs are too considerable for training to be offered in a purely ad

361

hoc way. A survey of broadcasting needs in Asia, conducted some years ago, showed that some 30,000 personnel would require training over a five year period; it was this discovery which led to the formation of the Malaysian training programme. Moreover, training generates its own needs — in new training techniques and materials — and it is no accident that a part of our forthcoming programme is devoted to building up training materials — handbooks, films, manuals, and in particular modular materials, which can be assembled in different ways to cater for a variety of different training needs. We have used the same approach in the family planning field, where handbooks, training films and slide sets are being produced as rapidly as resources permit. We have also begun to study the problem of training techniques with more intensity — applying to communication training techniques which have been long since applied to management and industry.

## The Communication Programme

This then is the structure which we have created, or are in the process of creating. But the principle of flexibility cannot be overriding; obviously we have a programme to execute, which has to be based upon value judgements of what we consider to be of importance.

The source of such judgements is varied. Partly it is on research findings — as an international agency we have access to a good deal of international research, more than we have time to sift or synthesize. Partly it is based upon the results of our own pilot and experimental programmes. Perhaps most of all it is based upon workshops, seminars and conferences — and specifically the biennial General Conference — which lay down the guidelines for our programme.

I had recently to set down, for a series, the main trends which we have seen over the past decade in the field of educational media and technology. I intend to retain the same grouping here, simply because it is a convenient way of describing how our programme is generated from an analysis of trends.

It seemed to me, on reflection, that the main trends are threefold.

The first relates to ways and means by which technology can be individualized and personalized. The problem is common, but the solutions are diverse — they range from the encouragement of local production services (at a community or institutional level) to the harnessing of the computer to education and educational management, the planned combination of different media and channels, the rediscovery of traditional and folk media, and the promotion of low cost and intermediate technologies.

The second trend affects systems working. Consideration of objectives, of precise functions, leads in the end to a more balanced use of media, a wider range of channels, and most important, to an insistence on the feedback loop for regeneration. It also insists upon the continuum between producers and extension agents — and by inference the relationship between mass and interpersonal channels.

Thirdly, there is the more recent trend towards audience involvement, access and participation — the insistence upon the rights of audiences and users, not only to select and talk back (within traditional media formats), but to involve themselves in the actual business of producing and programming.

Parts of our programme can be identified with each of these trends:

A lot of attention has been paid in recent years to harnessing a wider range of channels, ranging from very simple forms (for example the rural press) to complex computer configurations. I should say that, in our own sector, we are less interested in computerized applications than in the Education sector (except for questions of information storage, retrieval and transfer). Since our concern is mostly with developing countries in a context of general education, we have been at pains to examine simpler forms. In Africa, for example, we have had some success in promoting the rural periodical press — initially in francophone, shortly in anglophone Africa. The rural press is simply produced; it is usually in simple offset, even cyclostyled forms, and it concentrates on providing local material for local audiences. Its virtue is not only that it can afford to be parochial (since costs are low), but also that it requires a lower level of journalistic and management expertise than the traditional press, and of course distribution processes are more straightforward. It makes a particularly useful vehicle for literacy campaigns, since it can offer material suitable for neo-literates (usually a neglected group — in spite of all the attention given to literacy there is still a great shortage of material, especially in local languages, for new literates to read).

We are also interested in developing other mass media forms — radio and more recently television — in local situations. Recently, we have also come back to traditional media — folk forms, puppetry, mobile theatre — and attempted to combine these with mass media. And we have turned our attention again to low cost media (simple audio visual aids, which can be easily produced with a minimum of skills) and intermediate technologies (the adaptation of more sophisticated models to less well endowed environments).

Yet extending the range of media on its own is meaningless. Media in development are as good as the uses to which they are put, whether this is in education, family planning, health and welfare, literacy, community work. In such applied programmes, a balance has to be found between many different agencies, and the main problem is usually one of co-ordination and interdisciplinary working. The family planning programme in India uses radio and traditional folk forms; a literacy programme in the Arab States is experimenting with audio-cassettes and programmed materials to train monitors; a community development programme in the Caribbean employs local radio, mobile vehicles, video units, film materials. In each case, the relationships are different.

Once again, we are back to structures. The problem is of course more acute in the adult than in the school sphere — technology used in the school carries its own infrastructures and its own monitors. It is primarily a matter of training teachers in utilization, and equipping schools for reception and distribution; the flexibility of the system has to be provided through the teacher himself. Non-formal education is a different matter. There are few infrastructures (at least in the developing world); these have to be created.

If we are to depart from the direct transmission of information, to a more purposeful use of media, then we have to devise some system of extension agents, of listening groups, of study and discussion groups, which has in turn to conform to social environments. In spite of the many experiments in India, in Africa, in Indonesia, I have been surprised to see how poorly documented is this field. Few of the experiments have been methodically evaluted, and the basic models remain primitive.

It is easy enough to agree that the personalization of media demands special relationships between media workers and extension workers: a disciplined balance between mass and interpersonal channels. It is less easy to spell this out in practice. At the production end, who is to create the materials? How are they to be tested? How are they to be distributed? At the utilization end, who is to carry out training for extension workers? What character should this training have? How can results be evaluated, and fed back meaningfully to the production agency?

The answers to these questions, and many more like them, can only be provided empirically (they are mostly not normative answers; situations will vary from country to country, from community to community). By now we have a body of experience on which to draw and some general observations to make. We favour, for example, systems in which duplication of production resources is avoided — where small communication units, in special environments such as health and family planning ministries, offer content advice, produce simple printed materials, and act as a resource base, but leave expensive radio and television production to the broadcasting organizations. We favour systems in which utilization training is carried out by the specialist ministries, with an input from communication professionals. But the networks showing implementation are still undrawn.

The requirement is one of systems working — the problem is to delineate the entire communication system, before spelling out detailed functions of which media and channels to use, how they are to be evaluated, how can they be applied and interpreted.

We are still at the beginning of this learning process. I am at present engaged on a study of educational mass media in Thailand, in which some twenty experts in fields ranging from rural sociology to evaluation, media production and administration, curriculum and teacher education, have been looking at the educational needs of Thailand, in an attempt to construct a model for future development. All media were to be considered, and all audiences, both school and adult. The method of investigation has been somewhat novel. In the first phases of the study, we attempted to generalize objectives, and to create a matrix of possible media systems which might match these objectives. We then argued the alternatives, and on the basis of this argument a number of specific permutations were chosen by the Thai Government for deeper analysis. From this second investigation, a preferred critical path was isolated, and more concrete and detailed objectives. At present, the Government of Thailand is debating the choice, and in the final stages of the study the chosen system will be explored in depth.

The study has been interesting in a number of ways. It is first of all the work of an interdisciplinary team, and a variety of viewpoints and emphases have had to be accommodated in the system; the process of elimination reminded me at many times of the process of course construction used within the Open University. Systems planning in reality is rather different from the theory — in this context, not only have different personalities and opinions had to be reconciled, but the Thai Government has at each stage laid down parameters (of cost, educational priority, etc.) which had to be followed. To date we have achieved consensus, though by no means unanimity. But the most interesting aspect of all has been the sense of members of the team — however specialized their rôle — that we are dealing, not with a media system, but with innovation within the educational and social system as a whole. It has not been simply a question of matching, say, curriculum reform to media provision; we have been forced to consider the whole rationales of innovation. In designing an evaluation system we finally came to the conclusion that evaluation could, without too much extra expense and with considerable advantage, be extended to cover the whole educational system, and to the measurement of innovation in general. I suspect that at the end of it all the team will have learned quite as much as the Government of Thailand.

This is probably the biggest growth point of all — the consciousness (not simply the discovery) that media are not something attached to educational processes, but are a part of those processes, and that planning for media provision is a functional aspect of all educational planning. The understanding is not confined to educational media — it is an argument which is being applied increasingly to all facets of communication planning. There is always a time lag between the articulation of a process, and its penetration and acceptance. (This is after all what

365

development is about). During the interval, odd things happen. Fashions are created, often on the basis of an imperfect understanding; technologies are sold in currencies of enthusiasm, novelty, political superiority.

But there is no doubt that we have profited from the clarity of thought which is demanded within systems planning. The specification of objectives in terms which can be measured, identified and evaluated forces the practitioner back upon his own rationale.

As a minor illustration, I can cite a small project with which we are engaged in the University of Science, Malaysia, in the island of Penang. The demands in this project were of a rather unusual kind. A facility was required which could offer practical training and exposure in instructional technology for education students, a flexible production service for the University as a whole, and a training facility for students taking a communication degree.

The demands were unusual because they were influenced by both European and American models. The University itself is organized generally upon European lines, but the presence of a communication course was certainly American; such courses are still little known in Europe.

The University is new, and it is responding to interests and enthusiasms generated among its academic staff, after study tours and visits to other universities in many other countries. There is a commitment to innovation and experiment, which is not always consolidated or coherent.

At one time, in an unthinking transfer of models from the developed world, several solutions might have been offered. The standard package for a communication training course assumes a miniature production complex for TV and radio, with observation facilities for students, and a limited transmission capacity. The standard package for a University production centre involves CCTV production facilities, attached to a wired distribution system, and with some allowance for mobile work. If there is a standard package for educational technology courses, then it assumes laboratory and workshop facilities, portable video and audio recording and replay equipment, and other items usually in a modular assembly.

The results, in Penang, are not evaluated; the project has only recently begun. But the need to reconcile several different demands forced us back to first principles; the end result is more tentative than it might have been five years ago, with a small production resource which is capable of giving basic experiences to communication students, producing some general materials for those sectors which are interested to use them, and offering a range of equipment and laboratory spaces for education students to follow their own personal interests. There is no central distribution system, no final commitment to a particular form, which may condition growth too early. The possibility of expanding is there, but in several directions.

At the same time, we have been encouraged to build in links to other institutions. Communication training, for example, can be supported by both services and staff from the Malaysian National Broadcasting Training Centre. Teacher training in educational technology can be related to the demands and performance of a country-wide in-school media system which is now being developed. In other words, we are dealing, not only with the closed sub-system of the University, but with its function within the wider communication system of the country.

We do realize, of course, that there is more to systems working than empirical testing. We are interested in the whole field of communication management, and most particularly in developing management tools and training. One field is economics; our Division of Communication Research and Planning has recently revised (after testing in a number of countries) a set of guidelines for the economic evaluation of national communication systems. We have also brought together, in workshop situations, managers of major communication programmes, including satellite systems, to pool their experience.

One recent initiative was a study of operational planning for family planning communication programmes. The study was undertaken by three young economists, management and communication specialists from the European Institute of Business Administration; this choice was deliberate, an attempt to produce a fresh approach in thinking. The study begins by isolating economic variables in planning a communication strategy; it goes on to develop a co-ordination and management model; and finally lays down, in network form, communication flow lines, and allocates responsibilities between the various personnel involved. The model is general, but it is derived from data fed to the authors from a number of existing projects. It is now being refined, ready for trial in new country programmes. It is part of a real concern — to tap the considerable amount of business and management experience and apply it to areas which are currently the prerogative of the communication research worker or the media professional.

The third trend in our sequence is newer, both in the developed and in the developing countries. It concerns access to and participation in media — and it is a crystallization of earlier experiences — stemming, among other factors, from dissatisfaction with mass media performance. It has many objectives. One concerns the right of the individual to material — and the limitations on this right which are imposed by (for example) the restriction of channels on network television. Another discusses the 'impossibility' of feedback — and ways and means by which audience response can be recognized and built into programmes, ranging from 'phone-in' programmes to local broadcasting initiatives or community systems. A third argues that the production base of media should be widened — so that production is not simply a mystique reserved for an

367

elite, but something which can be put into the hands of individuals and groups.

The field is still tentative, and we are anxious to investigate it further. We have recently commissioned a series of studies, which are not so much research studies in their own right, as compilations of experience — because we feel that there is a great deal of information on access, which is still unsifted and unsynthesized. We have begun studies in the USA, in Canada (of cable systems), in Europe (of a whole range of new media formats) and general studies of the technology, the economic and the social inferences.

In the community development sphere we are already active. Following the experimental work of the National Film Board of Canada in its 'Challenge for Change' programme, and later experiments in Africa, we are now engaged in a pilot experiment in Tobago which, although technically labelled as a project in women's education, is actually an experiment in community self-help and self-determination. We have provided an adviser, and a range of limited audio-visual facilities. These include simple print production materials, a van equipped for film, slide and video demonstration (with video recording as well as replay equipment), audio-visual production equipment facilities for radio production. The use to which these are put depends upon the community. There are a number of local initiatives to follow — support for local health and welfare facilities; functional education, the improvement of tourism; increased employment opportunities — and training. The experiment is located, deliberately, in a community which is gradually being starved of its younger members, because of lack of employment, lack of involvement, lack of separate identity. The adviser is technical — he offers skills to help the community promote what they wish to achieve. To my mind, this experiment stems from exactly the same principle which, in the United Kingdom, prompted the BBC to set up its 'Open Door' programme, and offer a studio, a director and technicians for minority groups to make themselves heard.

## Transfer

I would like to end with a more specific reference to the transfer of experience from one environment to another, in the light of what has already been said.

Traditionally, transfer has been seen as a gift from the developed to the developing world. Traditionally, we have assumed that it is only in the developed world that adequate resources, impetus and expertise are at hand to experiment, evaluate and refine new models. Is this still the case?

Now that we are thinking more in terms of technologies which transform whole systems and societies, it may well be that these can only be practised and evaluated in the developing world. In the USA and Europe

we have seen that there is a great deal of investment in existing structures, methods and materials, which makes radical change difficult to
accept or to promote — in the developing world, the problems are more
urgent, and the infrastructures less solid. It is possible, in Malaysia,
Singapore or Thailand, to envisage a nationally based media system
associated with a nationally based programme of curriculum reform,
teacher re-orientation, even physical rebuilding. It has already proved
possible in the Ivory Coast and in El Salvador. In the West, how often
can such radical work be attempted — except in the case of something
like the Open University, which is a closed system, and is possible
simply because it does not strike at the existing foundations. I would
suggest that, today, the developed countries may have just as much to
learn from the developing world as vice versa.

I suspect that the simplicity (one might even say the crudity) with
which communication models are transferred from one environment to
another may surprise you. The standard approach runs generally as
follows.

In the course of its development planning, a country identifies its
main problem areas. It makes a request to an agency, either bilateral
or international, to assist with a particular problem. An 'expert'
(sometimes without developing country experience) is invited to visit the
country and offer a suitable plan. He does so, over the course of (at best)
a few months or (at worst) a few days, and produces a report. The report
is commented on, not only by the country in question, but by bureaucrats
and other specialists from the donor country, and is used as a base for
'project discussion'. A project is formulated, using standard criteria
which are normally evolved in the agency concerned, and discussion
with the Government takes place (though often mainly with the economic
development arm of Government, which has the closest relations with
the sponsoring agency).

Subsequently, long term experts are appointed. These are recruited
on the basis of brief advertisements, adopted (after evaluation) by the
recipient country, and imported, after a pre-briefing (much of which is
concerned with the agency's interests as well as the project in question).
The pattern of assistance which has been theoretically worked out is then
pursued; in practice little variation is possible. The overriding controls
are those of budget, though there may, in bilateral programmes, be other
considerations, such as the purchase of equipment from particular sources.

I deliberately overstate the situation; obviously, in practice, there
are local variations, which allow for local changes of attitude, and there
are many excellent projects. My point is that these are exceptional,
created by the competence of individual human beings on both sides, and
not endemic to the system. The system is mostly concerned with political satisfaction — and in practice this means those agencies which, in
both donor and recipient country, have the most frequent contact with
bilateral and international levels of action.

Patently this system offends against many of the conditions of learning which we favour and promote. It makes political and financial considerations paramount, rather than social or educational objectives. It does not seek for consensus at the professional level, only at the bureaucratic. It phases and plans according to generalized, not particular criteria. It does not allow for continuous feedback (as would happen even in the most traditional learning situation — that of the classroom) and it does not attempt to match teachers with environments.

Moreover, the approach may be guilty of even more major fallacies. It assumes, first of all, that the best, if not the only models, are to be found in the developed world, with a transplanting of foreign models to new environments. It trains counterparts in the universities and research institutions of the developed world.

This is not the time or place at which to enlarge on this process, but it does seem to me to be perfectly understandable that the developing world is having difficulty in creating its own values, models and techniques. I have been to conferences where Asian specialists have complained, for example, that research is too Western-oriented, but on each occasion no viable alternative has been offered — simply because the speakers have themselves been trained and disciplined in Western environments. There is an equal difficulty in finding suitable 'third world' experts; all too often applicants for expert posts are pallid imitations of Western models. This seems to me to be inevitable in a situation where transfer is thought of as a gift from West to East, from developed to developing territory.

I do not think that the situation can be quickly remedied. It would not help to insist upon giving developing countries complete autonomy in arranging their aid programmes, selecting their own experts, arranging their own fellowship programmes. They do not yet have the necessary talents, and they do not have the willingness to meet the financial burden, even if they possess the resources. The pattern and relationship of donor and recipient — of aid being offered, of being taken as a right — is too fixed, too much in the interest of both parties. Yet the system is not working, if the gap between developing and developed countries continually widens — in economic, educational and social terms. It is a vicious circle; the developed countries know the political advantages of aid, and the developing countires are too used to having their innovation financed externally to give it up without a struggle.

Again, it is the structures which impede. There is still no real co-ordination of international and bilateral aid; political and cultural considerations still figure largely in aid programmes; duplication of effort and resources is common.

Possibly the only real, long-term solution is for an exchange, on equal terms, between the two worlds. If students from the developed world could work, as students rather than as teachers, in the third world;

if developing country experts would serve as experts in the developed world; if roles could be sufficiently and frequently exchanged, then understanding might develop, and different balances and relationships emerge. But the achievement of this perspective is out of our hands, and I suspect that it is still a very distant prospect.